ECUMENICAL
TESTIMONY

ECUMENICAL TESTIMONY

The Concern for Christian Unity
Within
the Reformed and Presbyterian Churches

by
JOHN T. McNEILL
and
JAMES HASTINGS NICHOLS

THE WESTMINSTER PRESS
Philadelphia

Book Design by Dorothy Alden Smith

Published by The Westminster Press®
Philadelphia, Pennsylvania

PRINTED IN THE UNITED STATES OF AMERICA

Library of Congress Cataloging in Publication Data

McNeill, John Thomas, 1885–
    Ecumenical testimony.

    Includes bibliographical references.
    1. Christian union—Reform Church.   2. Christian union—Presbyterian Church.   I. Nichols, James Hastings, 1915–   joint author.   II. Title.
BX8.2.M323   285   74–977
ISBN 0–664–20998–X

CONTENTS

INTRODUCTION

OF THE NUMEROUS CONTRASTS that mark the history of Christianity, one of the most striking consists in its constant avowal of the principle of unity and its too common practice of sectarian division. The conception of the church in its apostolic beginnings was of one fraternal society spread abroad through all the world. Yet discord appeared even among the first disciples, and Paul's exhortations to unity have in their background contention and schism. The ecumenical unity of the church, whether we conceive it as spiritual or as organizational, has always been an unrealized hope.

But it is a hope that earnest Christians cannot abandon. To be content with the segmentation of the modern church would be to surrender a significant part of the Christian faith. Most of us are ruefully aware that by reason of our disunion we deny in act what we profess in solemn words. We Christians have for many centuries diligently repeated the declaration that we believe in the Holy Catholic Church, while we have dwelt apart in autonomous units that have at times confronted each other in rivalry or outright mutual repudiation.

Undoubtedly Christians today are more ready than their forefathers were to recognize that a kind of apostasy is involved in this disruptiveness, a contradiction of one of the essential tenets of Christianity. We know too that it entails an impoverishment of Christian experience, a loss of the comforting and invigorating realization of membership in a worldwide fraternity sharing a common faith. And not without shame we realize that the fragmentation of the church deplorably reduces the persuasiveness of the Christian testimony before the world.

The majority of Christians have mentally joined the movement toward the goal of Christian unity and are prepared to follow wise leadership in that direction. The steps of progress toward this goal are necessarily slow, but the greatest step of all is a sincere commitment to the cause. It is, I believe, a safe judgment that such commitment is increasingly widespread and intense. There have been, and there may still be, groups or denominations so obsessed by self-approval as to have lost the sense of fraternal obligation to the far-flung church of Christ; but such a phenomenon must be rare indeed. I am not concerned here with the distinction made by Ernst Troeltsch between the "church type" and the "sect type"—a distinction drawn with reference to the attitude of the denomination to the total community and to the traditions of the past. The value of this terminology is affected by the fact of experience that within all denominations the members exhibit a good deal of variety with respect to their appreciation of the total church. We readily discover instances of a sectarian and spiritually segregationist spirit that would protect itself within a narrow patrimony, and in the same ecclesiastical household a growing number of those who in plenitude of faith and charity crave communion with all believers and seek spiritual nourishment from the full resources of Christian thought and devotion.

As advocates of ecumenical Christianity we need to realize vividly that our allies are not all our contemporaries. It will hardly be disputed that a latent belief in the principle of unity and an unquenchable hope of its attainment have been generally, even where courage to affirm them has been absent, deep-rooted factors in the Christian consciousness, silently surviving all the losses of separation. Through the centuries, too, the voices of innumerable prophets of ecclesiastical peace and unity have spoken, urging their divided brethren to take counsel together with a view to union. Though their good intentions were largely defeated by the disruptive forces of their times, we should not think negligible or irrelevant the thought and effort they gave to this high cause.

From each of the older divisions of Christianity countless utterances can be drawn giving expression to an irenical spirit and pointing what seemed the way to cooperation and the widening of communion. It would be of great service to ecumenical thinking today if scholars were to present to us an adequate documentation of such statements, emanating from past centuries and from all branches of the church. As division and alienation became a settled condition of modern churches, there was a tendency to forget this historic testimony, and it is not without surprise that many readers learn of it today. The obvious multiplication of separated units in the course of the Protestant era has been rashly ascribed to one or another emphasis in the teaching of the Reformation leaders, who in fact had no intention or desire to initiate tangential movements. The sixteenth-century Reformers were not in their own minds founders or creators of churches. Instead, they labored toward the renewal or revivification of *The Church*. In so doing, they took over in wide areas the management and altered the structure of the church visible, claiming Scriptural authority for these reforms. Admittedly, the organization was freely altered, as was also what went on within it; but the *ecclesia*—the worshiping body of believers—remained.

The Reformers habitually and emphatically assert the continuity of their churches with the Catholic Church of earlier ages. It was important for them that this continuity should not be broken, and that, where it seemed to have been lost through abuses and impieties and doctrinal corruptions, it should be restored by a fresh impulse from the Scriptures and the primitive church. In repudiating the bond with the papacy they did not say, "We will not be Catholic." They said rather, "You are not Catholic, therefore we cannot remain with you." They habitually went behind the Western Scholastics to the Church Fathers who had been the church's teachers during the era of the formation of ecumenical dogma, and, following the practice of the Fathers themselves, put their doctrines to the test of Scripture. So the framers of the Augsburg Confession were able to claim that its articles contained "nothing which is discrepant with Holy Scripture, or with the Catholic Church, or even with the Roman Church so far as that Church is known from the writings of the Fathers." [1] This affirmation of catholicity and of continuity is characteristic of the propaganda of the Reformation and represents a sincere conviction of Christian solidarity throughout the centuries and throughout the world.

Though the sincerity of the Reformation espousal of this principle was challenged by opponents, and though the principle itself has often been lost from sight in our sectarian confusion, it is no less essential to original Protestantism than the doctrine of justification or of the priesthood of believers. The story of ecumenism in Protestantism, as well as in Anglicanism and in Orthodoxy, has been somewhat extensively explored in our century.[2] But the source materials are very abundant and their interpretation is still inadequate, although the work goes on apace in an increasing number of competent books and articles.

When in 1962 the invitation to write this book came from the Presbyterian Historical Society, the date of its completion had to be left open. In 1967 a manuscript was submitted that contained substantially the present Chapters I to VII and XIII. With a sense of my inadequate familiarity with American and other modern and recent aspects of the history, I sought a colleague who would have unquestioned qualifications in these areas. Happily it was possible for Professor James Nichols to undertake the additional chapters. While amid crowding academic tasks Dr. Nichols was engaged in writing these, the manuscript of the others underwent some minor revision in the light of new studies. We have now completed what we hope will be found to be an integrated text in which the little-known story of ecumenical proposals, strivings, and achievements emanating from Reformed and Presbyterian circles is narrated with some fullness. Throughout the book we have attempted to bring to the reader's attention essential source materials and to acquaint him with the personalities and the situations involved.

This small volume, as its title indicates, deals with only one province of historical ecumenical concern, that of the closely related family of churches commonly designated "Reformed" or "Presbyterian." Within this field the treatment is far from exhaustive. But it is such as to make evident an impressive continuity, within one widely extended communion through four centuries, of desire for the unity of Christ's church, and of attempts to move toward that elusive goal. The torch has been borne by some eminent leaders who are well known in history for other acts and utterances than those here recalled, and by many unrenowned but enterprising men of faith who courageously sought the wholeness of the church undaunted by the adverse forces which they could not overcome. The story could not be told without introducing a good many such personalities of whom historians have little to say. In the selection of materials we have tried to observe proportion. The notes, we hope, will help the industrious reader to look further.

The book seeks the attention of that unidentifiable but duly respected personage, the general reader. But it goes forth with the hope that scholars under whose judgment it may fall may not be too much exasperated by its limitations. At least they will find some attention given to matters rarely referred to in current discussions; and if they should be led to undertake fuller research, and to present improved interpretations, the authors will feel themselves well rewarded. In matters ecclesiastical, and not least in ecumenical discussions, history is indispensable. Without being bound by events and decisions of past centuries, we must make terms with them. Denominationally we must ransack our records anew in this generation, with honest appraisal, and charity for all. In the total record of any church, there is much to be repented of rather than defended; there is always a danger that in approving our peculiar traditions we shall glory in our very shame. Within the tradition here under review (as in other traditions) there has been too much of intransigent denominationalism not prepared to make response to the larger thoughts of ecumenical minds. To expose these elements was not the function of this essay. From the chapters that follow, it will appear, however, that the leaven of a higher loyalty, a primary attachment to the one Holy Catholic Church, was all the time at work, and that its force endured into our own era and helped to set in motion the more general ecumenical revival that in recent decades has stirred all churches the world around. Twentieth-century ecumenism has achieved many successes. It has also encountered some setbacks, but these should not be magnified to such proportions as to be thought of as reversing the ecumenical trend. A vast variety of negotiation is proceeding in which many churches throughout the world are engaged with a view to union, and projects of this kind are entertained that a generation ago would have been thought too wide-reaching to come under discussion.

But this book is primarily the history of a testimony and only secondarily a record of achievement. It goes forth with the hope on the part of its sponsors and writers that it may serve to lend a certain historical dimension to the ecumenical interest of today. We hope, too, that it may prove useful to students of ecclesiastical history by shedding light on some unfamiliar tracts of church relationships and literature since the Reformation. Perhaps it may also have suggestions for those entrusted with local or larger leadership where they are called upon, as agents of their churches, to meet the ecumenical opportunities that lie open today.

I

CALVIN
AS AN ECUMENICAL CHURCHMAN[1]

THE REFORMED and Presbyterian churches with which we are
here concerned are sometimes referred to as "Calvinist." It is un-
deniable that John Calvin (1509–1564) more than anyone else shaped
their theology, worship, and discipline and imparted to them most
of what went to form their sense of churchmanship. But Calvin would
have been highly embarrassed, even incensed, by such a use of his
name. For this and other weighty reasons we do well to avoid the
term "Calvinist" when speaking of churches. Calvin's leadership was,
however, so determinative for the strain of ecumenism in his followers that without question we must begin our story with him. Calvin
in his work and writings addressed himself not to a locality or a sect
but to the whole church in the whole world. It was characteristic of
him that in his last brief letter sent from his deathbed to William
Farel, the companion of his first reforming work in Geneva, he should
take comfort in the belief that their companionship had been "useful
to the church of God." [2] Never did he think of his obligations as
confined to Geneva or to any circumscribed area of service. His was,
rather, a primary loyalty to the church of God, the Holy Catholic
Church which has no boundaries in time or space. In their interpretations of the Apostles' Creed both Luther and Calvin held the terms
"Holy Catholic Church" and "Communion of Saints" to refer to the
same entity. Membership in the Holy Catholic Church implies fruitful participation in its communion. This point is often stressed by
Calvin with solemn exhortation. In a well-known passage he writes:

> For the Lord esteems the communion of his church so
> highly that he counts as a traitor and apostate from Christi-

13

anity anyone who arrogantly leaves any Christian society, provided it cherishes the true ministry of Word and sacraments.[3]

We come close to the heart of the Reformation when we say that it sincerely sought such a transformation of the visible church as would secure within its life a true communion of saints. Calvin could never think narrowly of this communion. The congregation in which it was experienced was made aware that it was but a local manifestation of the church universal, and the worshiper's membership in this was primary. We are to be "in brotherly agreement with all God's children." The communion of saints implies "that the saints are gathered into the society of Christ on the stipulation that they communicate to each other whatever benefits God confers on them." [4] In his reply to Cardinal Sadoleto he defines the true church as:

> the society of all the saints which, spread over the whole world and existing in all ages, yet bound together by the doctrine and by the one spirit of Christ, cultivates and observes unity and brotherly concord. With this Church [he adds] we deny that we have any disagreement. Rather as we revere her as our Mother we desire to remain in her bosom.[5]

The church as Mother of the faithful, a concept developed by Cyprian and Augustine, is a frequent theme of Calvin. In *Institutes* IV.i.4, he begins a discussion of the visible church with reference to the title "Mother," and declares:

> For there is no other way to enter into life unless this mother conceive us in her womb, give us birth, nourish us at her breast. . . . Our weakness does not allow us to be dismissed from her school until we have been pupils all our lives. . . . It is always disastrous to leave the church.

In his commentary on the words "the unity of the faith" in Eph. 4:13 he has this crisp, comprehensive sentence:

> The church is the common mother of all the godly, which bears, nourishes, and brings up children to God, kings and peasants alike; and this is done by the ministry.

With such a spacious concept of the church, it was impossible for Calvin to be patient with the spirit of sectarianism. He expounds the thought of Paul in I Cor. 14:36, "Did the word of God come out from you?" in terms of mutual acceptance among churches even if differences exist:

> No church can be taken up with itself exclusively. . . .
> They ought all . . . to hold out the right hand to each other,
> . . . cherishing mutual fellowship. . . . Let there be noth-
> ing of pride and contempt for other churches, let there be,
> on the other hand, a desire to edify; let there be moderation
> and prudence; and in that case, amid a diversity of observ-
> ances, there will be nothing worthy of reproof.

Thus it is a grave sin to alienate ourselves from other Christians on the ground of a difference in "observances." Calvin's advice to the English refugees at Frankfort and at Wesel, where they were in touch, respectively, with Anglicans and Lutherans, was in accord with this teaching.

For Calvin the Holy Catholic Church has always been and will always be divinely preserved and have some visible manifestation in the world. Continuity with all that is true and good in the church of past centuries is an aspect of the church's catholicity. The Catholic Church is an entity that extends through all time as well as through the spaces of the world. Perpetuity no less than universality is a quality of the church on earth. Any future extinction of God's church in the human scene was not to be thought of. He finds not only in the New but in the Old Testament, especially in certain chapters of Isaiah, assurances of its perpetual duration. Nothing is more ancient than the church, and nothing shall outlast it.[6] Since it is the body of which Christ is the head, it is indestructible. This holy society, spread over the whole world and existing through all ages, is held together by agreement in sound doctrine and in brotherly love. Its members are children of a common Father and "being united in brotherly love they cannot but share their benefits with one another."[7] To be a Christian involves this irresistible craving for unity and an interchange of spiritual values with all the Christian family, so excluding a divisive spirit. "All the elect are so united in Christ that, as they are dependent on one Head, they also grow together into one body."[8]

It will be noted that Calvin conceives of the church as normally having a vigorous internal life. Membership in it is no nominal attachment to an organization, but involves commitment and active participation. He lays emphasis on the continual forgiveness of sins within the communion of saints. This takes place both through the ministry of presbyters and bishops in their appointed functions and also in the mutual relations of the members. To "share with one another" involves a mutual ministry of confession of sins in which "we lay our infirmities on one another's breasts and receive among our-selves mutual counsel, mutual compassion and mutual consolation." [9] He was particularly exasperated with those sectaries who set up a requirement of sinless perfection as a qualification for membership in their company. We believe in the forgiveness of sins, and while we live, there are always sins to be forgiven. The church is "holy" in-deed, but in the sense that it earnestly seeks after and continually progresses toward holiness, not that holiness has been fully attained. The contrary assumption he regards as evidence of pride and arro-gance. Mutually acknowledging our sinfulness, we are to join in mutual admonition and fraternal correction. This important practice is to be carried on with mutual forbearance, humility, and gentle-ness, not with the harshness of pretenders to superior attainment. "Holy Scripture bids us correct our brothers' vices with more moder-ate care, while preserving sincerity of love and the unity of peace," and so avoiding "the sacrilege of schism." [10]

Calvin draws a sharp line between the schismatic spirit of inter-church faultfinding and the Scriptural sort of fraternal admonition that functions within Christian fellowship. He greatly believed in the value of talking out together differences and grievances among Christians rather than permitting them to rankle. It is notable that he carried this into the political realm. He established the practice of a meeting of the Little Council of Geneva, monthly or quarterly as might be desirable, for frank mutual criticism in a spirit of brotherly love and under pledge of secrecy. Consistently with this principle of fraternal conference he heartily favored the method of frank conversations between churches, which might take the form of planned conferences or synods, to resolve their differences and bring unity.

Numerous incidents in Calvin's life and countless passages in his correspondence afford evidence of his continual practical concern with the peace and unity of the church. His letters of irenical advice to reforming leaders and to ruling magistrates and princes in various countries have been examined in a dissertation by Willem Nijen-huis.[11] After his forced departure from Geneva in 1538 he was concerned about rumored controversy in that city. Writing from Strassburg to his former flock, October 1, 1538, he takes God to witness that when with them his whole study had been "to keep you together in happy union and concord." He laments that a divisive faction has now arisen to disturb the church and the city, and warns against all embittered strife. On the broader canvas of Swiss Protestantism he took the initiative in trying to lay a basis for unity. There was a possibility that the German-Swiss and French-Swiss churches would drift into alienation. It was Calvin who prevented this. As early as February 21, 1538, we find him proposing to Bullinger, Zwingli's able successor at Zurich, the meeting of a "public synod" in order to reach a common decision on discipline. Those attending this meeting could bring their own suggestions for the benefit of the church, and the decisions might be confirmed by the cities and princes. Calvin had made the acquaintance of Bullinger two or three years earlier at Basel, and he here addresses him as "most respected and learned brother." "How I wish," he exclaims, "that we could have a single day of free communication together!" A few months later Calvin and Farel were forced out of Geneva. They went to Berne, and thence to a synod called to act on their case in which Zurich, Berne, Basel, and other cantonal churches were represented which met in Zurich on April 28, 1538. Hearing the report of the expelled ministers, the synod approved their actions, and at its request Berne attempted to bring about their reinstatement in Geneva. They were not permitted to return, but the common action of the synod offered promise of peace and unity for the future.

Calvin's colleague and friend at Strassburg, Martin Bucer, was already seeking to mediate between the Swiss Zwinglians and the Lutherans; but Bucer had been unfavorably received in Zurich. A letter of Calvin to Farel, February 28, 1540, shows him much concerned about this. Incidentally in this letter while he holds Zwingli in "honorable esteem" he greatly prefers Luther. Shortly afterward (March 12) he wrote to Bullinger in an effort to heal the breach between Strassburg and Zurich.

> What [he asks] should more concern us in writing at this
> time than to keep up and strengthen brotherly friendship
> between us by all possible means? We see how much it con-
> cerns not our church alone but all Christianity that all to
> whom the Lord has intrusted any charge in his church should

agree in true concord. . . . We must therefore purposefully
and carefully cherish association and friendship with all true
ministers of Christ . . . in order that the churches to which
we minister the Word of God may faithfully agree together.
. . . As for me, so far as in me lies I will always labor to that
end.[12]

To overcome Bullinger's distrust he testifies to Bucer's modesty, sincere desire to cast aside all discord, and willingness to be admonished
if he should be found in error. Here again Calvin desires to converse
familiarly with Bullinger and sift the issues that hinder full agreement. Calvin wrote this well-considered irenical letter from Strassburg, where he was at Bucer's side, and in all probability it went
far to bring the desired result.

His further communications with Bullinger are of interest for us.
One cannot fail to see that Calvin had conceived a certain personal
regard for the Zurich leader. In one letter (November 8, 1542), apolo-
gizing for writing too hastily under pressure, he says: "You are well
aware how much from the heart I love you." It is remarkable how
far a craving for a fruitful friendship with Bullinger accompanied
Calvin's approach to formal agreement with him. But beyond this
it was his earnest wish that all the major Reformers—Luther, Melanchthon, Bucer, Cranmer—should be united with him in personal
trust and friendship. A mere doctrinal agreement without the attachment of a bond of friendliness would not have served his purpose.
He was distressed by personal hostilities within the Reformation
camp. When in 1544 Luther wrote a violent pamphlet against Zwingli
and his followers Calvin tried his utmost to stanch the wounds. He
wrote to Bullinger, November 25, 1544, to suggest a moderate reply.
He begs Bullinger and his colleagues to remember that Luther, despite his vehemence, is "a most distinguished servant of Christ." To
reply in kind would be to afford sport to the wicked and to make
shipwreck of the church. Even if Luther should call him a devil,
Calvin would still acknowledge him "an illustrious servant of God."

To Luther himself Calvin wrote, January 21, 1545, with reference
to troublesome issues among French Protestants but obviously with
a view to obtaining a conciliatory response of larger significance. He
sends along two treatises he has written and asks Luther to read and
judge them. Luther is here addressed in high terms of appreciation
as "most distinguished minister of Christ and my ever honored fa-

ther." "Would to God," he exclaims here, "I could hasten to you, were it but to enjoy a few hours of your conversation!" But Luther's years were running out, and the two most eminent Reformers were never to confer. Nor did the letter itself ever reach Luther's hands. With it went by the hand of a messenger another to Melanchthon, in which Calvin deplores the attack on the dead leaders Zwingli and "that holy servant of God, Oecolampadius." Melanchthon intervened to withold the letter to Luther on the ground that Luther was in a mood of suspicion.

The doctrinal center of confusion was the interpretation of the Lord's Supper, the very sacrament of unity and bond of fellowship. On this doctrine Calvin was in substantial agreement with Philip Melanchthon and Martin Bucer; and with Bucer he felt no final hindrance to agreement with Bullinger. This special problem was the subject of a number of exchanges between Bullinger and Calvin. Having read a memorandum by Bullinger, Calvin wrote to him, March 1, 1548: "Although I am conscious in myself of a more inti-mate union with Christ in the sacrament than you express in your words, yet this ought not to prevent our having the same Christ, or being one in him." Another of his letters to Bullinger, June 26, 1548, contains a commendation of Bucer, and is concerned with the doctrine of the Supper. Bucer had failed to obtain Swiss approval of the Wittenberg Concord of 1536, which he had hoped would become the basis of a general settlement. Calvin now presents a series of statements which he hopes will be acceptable to Bullinger; these were to become the basis of the fuller declaration given in the Consensus of Zurich in the next year.

He lets Bullinger know, too, that he is shocked by the latter's refusal to permit young men from Zurich to take communion in Strassburg, though they were asked to assent only to the Swiss Con-fession. Here, as frequently, we see the importance for Calvin of the establishment of intercommunion among the Reformation churches. He kept reiterating a principle not often fully affirmed in his time: that mere differences of opinion ought never to be a cause of dis-cord among Christians. The ideal relationship involved mutual en-richment by admonition and criticism within the bounds of love and esteem. He was obviously trying to establish on this basis a firm bond with Bullinger such as already existed between him and Bucer. In this letter he says of Bucer: "My love and reverence for him are such that I freely admonish him as often as I think fit." Half a year later he wrote to Bullinger: "Although I differ from you in opinion, this does not imply the least severance of affection; just as I cultivate the friendship of Bucer and yet am free to dissent occasionally from his views." (January 21, 1549.)

All this is background for the formation of the Consensus of Zurich, an important agreement in the history of the Reformed churches. It was Calvin and Farel, not Bullinger, who took the initiative in this. Indeed, Bullinger's aloofness would have discouraged any but an ardent advocate of unity. Bullinger's kindness and generosity to Reformation refugees from many lands can hardly be exaggerated, and in this respect his was truly an ecumenical spirit. But he was as hesitant to engage in conferences to decide terms of agreement as Calvin was always eager and ready for such activities. Calvin, however, would not let him rest. He kept occasionally suggesting a conference. In November, 1548, he sent to Bullinger a set of twenty-four articles on the sacraments, and to these he received an encouraging response. With his Geneva colleagues he sent, March 12, 1549, a letter to be presented at a synod of pastors presently to be held in Berne, warmly urging agreement on the Lord's Supper and with a set of twenty articles appended, designed to elevate the doctrine of the Supper above the minimal conception of mere empty signs. The response to these was less favorable.

Calvin felt the paramount importance of wide-reaching declared unity among the Reformation churches, and pressed for this in the fear that disruptive forces would get quite out of hand. Some have traced this characteristic of Calvin's mind to the influence of Bucer, who had been from the first enthusiastic and active in the cause of unity. But it is hardly possible to prove that Calvin did not adopt this attitude independently of Bucer. As early as October, 1538, Calvin, who had just reached Strassburg from Geneva, provided Bucer with a letter to be presented by him to Philip of Hesse and later to the Wittenbergers, to which were appended twelve articles designed by Calvin to bring Lutheran-Reformed agreement. It is in a letter to Farel that we learn of this, and Calvin says that in his haste he has not kept a copy of the articles. He could always be confident that Farel would lend to such efforts his hearty approval. Farel had well proved his own ecumenical interests since his association with the Waldenses in 1532. His lasting friendship and familiar correspondence with Calvin should prevent us from disregarding the possibility of his influence in forming Calvin's ecumenical outlook. In these matters we are, however, in a region of conjecture.

But certainly in the final action that brought the Zurich Consensus, Farel had a decisive part. It was on Farel's encouragement that Calvin, then recently bereaved of his beloved wife, started on his way to Zurich, May 20, 1549. He went by way of Neuchâtel, where Farel joined him. Hastening to Zurich, they participated together in the brief and cordial meeting with Bullinger and the other Zurich pastors, in which the Consensus took form. When Calvin afterward sent to Zurich (August 7, 1549) for confirmation his copy of the Consensus, his accompanying letter gives credit to his "venerable colleague" Farel for having suggested and advised the visit and further indicates that he and Farel have worked over the wording together. The warm response to this from the Zurich pastors (August 30) mentions "the visit which you and our venerable brother, the reverend William Farel, paid to us." Soon afterward (November 27) Calvin wrote to Oswald Myconius that Farel had unceasingly exhorted him to go to Zurich to treat the question "with living voice." But while it is fair to associate Farel intimately with the achievement, we need not doubt that the document itself owes most to Calvin's pen, just as the alliance it attested had long been Calvin's dream.

The twenty-six articles of the Consensus form a clear statement of Eucharistic doctrine and are substantially in accord with Calvin's *Little Treatise on the Holy Supper of Our Lord* (1540) and his other writings on this topic. The first six articles are Christological, leading to the point of our spiritual communion with Christ in the sacraments. In those that follow, the sacraments are represented as impressing on our senses what is announced in the Word. They are seals of the grace of Christ and of "the blessings once exhibited on the cross and which we daily receive by faith." They are God's instruments and are effectual only if God makes them so. The limitations of the efficacy of the sacraments are indicated in articles 16 to 20; the signs are administered to all the participants, but the reality reaches only the elect. In the remaining articles, certain special interpretations recognizable as Lutheran and Roman Catholic are expressly repudiated. "This is my body" is to be taken as metonymy. The body of Christ is in heaven, "though philosophically speaking there is no place above the skies." Christ is not to be worshiped as enclosed in the bread, making an idol of it. In its rejection of opinions already widely accepted in Lutheranism, the Consensus leans rather more to a Zwinglian position than might have been expected from Calvin. We may assume that Calvin was not entirely pleased with its language; but he was using it as an instrument by which to weld the

Swiss Reformed into one communion, and to this end it was largely effective. Not only the Zurichers but within about two years Basel, Berne, and the other cantonal Reformed churches adopted the Consensus. It was gladly approved by Bucer and John à Lasco, who were then in England; by Bullinger's English admirer, John Hooper; and by many others who desired Protestant unity and saw in it a notable achievement toward this goal. The comment of a Scottish scholar may be confidently accepted:

> If Calvin was the author of this Consensus, which linked together the Churches of Geneva and Zurich, and found acceptance in other countries, the influence of Bullinger pervades it, and it served as a welcome proof of the essential kinship of the two schools. Henceforward there was a theological harmony in Protestant Switzerland, and Melanchthon, though he rejected the clauses that made election the condition of the efficacy of the sacraments, abandoned all suspicion and hostility toward the Swiss.[13]

For Calvin the Consensus was a step toward wider union; for Bullinger it was final. He shrank from negotiations with Lutherans as likely to produce only renewed strife. Yet it is fair to Bullinger to say that he is not wrongly designated by his biographer, André Bouvier, as "Reformer and Ecumenical Counsellor." For him the concept of the universal church was a vital one; but he stressed its local existence, since there could be no assembly in which the worldwide church could make decisions for all its parts and members. Insofar as it is visible the church for him consists in the sum of the distributed local churches. In the First Swiss Confession, partly his work, and in the Second Swiss Confession, of which he was the author, he stresses the unity of "the Catholic and Holy Church of God," the communion of all saints, and warns against separation and against rashly excluding from fellowship those whom the Lord would not exclude. The active and considerate hospitality of Bullinger and his gracious wife to countless refugees testifies to the liberality of his spirit. With all his reservations, he wrote to Beza, December 15, 1557, expressing his desire for "a holy concord" with those in Germany "who profess Christ with us." Through the circulation of his writings he came to exercise a wide influence throughout Europe. But he resembles a good many modern Christians who hesitate to engage in serious interchurch conversations lest cherished values be imperiled.

Calvin was deluded in his hope that the Consensus would, with its doctrine of Christ's presence, commend the Zurichers to the Lutherans. Even Melanchthon withheld his public approval; and Melanchthon's Lutheran critics opened a pamphlet attack on the Consensus and its signatories. It would be unprofitable here to narrate the incidents of the controversy that followed, which for years consumed much of Calvin's energy. While unity within the Reformed churches was secured, Calvin's hope of total Protestant unity receded in his later years. Calvin's disappointment over the limited result of his effort can be seen in much that he wrote against the assailants of the Zurich Consensus. He repeatedly appealed to Melanchthon for his outspoken support. In a letter to John Marbach in Strassburg, August 26, 1554, he makes the claim that Luther, "that excellent servant of the Lord and doctor of the church," were he yet alive, would readily consent to the doctrines of the Consensus. This is not realistic; though his ultra-Lutheran adversaries represented Luther as more at variance from Calvin than he really was.[14] Calvin's claim here testifies to his almost pathetic craving for Lutheran-Reformed pacification and unity.

Some further attention to Calvin's ecumenical activities will require notice in chapters to follow. We have seen evidence of his willingness to be in communion with Christians who differed from him in what he held to be secondary matters, theological, liturgical, or organizational. A word is needed about the limits he habitually set regarding those qualified for inclusion within the true church. He recoiled from the self-approving leftists of all eras of Christianity, including his own. These were the *aerii daemones* ("airy spirits") or "angels of Paradise" such as the Donatists of old and "some of the Anabaptists," who claiming superior holiness mercilessly cast off offending members.[15] While he strongly opposed the Anabaptists on this and other grounds, he was in congenial company with the Waldenses and Bohemian Brethren, and encouraged those under his influence to unite with these pre-Reformation Biblical Christians. Holding firmly to the ancient creeds, he was antagonistic to all varieties of disbelief in the doctrine of the Trinity. More frequently we find him repudiating teachings and practices of the Roman church of his time. When sent by the Strassburgers to participate in the conference at Regensburg (Ratisbon) in 1541 he seems to have had little expectation of any fruitful interchange and to have left the presentation of the Protestant viewpoints mainly to his seniors Melanchthon and Bucer, more anxious to avoid or heal rifts among Protestants than to come to agreement with the Roman negotiators. He viewed adversely the "ambiguous formulas" on transubstantiation which, as he wrote to Farel on May 12, 1541, Melanchthon and Bucer had drawn up in the hope of a verbal agreement with the papal emissaries. Moreover, he vigorously criticized the papal policy in connection with this conference. In April, 1541, he published at Strassburg, under the pseudonym of Eusebius Pamphilus, a lengthy arraignment of Paul III's action in using a limited and controlled colloquy instead of calling a free and universal council. The pope, he argues, ought not to reject the plan set forth by the Council of Constance for a general council every ten years to reform and guide the church. The attack is primarily directed at Paul's instructions sent to the Colloquy by the hand of his young nephew. While Protestants had been associated with the three colloquies of Hagenau, Worms, and Regensburg, the pope, Calvin complains, had himself called them "worse than the Turks." Calvin is caustic on the cynicism and political artifices of the Roman Curia. Incidentally, he here uses the expression *catholici protestantes* of those who desire with him to see emerge one united communion, catholic and reformed.[16]

While he not infrequently asserts that there are true Christians in the Roman obedience, he usually appears completely alienated from the papal church of his time. He had hoped, as this tract shows, for a general council in which the demands of reformers would be heard and met. In a kind of encyclical letter to the Reformed churches of France, December, 1560, he set down conditions for holding "a free and universal council" which would "put an end to the divisions in Christendom." It should be centrally located and should be attended by elected representatives of those desiring reform, as well as by the prelates. While he insists that it be free from the management and control of the pope, he is disposed to concede that the pope should preside in it, but on the stipulation that he abdicate his domination and submit to its decisions. The Reformation churches must on their part also undertake to "accept the council" or be declared schismatics. However, when a few months later French Protestants were invited to confer with the French bishops at Poissy, Calvin was prevented from going only by the advice of his friends and the veto of the Geneva magistrates, who feared for his life in France. He fully approved of the participation of his colleague Beza and associated French ministers. On August 17, 1561, on the eve of the Poissy Colloquy, he wrote to Peter Martyr: "We should allow no opportunity of a happy arrangement to escape us." And it is not inappropriate to recall the earnest words with which he ends his animated reply to Cardinal Sadoleto—a prayerful glimpse of ecumenical unity amid the storms of the Reformation:

> The Lord grant, Sadolet, that you and all your party may at length perceive that the only true bond of ecclesiastical unity consists in this, that Christ the Lord, who has reconciled us to God the Father, gather us out of our present dispersion into the fellowship of his body, that so, through his one Word and Spirit, we may join together with one heart and one soul.[17]

With this may be compared a passage at the end of his last pamphlet against another opponent, the Lutheran Joachim Westphal (1557):

> But so long as any hope of pacification appears, it will not be my fault if mutual good-will is not maintained. Though from being unworthily provoked I have been more vehement in this writing than I was inclined to be, still were a time and place appointed for friendly discussion, I declare and promise that I will be ready to attend, and manifest a spirit of lenity which will not retard the desired success of a pious and holy concord. . . . Meanwhile I will beseech my Saviour whose proper office it is to gather together all that lies scattered throughout the world, that while our adversaries give no hope, he himself would find a remedy for this unhappy dissension.[18]

Calvin in various contexts voices his admiration for the ancient bishops and approves a jurisdictional episcopate for orderly administration and discipline, if it is strictly pastoral and free from tyrannical lordship.[19] It is not surprising, therefore, to find that he recommended to a Polish king a policy of reform by the agency of evangelical bishops (see below, p. 77). It was natural, too, that he should have sought the most cordial relations with Anglicans. This is plain from his correspondence not only with Cranmer but also with William Cecil and Archbishop Matthew Parker in Elizabeth's reign. It was Parker's wish that Calvin should attend the Colloquy at Poissy (see below, p. 30 ff.). In 1561 Calvin wrote to Parker to renew the proposals originated by Cranmer in the reign of Edward VI. His broad project here is "a general assembly of all the Protestant clergy wherever dispersed" as prelude to the forging of a union of "all the Reformed and Evangelic churches." Parker took the letter to the royal Council and was advised to reply favorably, with the condition that the English church would retain episcopacy, bestowed, as was claimed, by Joseph of Arimathea. But Parker had his hands full at home, and no action followed this exchange.[20]

Calvin was often harsh and vituperative toward those whom he believed to be in grave error, and even his well-meant criticisms of beloved colleagues may have taxed their patience. But his thought of the Holy Catholic Church was broad and deep, and he longed to see it visible and whole.

II

BEZA'S ECUMENICAL INTERESTS AND THE *HARMONY OF CONFESSIONS*

DURING Calvin's later years his colleagues Beza in Geneva and Farel in Neuchâtel were not less active than he in the quest of Christian union. Their efforts were not undertaken solely at his direction, nor were they discontinued at his death. William Farel (1489–1565) was in full career as a fiery preacher of reform before Calvin's conversion. It was to Farel that the eminent pre-Reformer Jacques Lefèvre d'Étaples exclaimed in 1512, "God will transform his church, and you will live to see it." Having for some time gathered congregations in towns of the Pays de Vaud, he first entered Geneva in 1532. In September of that year he attended an important synod of the Waldenses at Chanforan, and was largely instrumental in bringing that medieval Biblical sect into the circle of the Reformed churches. France now controlled an area formerly within the duchy of Savoy that was populated by Waldenses. In 1545 Francis I on false information sent troops among them, and many were put to the sword. At that time Calvin did his utmost to induce the German princes and Swiss magistrates to protest against the French king's action, to obtain relief for the impoverished survivors, and to settle Waldensian refugees in Geneva. A new persecution by Henry II in 1555 called forth similar activity on the part of Beza and Farel. In behalf of the Waldenses they visited the Protestant cantons of Switzerland. As a result Zurich, led by Bullinger, sent emissaries to Henry to plead for his Protestant and Waldensian subjects. Beza and Farel then went on to Strassburg and Heidelberg, ostensibly on the same errand. But they took the opportunity to bring Lutheran and Reformed ministers into discussion with a view to agreement. One of the Lutherans, John Marbach of Strassburg, had been in correspondence with Calvin, who tried to assure him that Luther, had he lived, would not have rejected the Zurich Consensus. Another was John Brenz of Stuttgart, with whom John à Lasco had held a futile two-day conference a year earlier. Both these Lutheran theologians proved unresponsive to the visitors, even though the latter went beyond Calvin in concessions to Lutheran positions. Beza framed, and with him Farel signed, May 10, 1557, a document, which seems somewhat alien to Reformed teaching. It states that "the true body and true blood are truly present, given and offered" in the sacrament, and its phrase "true flesh" (*vera carnis*) was startling to Calvin and particularly to Bullinger. Neither of them had been consulted on the terms exchanged. Calvin learned of the conference only in a letter from Francis Hotman written May 28. His chief anxiety, however, was to soothe Bullinger's wounded sensibilities. The incident did not lessen Bullinger's suspicion of danger in the mixed colloquies in which the Genevans were prone to engage.[1]

Fresh persecutions in France led Beza and Farel to attend a meeting of Lutheran theologians at Worms in October, 1557, to present to them the cause of the French Protestants. On their behalf Beza presented to the Lutherans a new confession. Its treatment of the Lord's Supper is comparable to that of the Zurich Consensus in the differentiation of Reformed teaching from that which would make of the sacrament a "mere sign." The document further proposes a conference to discuss this question with a view to complete definition and agreement. On other doctrines it is claimed that agreement already exists, so that the Reformed with the Lutherans already "form one true church of the Son of God." Calvin appears to have had knowledge of this statement in advance, since he wrote to Bullinger on October 7, one day before it was presented, "A confession of faith was also demanded, in which you will see that our brethren did not disguise their sentiments." What Calvin did not expect was that Brenz and Marbach would approve the document, but their signatures, with that of Melanchthon, were appended.[2] In this letter Calvin characteristically tries to overcome Bullinger's reluctance to meet with Lutherans in the unlikely event of a conference being arranged. In response to Beza's plea the German princes at Worms undertook to send a deputation to lodge a protest against the French persecutions; but on erroneous information that these had ceased, the matter was dropped until Beza had made another visit to Germany in 1558. A vigorously worded protest was then sent, but it did not affect King

Henry's policy. In 1559 Beza made a fourth journey with a renewed project for a consensus; but he found only the Strassburgers, among whom some memory of Bucer and Calvin remained, in any degree responsive to his persuasions. No general convention to frame a mutual agreement was now in sight, and such local conferences as there were proved quite futile. A few prominent theologians from each side conferred at Maulbronn in Württemberg in April, 1564: Brenz and Jacob Andreae for the Lutherans; Olevianus and Ursinus for the Reformed. The chief topic of discussion was the Lutheran doctrine of the ubiquity of Christ's resurrected body, and the result was only to register disagreement.[3]

A month later John Calvin died, and Beza succeeded to the leadership not only of the church of Geneva but of the whole growing nexus of Reformed churches in Europe. From about 1550, Calvinism began to spread into areas and nations far distant from Geneva. It was then that Calvinist worshiping groups appeared in Poland. The celebrated John à Lasco (Jan Laski), nephew and namesake of an influential Polish archbishop, having served Reformed churches in the West with distinction, spent his last years (1556–1560) in Poland seeking to promote the unity of the Protestant elements which had already gained some strength in that country. In Hungary after some decades of Lutheran influence the Protestant movement turned mainly Calvinist under the influence of Matthew Devay. Under the theological guidance of Peter Melius, the confessions of Debrecen (1560) and of Czenger (1570), the Hungarian and Transylvanian Calvinists set forth their beliefs in repudiation of Socinianism, which also had large acceptance. Some relevant later developments in these nations of eastern Europe will require attention in Chapter V. In the Netherlands a Bible-based movement largely influenced by Lutheranism had many resolute adherents, some of whom paid for their faith with their lives under the Hapsburg regime. But the national uprising for liberation from Spanish rule was accompanied by a rising tide of Calvinism which gained acceptance through the eloquent preaching of Francis Junius (du Jon) and other Geneva-trained ministers, and through the hearty singing in public assemblages of the psalms in French and Dutch. The Belgic Confession of Guido de Brès (1561), in its French original or in a Dutch version, served as a doctrinal standard; a Latin translation with some changes was prepared by Junius and adopted in 1566.

One of the greatest accessions to Calvinism was its adoption as the established form of religion by the great German electorate of the Palatinate. There the elector Frederick III (1559–1576) turned strongly from Lutheranism as then advocated, to Calvinism. He cooperated personally with his theological advisers Caspar Olevianus and Zacharias Ursinus in the preparation of the Heidelberg Catechism, promulgated in 1563, a document of wide influence and acceptance in Reformed churches. We shall resume our attention to these developments in Chapter IV.

Thus as consulting leader of the Calvinist parts of Europe, Beza inherited from Calvin an important and enlarging role. Historians of doctrine have left an impression of Beza as a rigid Calvinist who tightened Calvin's cautious treatment of the manner of predestination by adding an explicit supralapsarianism. But in some contrast with his theology, Beza's ecclesiology was, like Calvin's, elastic enough to bring him into hopeful discussions with both Lutherans and Roman Catholics. With the latter he had already conferred peaceably, in the hope of obtaining some toleration for the French Protestants and of contributing to the pacification of France. When in July, 1561, the queen mother, Catherine de Medici, invited the Reformed party to state their case before the French bishops, hoping thereby to secure the peace of the realm, the Protestants looked to Geneva for assistance. Calvin, as we have seen, on a decision not his own, was prevented from exposing himself to danger on French soil. But Beza, responding to the request of the ministers of Paris, undertook the mission. On August 22 he was at Saint-Germain-en-Laye, where he first met both Catherine and the cardinal of Lorraine, Charles de Guise. The formal Colloquy opened at Poissy on September 9 and was prorogued on the sixteenth; but ensuing conversations lasted until October 14. The meeting, to be sure, is not comparable to the conference at Regensburg twenty years earlier which began with some hope of discovering a way to a general reunion of the Western church. What Catherine and her chancellor, Michel de l'Hôpital, had in mind, for the present at least, was the more modest objective of establishing peace by mutual toleration within France.

Inevitably the Protestants were treated, however, not as equal partners in a peace-seeking effort, but as outsiders presenting a case for their existence before the bishops who were the religious establishment of France. Besides Beza, eleven French protestant ministers were present, including three or four who were scholarly writers, but no speeches from them are on record. The chancellor made at the outset a brief and conciliatory address, and Beza was given opportunity to speak. He first led the assembly in prayer, using the prayer of confession of sins in Calvin's Liturgy, and adding a petition that their meeting might conduce to "the comfort of all christendom and especially of this kingdom." He then delivered an hour-long eloquent defense of the cause of the Protestant minority, reciting first the numerous points of doctrine on which all were agreed and then explaining the evangelical affirmations on matters in debate, especially the Lord's Supper, which he expounded in typically Calvinist terms. One imprudently rhetorical sentence, however, aroused angry outcries. The body of Christ, he said, is in the sacrament "as far removed from the bread and wine as the highest heaven from the earth." There were loud exclamations of *"Blasphemavit Deum!"* and only Catherine's intervention made possible the continuance of his speech. Implying rather than fully reciting the abuses prevalent in the prelatical church, he called for the restoration of it to its pristine purity.

The bishops were offended, but were not ready to reply. By September 16 the Cardinal of Lorraine spoke for an hour and a half, following, however, a line of argument that had little to do with Beza's thought. Peter Martyr, who had been invited from Zurich and had arrived after Beza's address, reported that the Cardinal stressed the apostolical succession of bishops and the church's authority to judge tradition and Scripture, and that his treatment of the Eucharist avoided transubstantiation and the Mass but followed Lutheran lines. The Reformers craved an opportunity for rebuttal. Beza wrote to Calvin, September 17, that the Cardinal's speech had nauseated him.

The Protestant participants were convinced that Lorraine's introduction of the Lutheran doctrines was an attempt to divide them and to turn aside the thrust of Beza's arguments. Here and in the discussions that followed he demanded of the Protestants approval of the Augsburg Confession, although on their inquiry he himself declined to approve it. Benjamin Paist, in his valuable study of Martyr's part in the Colloquy, notes Martyr's repeated insistence on the spiritual nature of the sacrament and his tendency to speak independently of Beza and the others. Martyr had the advantage of speaking Italian with the Queen Mother, and the disadvantage of not speaking French, which, because of the presence of many laymen, had been made the language of the meeting. Martyr's opponents complained when he spoke Italian. But when the general of the Jesuits,

Diego Laynez, arrived, they welcomed his heated speech in that language. Laynez argued against any action by the Colloquy and urged the reference of the whole issue to the Council of Trent, then soon to reconvene. After his address, to escape a quarrelsome atmosphere, a joint committee of five on each side was put to work. The ten seriously tried to produce a workable agreement. They actually adopted a formula, but under influences emanating from the Sorbonne this was promptly rejected by the assembled prelates, and on October 19 the Colloquy broke up. On the same day, for reasons not made clear but apparently at the Cardinal of Lorraine's invitation, five German theologians of divergent views, sent by the princes of Württemberg and the Palatinate, arrived at Poissy, but they were too late to form vital contacts with members of the Colloquy.

It can hardly be said that the Colloquy of Poissy contributed anything toward the solution of the religious cleavage of France and of Europe. But some men had their minds changed by attending its sessions. Having listened to Beza and the Cardinal, Peter Ramus, the celebrated philosopher, became a Protestant. The Neapolitan Antoine Caracciolo, bishop of Troyes, was so impressed by the arguments of Martyr, who had once been his teacher, that after conversation with him he allowed himself to become bishop over the Protestant churches in his diocese, and often directed their worship after celebrating Mass in his cathedral. He was deposed by papal action, and died a Protestant in 1570. Despite some variations of approach and moments of mutual embarrassment, Martyr and Beza cemented a warm friendship, as their later correspondence shows; and this undoubtedly helped to maintain the link between Zurich and Geneva that had been formed by Calvin and Bullinger in 1549. Joseph C. McLelland has shown that Calvin, Bucer, and Martyr were in full agreement on the presence of Christ in the Eucharist. It is noteworthy that Bullinger, though he had parted company with Bucer and in 1557 complained of Calvin's involvement in Bucer's "overactivity" in seeking agreement through conferences, was in close correspondence with Martyr during the Colloquy and was seemingly content to let Martyr speak for the Zurich church. The meeting had not closed in anger, and there seemed indeed at its close some reason to hope that a more pacific spirit might pervade religiously divided Europe. It evidently gave some encouragement to the policy of toleration of Catherine and l'Hôpital which was to find expression in the edict of January 17, 1562.[4] But the peace that seemed thereby established in

France was to be shattered in one reckless act, the Massacre of Vassy, by the Duke of Guise (March 1), and France was plunged into the anguish of religious war.

An anonymous tractate attributed to Beza, *On Establishing the Peace of the Christian Churches*,[5] was published in Geneva in 1566. It is addressed to the emperor and the German estates assembled at Augsburg. The author's reason for concealing his name is that thereby his book may be read without prejudice. He hopes for a general council to bring the deplorably divided church to peace and unity. He exhorts the emperor (Maximilian II) to follow the example of his fourth- and fifth-century predecessors and take the initiative in calling a council. The ecumenical council of Chalcedon, for example, was summoned by the emperor to a place of his choice, away from Italy. There follows a discussion of the debated doctrine of the Lord's Supper. It is argued that "the bread is not elsewhere than on earth, the body of Christ not elsewhere than in heaven." To the question "in what sense the sacred bread and wine are body and blood" the answer is that "the corporal signs have sacramentally joined with the *res ipsas*, the body and blood of the Lord." Three initial requirements for effective union are presented: the abolition of superstitious non-Scriptural elements; the removal of things useless, though with consideration of circumstances; and taking the upbuilding of the church as the sole guiding principle with regard to what is discarded or established. If, as seems probable, this is a work of Beza, it is hardly one of his more brilliant writings.

In 1566 Beza was led by English Puritan correspondents to take an unfavorable view of the Church of England, which he regarded as only partly reformed and marred by papistical defects. Convinced that Queen Elizabeth had a hatred of Geneva, since she had been offended by the books of Knox and Goodman published there, he urged Bullinger to use his influence with the queen and the bishops in the cause of Puritan reform. Bullinger, however, was not disposed to provoke contention in England and from his knowledge of the complainants sensed that they were filled with animus against the bishops, whom he judged to be "men of piety and integrity." [6] Later Beza became more appreciative of the English church. With Archbishop Whitgift he engaged in frequent and mutually appreciative correspondence, a fact emphasized in Sir George Paule's *Life of Archbishop Whitgift* (1612). Whitgift, we are told, aided Beza out of his own purse and encouraged public contributions to Geneva, while

Beza in a letter of March 8, 1591, declared that he had never intended to impugn the ecclesiastical polity of the Church of England and hoped its "holy college of bishops" would ever continue to govern it in equity and moderation. He even calls Elizabeth the "nursing mother of the Church of Christ" and the English church "the pre-server of the other reformed churches." [7]

The problem of relations between the Reformed and the Lutheran churches in Beza's time was enhanced by disputes and changes within Lutheranism itself. Melanchthon had been a friend of Calvin and his work led in the direction of Christian agreement wherever possible. To this end he had been joint compiler with Martin Bucer of the Wittenberg Concord of 1536, of which Luther was a signatory. But the tide turned against him, and some years before his death he lost all confidence in synodical conferences as a method of resolving theological disputes. At the conference held at Worms following an imperial diet in 1557, Flacius Illyricus and others who took their stand on Luther's doctrine of the "ubiquity" of Christ's body in the sacrament, assailed Melanchthon bitterly, and all his eloquence in reply proved ineffective.[8] Not long afterward, the Huguenot scholar and international agent Hubert Languet interviewed him, and reported him outspokenly opposed to extremists such as Westphal, but crushed by the toil of the years and the calumnies of his opponents, and quite devoid of his wonted *hilaritas*.[9]

German Lutheranism, indeed, ever since Luther's death (1546) had been torn by strife over a number of theological issues. In the period following Melanchthon's death (1560) a great effort was put forth to bring an end to these contentions. Amid all the advocates of special theological positions there emerged mainly two parties. One of these, centered for a time at Wittenberg, adhered to the teachings of Melanchthon even where these diverged from Luther's in the direction of Calvinism. From Melanchthon's first name they were called Philippists. Their opponents, led by Flacius Illyricus, were often called Flacians. In many contexts the former are dubbed Crypto-Calvinists, since they were accused of a secret or concealed attachment to Calvinism, while the latter were sometimes called Gnesio-Lutherans on the view that they were the genuine followers of Luther himself. It was increasingly evident that the rigid party was gaining ground; but most were weary of the conflict, and in the 1570's a strong effort was made to find a basis for Lutheran pacification. With great labor a group of theologians compiled the Formula of Concord. This long and scholastic statement of doctrine was completed in 1577, and in 1580 it was adopted by the chief Lutheran governments as of authority within their territories. Its authorization was felt by Calvinists generally to be an intended rebuff since it definitely excluded them from fellowship. While it rejects many of the more extreme positions of the Flacians and can be shown to be at many points in agreement with Reformed theology, it nevertheless repudiates in the strongest language what it represents as Calvin's position on the Lord's Supper. The Calvinist "Sacramentarians" are declared to be more dangerous than the Zwinglians in that they are crafty in concealing gross opinions under high-sounding phrases.[10] The adoption of this standard of faith marked the complete rejection in official Lutheranism of the Melanchthonian element conciliatory to Calvinism. Some years earlier, indeed, the Philippists had lost their stronghold in Wittenberg. By action of the elector Augustus of Saxony a sudden purge of the university took place in 1574. The prince's motives seem to have been mixed; and his Danish consort Anne had an influence upon him. She conceived an intense dislike for Casper Peucer, Melanchthon's son-in-law, the elector's physician, especially after her infant son had been held in Peucer's hands at baptism and soon after died. Peucer, though a medical professor, was deep in theology, and carried Melanchthon's teachings farther in the direction of Calvinism. Augustus was persuaded that Peucer was the author of a boldly pro-Calvinist book (really written by a Silesian, Joachim Curaeus) which appeared in January, 1574, and was angered on the mistaken ground that he had been deceived over this. Peucer was imprisoned at Leipzig until the death of the electress twelve years later. Members of the theological faculty were scattered, to find employment in Hesse, Hamburg, and Nassau where the Formula would not be adopted and Calvinism was in favor.[11]

Convinced ecumenists are apt to be incurable optimists. Not even the adoption of the Formula in most of Lutheran Germany was sufficient to discourage Beza from continuing his irenical efforts. His former associate, Farel, was now deceased (1565), but he had the support of his Genevan colleagues, and the French Protestant leaders were active in the same cause. While some of the German principalities were still indisposed to accept the Formula a notable international conference took place at Frankfort attended by representatives of England and the Continental Reformed states and churches (1577).[12] There the Prince Palatine, John Casimir, urged that steps be taken to unite all the "Reformed and Protestant churches of the world." In response, the French national synod of Sainte-Foy in 1578 determined to send a delegation of four ministers, headed by Antoine de Chandieu, together with representatives of all the twenty-four provincial synods of France, to visit the Lutheran churches of Germany and treat with them on the unity issue. The national synod meeting at Figeac a year later proposed steps toward the preparation of a common confession for Protestants, and resolved "to seek and obtain all suitable means for uniting all the faithful of the particular confessions of the Protestant nations in a single confession of faith." The national synod of Gap (1603), on an overture from the provincial synod of Dauphiné, in order to end "the schism between us and them," authorized the sending of "letters to the orthodox universities of Germany, England, Scotland, Geneva, Basel, and Leiden (and to certain persons in London) entreating them to labor with us to effect this holy union." [13]

These proposals are in accord with the normal attitude of Reformed leaders in that age, but they were called forth by the rising tide of adverse Lutheran opinion about the time of the completion of the Formula of Concord, and in the fading hope of forestalling the final adoption of this statement which seemed irrevocably to exclude the Reformed from communion. At the Frankfort conference Jerome Zanchi, then professor at Heidelberg, won approval for his proposal to prepare a new confession of faith, but without result. A year before the adoption of the Formula by the Lutheran states, the ministers of Zurich put forth a project for compiling a book to exhibit the essential agreement of the existing Protestant confessions (1579). Such agreement in essentials had constantly been claimed, but to make the point obvious in a comparative display of texts would at least help to lodge it in the minds of readers. The Zurichers' suggestion was soon to bear fruit; but it was in Geneva, not in Zurich, that the work was produced.

The impressive volume *Harmonia confessionum fidei* appeared in Geneva in 1581. It was largely on Beza's initiative that this work was undertaken and brought to completion, though it was apparently chiefly penned by others. It was circulated under the name of "Monsieur Salnar," an error for [Jean François] Salvard or Salvart, who, with Antoine de Chandieu, the well-known leader of the French church and editor of the French Confession of 1559, the scholar and author Lambert Daneau, and the pastor and poet Simon Goulart, assisted in compiling the book.[14] It contained in its first edition extensive extracts from eleven confessions, Lutheran, Reformed, and Anglican, arranged under nineteen theological topics, so as to exhibit the essential agreement of these authoritative Protestant statements. There is added in the English edition of 1586 "A Preface in the Name of the Churches of France and Belgia," evidently by the compilers, in which it is claimed that the Reformed have always been "desirous of peace and agreement." Regret is expressed that the state of the times has not permitted the holding of a general council, but the writers look forward to some future "common councell of the churches of well-nigh all of Europe" to frame a common confession. The book bears testimony to the attachment of the communions represented to "the holie and truelie Catholick Church of God" and is designed "to knit all the churches of Christ together with one band of brotherlie love." Thus it is evident that the *Harmony* was intended not merely as proof of existing doctrinal agreement in essentials but also as a reminder that the unitive assembly that had so often been advocated was still, despite all discouragement, a vivid hope in Reformed circles. The English version, containing as an appendix the First Scots Confession of 1560, was reprinted at the time of the Westminster Assembly (1643), and in 1842 appeared in a critical revision, with ample bibliographical and other notes, by Peter Hall. The Scottish Confession is here incorporated in the main work, and the Thirty-nine Articles, the Irish Articles of 1615, the Decrees of the Synod of Dort, and the Westminster Assembly's Confession of Faith are appended. The addition of an admirable index (by Thomas Timpson) makes this substantial volume a highly useful reference work, despite some obvious limitations of the editor's mind and era.[15]

The *Harmony* was welcomed everywhere in Reformed circles. It was formally approved in 1583 by the national Reformed Synod of Vitré, which called for the circulation of a French translation. But its influence could be educative only, not otherwise creative. It did not contain even the first draft of a confession for common use, much less lay down a procedure for the establishment of unity.

Beza and his associates still followed the gleam of a consensus solution. Through a strange chain of events he obtained an opportunity to confer with Jacob Andreae of Tübingen, the chief framer of the Formula of Concord. The comté of Montbéliard had earlier come under the control of the dukes of Württemberg, although it lay across the Rhine from that state and its people were French-speaking.

It had been protestantized through Farel's evangelical preaching, but was now under pressure to abandon its Reformed practices. The late duke of Württemberg, Christopher (d. 1568), had been a warm correspondent of Calvin who dedicated to him his Commentary on Galatians. His successor, Louis, however, was pressing the cause of exclusive Lutheranism and urging his minister at Montbéliard, Count Frederick, to make changes accordingly in his district. But the comté had not in 1586 been brought under the Formula of Concord and Frederick himself desired a peaceful settlement. On his invitation, Beza went to Montbéliard to discuss the situation with Andreae. In March of 1586 they engaged in a protracted but fruitless discussion. The only result was to confirm the lasting disagreement between the two branches of Protestantism which the Formula had declared. When they parted, Andreae refused to Beza "the hand of brotherhood," offering instead only "the hand of benevolence and humanity," which Beza in turn declined.[16]

Beza began as a humanist scholar and his importance for the Reformation rests in part on his textual work on the New Testament for which he provided an authoritative Greek text and a Latin translation. Of wide service and influence, too, was his French edition of the Psalter which, with similar versions in other languages, gave to the Reformed churches a singing voice. A numerous army of ministers went forth from the Geneva Academy, which he headed, to spread the Reformed message in many lands. It is sometimes forgotten when these facts are called to mind that Beza was also an active advocate of church unity, always eager to be in conference with those who differed from him, with one comprehensive aim in view: "to knit all the churches of Christ together with one band of brotherly love."

Mention should here be made of another close friend of Calvin, Pierre Viret (1511–1571), a convert of Farel who after a notable work of reform and educational effort at Lausanne, punctuated by periods at Calvin's side in Geneva, spent his later years building and serving Reformed congregations in southern France. Viret was an irenical spirit. He was at one time accused by the Bernese of being a Lutheran and a Bucerian because of his fraternal attitude to Lutherans and his strong sense of the essential unity of all evangelical Christians. But he was hardly more inclined than Bullinger to enter into negotiations for formal acts of union. This is to be associated with his view of the autonomy of the worshiping congregation. The English translation in 1573 of selections from his *Christian Instruction* may, as Robert Dean Linder has suggested, have exercised some influence on the rise of congregationalist ideas in England. He seems not to have felt hopeful that conferences or synods would produce any unitive results. This involved in his case no harsh judgments of Lutherans or others. A high estimate of the democratically organized local church was coupled in his mind with a kindly tolerance of divergent elements in other churches and a consciousness of the reality and mystical unity of the universal church of all true believers. He thought it a heinous crime "to take away life in the name of God," and from John, chs. 10 and 13, reminded both Roman Catholics and Huguenots that Christ taught his followers to love not only their friends but also their enemies. He believed in the persuasive force of Christian love, and looked toward a future reunion on this basis, by mutual consent and in obedience to the Word of God. In April, 1562, the war in France having begun, a Jesuit priest, Emond Auger, was menaced by a Protestant mob in Valence, when Viret boldly intervened to save his life. He was later in written controversy with Auger, and apparently engaged in peaceful dialogue with him at Lyon in 1564. In an open letter to the citizens of Lyon "of both religions" written in April of that year he advocated efforts to solve the religious strife by means of friendly private conversations. Nothing resulted from this interchange except mutual respect; and a year later Auger, taking offense at another of Viret's writings, was instrumental in having him expelled from French territory. He soon ventured back, but apparently his efforts were now wholly connected with the internal problems of his own communion.[17] He represents an approach to church unity problems very different from that of Calvin and Beza, and seems to have had nothing to do publicly with their efforts in this field; yet he remained in warm fraternal relations with them both, and to a remarkable degree shared Calvin's personal confidences in times of crisis. Viret is evidently not typical of Reformed churchmen in his ecumenical outlook. The others would not censure him for his private-conversation procedure, but they usually thought in terms of structured assemblies in which the participants would represent organized churches and be empowered to commit these to unitive action.

III

FRENCH AND SWISS REFORMED PROPONENTS OF PROTESTANT UNITY

THE REFORMED churches of France and Switzerland maintained close ties through the seventeenth and eighteenth centuries. In both countries there were at all times numerous leaders and writers who gave testimony to their vital interest in the unification of the churches of the Reformation. The acts of the synods of Sainte-Foy (1578) and Figeac (1579)[1] are indicative of the normal attitude of the Reformed through the entire period. In a later typical avowal of the unitive principle, Jean Alphonse Turretin of Geneva, replying in 1707 to an inquiry of the king of Prussia, was able to affirm that it had been the constant and unanimous attitude of his church that there existed no doctrinal impediment to its union with Lutherans. Individual theologians of both Lutheran and Reformed affiliation from time to time formed friendly relations with Anglican scholars; and an interesting book could be written about French Protestant personalities who played a part in the ranks of the Anglican clergy. At the same time, a considerable number of Scottish Presbyterians found a career in the service of the Huguenot academies or in the pastorate in France and Holland. After the new philosophical and political liberalism stemming from Descartes, Spinoza, Bayle, Leibnitz, and Locke began to alter the tone of theology, the earlier type of impassioned controversial writing lost much of its appeal. A new tolerance tended to dissolve the dogmatism that made for discord. But this detachment from some of the old divisive causes was in itself impotent to abolish the divisions. The lasting condition of separation, hardened by custom and strengthened by loyalty to forebears, would be hard to alter. It was only after Pietism and Evangelicalism and nineteenth-century Biblical and historical scholarship had enlivened the churches

40

that a more positive religious concern for unity brought forth the beginnings of the ecumenical revival that is stirring in all sections of Christianity today. Nevertheless it is well worth our while to pass in review some of the efforts and ideas of leading advocates of unity in that era, the spiritual antecedents of those in our century who have given more successful leadership in the same cause.

The French church had the services of numerous able theological scholars, but, conditioned as it was by an unfavorable political environment, it relied for leadership in no small degree on certain eminent laymen who were deeply involved in politics. One of these was Gaspard de Coligny, admiral of France, whose assassination in 1572 was the opening act in the Massacre of St. Bartholomew. Coligny was one of the few sixteenth-century statesmen who had a grasp of the affairs of Europe and a vision of the possibilities of America. He hoped to plant Protestant colonies of France in the New World, and attempted this in Brazil (1556) and in northern Florida (1564). His aim in promoting these adventures was to establish a footing for France in those areas of the New World dominated by her colonial rivals Portugal and Spain, while securing there for the future freedom for the Huguenots to profess and practice their religion.[2] Coligny was described even by an enemy as "a man wholly religious,"[3] and his political integrity and humanity in war have often been praised. Yet his policy of uniting the contending religious parties in France by having them join in a war against the Spaniards in the Netherlands cannot be commended on grounds either of religion or of prudence. The disastrous outcome helped to bring on Catherine de Medici's desperate decision to destroy Coligny and exterminate the Huguenots in the St. Bartholomew massacre, 1572.

After "the slaughter of the Huguenots," there were, however, many survivors who would be heard from. The French Protestant layman who after Coligny most obviously possessed similar qualities of greatness was Philip du Plessis Mornay (1549–1623), a versatile and vivid personality—statesman, soldier, and writer. Born at the period of the perilous beginnings of organized Protestantism in France, he early encountered experiences calculated to alert his mind to the religious tension, while the influence of his mother and of his tutors in the sacred languages turned him strongly to evangelical religion. While still in his teens, Mornay engaged in "an amiable conference" with clerical disputants, whom he surprised by his superior competence in Greek and Hebrew. A traveling scholar, he paid extended visits to many schools in Italy and Germany, and profited especially in Heidelberg, Frankfort, and Padua. He also made leisurely tours, making the acquaintance of scholars in Moravia, Bohemia, Austria, the Netherlands, and England. When he was twenty-two he was engaged in a protracted and courteous disputation with a Portuguese priest and theologian at Cologne. At Frankfort he first met the Burgundian Hubert Languet, an experienced and trusted international Protestant errand man, friend and correspondent of Calvin, who had spent much time at Wittenberg and felt the influence of Melanchthon. Mornay formed with this elder statesman an intimate and lasting friendship, signalized later by their joint authorship of a famous book, the *Defense Against Tyrants* (*Vindiciae contra tyrannos*). With these two, Sir Philip Sidney, five years Mornay's junior, came to form a strange international triumvirate. All three were in Paris at the time of the Massacre of St. Bartholomew, young Sidney being sheltered in the house of the English ambassador Sir Francis Walsingham, whose daughter he would marry. While the carnage still raged, Mornay, with help from Walsingham and Languet, made his escape to England. Walsingham would later prove a political favorer of the presbyterian puritans in England. Sidney's correspondence with Languet, largely concerned with the international interests of Protestantism, has a certain bearing on the theme of this book, and will find mention below.

The fact that the destined lay leader of the Reformed in France had such connections as these outside his country undoubtedly had a part in arousing in his mind an ecumenical interest. At a very early age he is known to have shared the counsels of Coligny, and is even credited with the writing of Coligny's proposal to King Charles IX for the Netherlands war.[4] He entered the service of Henry of Navarre, and much of his activity was in military and political operations on behalf of that prince. It was chiefly after Henry's assassination (1610) that he played a notable role in the decisions of his church. He remained in Henry's confidence long after the king's prudential conversion to Roman Catholicism in 1593. Before that date, however, writings of Mornay put forth in Henry's name called for a meeting of a free general or national council on religion (*un bon, legitime et libre concile général ou national*) with a view to the pacification of France and of Europe (1588, 1589). Though busy with public affairs, he found time to be the author of books of distinction. Apart from the *Vindiciae*[5] (a political work of significance marked by a strong

Calvinist piety, part of which was from the pen of his friend Languet) most of his writings belong directly in the field of religion and theology. Best known of these is *The Truth of the Christian Religion* (1581), a theological and philosophical confutation of atheism and of the chief non-Christian religions. Sidney's translation of this Latin work was interrupted by his death from wounds at Zutphen (1586); it was completed, as Sidney had asked, by his friend Arthur Golding, and was much read in England. It won the appreciation of Roman Catholics as well as Protestants. Apparently Mornay was the author of an anonymous treatise entitled *Exhortation to Peace, to the French Catholics* (1574); and in many utterances he expressed a longing for the religious pacification of France. Mornay's *Treatise on the Church,* published in London (1579) and widely translated, is primarily a defense of the Reformation, with ample citations from the Bible, the Fathers, and the early councils. A feature of the argument is an assertion of the continuity of the Reformation with the late medieval resistance to the papacy, particularly at the Council of Constance. Having attacked the corruptions of the Roman church, Mornay denies that his fellow believers have broken the communion of the church and raised altar against altar:

> We hold to be true members of Christ all those who worship the one God in spirit and in truth, and hope for their salvation in Jesus Christ alone. . . . We desire complete union with those who (in whatever country or region they may be, and whatever may remain among them of corruption, not only of morals but in some points of doctrine) deplore the servitude, corporal or spiritual, which they endure and pray to the Lord of light that it may please him to enlighten them more and more by his Holy Spirit.[6]

Perhaps his most laborious theological work, weighted with patristic learning, was on *The Holy Sacrament of the Eucharist* (1598). Some of his writings are devotional, such as his *Discourse on Life and Death,* a marriage gift to his bride, Charlotte Arbaleste, who was to write an informing account of his life through the period 1584 to 1606.

It is not surprising that a layman so theologically competent, and so eminent in public affairs, should have great influence in the national synods of his church. We have noted above the irenical acts of the synods of 1578 and 1579.[7] The Synod of Vitré in 1583 not only adopted the *Harmony of Confessions* but also, under Mornay's influence and with the backing of Henry of Navarre, sent an emissary, Jacques Ségur, Seigneur de Pardaillon, on a mission that lasted for eighteen months, to England, the Netherlands, Denmark, and Germany, to lodge an appeal against the characterization of Reformed theology in the Formula of Concord, to call attention to the perils of Protestant division, and to propose a meeting of a general synod to frame the terms of Protestant union.[8] The Synod of Vitré also approved Mornay's *Treatise on the Church,* defending it from numerous assailants.

The Guise faction in France was eager to exploit the Lutheran rejection of the Reformed. The rebuff suffered by Beza at Montbéliard in 1586 encouraged the Guises and the Catholic League in their hope to bring about the extinction of Protestantism in France. We are here in the era of the political and military activity of the Huguenots, and their desire for international Protestant unity is frankly motivated in part by the peril to their survival posed by the Catholic League. But, for that matter, Lutheran states were also imperiled. Some of them, led by Hesse, had declined to adopt the Formula of Concord, a fact that gave some encouragement to the French advances. Had the scheme for a political and religious alliance of Protestantism succeeded, the course of subsequent Western history would almost certainly have been vastly altered. But we should go far wrong to conclude that the motivation of the French Protestant unity proposals was solely to ward off the danger of suppression. The religious desire for a wider communion among Christians was always a yeast in Calvinism.

England had reason to watch Continental religious affairs, especially after the papal excommunication of Elizabeth I in 1570, and English sympathy was largely with the Reformed churches. With Walsingham as secretary of state (1573–1590), this sympathy had occasional expression in foreign policy. In 1577 Elizabeth sent Sidney, accompanied by his distinguished literary friends Fulke Greville and Sir Edward Dyer, to visit the new emperor, Rudolf II, and John Casimir of the Palatinate, a leading Reformed prince in Germany, who ten years earlier had fought in the cause of the Huguenots, and who now shared with Sidney utopian plans for a *foedus evangelicum* throughout Europe. "This was," says Malcolm Wallace, a competent biographer of Sidney, "a project dear to Sidney's heart." He further states that "from the time of his return to England in 1577 Sidney's one absorbing interest during the remainder of his life was in the cause of continental Protestantism with which he believed the welfare of England to be bound up." [9] Before his return Mornay had begun a two-year stay in England in the interest of the Huguenots and their European policies, and, as Mme. de Mornay later wrote, his most intimate friends there were Walsingham and Sidney. Mornay was in a position to represent the still Protestant Henry of Navarre, the Huguenot chiefs and the Reformed Church of France. Besides dealing with Elizabeth's ministers, he formed a relationship with James VI of Scotland, soon to be James I of England. When James came to the English throne Mornay had great expectations of his possible role in the unification of the Reformation churches of Europe. He soon found much to regret in James's policy, including his unnecessarily vehement blasts against both the pope and the Puritans. But in 1611 Mornay dedicated to James the Latin edition of a work severely hostile to the papal claims; and two years later the marriage of James's daughter Elizabeth to Frederick V of the Palatinate (that ill-starred victim of the early phase of the Thirty Years' War) seemed to promise well for English cooperation with French Protestant union plans. James was indeed, though cautious, somewhat more disposed than Elizabeth had been to promote the common cause of European Protestantism, and had lent financial aid to the Protestants of Paris.

The Paris minister Pierre du Moulin (1568–1658), one of the ablest of the French Protestant pastors of that age, was associated with Mornay in his irenical efforts. Like Mornay, he had spent years in England, partly as a student at Cambridge under the Calvinist Anglican William Whitaker. Later, keeping in touch with English church affairs, he showed a qualified admiration for Anglicanism. He was committed to the cause of Protestant union, and looked to King James to play a central role in promoting it. The king, on his part, was pleased by Du Moulin's *Defense of the Catholic Faith* (1610), a work written in support of the opinions of James to refute a Dominican pamphleteer. After a conference with Du Moulin, Mornay wrote, October 4, 1613, to the English ambassador Sir Thomas Edmonds, seeking to enlist the king's patronage of a "salutary design" for the union of the churches. Mornay wrote a memorandum of the same date approving a project for unity which Du Moulin had prepared. Lucien Rimbault in his book on Du Moulin has identified the original proposal with the nineteen articles entitled *Ouvertures pour travailler à l'union des églises de chrétienté* (1613?), which, with Mornay's alterations, emerged as the twenty-one articles presented to the national Synod of Tonneins in May, 1614.

It was the Scot David Home (or Hume), then pastor of Duras in Gascony, who presented the project to the Synod. Having visited his homeland and conferred with King James in London, Home was able to bring to the Synod a letter from the king, which he was authorized to amplify by word of mouth. The letter expressed the British sovereign's ardent desire for peace and union among all sincere professors of the Christian faith, but without any commitment to the specific project. James had a pained reference to a theological quarrel internal to the French church, in which Du Moulin was one of the contestants, and the Synod took action to bring about "a holy reconciliation" and, by the destruction of the angry pamphlets exchanged, to "abolish the memory of the dispute." [10] But Home took occasion to present the detailed project for union which had originated with Du Moulin, and came with the revisions of Mornay. It was to embrace "the Christian churches that have cast off the yoke of the pope." As a first step a colloquy is projected, to meet preferably in Zealand as having ready access to England, with delegates from England, Scotland, France, the Netherlands, Switzerland, the Palatinate, etc. By this body a document would be compiled containing fundamental materials from the various Reformed confessions and bypassing controversial points. All the deputies would partake of communion together, following a religious fast. Only peaceable, grave, God-fearing and prudent men were to be commissioned to this meeting. During the session there would be fasting and prayer among the churches for the good success of the pious design. King James is several times referred to with great respect, and is indeed looked to as the patron of the scheme. Following the first stage, a second representative assembly is to be convoked. In the meanwhile His Majesty of Great Britain would be expected to join in requesting the Lutheran princes and churches to cooperate, and to send "pastors and doctors to work in concert with us." Numerous points of difference between Lutherans and Reformed, including the doctrine of ubiquity, are briefly treated in a noncontroversial way. While disagreements are looked upon as consisting in matters not essential, it is recognized that some of them will remain. But it is proposed to bring controversy over them to an end and to live in fraternal unity awaiting further light from God. The procedure in the second assembly would be the same as in the first, and it would conclude with a fast and celebration of the Lord's Supper, Lutheran and Reformed ministers communicating together. The uniting churches would now no longer be called Lutheran, Calvinist, or Sacramentary, all such odious distinctions being abolished, but "Christian Reformed Churches." It is not proposed that they become one church except in the sense that full intercommunion is established. The Consensus of Sendomir, a pact of brotherly friendship formed by the Polish Protestants in 1570, was to be circulated as a helpful example of the union proposed. The result, at least for the time being, would be a federation of churches territorially organized, mutually supporting each other and practicing full intercommunion. This end having been achieved it would be time to make overtures to the Church of Rome, though there appeared now little hope for a favorable response in that quarter.

The document was neither formally approved nor rejected by the Synod. It was declared "worthy of a great king," but action on it was courteously postponed to a more convenient season. Most of the points just recited are in the original "Ouvertures" of Du Moulin. It is to be regretted that, with other French delegates, he was forbidden by Louis XIII to attend the Synod of Dort, where his presence might have widened the ecclesiastical horizon.

As governor of Saumur, Mornay instituted there in 1599 a famous Protestant academy which was to represent the avant-garde factor in Reformed theology until its suppression by Louis XIV, in January, 1684, shortly before the Revocation. The faculty was an international one, as we are reminded by the brilliant names of Francis Gomarus, brought from Amsterdam, Mark Duncan from Edinburgh, and John Cameron from Glasgow; while English, Scottish, Swiss, Dutch, German, and Hungarian students mingled with Frenchmen in the classrooms.[11] The most eminent name among the Saumur teachers is that of Moïse Amyraut (1596–1664), whom Richard Stauffer has characterized, in a closely written study,[12] as "a French herald of ecumenism." We may here refer only to two phases of the ecumenical record of Amyraut. He was the man chiefly responsible for the formal admission of Lutherans by the national Synod of Charenton (1631) to the rites and communion of the Reformed church of France. It was declared that "since the Churches of the Confession of Augsburg are in agreement with the other Reformed Churches with regard to the fundamental points of sound religion, and have in their worship neither superstition nor idolatry," they may, without abjuring their Lutheran opinions, "be received with us at the Lord's Table, con-

tract marriages with the faithful of our confession," and as parents
present their children for baptism, promising to instruct them in the
doctrines that are held in common between the two confessions. This
notable "decree of Charenton" [13] called forth strange responses. A
Protestant gentleman, Théophile Brachet de Milletière, assailed it as
a proposal for a "shameful syncretism." He was answered by the
distinguished historical scholar David Blondel, secretary of a score
of the national synods, whose hand had probably shaped the document. On the other hand some Roman Catholics inferred that since
the door was opened for believers in consubstantiation it would also
be opened for believers in transubstantiation; but John Daillé, chaplain to Mornay and defender of the theology of Amyraut, interpreted
the decree otherwise. This was in accord with the general attitude
of the French and other Reformed churches. They applied the word
"idolatry" to the Roman Mass, not to Lutheran rites. As Elie Benoit
later wrote, they regarded Lutheran error as not poisonous and
Lutheran worship as not idolatrous.[14]

The other part of Amyraut's contribution lies in his two treatises
on topics connected with ecumenism. In 1647 he published *A Discussion of Secession from the Roman Church and of a Plan to Bring
about Peace among Evangelicals in Matters of Religion.* This is in
reality a defense of the policy involved in the Charenton Decree, of
seeking communion with the Lutherans while remaining in separation
from the Church of Rome. It was dedicated to a young German
prince, William VI of Hesse, who had attracted Amyraut's notice
while spending some months in the environs of Saumur. The other
treatise, *Eirenicon, or Advice on a Plan to Bring about among Evangelicals Peace in Matters of Religion,* appeared in 1662. It was written
in response to a request from persons under the influence of John
Dury, following the Colloquy of Cassel, June, 1661. This important
meeting was held at the call of the landgrave William VI of Hesse,
to whom Amyraut had addressed the earlier treatise. Jean Melet,
through whom the request came, was a disciple of Dury and chaplain
to Anne of Chantilly, a great-granddaughter of Coligny, and herself
interested in Reformed-Lutheran relations.

The *Eirenicon* is now an extremely rare book and Professor Stauffer
is the first modern historian to examine it with precision. Amyraut
is here primarily concerned with the issue of intercommunion with
the Lutherans. As with earlier Reformed advocates of this (including
Pareus, who will be discussed below, whose *Irenicum* Amyraut alludes

to only once), he lays stress on the existing common element of belief, embracing the fundamental articles of sound religion.[15] He reviews the differences in polity among the churches, and admits the legitimacy of a variety of ecclesiastical governments, including the Lutheran system of superintendents and the Anglican episcopate. Just as states differently governed may form treaties of alliance, so churches may join together despite differences of polity. With respect to worship, Amyraut is prepared to concede to the Lutherans the use of images, altars, candles, the sign of the cross in baptism, kneeling in the reception of the Eucharist. In doctrine he finds that the differences lie in matters nonessential. He desires to see these differences reduced as far as possible through discussion, and, beyond that, mutually tolerated. He examines in some detail variations in the interpretation of the sacraments, including the Lutheran exposition of the *communicatio idiomatum* and the doctrine of ubiquity (erroneously supposing that the latter was introduced after Luther), and points to the fact that these conceptions are not embodied in the Lutheran liturgies. To be sure, he says, "we would like to convince the Lutherans, [but failing this] let them keep their opinions; we tolerate them willingly, since we judge them to contain no pernicious poison. Let the Lutherans undertake to win us to their ideas, if they can. . . . Our wish is that the Lutherans refuse not to take the Supper with us, since we require them to abjure nothing, and permit us to commune with them, without demanding that we renounce our doctrine." He further proposes, in accord with the Decree of Charenton, that a confession be prepared with a revised joint statement on the Eucharist, in which the manner of the presence may be expressed by the words *realiter* and *sacramentaliter*. He goes beyond mere intercommunion to propose that ministers of each confession be eligible to serve in congregations of the other, and that interchange of pulpits should be begun without delay. Both Amyraut and his associate John Daillé believed that the doctrine of hypothetical predestination which Amyraut had received from John Cameron, and for which he had to answer before two national synods, in its departure from the predestination doctrine of the Synod of Dort, would help to conciliate Lutheran opinion in that field. However, his treatise on predestination (1634) long preceded his ecumenical treatise, and did not arise from his irenic interests. Stauffer in his conclusion describes Amyraut as "a believer and a theologian; a believer who, wholly attached to his church, longed for the *Una Sancta* with all his soul." The fact that young William Penn was closely associated with Amyraut in his studies for three years, during which time the *Eirenicon* was written, may not improbably have had some effect on Penn's irenic approach to politics marked by his *Essay toward the Present and Future Peace of Europe.*

Opposition to Amyraut arose on the part of some of his fellow ministers; but this was in criticism of his novel interpretation of predestination and did not involve a rejection of his irenic ideas. One of his doctrinal opponents was Pierre du Moulin; but Du Moulin supported the Charenton Decree, and on behalf of the pastors and professors of Sedan wrote in 1633 to Archbishop Abbot asking him "to promote the meeting of a general synod of the Protestant churches for the purpose of reconciling their differences." The reply came from Archbishop Laud in the name of King Charles I, and was non-committal.[16]

A more liberal strain of irenic and unitive thought was already finding expression. It was early exemplified in the writings of Isaac Casaubon (d. 1614), son of a French pastor, alumnus of the Geneva Academy and teacher there, friend of Mornay and librarian to Henry IV in Paris. Casaubon, whose father introduced him to Greek while in the woods hiding from persecutors, was already in high repute as a Greek scholar when on Henry IV's assassination he responded to Archbishop Bancroft's invitation to Canterbury (1610). Although he had no mind for religious contention, he was induced to undertake controversial writings on behalf of King James. He assailed Archbishop Perron's denial to James of any claim to be called a Catholic king, and defended against Cardinal Bellarmine the filiation of the Reformation from the early church. Also at the bidding of the king he undertook the refutation of the famous *Annales* of Baronius, a task that occupied his latest years and was left far from complete. While Casaubon remained a loyal son of the Reformation, he earnestly desired the general reunion of the church. In works of 1611 and 1612 he sets forth as a basis of unity a doctrine of the Catholic Church as it can be described from the patristic writings of the first six centuries, while he defends the Reformation as essentially in agreement with these. He was of course aware that a similar reference back to the Church Fathers as guides to the one true church had been common in the sixteenth century. On the Protestant side, the Fathers were appealed to as interpreters of Scripture, while Roman Catholics tended to see in them witnesses to tradition. The formula of Vincent of Lérins (ca. 430), "what has been believed always, everywhere and by all," had been adopted by George Cassander in his celebrated *Con-*

sultatio inter Catholicos et Protestantes (1564). Calvin did not live to
see this work. He had, indeed, expressed a dislike for Cassander as a
deceiver; but this attitude was formed through Cassander's association with Francis Baudouin, who had access to Calvin's files and
grossly betrayed him.[17] Actually this approach has affinities with
Calvin's reading of church history, in which the great apostasy of the
church is linked with the papal assumption of world power after the
pontificate of Gregory the Great. Cassander's view not only was revived
by Casaubon but was also an anticipation of the proposal put forth
by the Lutheran George Calixtus (d. 1656) for union on the basis of
"the first five centuries." It is noteworthy that Calixtus made Casaubon's acquaintance on a visit to London in 1612.[18] Though intellectu-
ally a product of Geneva, Casaubon was perhaps almost as much an
Erasmian as a Calvinist in his outlook on the divided church. Nevertheless he definitely belongs in the present context, since he gave his
allegiance to the Reformers in a warm general approval of their
principles and in his testimony to their agreement with the Fathers.

Throughout the seventeenth century, tracts on Christian unity emanating from French Reformed ministers were numerous. In 1655 David
Blondel placed on record many of the declarations that had been
made by the Reformed churches in this cause. His title deserves translation in full: *Authentic Acts of the Reformed Churches of France,
Germany, Great Britain, Poland, Hungary, the Netherlands, etc.,
concerning the Peace and Brotherly Charity which all the Servants of
God ought to Preserve as Sacred, with the Protestants who have some
Diversity either in Expression or Method or even Opinion; Compiled
in One for the Comfort and Confirmation of Pious Souls and for the
Instruction of Posterity.* In a dedicatory epistle and an introductory
essay he refers in some detail to synods of the churches of the Netherlands, France, Poland, Great Britain, Brandenburg, Hesse, Bremen,
and to some appropriate utterances of theologians. Though the documentation is by no means comprehensive, it is extensive enough to
be useful. Blondel includes, for example, the Consensus of Sendomir
(1570), which irenicists of his time looked upon as a landmark.[19] He
appeals to the churches mutually to cultivate such close association
that if controversy arises, no decision be made without the consent of
all. Like his colleagues in the ministry, he looks toward a meeting
with spokesmen of Lutheranism, and ultimately to the replacement
of the separative names "Lutheran," "Calvinist," and "Sacramentarian"
by the common designation "Christian Reformed."

Another writer of some note was Pierre du Moulin *fils* (1601–1684), whose father has been mentioned above. He early removed to England and entered the ranks of the Anglican clergy. He remained a royalist during the Cromwellian era, and later became one of Charles II's chaplains. In his *Treatise of Peace and Contentment of Mind* (1687), which soon had fifteen English printings and also appeared in French, he sees religious controversy as a product of inner disquiet and would look for the peace of the church as associated with, and consequent upon, the peace of the soul. He deplores the habit of taking offense at the things on which we differ instead of considering with thankfulness the matters in which we agree. If to preserve the faith we destroy charity, we throw down the roof of the church to patch the walls. His younger brother, Cyrus du Moulin, in a book entitled *The Peace of the Church* (1665), does little more than defend the Reformed churches from the charge of schism. But Benedict Pictet (d. 1724), an able and influential Geneva theologian, in 1700 replied to a Lutheran critic of his earlier proposals for unity in a weighty Latin treatise: *Defense of the Dissertation on Consensus and Dissensus between the Reformed and the Brethren of the Augsburg Confession.* Pictet here goes to history to show that Melanchthon's *Augustana variata* of 1540 had been acknowledged by Reformed and Lutheran princes alike. If it is claimed that Luther objected to this confession, why is no objection found in his writings? And on a more religious note, he asks his adversary whether a man who flees to Christ in true faith, hungers and thirsts after righteousness, approaches the Holy Supper with piety and earnest prayer for pardon, is not a partaker of the body and blood of Christ.[20]

It is to be recognized that the Reformed showed among themselves some variation and even disagreement in their union proposals. This was manifestly due in part to the changing thought patterns of the age. Not long after Amyraut's death Isaac d'Huisseau, a learned pastor of Saumur, who though not a professor had been three times rector of the academy, scandalized his associates with his book *The Reunion of Christianity, or the Way to Unite all Christians under One Confession of Faith* (1670). There is grandeur in d'Huisseau's conception of the reunion of all Christianity in each of the two great areas of the East and the West, but the project is developed with a reckless indifference to received doctrines. While professing to take as basic the Scripture and the Apostles' Creed, he abandons the scholastic approach to lay stress on contemporary issues, and limits sharply the class of necessary articles of faith. In his attitude to Trinitarian and Christological dogmas he is not far from Socinus, and he would exclude from discussion the "divine decrees" with other "thorny questions of the schools." In a theological appropriation of Descartes's hypothetical doubt, he holds it necessary in seeking reunion to set aside all preconceived opinions and to begin from simple propositions not contested by reasonable men. As analyzed by his latest interpreter, Richard Stauffer, neither his theology nor his ecclesiology appears to have been either Reformed or Catholic. It is morality that has importance for him, not Christian belief or church order. A storm of criticism greeted d'Huisseau's treatise, and he was promptly excommunicated by the local consistory and by a provincial synod. Among his most vehement assailants was Pierre Jurieu, later of the Academy of Sedan, in his *Critique* (French: *Examen*) *of the Book on the Reunion of Christianity* (1671).[21]

It was an extremely difficult time for the French Reformed churches. The painful infringements and final revocation (1685) of the Edict of Nantes, on which their legal existence depended, resulted in a great migration of Huguenots from France to the Netherlands, England, Germany, and other lands. Many of these émigrés were scholars and many now became, especially in the Netherlands, prolific writers. Jurieu reached the Netherlands years before the Revocation. Always a vehement defender of the Reformed doctrines, he dealt polemically in several of his works with approaches to church unity made by opponents. The Jansenist Pierre Nicole had devoted a treatise to the charge of schism against the Calvinists, and in another had discussed church unity from a Roman Catholic viewpoint. The hierarchical church was for Nicole the Ark of Noah. Jurieu's *Treatise on the Unity of the Church and the Fundamental Points* (1688) bears down with Hebrew scholarship on Nicole's Ark of Noah argument for the Roman communion. The Ark is the total church of Christ; that of Rome is Western only. In the manner of many seekers of unity, Jurieu expounds certain fundamental articles of religion on which unity should be built. He elsewhere assailed with passion the doctrinal indifference of his fellow exile Bayle. Like other Calvinists, however, he seriously sought a reconciliation with the Lutherans, but frankly with a view to combined resistance to political Roman Catholicism. This is the theme of his *Avis aux protestants de l'Europe* (1685), which later appeared in English as *Seasonable Advice to All Protestants in Europe of what Persuasion Soever for Uniting and Defending Themselves against the Popish Tyranny* (1689). Another of his numerous treatises discussing aspects of the unity topic is his *Essay on Bringing Peace among Protestants* (1688),[22] where he finds the differences on the doctrine of grace, which now "delay protestant union," not insurmountable, but frankly calls for the intervention of princes to use their authority, in accordance with the Erastian theory of Hugo Grotius, to impose peace on their ecclesiastical subjects.[23] Jurieu, the irascible controversialist, was by habit and temper ill-equipped as an irenical writer, and he seems to have been quite ineffective in that role.

It is an impressive fact of seventeenth-century Reformed church history in France that the academies of Montauban, Montpellier, and Sedan maintained until their suppression such standards as to secure for the church a learned and competent ministry. But fresh perils and conflicts marked the reign of Louis XIII (1610–1643), and under Louis XIV (1643–1715) the rights of the Huguenots were progressively withdrawn until the attempt was made to extinguish the Protestant minority by the revocation of the Edict of Nantes in 1685. Armed resistance was maintained in the Cévennes until 1707. Meanwhile about half a million Protestants managed to make their escape from France, chiefly to Brandenburg, England, Ireland, Holland, and Switzerland, where many of them were to make notable contributions to learning, theology, and church life. A substantial body, however, remained in France, and their worshiping groups survived, despite all measures of suppression. In some instances, such as Lisle and Montauban, the local governments accorded them the rights of citizens, thereby attracting a Protestant element to reside within their jurisdiction. The number of the Reformed actually increased, reaching about 2,000,000 by the time of the Revolution. But in general the higher learning was now inaccessible to the Protestants, and the French Reformed scholars and writers were not in France.

The ecumenism of the French and Swiss churches in the eighteenth century could not fail to reflect the liberal and latitudinarian trend set in motion earlier by a flood of new ideas in philosophy, science, and religion. There is everywhere a relaxation of the earlier sense of the importance of exact doctrinal definition. Pietistic elements were also present, helping to prevent the broader perspective from leading to mere indifferentism. In that century we find some of the most lively and emancipated proponents of unity to meet us anywhere in this history. Their failure to obtain tangible results does not necessarily invalidate their proposals, nor does it justify relegating them to oblivion. They faced not so much now the barriers of antagonism as the inertia of comfortable church establishments. The confessional and territorial segmentation of the Reformation churches had become a set pattern which could not be disturbed without discomfort. The divided state of Christianity was, to be sure, not thought of as ideal, but the way to unity seemed too difficult to try. Advocates of, and workers for, Christian unity nonetheless continued to appear. French Protestantism, shattered by repression, could produce no leadership on French soil. But the Swiss Reformed churchmen were from time to time speaking with the old accents. There is little that is startlingly original in their approach except perhaps their pronounced emphasis on the cultivation of brotherly charity, piety, and a holy life as the precondition of true unity.

This is characteristic of the three eminent teachers of Geneva, Basel, and Neuchâtel who are known as the Swiss Triumvirate: Jean Alphonse Turretin (d. 1737), Samuel Werenfels (d. 1740), and Jean Frédéric Ostervald (d. 1741). Turretin belonged to a distinguished Geneva family, descendants of Francesco Turretini, who came from Lucca to Geneva in 1579. François Turretin, the father of Jean Alphonse, had been a rigid Calvinist theologian who took alarm at Amyraut's disturbing ideas and joined with Johann Heidegger of Basel in the *Formula consensus Helvetica* (1675), a reactionary statement. The son was of a different type, and was largely instrumental in the rejection (1706) of this crippling formula. His motive in this was partly to improve relations with the Anglican and the Lutheran churches.

In 1707 he was consulted by Frederick I of Prussia, who had in mind a union of his Lutheran and Reformed subjects. On behalf of the ministers of Geneva, Turretin said in his reply to the king: "The constant and unanimous opinion of our church has been that the Protestants of both communions are in agreement concerning every important and essential point concerning religion." He held the differences between them too slight to be allowed to prevent their brotherly association and joining in one communion. Turretin was made a member of the Prussian Academy, but the unitive action he and the king desired was prevented by Frederick's death (1713). He was one of the numerous Continental correspondents of William Wake, archbishop of Canterbury (1716–1737), and from this and other outside contacts was led to write a notable contribution to irenic literature, *The Cloud of Witnesses for . . . Establishing Concord*

among Protestants.[24] Turretin's position is that differences among
Protestants are nonfundamental, while their differences from Rome
are fundamental. He agrees with Calvin that in some things good
men may differ without prejudice to piety or mutual love. He treats
with appreciation but not as finally adequate such ancient formulations as Tertullian's Rule of Faith, the Vincentian Canon, and the
Apostles' Creed. The Creed contains such nonessentials as the name of
Pilate and the descent into hell, while it omits some things more important. When it comes to determining the fundamentals, Turretin
is a relativist. They are not the same for men of different capacities.
The number of fundamental articles is not determined. A man has
what is fundamental if he sincerely loves truth and seeks it heartily,
begging help from God and making use of those who are capable
of giving him light. It is our duty to cultivate communion with all
disciples of Christ: and he stresses the point that not all differences
dissolve the communion of saints. Through many chapters Turretin's
favorite word is *tolerantia,* usually rendered "forbearance" by the
translator. In the exercise of this virtue, truth is found: *"Tolerantia
veritati amicissima"* (p. 30); tolerance or forbearance is truth's best
friend. In dealing with the Lutheran-Reformed disagreements he
seizes on a sentence from Bullinger, who "would not quarrel over
issues that rest solely in the mind, not in worship or practice." The
whole intent of this book is to cultivate an irenic and charitable
spirit among the Protestant communions, and it shows scant concern for doctrinal definitions.

Samuel Werenfels also had Europe-wide contacts and interests. The
panegyric spoken by Petrus Ryhinerus at the time of Werenfels' death
refers to his descent from Simon Grynaeus, Calvin's friend in Basel,
to his conversations in 1686 with Gilbert Burnet, later bishop of
Salisbury, and to his association with the English Society for the Propagation of the Gospel, and with the Prussian Academy. Ryhinerus
describes him as *"si pacificus, quoque veritatis amantissimus"*—a man
of peace but also a great lover of truth.[25] Werenfels deplored the
"strife of words" by which believers were unnaturally divided, and
diverted from things central. He had no hesitation in making a friend
of Count Zinzendorf and accepting leadership among the Moravians
of Basel. At the age of sixty he retired from his public ministry to
live a life of devotion. He was a large-minded advocate of unity, and
particularly concerned with the problem in its Reformed-Lutheran
context. One of Werenfels' treatises is *General Considerations on the*

Way of Uniting the Protestant Churches usually distinguished as Lutheran and Reformed. In this work Werenfels sings again the old song of the Reformed advocates of Protestant unity, with the conditions of his time in mind. A full and complete consensus is not the way, and is not possible. Christians will always present variety in nature and temperament. They can be asked to agree only on matters essential to salvation. Such mutual tolerance should be cultivated that despite differences the parties are not hindered from recognizing each other as true brothers in Christ and loving one another in sincerity, no less in their disagreements than in their agreements. No Christian is perfect, but erring members belong still to the mystical body of the church. All that should be demanded is that they testify by words and works what they believe in their heart and, agreeing on the fundamentals, tolerate each other's peculiarities. As the best remedy for tumults in the church, Christ prescribed charity, humility, gentleness, toleration, love of peace. These are always requisite for the maintenance of peace. One of the prime causes of dissension is the rarity of Christian humility. He adduces Calvin's short list of necessary doctrines (*Institutes* IV.i.12) and his reminder that nobody is without some little cloud (*nubecula*) of ignorance. He also makes use of Pareus' *Irenicum* (see below, pp. 71 f.) on the fundamental articles and in this connection observes that ignorance of the catholic articles is damnable, doubt is dangerous and denial heretical and irreligious (*impia*), while ignorance of theological propositions is not damnable, nor is doubt or denial of them heretical or irreligious.[26]

Ostervald was probably more widely read in his time than the others of the triumvirate, since his works in Biblical and pastoral theology were extensively translated. As a student at Saumur, Geneva, Orléans, and Paris, he acquired some bold opinions. He became severely critical of the Reformed liturgies, including that of Calvin, and was somewhat fascinated by certain features of Anglicanism. His Neuchâtel Liturgy of 1713 shows the influence of the English Prayer Book. But in his correspondence with Wake he finally reacted unfavorably to the archbishop's insistence on the establishment of the episcopate in the Reformed churches as the condition of union.[27]

These three companions in ecumenical thought, in a greater degree than their predecessors, endeavored to cultivate a fraternal spirit among Christians and among the spokesmen of the churches. "Again and again," writes Martin Schmidt, "in correspondence between

Werenfels and Turretini one finds the words 'peace,' 'moderation,' 'equity' and 'gentleness,' and the first qualification for genuine theological thought is held to be an earnest desire for peace."

A work of somewhat similar qualities appeared in French anonymously at Heidelberg in 1723: *Thoughts on the Reunion of the Protestant Churches.* It was from the pen of Philip Adam Brucker (1676–1751), Swiss pastor and scholar.[28] Brucker here writes as a Protestant rather than from a defensively Reformed position. He favors the Augsburg Confession as a basic document from which to move toward union, and he would disregard both the Decrees of Dort and the Formula of Concord. He argues along historical lines, and regrets that the Reformers followed in their disputations and condemnations the unedifying example of the Church Fathers. Like Turretin, he urges mutual tolerance among Protestants. As virtue may lie midway between two vices, so truth may be the middle point between two errors. The effect of his treatment of disputation through Christian history is to set the Protestant controversies in a wide historical setting. Characteristically, he takes Cyprian's citation of Peter's yielding to Paul's rebuke as an example of the duty to avoid an opinionated attachment to one's ideas. Symbols of faith should be bonds of unity, not grounds of dispute. It is useless to raise a dispute between the Augustana Variata and Invariata; and no formula is to be equated with the Word of God. He thinks the episcopate entered the church after Paul's lifetime, and notes that it was those bishops who resisted reform against whom the Reformers preached; where bishops consented to the Reformation, they were retained. Brucker, though a liberal, and notably indifferent to sharp dogmatic distinctions, is earnestly loyal to the historic church and desires its visible restoration as one, catholic and holy.

Among the writers discussed in this chapter there is a constant recurrence of the theme of fundamental doctrines, but a failure to list and define these with confidence and a sense of finality. The seekers of unity are aware of the human limitations that beset attempts at doctrinal definition, and they hold existing formulations as not irreformable. They are men weary of the embittered doctrinal strife in which their fathers had spiritedly contended. It is a sincere Christian brotherliness by which they are primarily moved; they wish to give expression to this in the unification of the severed churches. But this brotherly feeling hardly extends beyond the churches that had espoused the Reformation. Reunion with Rome is for them hardly a practical issue, and is at most a far-off possibility. Protestant union is, indeed, often recommended as a means of obtaining political strength for protection against discrimination and persecution in states adhering to the papacy. In the absence from their writings of specific proposals for an approach to Roman Catholicism they stand in contrast with some contemporary leaders of thought in other churches, such as Leibnitz, Wake, and Zinzendorf. Roman Catholics lay largely, though not entirely, outside the range of their charity, as did those of the leftist sects. Yet in this realm they are not embittered partisans. The tendency of their writings was to enlarge the horizon of Christian fraternity for many readers, and to maintain and increase the realization of membership in the Holy Catholic Church. Side by side with their respect for reason was a sincere devoutness that is sometimes described as pietistic. The use of this term may or may not assume that the persons concerned were under the influence of Spener's German pietism. There was a Reformed pietism, chiefly developed in the Netherlands, where Lewis Bayly's *Practice of Piety* was circulated in Dutch translation from 1620. The first German translation of this influential book was published not in Germany but in Zurich, in 1629, while Spener's epoch-making *Pia desideria* appeared only in 1675.[29]

In the eighteenth century the Lutheran and Reformed pietism became somewhat intermingled, and at certain points elements of Roman Catholic mysticism entered into Protestant patterns of devotion. Although the evangelical movement of that era was not marked by mysticism, it felt the influence of pietism and of the Moravianism of Zinzendorf. An unpretentious but influential Swiss pastor near Basel, Hieronymus Annoni, who had come under these influences, founded a society for Christian cooperation called the Fellowship of Good Friends (1756). This group promoted interest in news of the churches and of missions, and in a spirit of brotherly love undertook emergency tasks where need arose. The Fellowship became the model for the German Christian Fellowship instituted in Basel in 1779–1780 by the Lutheran Johann August Urlsperger. This organization rapidly grew to be a wide international brotherhood in which were joined Lutherans, Reformed, Moravians, Mennonites, Anglicans, and some Roman Catholics. It was, says Martin Schmidt, "consciously ecumenical in its aim. . . . Socially as well as ecclesiastically, it was catholic."[30] Being rather European than merely German in its membership and activities it led the way in providing

something of an ecumenical experience, and of the world consciousness that was to characterize the Evangelical Revival.

The extent to which the rank-and-file membership of the various
churches with which our irenicists were associated knew or realized
the nature of the proposals of these writers cannot be estimated. No
doubt a great many church members were wholly untouched by this
class of literature. Nowhere did it gain a wide popular response or
create a tidal movement such as to call forth immediate action. Each
church, operating within its own territorial milieu and responding
to crises growing out of its social and political involvements, tended
to put aside far-reaching issues. Even the pressures of a highly adverse
political situation such as the Reformed Church of France suffered,
failed to call forth an active movement to secure fraternal bonds with
other branches of Protestantism. It has been shown that in eighteenth-
century France seriously divergent attitudes toward the oppressive
government policy found expression. The bourgeois Huguenots,
finding themselves increasingly comfortable economically, were inclined to yield without protest to restrictions imposed affecting the
public exercise of their religion, while the "desert" congregations stood
immovably for the traditional doctrines and worship, suffering the
consequences.[31] Attempts to reach agreement between these parties
made little progress; the issue was to be resolved by the Revolution
of 1789. Meanwhile the lack of internal unity constituted a grave
hindrance to unified action on the part of the Huguenot church in
its relations with Protestantism elsewhere. The preoccupation of most
Protestants with other than ecumenical concerns was characteristic of
the era of the Enlightened Despots. The ecumenical ideal was not
extinguished, but its promotion seemed less urgent than the securing
of comfortable relations with the ruling powers.

IV

IRENICAL TREATISES BY GERMAN AND DUTCH REFORMED WRITERS

THE GREAT PERIOD of the expansion of the Reformed church in the German states was from the time of the Heidelberg Catechism, 1563, to the opening of the Thirty Years' War, 1618. Following open strife between Lutherans and Calvinists at Heidelberg University, the Palatinate under the government of the elector Frederick III (1559–1576) took its stand among Reformed states. The very gifted theologians who chiefly framed the Heidelberg Catechism—Zacharias Ursinus and Caspar Olevianus—had studied under Calvin. Olevianus had earlier followed Calvin's footsteps at Orléans and Bourges, while Ursinus had been a favored student of Melanchthon at Wittenberg and had also studied with Bullinger and Peter Martyr at Zurich. Frederick highly esteemed Melanchthon and received his advice on the Lord's Supper in terms that differed but slightly from Calvin's teaching. Frederick was distressed by the continuing conflicts within Lutheranism, and by the attitudes of some extreme Lutherans at Heidelberg. To his satisfaction, these were refuted by the French Calvinist Pierre Boquin (before his conversion a doctor of theology of Bourges) in a disputation held in June, 1580. As Bard Thompson has written, Frederick was now resolved "with the help of Calvinist theologians to erect a church catholic and reformed, faithful as far as humanly possible to the Scriptures." [1] The Heidelberg Reformed theology was from the first characteristically of an ecumenical cast. The Heidelberg Catechism, the least scholastic and most devout of the Reformation confessions, was soon approved by virtually all Reformed churches and became a prescribed basis of preaching in those of Germany and the Netherlands. It has never lost its status through all the changes in Reformed and Presbyterian organization.

61

"While the influence of Calvin and Peter Martyr is apparent throughout it," writes Thomas F. Torrance, "the exposition brings together
both Lutheran and Reformed teaching and as such has exercised a
powerful mediating influence." [2] It is noteworthy that this catechism,
so universally accepted in Reformed churches, omits altogether Calvin's doctrine of predestination. Under Question XXIII it recites the
Apostles' Creed.

In this connection we may note that it is characteristic of the history of the territorial and national units of the Reformed church that
they approved each other's statements of faith. Typical is the action
of the Synod of Emden (1571) which adopted the Belgic Confession
and approved with it the Gallican confession, that of Geneva, and
the Heidelberg Catechism. While in this book we sometimes for
convenience refer to them as churches, they really in their several
autonomous structures regarded themselves as together forming one
church. "Each church," wrote John Dickie in 1924,

> regarded itself and all the others as being the representative
> of the One Holy Catholic and Apostolic Church. The whole
> Reformed Church laid great stress upon unity and Catholicity
> as notes of the true visible Church of Christ on earth. . . .
> Any Reformed minister might receive a call or a professorial
> chair anywhere in the whole Reformed world.[3]

Dickie here refers especially to the hundred years following the
Reformation, but the sense of the universality of the church was kept
alive, and the exclusive denominationalism of the later age never
became characteristic of the Reformed and Presbyterian family.

The Palatinate Reformed church was suppressed by Frederick III's
heir in 1576 and restored under John Casimir in 1583. Meanwhile,
partly in opposition to the Formula of Concord, the Reformed doctrines and the Heidelberg Catechism were coming to acceptance in
other German areas. At Herborn in Nassau a new Reformed academy
was established. Calvinism gradually became paramount in Bremen,
though Lutheranism was not excluded. In Wesel, Calvinist refugees
laid the foundation of what became an expanding German Reformed
church. At Marburg in Hesse the influence of Melanchthon mingled
with that of Bucer and Calvin, and by a series of decisions ending
in 1610 Hesse distinctly entered the list of states maintaining Reformed churches. In Brandenburg the prince John Sigismund became a Calvinist, adopting a policy of toleration toward the Lutheran

majority of his people (1614). Later a great number of French Protestant refugees from the oppressive rule of Louis XIV settled in Brandenburg. They were befriended by "the Great Elector," Frederick William (1640–1688). This prince was largely responsible for that provision of the Peace of Westphalia (1648) by which Calvinists acquired the same status as Lutherans within the empire. The Lower Palatinate had been devastated by hostile armies during the Thirty Years' War, but it now resumed its character as a Reformed principality, and so continued until it was laid waste by the armies of Louis XIV fifty years later.

In the same era, the Netherlands Reformed church, soon after its organization in the several northern provinces, endured an internal struggle over the doctrine of predestination—a struggle complicated by political and economic forces. Before the outbreak of the Arminian controversy the Netherlands church had been served by a number of able leaders and thinkers. Some of these, such as Dirk Coornhert and Caspar Coolhaes, developed ideas of toleration in religion that were shocking to most of their associates. Coornhert, assailed by strict Calvinists for such opinions, declared at Leiden: "I hold as brethren all God-fearing people who rest on the foundation of Christ, whether they be Papists, Monks, Baptists, Reformed or Lutheran." [4] Church synods dealt severely with both these irenic and tolerant ministers, who were some generations ahead of their time. A more acceptable theologian, Francis Junius, remarked of Coornhert that he was a man "of profound intellect but not favored by fortune." [5] A similar judgment might have been made of the firm Calvinist Guido de Brès, author (with Adrian Saravia, later a famous defender of Anglican episcopacy) of the first draft of the Belgic Confession. Amid his activities as a powerful evangelical preacher, de Brès was engaged in seeking accord between Lutherans and Reformed.[6] For this purpose he accompanied William of Orange to a conference at Metz in 1565.

Prince William was at this time emerging into prominence not only as the leader of the Netherlands in revolt against the Spanish oppression but also as a figure of significance in the balance of religious forces in Europe. The death of Frederick III of the Palatinate, October 12, 1576, and that of the tolerant emperor Maximilian II two days later, intensified the peril felt by all concerned for the Protestant cause. Queen Elizabeth, alive to the crisis on the Continent, dispatched Sir Philip Sidney with a considerable retinue to visit Frederick's sons at Heidelberg, to greet the new emperor, Rudolf II, at Prague, and to confer with William where he might be found. Sidney had already traveled widely on the Continent, and had lived for a winter in Vienna with his senior friend and monitor Hubert Languet (see above, pp. 42 f.). His interesting correspondence with Languet covers the years 1573 to 1580. It is evident that Sidney proposed to John Casimir a general Protestant league (*foedus evangelicorum*), and was encouraged by Casimir's response; but that on his return to Heidelberg he met Casimir's Lutheran brother Lewis and was coldly received. Sidney, aged twenty-two and unmarried, was looked upon as a possible candidate for an important international marriage. Ursula, sister of the Palatinate princes, was, according to rumor, mentioned in that connection by her brother Casimir. Languet undoubtedly wished to see Sidney marry a sister of William (which of several of William's sisters is a matter of conjecture). When the party visited William, Sidney stood godfather to the prince's daughter. But since Sidney's initiative with Casimir and his bold Protestant talk at Rudolf's court had probably gone beyond his queen's instructions, he treated the proposal of Languet cautiously; it was, he thought, uncertain how "Zenobia" would react; Languet would understand the wry reminder of Chrysostom's fate. The correspondence has cryptic references to some *magnum negotium,* or great affair to be undertaken, which had been proposed by Languet in a confidential conversation. It evidently involved a far-reaching project for Protestant union, to begin with a Dutch-English league and become a general alliance of Protestant states. Sidney, immortal poet and beloved hero, had early acquired a sincere attachment to evangelical religion, and like his father, Sir Henry, and Walsingham, who was to be his father-in-law, he favored the presbyterian-puritan cause in England.

Instead of marrying a Dutch princess, he gave his life in the Dutch war of liberation. When he lay dying after the battle of Zutphen in 1586, the minister whom he called to his side was George Gifford, an outed and exiled Presbyterian of London, who in 1584 had represented the ministers of Essex in a Presbyterian synod [7] and whom Bishop John Aylmer had called "a ringleader among the nonconformists." Men of this party were interested in forming foreign religious as well as political connections. Walsingham had visited Knox in Scotland; earlier under Knox in Geneva English Presbyterianism had first found organized existence. It continued to cherish its Continental ties.

Among the numerous energetic leaders and well-trained scholars of the later Reformation period, Francis Junius (François de Jon,

1545–1602) holds a place of some distinction. A Frenchman by race and birthplace (Bourges), he had been an impoverished refugee student in Geneva during Calvin's late years, and when hardly out of his teens earned a living by tutoring students in that city. He later held an influential pastorate in Antwerp, and while in that office revised the Confession of de Brès, which was then adopted by an Antwerp synod (1566). As professor in Leiden and during two periods in Heidelberg, Junius attained prominence as a teacher and writer. At the time of his death he had just accepted an invitation from Mornay to join the faculty of Saumur. At the completion of his second stay in Heidelberg he joined the Duc de Bourbon (whose predecessor had at one time sheltered de Brès) at Sedan, and had an interview with Henry IV. About the same time he completed his *Eirenicum,* a work that calls for our attention.[8] The book was dedicated to Maurice, landgrave of Hesse. It is likely that the French version of this work, which appeared in Leiden, *Le paisable chrétien, ou De la paix de L'Eglise Catholique,* was written before the Latin. The *Eirenicum,* which extends to about two hundred pages in Kuyper's edition, takes the form of a meditation in sermon style on Psalms 122 and 133. Junius exhorts the teachers of the church to cultivate the communion of saints. In vivid phrases he deplores the incurable itch for writing that animates the controversialists, praising by contrast medical scholars who use their knowledge to benefit all. "Beloved brethren," he exclaims, "let us strenuously endeavor at all times to contemplate, to lay hold of, and to defend the peace of the Lord." He desires unity on the basis of those fundamentals "without which the Christian church cannot exist." These for him consist of articles on the doctrine of God, on the foundation of our salvation, and on the unchanging object of our faith—all in adherence to the Scriptures. And where there is corruption of the faith itself "we should act very cautiously and tenderly" that the good now attained be not lost through our animosities. Greatly concerned by the prevailing temper of intolerance, he wonders at those who set no value on the great privilege of brotherly friendship, but disown their spiritual brethren though honoring natural relations. As for him, he will not yield to this: "If you will tear the brotherhood in pieces, I will do my best to put it together again. . . . If you renounce it, Christ will confirm it, and I with Him." Any Christian may be in some error, but "we believe in the forgiveness of sins. We are commanded to forgive those who injure us in earthly things; shall we not then forgive one who errs in a matter of faith? Faith is a gift of God, not from ourselves, and by nature all men are brothers, thus no one should be put to death for his religion." Junius offers no planned series of steps to bring organizational unity. Rather would he cultivate the attitudes prerequisite to any unifying act that is to be effective. Regardless of minor differences, we must learn to "dwell together in unity" (Ps. 133:1). Geeraert Brandt, the historian of the Reformation in the Netherlands, learned personally from Junius' son that in a late utterance he declared, "The rest of my books I wrote as a divine, but this as a Christian." [9]

Junius was succeeded at Leiden by the celebrated Jacob Arminius, who died in the midst of the controversy in which his name became attached to a theological movement that threads its way through later theology. It has often been the sad lot of peaceable men to be drawn into intense controversy, and certainly Arminius had no wish to cause strife or division. In 1606 he delivered a long oration entitled "On Reconciling the Dissensions among Christians." In this discourse, if not in his view of predestination, he writes like a pupil of Junius. But he goes on, much in the manner of Calvin, to project a general council of earnest Christians, representative of all the segments of Western Christianity, composed of "men burning with zeal for God . . . inflamed with love of truth and peace." In this meeting, freedom to express opinion must be assured; and if differences remain, the parties must give pledge not to rail at each other or to employ coercion.[10]

The widely celebrated Dutch scholar Hugo Grotius (d. 1645) spent years of his youth in the home of Francis Junius, whom on occasion he called his "father," and in the theological battle over predestination belonged to the party of Oldenbarneveldt and the Arminians. His consistent attitude to church controversies is well indicated by his resolution at the age of eighteen "to write nothing that is not catholic and ecumenical in the sense in which these words are used by the Fathers." Deeply indebted to Cassander and to Casaubon, he sought to promote a tolerant interconfessional fraternalism. At the same time he conceived specific schemes of union, and encouraged those proposed by others. After Grotius' mission to England in 1611 he was in lively correspondence with Casaubon on Christian union. He advocated (February 7, 1612) a Protestant synod, a fully ecumenical synod being at the time out of the question. Agreement in essentials among Protestants being established, the fact that they have retained some elements of the Roman ritual and forms of speech would afford an approach to the Roman church. Meanwhile we must unite to protect ourselves politically against the papacy. He next proposed that a new confession be framed by "wise and moderate men." From Casaubon he found that King James did not wish to assume the authority of calling a general synod, but had the opinion that the proposed confession would be better made in Holland. In April, Grotius was again in England and was able to confer with both Casaubon and James as well as with Archbishop Abbot and other bishops. A mutual dislike arose between him and Abbot. In 1614 he prepared for the Estates of Holland a "Resolution for the Peace of the Church," proposing a silence on the debated issue of Arminianism, which only incensed the theologians.[11]

It was as a result of the defeat of the Arminian party that he became an international figure. He was imprisoned but escaped, first to Germany, and then to France, where he was to spend most of his later life engaged in diplomatic employments and in writing his influential treatises. For some time he enjoyed friendly intercourse with Casaubon, whom he revered and largely followed. Later he welcomed the initiative of John Dury, and supported some of the teeming projects of the Scottish apostle of unity. It was after his first association with Dury in 1637 that Grotius made his most notable literary contributions directly in this cause. According to David Masson, who examined many related documents, Dury "inoculated him with the idea" of linking the churches of England, Denmark, Sweden, and Norway by a common confession.[12] At any rate, Grotius warmly supported this scheme in a futile correspondence with Archbishop Laud. Like Cassander, Casaubon, and Calixtus, he remained a proponent of union on the basis of the patristic theology and the ecumenical dogmas of the early centuries. Thus in 1642 he republished, with favorable comment, Cassander's *Consultatio*. His application of this principle did not, however, preclude a vivid outlook on the contemporary church and a genuine concern for worldwide Christian missions.

Also in 1642 appeared both his *Way to Ecclesiastical Peace* and his *Prayer (Votum) for Ecclesiastical Peace*. In these writings Grotius made such concessions to the decrees of the Council of Trent that he was by some erroneously supposed to have become a convert to Roman Catholicism. Rather, he was a Christian humanist, who was prepared to tolerate a wide range of variation within the Christian society. On the way to complete unity his objective was to set on foot a plan by which Anglican, Lutheran, and Reformed churches might move toward a consensus. For this he envisioned a representative synod that would design a confession setting forth fundamental doctrines based on Scripture; and before treating with Rome he would have the Protestant churches make a united approach to Eastern Orthodoxy. There is, in fact, a fairly close parallel between the practical proposals of Grotius and those promulgated by the French Reformed synods that we have considered; while his theological liberalism differentiates him from the sponsors of these synodical decisions. That he was in agreement with Amyraut in viewing favorably Dury's projects should remind us that as an ecumenist he had affinities with the Saumur school.[13]

The Synod of Dort (1618–1619), called to end the Arminian controversy, was to some degree international in membership. Delegates came from England, Geneva, Zurich, Basel, Berne, Schaffhausen, Hesse, Bremen, the Palatinate, and Brandenburg. It was, however, controlled by the anti-Arminian Calvinists of the Netherlands, and the Arminian minority were not allowed a hearing. It was followed by the ejection of Arminian ministers and the prohibition of their teachings in the Netherlands; but after 1625 under the tolerant policy of Prince Frederick Henry, this ban was lifted. It must be recognized that this Synod, remarkable as it was for the learning of its members, while attempting with limited success to unify the Reformed, took no action toward better relations with the Lutherans. The latter, indeed, tended to interpret its decrees as directed against Lutheran theology. Philip Schaff compared its effect with that of the Formula of Concord in that "both consolidated orthodoxy at the expense of freedom." [14] There are many fine insights in its ably written decrees. But, confined as they are to a single disputed doctrine, they open no window on the Holy Catholic Church, the Communion of Saints, or on the problem of unity. On the whole they exhibit a Calvinism devoid of that element of devout elasticity which is prerequisite to ecumenical relationships. In this the Synod did not fully express the mind of many of its participants, some of whom were themselves authors of irenic treatises.

One of these was Ludwig Crocius of Bremen (1586–1673), a great admirer of Junius, who in 1615 had republished Junius' *Eirenicum*[15] with a preface to the reader which contains a passage in praise of Junius and a lament over the bitterness that marks the writings of pontiffs and Protestants alike, whereby Christian charity is almost extinguished.[16] When before the Synod convened Francis Gomarus was receiving the delegates from Bremen, Crocius offended him by a reference to *"Arminius piae memoriae."* Such a sentiment had no acceptance with the majority of the Synod. One of its brilliant younger members was Gisbert Voetius of Utrecht, who in a long life (1588–1676) was to become the most eminent of Dutch theological scholars. He eagerly espoused the cause of the anti-Arminians; but he is better known as the most active antagonist of both Cocceius and Descartes. His reputation as a controversialist, however, should not be allowed to eclipse those devotional and irenic interests that from time to time occupied his pen. Voetius was the author of a dissertation entitled *The Union and Conjunction (syncretismo) of Separated Churches.*[17] This is a highly analytic and comprehensive treatment of the problems and possibilities of the reunion of separated churches by a master of Protestant scholastic theology. It is in two sections of which the first deals with the nature and history of separation, the second with the restoration of unity and the combining together of the severed branches of the church. Section 1 is of little profit for us, with its recurring theme of Jerome, Paula, and Eustochium leaving Rome for Bethlehem. In Section 2, however, we are in touch with matters of the author's era. Voetius sets forth the conditions of any acceptable "syncretism." It must be spiritual, not political; free and not forced, must presuppose agreement in fundamentals and be framed without deceptive ambiguities, and it must be planned with provision for future eventualities. In dealing with the means of bringing about such a syncretism he includes the use of those unitive writings (*scripta henotica*) made available by such writers as Pareus and "the reverend man and friend of ours, the British Doctor John Dury who with great labor and pious zeal has been these many years engaged in the business of syncretism." Voetius had met Dury in 1655, and with his colleagues at Utrecht had approved the projects of the Scottish apostle (see below, Ch. VI). With all his admiration for, and repeated citation of, such authors, Voetius cautions against injudicious ties with the Lutherans, many of whom show hostility to the Reformed. He interests himself, too, in the relations of the Dutch Reformed with the English Independents in the Netherlands and in New England, whose writings are known to him. His view of any project for coming to terms with Rome is unequivocally negative, and here he fortifies himself by citing another British author, Bishop Joseph Hall, in the latter's *Roma irreconciliabilis* (No Peace with Rome). Appended to the tractate are twenty-two pages of documents on the inception of the Colloquy of Thorn, 1645. A laborious rather than a spirited writer, in this work Voetius revels in numbered distinctions and fails to convey a cumulative impression.

Veritas pacifica (The Peaceable Truth) is the title of a not very impressive treatise by Timann Gesselius[18] which begins with an analysis of the causes of religious division, its pernicious effects, and the principal remedies proposed. Gesselius advocates a return to a few "certain and necessary" doctrines and emphasizes the necessity of a "zeal of charity and piety" in composing differences. He would heed the lesson of Zech. 8:19: "Therefore love truth and peace." But, since the prophet did not add "brevity," Gesselius' enumeration of the "necessary" doctrines expands into what is essentially a new Reformed confession in fifty-seven articles occupying more than one hundred pages. Though not without merit, this was hardly an appropriate contribution at the time. More interesting to us is the treatise by Cornelius Trigland, written for William of Orange (later William III of England) in 1666 on the *Image of a Christian Prince*.[19] He urgently exhorts William to afford shelter to "the pilgrim church" in its distress in the world:

> We behold the Christian world for many years divided by schisms, all nations in confusion for this cause. . . . Consider what fervent love, what glory among future generations and what felicity in his own soul would be won by the prince who would repair the temple of God, . . . reconcile the factions in church and state. Such, then, are the joys that I desire for our prince.[20]

Prince William, then aged sixteen and facing many troubles, was not unsympathetic with Trigland's desire for him. Trigland, who was his tutor, on occasion came upon him at prayer over the matter. At a later stage William thought in terms of a league of European powers in the interests of political and religious peace, to include his natural adversary, Louis XIV (1681). Yet he never attempted to assume the grand role of supreme peacemaker to all the churches, and was in general content with diplomatic and limited military cooperation with Protestant powers.

During the first half of the seventeenth century, true to the spirit of their church, the faculty of Heidelberg University in a series of writings took leadership in giving expression to the Reformed irenic interest. In 1606 appeared *A Sincere Exhortation of the Churches of the Palatinate to All the Evangelical Churches of Germany, that They May Yet Heed the Great Danger which Threatens Them as Well as Us from the Papacy and One Day in a Christian and Brotherly Spirit Help Us to Remove or Allay the Internal Unnecessary Strife Which has Already Been Sufficiently Investigated.*[21] It is here argued that since the states attached to the papacy treat Lutherans and Reformed alike and expel both from their borders, it is time to abandon the points of controversy between the two confessions. The difference over the Lord's Supper is not a matter on which salvation depends. The Reformed do not demand that Lutherans abandon what they hold to be true: let them only refrain from assailing the presumed errors of the Reformed in their writings and sermons. The Reformed on their part, while retaining their view of the Holy Supper, will not condemn the Lutherans but hold them as brethren in Christ.

The Silesian David Wängler, known to his readers as David Pareus, was the author of the weightiest of the Heidelberg treatises of this class. Pareus enjoyed a great reputation as a theologian and drew to Heidelberg students from many lands. Having written against Lutheran views of the Lord's Supper, he began about 1603 to take a more conciliatory approach and to employ the words *essentialiter* and *substantialiter* of Christ's bodily presence.[22] He subsequently moved out of the controversial realm and produced his substantial work, possibly written some years before its publication in 1614, *Irenicum, sive de unione et synodo evangelicorum liber votivus.* The central feature of this treatise is the proposal, not new but more than elsewhere specific, for a general synod of all the "evangelical" churches to initiate the process of unification. The synod should be held in a free city, and during summer. Participants should be learned, wise, and mature men of unquestionable piety and love of truth. This assembly of the best and weightiest men from every part of the Christian world will be charged with the task of determining what are the fundamental articles of the faith on which a union of evangelical churches must rest. Recalling the advice of Paphnutius at Nicaea, Pareus is confident that in such a synod truth will triumph, since Christ will not desert his church. The people of all the churches are to participate in their congregations by offering a prepared form of prayer during the period of the sessions. Against the papacy and the political menace of Roman Catholic powers, Pareus would have Protestants combine in a *"pius syncretismus."* The phrase is here an

echo of the then recent proposal of Paul Windeck, a priest of March-
dorf, for a "syncretism" of Catholic forces. But "syncretism" was not
a new word; it had been used in a favorable sense by Erasmus,
Zwingli, Melanchthon, Calvin, and Bucer. Essentially it meant the
making of a common cause with others who are confronted by the
same enemy. It was soon to be much employed in the internal controversies of Lutherans with special reference to the irenic teaching
of George Calixtus of Helmstadt (d. 1656). The opponents of Calixtus
made it a term of reproach, as suggesting theological indifference.
Pareus was not disposed to alter his essentially Calvinistic theology;
but he was anxious to secure, under the general rule of Scripture,
agreement on essentials and "mutual Christian toleration" on the
matters, which he held nonessential, on which disagreement remained.
This work anticipated by eight years the *Paraenesis votiva pro pace
ecclesiae* (1626)[23] of Peter Meiderlin ("Rupert Meldenius") of Augsburg, addressed to his fellow Lutherans, which contained the oft-
quoted ecumenical motto: *"In necessariis unitas; in non necessariis
libertas; in utrisque caritas."* Sixteenth- and seventeenth-century writers, as we have seen, often point to the distinction between necessary,
or "fundamental," and nonnecessary points of doctrine.[24] The close
similarity of the proposal of Pareus to that of the Synod of Tonneins
of the same year justly raises the question of interdependence; but
this, I believe, cannot be shown. Both arise naturally enough from
the attitudes of Calvin and Beza and of their disciple Francis Junius.

It is obvious that the German Reformed advocates of a united
Protestantism in this period had constantly in mind the problem of
Germany and of accord with the German Lutherans. They frequently
put forward the claim that the Reformed had a right to the benefits
accorded to the party of the Augsburg Confession by the terms of the
Peace of Augsburg (1555), and by later agreements valid within the
empire. This claim is expounded by another Heidelberg teacher, John
Henry Alting (1583–1644), in his *Logical and Theological Exegesis of
the Augsburg Confession* (1647).[25] Alting argues syllogistically that
those who have defended the Augsburg Confession deserve to share
its benefits. Calvin and other Reformed theologians contended, side
by side with Melanchthon and other Lutherans, for the doctrines of
the Confession at the conferences of Hagenau, Worms, and Regensburg in 1540–1541, and Calvin was appointed by the Church of
Strassburg to be a delegate to the Council of Trent. Therefore, in
Alting's syllogism, the adherents and successors of these Reformers

ought now to be recognized by the Lutheran churches as associates (*pro sociis*). Alting gives us here an example of the constant effort of the Reformed advocates of unity to go behind the Formula of Concord to the Augsburg Confession in their approach to Lutheranism. Apart from its syllogistic form, the argument of Alting accords well with the position that had been stated with intense personal conviction by the elector Frederick III of the Palatinate, when he defended his adherence to the Heidelberg Catechism and the Reformed doctrines at the Diet of Augsburg in 1566, before the Formula of Concord was compiled.[26]

Another Reformed teacher and leader, Samuel Strimesius (1649–1730) was a somewhat copious writer and an ardent ecumenist. The son of a well-educated merchant of Utrecht, he studied in Königsberg, Berlin, Cambridge, and Oxford, and in 1679 became professor in the University of Frankfort on the Oder. He was five times rector of that university. In 1703 he participated in a colloquium (*"collegium caritativum"*) that met in Berlin at the call of Frederick I of Prussia to promote unity between Lutherans and Calvinists. Frederick's second wife, Sophie Charlotte, an energetic and cultured princess and the sister of George I of England, broadened the king's interest in ecclesiastical union through her connections with Hanover where Leibnitz had been especially influential. The Berlin meeting was amicable, but was rendered futile by the fact that a scheme of state-enforced union secretly presented to the king in advance by the Magdeburg Lutheran superintendent John Joseph Winckler was given publicity by opponents of the union policy. At the meeting, Strimesius conferred with a number of Lutheran divines, including Gerhard Walter Molanus, celebrated for his correspondence with Bishop Bossuet, and also made the acquaintance of that ecclesiastically ambiguous but very sincere Christian, Ernst Jablonski, grandson of John Amos Comenius, Reformed chaplain and court preacher at Berlin, who still retained his connection with the Moravian church of his ancestors—at that time a mere remnant but soon to be revived. Jablonski was already an eager advocate of unity among the Reformed, Lutheran, and Anglican churches. The irenical writings of Strimesius appeared chiefly within the decade following the Berlin colloquy. They include: *Statement of the Agreement of the Evangelicals in the Basis of Faith* (1704); *Theological Instruction on the Peace of the Church* (1705); *Frank Inquiry into the Controversies of Evangelicals* (1708); *Two Tractates on Ecclesiastical Union of Evangelicals*

(1711). In his own way Strimesius states a position typical of many Reformed predecessors. In the *Frank Inquiry* he stresses the existing agreement of the confessions on fundamental doctrines. Where there are disagreements, as on oral manducation of the bread in the Eucharist and participation of unbelievers in the sacrament, he holds the differences of no importance for salvation. His forecast is of two stages of progress toward unification. In the first of these, Christians of both confessions should exercise tolerance and recognize each other's freedom from fundamental error. The higher stage would be the achievement of organic union itself. He is prepared to receive the unaltered Augsburg Confession; but he holds it necessary that both the Formula of Concord and the Decrees of Dort be subjected to reconsideration, as being alterable, in the light of Scripture itself.

In his *Two Tractates on Ecclesiastical Union,* Strimesius distinguishes plain (*nudae*) truths from a posterior category of truths treated by theologians. He points to a number of historical instances in which Lutherans and Reformed have expressed basic agreement, and to the unwarrantable extension of the alleged fundamentals by some Reformed, Anglican, and Lutheran doctors. We find him quoting with approval such of his contemporaries as John Dury, Joseph Hall, James Ussher, David Pareus, George Calixtus, and John Daillé. In the second tractate he urges mutual forbearance (*toleratio*) and fraternal charity. Union is not to be simply external, but an inward coming together (*coitio interna*) of the churches and of all their members. The work gives proof both of the author's eager interest in Protestant unity and of his generous and discerning mind.[27]

After Frederick I, Prussia was ruled by Frederick William I (1713–1740). The impulse toward church union that marked his reign was in part a response to the work of two pietistically oriented Lutherans of Tübingen, Johann Christian Klemm and Christoff Matthaeus Pfaff. They won approval by the Protestant princes, in a conference of their organization (the "Corpus Evangelicorum") at Regensburg in 1722, for a plan of union to rest upon acknowledgment of existing agreement in the essentials of faith. This typically Reformed approach was probably adopted, as Otto Ritschl indicates, under the influence of Jean Alphonse Turretin. But the project met with hearty disapproval on the part of most Lutheran theologians, and came to nothing.[28]

In the Netherlands certain Arminian writers were in this era concerned with ecclesiastical peace and reconciliation. They were under the influence not only of Arminius and Grotius but also of Jacob

Acontius, author of *The Stratagems of Satan,* an able and sweeping attack on religious persecution. Acontius, born in Trent, escaped the arm of the Inquisition by flight to England, where he was naturalized and became distinguished as an engineer. He dedicated this subsequently famous book in classical fashion to Queen Elizabeth (*Divae Elizabethae*) and had it published in Basel (1565).[29] It was widely read, praised and attacked during the seventeenth century. Arminius was one of those who esteemed it highly, as did also that prodigiously learned Arminian theologian of Amsterdam, Philip van Limborch (1633–1712), whose weighty treatise, *Christian Theology,* was, according to its full title, "particularly designed for the practice of piety and the promotion of Christian peace." [30] Like Acontius and his friendly correspondent, John Locke, Limborch rejected all persecution and in the interests of Christian unity advocated the cultivation of mutual tolerance. He not only follows the distinction between fundamental, saving, doctrines but also holds that controversies have been largely caused not by differences in the fundamentals themselves but in the ways (*modus*) in which they are presented. Limborch is concerned for intercommunion as well as for toleration, and urges the maintenance of communion even where some disagreement occurs. He proposes the attainment of union by reversing the order of the steps that were taken in schism; but first of all, we are to extirpate hatred.[31]

V

REFORMED UNITIVE ACTIVITY
IN EASTERN EUROPE

IN THE EARLY SIXTEENTH CENTURY three kingdoms lay east
of Germany and Austria and west of the Russian border: Poland,
Bohemia, and Hungary. The westward advance of the Turks resulted in repeated partitions of Hungary and Bohemia, in each of
which after 1526 Ferdinand of Austria, brother of Charles V, ruled a
considerable area. Despite hostile governments, both Lutheranism
and Calvinism, together with Anabaptist and Unitarian elements,
entered each of these states; and their religious as well as their
political history is, throughout the century, marked by variety, struggle, and controversy. The Western humanist learning of the period
found a keen response in these countries, and a host of eager students
from each of them attended Western schools, including the Reformation centers of study in Germany and Switzerland. Many of these
returned to their homelands as competent scholars and convinced
Protestants. The Reformation leaders, Luther, Melanchthon, Calvin,
Bucer, Bullinger, and others, took an interest in the rising Protestant
movement in eastern Europe, and did what they could to promote it.
The personal relationships formed in this connection were numerous
and complicated. A considerable body of extant correspondence bears
record to this. Our interest here must be confined to the Reformed
churches and the activities and attitudes of their leaders.

Although the writings of Bullinger were widely read in all these
nations, it was from Calvin and Geneva that the strongest influence
was exerted. We find him writing repeatedly to men of influence and
power who were concerned for church reform in Poland, including
King Sigismund Augustus II (1548–1572), Prince Nicholas Radziwill
of the Grand Duchy of Lithuania, whose sister, Barbara, was Sigis-

mund's queen consort and a convinced Calvinist, and Count Tarnowski, governor of Cracow. It was Prince Radziwill who bore the expense of the Polish translation of the Bible. He helped to promote Calvinism in Lithuania, where for a time it was in high favor with the people. A recent historian judges that throughout the seven hundred parishes of the territory the sentiment was Calvinist 1000 to one.[1] In 1549 King Sigismund accepted Calvin's dedication of his Commentary on Hebrews. On December 5, 1554, learning of the king's favorable attitude, Calvin addressed to him a long letter of advice on the Reformation of the church in the Polish kingdom. Francis Lismanini, an Italian who had been confessor to the king's mother but was now a Protestant, was about this time acting virtually as an emissary of the Swiss churches in Poland. He had the full approval of both Calvin and Bullinger, and for years he enjoyed the favor of the king. Calvin had hopes of a Polish church, united and reformed, that might take shape under Sigismund's guidance. He advised the king to abolish the papal hierarchy in Poland and institute a new ministry on the model of the ancient church with its patriarchs and primates. In Poland one archbishop would have "a certain pre-eminence" in synods, and would "cherish a holy unity" among his colleagues and brethren in local episcopates. The scheme is utopian, and appears to have been put forward as a suggestion to be considered rather than as a plan to which the writer was unalterably committed. The religious elements in Poland were already so diverse that unity was far to seek. The king, though an admiring reader of Calvin's writings, did not come to a decision favorable to the Reformer's advice, or take any decisive action on church reform.[2] In his reign, Lithuania, with such cities as Vilna and Brest, became a definite part of the Polish kingdom (1569).

A large migration into Great Poland and East Prussia of the Bohemian Unity of Brethren (Unitas Fratrum), an outgrowth of the work of John Huss, had now taken place (1548). (Great and Little Poland were roughly divided by the rivers Pelica and Bug, tributaries of the Vistula. Warsaw was in Great Poland.) The Reformed congregations were formed chiefly in Little Poland, centered in Cracow and Posen. In this area Luther's writings had been in circulation, and numerous Lutheran churches had been formed, chiefly of the bourgeois class. The Polish nobility, however, with a traditional distrust of Germans, welcomed more the French or Swiss sources of the Reformation. Despite repressive measures under Sigismund I, and continued strong resistance from the bishops, the growth of Calvinism was rapid through the period 1540–1573.[3] There were many conversions of Polish Dominicans and other scholars. Polish humanism tended to adopt or to favor the Calvinist theology, and as a result the humanist trend in the Reformed church of Poland was perhaps greater than elsewhere, and marked it with a tolerant attitude toward Lutherans and Brethren. The humanist and Calvinist Nicholas Rey (1505–1569), author of poetic satires in Polish and of a translation of the Psalms, has been dubbed "the father of Polish literature." Printers played a great part in spreading the literature of reform, and the king's printer, Michael Wierzbieta, like many others of his calling, was a Calvinist.

An early result of the spirit of tolerance and unity in Polish Calvinism was the adoption of a common statement of faith by the Calvinists and the Unity of Brethren. This was done on the initiative of Felix Krzyzak (Cruciger), superintendent of Calvinist congregations of Little Poland, who had made the acquaintance of the Brethren of Great Poland when in 1551 he was forced to seek safety there. After preliminary conferences in both provinces, a synod of the two churches met in August, 1555, at Kozminek. The confession adopted with unanimity in this meeting was in fact that compiled by John Augusta (1500–1569) for the Brethren in Bohemia, where it had been in use for twenty years. Before parting, the members of the joint synod celebrated the Lord's Supper together, using what was essentially a liturgy of the Brethren. While the two churches had thus established intercommunion, being separate in location they did not coalesce under a single constitution, but rather cultivated a spirit of fraternity and practiced cooperation. Calvin welcomed the agreement with enthusiasm and eager hope. With reference to it he wrote to a Polish knight, December 29, 1555: "I am hoping for very good results from your consensus with the Waldenses [his name for the Brethren], not only because God blesses the holy unity in which the members of Christ come together, but because, amid these beginnings the experienced skill (*peritia*) of the Waldenses, which the Lord has exercised in long practice, will, I hope, be of no small help to yourselves." [4] The link thus forged in 1555 was never to be broken.

Poland gave to the Reformation one eminent international figure in the person of John à Lasco (1499–1560), son of a Polish magnate and nephew of a powerful prelate. In his youth à Lasco became intimate with Erasmus at Basel and purchased the reversion of his library. But he found religious guidance in Zwingli and moved into circles of the Reformed church. Returning to Poland, he became bishop of Vesprim, but married and resigned his office. He returned to the West, where he was to give distinguished service, especially at Emden in East Friesland and as chief pastor of the presbyterially organized church of the foreign exiles (*Ecclesia Peregrinorum*) in London. As a result of the agreement of Kozminek and by action of the reform-demanding Diet of Piotrkow in the same year, à Lasco was invited to return to his homeland. He was at the time in Frankfort, consulting with Lutherans in the hope of bettering Lutheran-Reformed relations in Germany. The Polish diets of that period were strongly pro-Protestant and were usually presided over by Calvinists.[5] Not only à Lasco but also Calvin, Melanchthon, and Beza were named in the Diet of Piotrkow's project, the others to be consultants at the meeting of a proposed national reforming synod. The influence of the Polish bishops annulled this bold plan; and the king's request to Pope Paul IV for a liturgy in Polish, communion in both kinds, marriage of the clergy, and approval of a national synod brought only the dispatch of a special papal legate to Poland. À Lasco, however, turned his steps homeward, having first written to the king an urgent plea for measures of church reform. Arriving in December, 1556, he soon became superintendent of the Reformed congregations in Little Poland. During the following March he paid a visit to King Sigismund and Prince Radziwill at Vilna, the capital of Lithuania. The fact of this meeting with the king is well attested by the letters of John Utenhovius to Calvin, and to Bullinger and Martyr in Zurich. The Dutch scholar had been an elder in the Church of the Strangers in London, had there translated à Lasco's liturgy into Dutch, and was now his companion in travel from Cracow to Vilna, where he shared the Reformer's conferences with the king. Sigismund was extremely gracious; but any decisive response he might have made to à Lasco's exhortations was prevented through the objections raised by the clergy present. In private talks Sigismund promised à Lasco protection and permission to hold meetings, but indicated that he was unable to overcome the resistance to reform. The visitors were for a month thereafter the guests of Prince Radziwill in his Vilna mansion. During this time, à Lasco was allowed to preach in Vilna. He and Utenhovius also conferred, through an interpreter, with seven Basilian monks, refugees from Moscow, who gave such an account of their Scriptural knowledge and Eucharistic doctrine that Utenhovius happily remarks: "We recognized them all as our friends, and owned

them as brethren." Thus the Pole and the Dutchman were among
the first Protestants to be in dialogue with Eastern Orthodox Christians.[6]

À Lasco's main object was the integration of the Polish Lutherans with the existing communion of Reformed and Brethren. He
presided in a Reformed synod at Brest in June, 1557, which reaffirmed union with the Brethren, with a proviso intended to be
inviting to the Lutherans: "saving Christian liberty according to
God's Word, and without prejudice to other churches of Christ."
For agreement with the Lutherans he felt it necessary to revise the
confession adopted at Kozminek, and to alter the requirements for
ordination. "Pray you," he wrote to the East Prussian Lutherans in
1558, "that sometime we may think and speak as one about everything; meanwhile let us comport ourselves with charity and Christian brotherliness." But both the Polish Lutherans and the Königsberg
theologians whose help he sought in persuading them, discouraged
his efforts. Fox sums this up by saying: "He worked faithfully, though
fruitlessly, for a union of the Lutherans with the other two already
united Protestant bodies, the Calvinists of Little Poland and the
Bohemian Brethren of Great Poland."[7] However, seeds were sown
that would bear fruit ten years after his death.

Another irenic figure in Polish Protestantism was Andrew Frycz
Modrzewski (Modrevius) (1503–1572), a former Wittenberg student
and house guest of Melanchthon, an admirer of Bucer, and a correspondent of à Lasco when both were in Western lands, who in Poland leaned toward Calvinism. For thirty years he was secretary to
the king, and in the late 1540's was sent by him as an emissary to
various countries. In Bohemia he formed a favorable view of the
Czech Brethren. As a humanist, Modrevius showed wide sympathies
even for left-wing sectarians. He strongly urged reform of the corrupt clergy, but never allied himself with the Reformed church. In
his address "On Sending Delegates to a Christian Council" (ca. 1546),
occasioned by the early sessions of the Council of Trent, he advocated a universal free Christian council, of delegates chosen by the
people of each diocese, to reform and unite the church. In Poland,
Modrevius does not seem to have cooperated directly with à Lasco,
but the influence of his thought was undoubtedly favorable to religious accord, and may have helped to bring about the events of
1570 and 1573 now to be noticed.

Melanchthon died three months after à Lasco, but Wittenberg was still Melanchthonian, or, as described by its Lutheran critics, "Crypto-Calvinist," a fact of importance for the negotiation of the Consensus of Sendomir (Sendomierz) in April, 1570. In this agreement, unique in its time, Lutherans, Calvinists, and Brethren solemnly and sincerely joined; and we may say that the common interests of the deceased leaders, Melanchthon, Calvin, and à Lasco were well represented. The Lutherans here acted on the advice of the Wittenberg faculty, to whom they had appealed by agreement with the Brethren in order to settle a controversy. The *Consensus Sendomiriensis* as published in 1586 bore the signatures of the general superintendents of the three consenting churches and included certain expository resolutions added by subsequent synods. On the much-disputed doctrine of the Eucharist it affirms with Irenaeus (*Against Heresies* IV.xvii.5) that the consecrated bread is no longer common bread, but consists of two realities, an earthly and a heavenly. The elements are not bare and empty signs, but there is a substantial "presence of Christ" in the sacrament. The Lutherans would have preferred "presence of the body of Christ," but were persuaded instead to accept the phraseology of Melanchthon's Saxon Confession, prepared for the Saxon delegates to the Council of Trent in 1551, which reads *"vere et substantialiter adesse Christum,"* not *"Corpus Christi."* [8] This historic document is of much more than Polish significance, both in its origin and in its influence. It was to be referred to as a guide to Protestant union in many later treatises and proposals, and is still worth the attention of ecumenical minds. Yet it did not cement the churches concerned into one organic body. Rather, it pledged them to mutual peace and charity. Each church was to regard the others as Christian and orthodox, and to cooperate with them amicably for the good of the whole church of Christ. General synods were to be held; intercommunion and the interchange of pulpit ministries were to be freely practiced. These provisions were maintained against increasing pressure from the forces of the Counter-Reformation for a quarter of a century. The Consensus was repeatedly reaffirmed in joint synods, of which the last and largest was that of 1595 at Thorn.[9]

An interim of some political confusion followed the death of Sigismund II in 1572, at the close of which the Polish diet elected Henry of Anjou, later Henry III of France, to be their king. Before he reached Poland a convention of nobles drew up at Warsaw, in January, 1573, a remarkable constitution for securing religious peace. This is known, by an abbreviation of its title, as *Pax dissidentium*

(The Peace of the Dissident Sects). It called for a policy of religious peace, toleration, and nondiscrimination among all religious units equally: no harm was to be done to anyone on religious grounds. It was approved by the national diet (in which the Calvinists were numerically strong), and presented by its Lutheran president to King Henry for his assent before his accession to the throne. Henry had no alternative but to accept. After his short reign, his successors Stephen Batory and Sigismund III also found it advantageous to confirm the royal approval of the *Pax dissidentium,* though they both departed from it in their partiality for the Roman church. A religious toleration so comprehensive was hardly feasible in that age. By 1607 Sigismund's measures against Protestants called forth a futile revolt followed by the enforced suppression and progressive extinction of Protestant organizations. But the *Pax dissidentium* remains on Poland's record as a landmark of mutual religious tolerance.

The powerful influence of Luther in Bohemia during the 1520's and 1530's gave place to that of Bucer and Calvin from about 1540. In that year Bucer began a correspondence with ministers of the Unity of Brethren, and three young men delegated by the Unity were students at Strassburg, where they came in touch with Calvin. One of these, Matthew Cervenka, had a dinner conversation with him, and this was followed, as Cervenka himself reports, by "frequent and lengthy discussions." [10] Calvin inquired closely of the Brethren's church order, and was impressed by what he learned of their faithful ministers and good discipline. He was afterward in correspondence with John Augusta (1500–1572), an important figure among the Brethren, who had formed warm relationships with Luther and Melanchthon at Wittenberg and later paid visits to Bucer and Calvin. Augusta was the compiler of the First Bohemian Confession of 1535, approved with changes suggested by Luther in 1538, and adopted, as noted above, by the Polish Calvinists in 1555. Having suffered torture and endured a twelve-year imprisonment, Augusta suffered the further misfortune of a tragic misjudgment on the part of his own communion. The tendency of the Brethren, who craved a strong discipline, was toward affiliation with the Reformed branch of Protestantism. They also felt all the while the influence of the Waldenses, many of whom had earlier found refuge in Bohemia. Under the liberal policy inaugurated by Maximilian II (1564–1576), and with his personal encouragement, the Brethren, Utraquists, Lutherans, and Reformed, making a common front against the Counter-Reformation, joined together in adopting the so-called Second Bohemian Confession. It was presented to Maximilian at the Diet of Prague, May 17, 1575. The emperor expressed his satisfaction and promised to protect its adherents. This document in twenty-five articles remarkably combines the doctrinal teachings of the Augsburg Confession as revised by Melanchthon with Calvinist and Moravian elements.[11] It was edited by John Amos Comenius in 1662, and is a standard of the modern Czech Brethren Evangelical Church.

Until 1620 the united Protestantism of Bohemia withstood the hostility of Maximilian's successors. In his *Maiestätsbrief*, or royal charter, of July 9, 1609, Rudolf II, for reasons of policy, yielded large concessions to those affirming the Confession of 1575; but his pledge was soon violated. It was renewed by his intriguing brother and successor Matthias, and after him by King Ferdinand III, both of whom, however, permitted such infringements as to nullify their pledges. The combined groups affected by the Hapsburg policy of repression, according to Matthew Spinka, numbered more than 90 percent of the population.[12] The situation made for tragedy. A company of Bohemian nobles in an act of rebellion threw certain agents of Matthias from a high window of Hradčany Castle (the Defenestration of Prague) on May 23, 1618, thus precipitating the Thirty Years' War.

The war brought a chapter of disasters for Bohemia, in the course of which the adherents of the Confession were reduced to a remnant of impoverished survivors in exile. Among the exiled Brethren there arose one of the geniuses of the "century of genius," John Amos . Comenius (Komensky) (1592–1670). Through provision made by Count Charles Zerotin, who had studied in Geneva and was a friend of Mornay, young Comenius was sent with others to the Reformed seminary at Herborn in Nassau. There he studied under the wide-ranging scholar John Henry Alsted (1588–1638), author of the first well-ordered encyclopedia. His next teacher was the then celebrated David Pareus in Heidelberg, whose *Irenicum* has already gained our attention. In the year of its publication, Comenius ventured back to Bohemia (1614). He was ordained to the ministry and for ten years held a pastorate at Fulnek near the Silesian border. Fresh legislation designed to exterminate the Church of the Brethren required all but nobles to join the Roman communion, and gave to nobles the option of submission or emigration with loss of property. With many other refugees, Comenius settled at Leczno (Lissa) in Poland in 1628, and four years later was, by a general synod of the Unity, elected a bishop. Within Bohemia the Unity of Brethren was now extinct as an organization, and Comenius exercised his episcopate in the Polish branch of the church, whose harassed existence he shared until he and his people in Leczno were finally left homeless by an incendiary fire, and driven out, in 1656. Meanwhile he had visited various places in the West, and written many books. In 1650 he wrote the moving obituary of the church of his fathers, *The Bequest of the Unity of Brethren*,[13] characteristically turning the sorrowful story into a series of appeals for repentance, reform, and unity to the other branches of Protestantism, not omitting a word to the Church of Rome, "our mother who hast become our stepmother."

The originality and versatility of Comenius in educational method, and in his proposed universal classification of ascertained knowledge, have in recent times been recognized by historians; and church historians have been similarly impressed by the range of his ecumenical outlook and interests. For Comenius there was not the slightest incongruity in associating the interests of Christianity with the promotion of all knowledge; all men everywhere needed both; he loved all men, and the unity of knowledge would support unity of faith. For the spread and sharing of knowledge, he desired the invention of a universal language. While in England, he sought to institute a permanent bureau of world learning at Chelsea College, an impecunious foundation in which Matthew Sutcliffe had assembled a store of books. There would follow, he fondly hoped, such a universal culture that men would "become, as it were, one race, . . . one school of God." His *Way of Light*, though first published in 1668, was written in England in 1641. His idea of a "pansophic college" was influential with some who were to be associated with the formation of the Royal Society (1662) and he dedicated this book, at once prophetic and utopian, "to the Torch-bearers of the Enlightened Age, Members of the Royal Society of London." [14] The utopianism of Comenius stems from a deep faith in God and a sound understanding of man's nature and needs. It is true that in his enthusiasm he was at times gullible, and that he expected too much too soon; but such faults are likely to go with a mind of great range and constructive imagination.

In one of Comenius' earliest books, *The Labyrinth of the World and the Paradise of the Heart* (1623), he approaches the issue of sectarianism and unity with brilliant satire and well-contrived allegory. It is hardly too much to say that he here rivals both the sprightly satire of Erasmus and the spiritual allegory of Bunyan.[15] A number

of Comenius' treatises were devoted specifically to ecumenical proposals. His *Haggaeus redivivus* (1632) has special reference to the
Bohemian churches in distress, but with general implications for
Christianity. With his fellow bishops of the Unity he wrote in 1637
The Way of Peace, in which, in the manner of many Reformed writers,
he lays stress on the already existing agreement on Scriptural fundamentals shared even by hot contenders for other details of doctrine.
Like others, too, he employs materials from the Church Fathers and
early councils as affording useful interpretations of Scripture. In
1643, when residing at Elbing and serving the Swedish government
as educational adviser, he wrote his *Memorandum on the Reconciliation of the Christian Sects.*[16] Here he brings within his purview all
segments of Christianity, and coolly lays out a project for a general
representative council. In 1660 he dedicated to Charles II, on the
king's return to England, another treatise bearing on this topic, his
De bono unitatis, which in the following year appeared in English
as *An Exhortation of the Church of Bohemia to the Church of England.* He commends to Charles the polity of the Brethren church as a
model for England and "for the diswaging of animosities and enlarging of good affections"; then goes on to address "Christian people,
dispersed through Europe, Asia, Africa and America, and the Islands
of the Sea," praying that God will bring them to unity and give them
vital breath like the bones in Ezekiel's vision. Every man, says
Comenius, seeks after that which he loves; his own love is for the
unity, order, settlement and vigorous life of the church. Having lost
all this in his small homeland he prays for it throughout all Christendom. He even attempted to set on foot a plan for the translation of
the Bible into Turkish, and in this connection wrote a preface addressed to the Sultan, urging him to read the Scriptures since he was
the ruler of many Christians. At the end of his life Comenius reflected somewhat sadly on the failure of his "irenic labors," but not
without hope that they would yet prove fruitful. He found resistance
in "the obstinacy of Christians one to another." He saw his life task
in most comprehensive terms, "an endeavor to reconcile the whole
human race, which is out of harmony with things, with each other
and with God." [17]

  As bishop of the Community of Brethren, Comenius had many
contacts with Lutheran, Reformed, and Anglican churchmen and
scholars. A devout and prayerful soul, he was indifferent to the
niceties of dogma. What mattered to him was the healing of the

church's disabling sectarianism. In his last book, *The One Thing Needful,* he paraphrases the threefold requirement of "Rupert Meldenius" (see above, p. 72) in the words: "In all things essential, unity; in those less needful (which are called additions), freedom; and in all things, love to all." A true friend of all sincere seekers of unity, he was in correspondence with John Dury, and conferred with him when both were temporarily resident in Amsterdam (1656–1657), in order to further Dury's projects and missions. At the Colloquy of Thorn, assembled in the interest of unity by Ladislas IV of Poland in 1645, Comenius with others of the Brethren was associated with the Reformed theologians, and to him was assigned the task of trying to persuade the Lutheran John Hülsemann to cooperate. He was unsuccessful, and the meeting was without positive result. While strictly speaking he was not within the Reformed church, he was affiliated with it not only through the Bohemian Confession of 1575, which he reedited, but by habitual cooperation with men of the Reformed tradition. Educationally he was much indebted to the Reformed scholars Alsted and Pareus. While he was well disposed to all other Christians, he was so linked with the Reformed branch of Protestantism that his appearance in these pages was unavoidable.

The Magyar people of Hungary, racially unrelated to the Slavic inhabitants of Poland and Bohemia, were, like them, on the fringe of Hapsburg power. They were also peculiarly exposed to Turkish aggression. From the disaster of Mohacs in 1526, Hungary was a subjected and divided nation. Lutheranism had already gained adherents, chiefly among the German-speaking people of the towns. The Magyar youth studying in the schools of the West now brought back both Lutheran and Swiss reforming ideas. In some of these traveled scholars there is seen a tendency to turn for guidance from Wittenberg to Zurich and Geneva. One of the first Hungarians to meet Calvin, and, so far as known, the first to correspond with him, was Gregory Belenyesi, who was a student in Strassburg when Calvin visited it in 1543, and in 1544 spent some time in Geneva.[18] Calvin's writings were from this period widely read by Hungarians. Like the Poles and the Czechs, the Hungarian Magyars had a tendency to distrust Germans because of their experience of Hapsburg rule. Here too, the humanist element in culture led more naturally to Calvinism than to Lutheranism. From about the middle of the century, the spread of Reformed congregations was rapid. In Transylvania, where the Turks were in control and were contemptuously indifferent to the varieties of Chris-

tianity, the Calvinist trend was particularly manifest. The pioneer of
the Swiss teachings there was Martin Santa Kalmancsehi (d. 1557),
a refugee from the Hapsburg to the Turkish area.

Among the Protestant beginners in Hungary, Matthew Biro Devay
(d. 1545), an alumnus of Wittenberg, in the Synod of Erdöd (1545)
approved the adoption of the Augsburg Confession, while he held a
doctrine resembling Calvin's of the spiritual communication of the
body and blood of Christ in the sacrament. The scholarly Stephen
Kis of Szeged (1505–1572) after obtaining a doctorate at Wittenberg
survived imprisonment and torture in Hungary to become an influential preacher and the rector of an academy. About 1550 he became
an enthusiastic reader of Calvin and Bullinger. Through his direct
influence and his posthumously published writings Kis was "one of
the potent fashioners of the Hungarian Reformed Church." [19] A
vigorous contender against the antitrinitarians, he was otherwise a
man of irenic temper. Like him in both these respects was his convert and co-worker Peter Juhasz Melius (1515–1572). As pastor and
leader of reform in Debrecen, Melius made that city a Calvinist stronghold. He was the chief compiler of the Catholic Confession of 1562,
which was soon adopted by synods in both Hapsburg Hungary and
Transylvania. It was the hope of the framers of this Confession that
it would form a bond of Protestant unity in all Hungary; and indeed
it was subscribed by many Lutherans in Transylvania. On the Lord's
Supper it affirms "a spiritual communication of Christ's real body,"
and claims for this the approval of all the Fathers. But in the outcome
it failed of its purpose as a unifying standard, and no general consolidation of Protestant elements took place. In 1591, after the severity
of Rudolf II's policy had become apparent, the Lutheran bishop
Stephen Beythe and a local ruler, Francis Nadasdy, brought about a
conference of the parties at Csepreg, but it achieved nothing. Even
after the acceptance by the Hungarian Lutherans of the Formula of
Concord (1598) the Transylvanian Reformed statesman Stephen
Bocskay, who became the uncrowned prince of Hungary, pursued a
policy of toleration and tried to bring about Protestant agreement.
But his term of rule was shortened, it is thought by poison, and
nothing of this had been accomplished at his death (1606). From 1613
to 1648 two other rulers of Reformed faith governed Hungary. While
their policies were directed to the securing of religious liberty, they
showed little interest in Christian unity.[20]

It is not inappropriate to add here a word about the Ecumenical

Patriarch who was a convinced Calvinist, the celebrated Cyril Lucaris (1572–1638). This brilliant Cretan while he advanced rapidly in the Greek church became deeply interested in the Reformed and Anglican branches of Western Christianity. He was in touch with the Dutch and English ambassadors in Constantinople, and through the latter, Sir Thomas Roe, the friend and helper of John Dury, made important contacts with England and presented to James I the precious Codex Alexandrinus. One of his young officials was sent to study at Oxford, and on his way back conferred with Geneva scholars. Antoine Léger, an emissary of Geneva, was also for years at his side in Constantinople, and in 1629 had Cyril's plainly Calvinist confession of faith printed in Geneva. Lucaris actively sought to bring about Orthodox alignment with the churches of the West separated from Rome. He formed a relationship with Gustavus Adolphus, Lutheran champion of the Protestant cause, and with Bethlen Gabor, then the Calvinist ruler of Hungary. His greatest enemies were the Jesuits, then active in Constantinople; he also offended against traditional Orthodoxy; but it was the Turks who strangled him. In whatever measure he was politically motivated in seeking wide alliances, he was personally a believer in the Reformed doctrines and a brave advocate of the general coordination of the forces of non-Roman Christianity.[21]

VI

SCOTTISH AND ENGLISH ADVOCATES OF CHRISTIAN REUNION: JOHN DURY; RICHARD BAXTER

THE NAME of John Dury has several times appeared in these pages because of his innumerable contacts with Continental advocates of church unity who were his co-workers and correspondents. His long life (1596–1680) embraced a full half-century of unremitting and un-discouraged effort in this apostolate without parallel for both dedication and duration. The very multiplicity of data concerning his travels, labors, and writings makes very difficult a sketch and evaluation brief enough for our present purpose. An unusual example of the "wandering Scot," he requires of us some attempt to follow him in his wanderings while we observe the variety of his unitive projects together with the single purpose and unflagging zeal in which they were conceived and born.[1]

Dury's grandfather, also John Dury, left a monastery to become a Reformation minister of distinction, and his three sons labored in the same calling. One of these, Robert, interrupted his ministry in Anstruther to carry on a mission in the Hebrides, Orkneys, and Shetlands, establishing Reformed parishes. His resistance to King James in arranging, with Andrew Melville and others, a forbidden meeting of the Scottish General Assembly, brought him imprisonment and exile. Our John Dury, born in Edinburgh in 1596, was thus cradled in the Scottish Kirk, but he was taken with his parents to the Netherlands at the age of ten and at fifteen entered the University of Leiden. The school was then agitated by the Arminian controversy. His father's former colleague, Melville, was also in exile, and a professor in the academy of Sedan. John Dury studied there for some years, and Melville wrote to Robert Dury in 1616 expressing "great hope he shall be a good instrument after our departing." His talents were already receiving attention. After further study at Leiden and Amsterdam he became a traveling tutor to a merchant's son, and made the acquaintance of some French Protestant leaders, including Amyraut. In 1624 he had a short sojourn in Oxford. In the same year he was ordained in Holland and became minister to a community of Scottish and English Presbyterian merchants in Elbing, East Prussia. Here he met Samuel Hartlib (1595–1662), a merchant deeply concerned for religion and learning, friend and correspondent of Comenius and of the Lutheran John Valentine Andreae in Calw, whose visit to Geneva called forth his *Christianopolis* (1621), the sketch of a Christian utopia. Dury and Hartlib shared many religious and intellectual interests, and so cooperated for many years that in 1650 Hartlib referred to Dury as his "dear and precious friend" and to himself as Dury's "co-agent." In 1626 Gustavus Adolphus took possession of Elbing and placed it under the administration of his councillor Caspar Godemann. Pursuant to the policies of Gustavus to unify the political forces of Protestantism, Godemann, a former professor of law and the son of a Lutheran proponent of Lutheran-Reformed cooperation, submitted to Dury's judgment a tract he had written on the Lord's Supper. The resulting conversations formed the occasion of Dury's life commitment to the peace of the church. Dury's own words are:

> Concerning myself, I do ingenuously confess that the mere love of peace and quietness, and the hope of doing good to the Church of God, did move me to embrace this endeavor when I was called thereunto in Prussia, by Dr. Godeman, a Chancellor of State to the late King of Sweden, in the year 1628.[2]

In the same year, encouraged by Godemann, Dury addressed to Gustavus a petition, in urgent and somewhat obsequious language, beseeching the king to assume leadership in the task of general pacification and reunion, and requesting an audience. He desired nothing so much as the king's approbation of the project for "the reuniting of the churches, rent in pieces meerly by the factious ambition of some of the clergy." Such phrases may indicate an awareness on Dury's part that Gustavus would find opposition to his work among some of the Swedish clergy, as indeed proved to be the case.[3] For an interview with Gustavus, however, Dury had to wait more than three years.

Meanwhile new doors had opened for the eager apostle. In 1629

Godemann introduced him to Sir Thomas Roe, who, fresh from discussions with Cyril Lucaris in Constantinople, came to Elbing on a mission from Charles I to act as mediator between Sweden and Poland. Roe and Dury, the one an Anglican and the other a Presbyterian, found themselves congenial spirits, and at once forged a bond of concern for Christian union. Roe approached Axel Oxenstierna, chancellor of Sweden, in order to gain support for the project to which Dury was now committed of bringing agreement between Lutherans and Reformed. But Roe was even more intent on enlisting the support of his own king and church. When in 1630 the English factory in Elbing was closed, Dury on Roe's advice went to England, where both Roe and Hartlib, who had taken residence in London, were prepared to aid his efforts.

Armed with commendatory letters from some ministers who had known him in East Prussia, and with Roe's letters of introduction to King Charles, Archbishop George Abbot, William Laud, bishop of London, who would soon be Abbot's successor, and other churchmen, Dury began his campaign to win the royal and ecclesiastical underwriting of his comprehensive project. But in England the tide was running in a direction opposite to that desired by Dury. Abbot was out of favor with the court, suspended from his archiepiscopal functions, and without influence in the church. Bishop John Davenant of Salisbury had just been disciplined and personally reproached by the king for alleged Calvinistic preaching. Laud was about to revoke the freedom to use their own worship assured by Elizabeth and James I to the foreign Protestant congregations in London. Charles left Dury's appeal to be dealt with by Abbot and Laud, thus really leaving it to Laud's decision. If Laud had in mind any conception of future reunion, it was not conceived in terms that would include the Reformed churches. Dury obtained interviews with Abbot and Laud together, and felt that Abbot was favorable to his proposal. Laud was apparently impressed by Dury's activities on the Continent, and willing to see them continued. But no official authorization was given. Following the meeting with the prelates, Dury wrote a letter to Laud to explain his plans. He speaks of the project entertained "beyond seas" and now laid before the learned clergy of England for their counsel and advice. It has been decided to approach both sides at once, first inducing them to follow "the rules of charity," not rushing into controversy. He came to England encouraged by Oxenstierna's cooperation. He earnestly prays "that this Church of England may be the corner stone; and that Your Honor may be the restorer of the breaches of many generations," content that he himself may be the meanest of instruments in it.

The most that Dury obtained from Laud was his permission to say in Germany that the English clergy would be ready to cooperate with him in his efforts there. It is believed that Dury assumed too much of approval in this statement, which in no way committed the English church to membership in one communion with Continental Protestants. In England, Dury visited a large number of the "learned clergy," and obtained where he could a private testimony to his "good and holy purpose." The signatories, thirty-eight in number, were not of the Laudian party, but chiefly men of known Puritan sympathies, such as Stephen Marshall and Thomas Goodwin; they also included three outstanding bishops: Davenant, just mentioned, Joseph Hall of Exeter, and William Bedell of Kilmore and Ardach in Ireland. Bedell backed his support of Dury with financial aid, and all three continued to favor his work. Dury later represented these communications as constituting an authoritative endorsement from the Anglican church. His indomitable optimism may largely account for this, but some lack of candor may have been involved. He was perhaps unwilling to admit to himself how meager the response to his efforts in England had really been.[4]

But he returned to the Continent in July, 1631, with undiminished energy and buoyed by fresh hopes. A colloquy had been held at Leipzig the previous March in connection with a Convention of Protestant Estates, in which three Reformed theologians with three Lutherans closely examined the Augsburg Confession, and found themselves not far from agreement. And Dury was presently further encouraged by the action of the Synod of Charenton in September (see above, pp. 47 f.), a record of which he published in the report *A Summarie Relation* (1633). His movements and conferences in Germany and the Netherlands now become too complicated to recite; but more of his time was spent at Frankfort than anywhere else. In eager haste he journeyed to Stettin and on to Würzburg to interview Gustavus, bearing with him the letters from England referred to above. His approach was aided by the English ambassador, Sir James Spens. The king courteously received him, listened with interest to his story, and sympathetically discussed ways and means of procedure. Gustavus offered to give him "promotorial letters," but Dury, perhaps unwisely, preferred to wait for these until he should have conferred with leading

Reformed divines and secured their opinions on the plan to be followed. This was in December, 1631; on the following November 6, Gustavus fell in battle. No one more than Dury felt the impact of this tragedy.

All the while, Dury was engaged in much correspondence with key persons in church and state. He kept Roe informed in frequent letters that are often intimate, helping us to understand the motivation of this often-disappointed but spiritually resourceful campaigner for Christian unity. On June 25, 1632, he writes that he has been discouraged, but again encouraged by new opportunities, and continues:

> I think myself obliged to do what I can so long as God shall show me any opportunity; for now I say thus: if this be God's work, God will do it, and if I be his servant he will do it by me . . . so long as conscience doth bind and opportunity doth not fail, I cannot fail to go forward; thus I rest on the invisible staff of God's providence.

On July 5 in a characteristic letter he has good news for Sir Thomas: two of the Reformed theologians who had attended the Leipzig colloquy have visited him at Frankfort. These were John Crocius and Theophilus Neuberger, both of Hesse-Cassel, "who were no less joyous to meet with me than I was to meet with them." They reported optimistically on the discussion at Leipzig with Mathias Hoe von Hoenegg, who seemed willing to pursue the negotiations. The differences registered were on the Lutheran doctrines of the *communicatio idiomatum* (interchange of properties, divine and human) and oral manducation in the Lord's Supper, and on the doctrine of predestination. Despite "calumnious aggravators" he has been assured that "the Saxon divines and the better sort of all other Lutherans are inclining to peace and unity." With Crocius and Neuberger, Dury will write to John Bergius, court preacher of Brandenburg, the third Reformed representative at Leipzig, with whom he was already in correspondence, to acquaint him with their conference. He is sending a copy of the letter to Hartlib.

This was one of the high points of expectation for Dury; but, as Westin and others point out, Hoe von Hoenegg's conciliatory mood soon gave place to his wonted antagonism to the Reformed, an attitude in full accord with the policy of the elector of Saxony whose court chaplain he was.[5] Dury was in touch with more favorable, if less influential, Lutherans, including John Valentine Andreae and George Calixtus.

Dury had a favorable reception at a meeting of the princes and theologians at Heilbronn in April, 1633, and thereafter had explicit encouragement from the Helmstadt professors and from their leader Calixtus, who was promoting an alliance of the churches of Brunswick-Lüneberg. But these men were so under attack within Lutheranism that their approbation could only further alienate the Lutheran majority. While anticipating the conference of the Evangelical Estates to be held at Frankfort in 1634, Dury spent some months in England in order to strengthen his relations with Laud and the Anglicans.

Laud, now archbishop, suggested, as a condition of his cooperation, that Dury accept ordination at the hands of an English bishop. It appears that Dury had already felt some disquiet about the regularity of his ordination by Dutch ministers in 1624. Believing the Church of England a true church of Christ, and in hope of obtaining needed support for his work, he accepted Laud's proposal and was ordained by Bishop Hall and English presbyters in February, 1634, on the understanding that he would continue his foreign activities. Laud undertook to supply financial support, but failed in this. It was Hartlib, with his friends, and Sir Thomas Roe who provided his livelihood and travel funds, but he was handicapped by the meagerness of this provision. In April, 1634, he hoped "to subsist in a mean way yet a year or two" so that the seed that had been sown might spring up. Though shabbily attired, he was able to attend the Frankfort convention that summer, and made such an impression as to obtain general approval of his work as a continuation of what had been begun at the Leipzig colloquy. Westin thinks Dury was here trying to use the politicians against the noncooperative Lutheran divines. He learned afterward that Laud's advice to the English emissary at the convention had "rather restrained than encouraged" any involvement with him.

To Frankfort came also Hugo Grotius, to confer with Oxenstierna about his appointment as Swedish ambassador to France. At once Dury and Grotius became friends and fellow contrivers of unity projects. In Dury's interest Grotius entered on a correspondence with Laud, which, as we have seen, proved futile.[6] A short visit to Scotland for interviews with Scottish church leaders followed; but his association with Laud was far from recommending him to the Scottish

Presbyterians. Only the "Aberdeen Doctors" warmly approved his mission; their ablest writer, John Forbes, had been his fellow student at Sedan twenty years earlier.

Encouraged by Grotius, Dury went to ply his propaganda in Sweden (1636–1638), accompanied and assisted by Peter Figulus, son-in-law of Comenius. He was permitted to address the professors of Uppsala and a synod of clergy at Stockholm. But his proposal for a new and simplified confession as a basis of union with the Reformed churches had little appeal to the Swedes, and aroused a series of bitter attacks from John Rudbeck, bishop of Westeräs. As a result, the peacemaker was banished as a disturber of the peace. He was ill at the time; but as soon as possible he resumed his work, meeting Roe in Hamburg, visiting Lübeck and Bremen, and fraternizing with Calixtus at Hildesheim.

The revolutionary situation now developing in England seemed to offer special possibilities for his irenic effort. Along with Comenius, Dury was now invited to England by a group of members of the Long Parliament. He arrived in August, 1641. With Comenius and Hartlib he was engaged in framing proposals for a system of education tending to "peace, piety and truth." As opportunity offered, he raised his voice for church unity. He had already enlisted the interest of the Scottish Presbyterian leader Alexander Henderson, and presented to the Scottish General Assembly "A Memorial concerning Peace Ecclesiasticall" urging Scottish and English Protestants to "live in the communion of saints one toward another." The Assembly, meeting at St. Andrew's (1641), took a favorable view of his designs for a broad unity. He also tried to secure consideration of his plans by the English Parliament. He was appointed a royal chaplain and was sent to The Hague to tutor the king's daughter, Mary, child-wife of Frederick Henry of Orange. But shortly after the opening of the Westminster Assembly, July 1, 1643, one of the members designate having died, Dury was appointed by Parliament to that body. However, as a chaplain of the king and an Anglican clergyman, he had lost status with the high Presbyterians in the Assembly, and he prudently remained for some time in the Netherlands, now ministering to an English congregation in Rotterdam. Here, as an Anglican, he made a free use of the Book of Common Prayer, and recommended it to Dutch and German friends.[7]

The Westminster Assembly was summoned "to procure and preserve the peace of the church at home and nearer agreement with the

Church of Scotland and other reformed churches abroad." With such a prospect the Assembly irresistibly attracted Dury for its possibilities as a unitive agency amid the disarray of the churches. He wrote from The Hague before going to Rotterdam to promise his attendance, noting that Oxenstierna had undertaken to promote reconciliation among Protestants. The Assembly heard the letter read, December 20, 1643; but he did not arrive until August 12, 1645. His coming was viewed with apprehension by Robert Baillie, watchful Scottish adversary of bishops and their liturgies, who wanted no "least tincture" of such elements among the Divines; but he later conferred with Dury, when a shipping mishap took him to Holland, and was partially reassured. Dury seems to have made himself agreeable to the Presbyterian majority of the Assembly, and he was an active participant. In a sermon before Parliament, November 26, 1645, on "Israel's call to march out of Babylon and unto Jerusalem," he warned: "Make not the walls of Jerusalem too narrow, but be mindful that ye ought to receive all that are going out of Babylon with you." Asking them not to forget the foreign Protestants, he pointed out that the Solemn League and Covenant to which they were pledged called for union efforts at home and abroad. In the years of the Assembly his grief was that he could not get most of those in it to see its task in the larger dimension in which he pictured it.[8]

Despite all efforts to make his aims known, Dury found it hard to come to terms of mutual understanding with men who represented the controversial mentality of his age. A man in dead earnest about the Holy Catholic Church may not feel called upon to label Charles I or Cromwell as angel or devil. Dury exposed himself to attack by shifting his allegiance. He was in turn a Presbyterian, an Anglican, and an instrument of Cromwell abroad. That Puritan extremist William Prynne in a bitter pamphlet assailed him as *The Time-serving Proteus and Ambidexter Divine,* to which Dury's reply was entitled *The Unchanged, Constant and Single-hearted Peacemaker* (1650). The reason for his indifference to the conflicting parties was his desire to be of "universal serviceableness in that which is good," following the principles of the gospel.

The Form of Church Government, adopted by the Westminster Assembly, under the heading "Of Synodical Assemblies," states that these "may lawfully be of several sorts, as provincial, national and oecumenical." The minutes of the Assembly do not tell us whether Dury suggested this language or not, but it represents his point of view. It is not unlikely that his colleagues in the Assembly thought of "oecumenical synods" in far more strictly Presbyterian terms than he did. While some of them were, to use modern parallels, thinking of such a synod as might speak for a world Alliance of Presbyterian and Reformed Churches, he was thinking of one that would be an organ of a World Council of Churches. Incidentally, this is an early use of the word "ecumenical," as a term in church polity and not as a label for the ancient creeds and councils.

When Cromwell laid his hand on the church, Presbyterianism was soon in eclipse. In "Pride's Purge," December 6, 1648, preparatory to the trial and execution of Charles I, Presbyterians were excluded from Parliament, though many were still ministers in the parishes. But in Cromwell's foreign policy Dury saw new opportunity for his proposals. Indeed Cromwell's well-known scheme for consolidating European Protestantism, as described by Gilbert Burnet, seems in some features to resemble the ideas of Comenius and Dury.[9] Not surprisingly, then, in 1654 Dury was back on the Continent under the aegis of Cromwell, explaining his plans in Zurich, Geneva, Basel, and many parts of Germany. In the Swiss centers he met with a very favorable response, tempered, however, by fear of French hostility. In Germany too the Reformed were generally favorable, though some would have nothing to do with an agent of the regicide Cromwell, and some looked upon Dury as an impractical visionary. A Lutheran group at Rintelin, and many elsewhere, were warmly cooperative; but these were only men who had lined up with Calixtus, and his opponents, the great majority of Lutherans, were Dury's opponents also. Going on to the Netherlands, he met with a good reception from a large section of the ministers, but these were chiefly of the liberal opposition party headed by John Coccieus. The decisive action of the Estates was to the effect that since the Lutherans had hitherto made no response to previous approaches, unitive action should be delayed until they were ready to initiate it.

Cromwell's plans were shifting, and Dury went back to England to make ready for a new campaign, and to secure, through Cromwell's Latin secretary, John Milton, authorization for this from the Lord Protector and the Parliament. To himself, at least, Dury's prospects looked hopeful again, when the whole scene was changed by Cromwell's death, September 3, 1658. As with the death of Gustavus in 1632, Dury's immediate designs were wrecked. He had always regarded the ruling powers as "ordained of God" whether king, parliament, or dictator, and was always ready to make use of any political help available for his ecclesiastical propaganda. At times he had expected much from the support of statesmen and rulers, but there remained now little prospect of such help. Charles II and his ministers rebuffed him coldly.

In this adverse turn of affairs, another man of his ripe age might have accepted defeat and gone into retirement. But Dury had embraced a lifetime calling, and he would still earn "the wages of going on." He was soon traveling new and old trails in Germany and Holland, conferring and persuading, and devising conferences. He prepared the ground for the colloquy between Lutheran and Reformed at Cassel, June, 1661. The parties reached here a large measure of agreement. They took strong ground against polemical preaching, but they failed to establish intercommunion. However, the Lutheran participants at Cassel were again men trained in the school of Calixtus. Their opponents within Lutheran ranks had louder voices which were soon heard. Prince William VI of Hesse, who had called the meeting, soon afterward died. His widow, Sophie, was to provide for Dury a residence at Cassel. He greatly wanted to be of use to Frederick William, the "Great Elector" of Prussia, but that prince, though he had an interest in Protestant union, persistently declined to permit Dury to take a hand in promoting it in his territories.

Among Dury's very numerous correspondents was Paul Ferry (1591–1669), pastor in Metz for fifty-eight years and a lifelong advocate of Christian unity. Jacques Bénigne Bossuet had challenged one of Ferry's early writings and the resulting debate ended in mutual respect and friendship which was maintained after Bossuet had become bishop of Meaux. On Ferry's invitation, Dury visited him in 1662, and the two veterans had a good time together conferring over Dury's union projects. Ferry's writings on the theme of union still remain unpublished.[10]

In his late years Dury's writings were hardly less abundant than before, but his travels were less extensive. The last period was spent at Cassel, where he worshiped in a church of French émigrés. His latest tractates won the praise of Philip Jacob Spener, founder of German Pietism, who had formerly lightly esteemed him. In 1677 Dury was visited by William Penn, who paused in a tour of Europe to see the aged peacemaker. On the mystical side, Dury had certain affinities with the Quakers, though he was not so tolerant as to wish them well in England. In 1674, six years before his death, he announced that he would henceforth labor for the union, not of Protestants only, but of Protestants with Roman Catholics, stressing the fact that both revered the Scriptures, and setting forth new principles of exegesis that he thought would lead to agreement. Hitherto he had neither contended with Roman Catholics nor conferred with them and now his strength was almost spent.

It is difficult to evaluate the career and labors of John Dury. The easiest judgment to offer is that his work was a failure; and with this may go the characterization of him as a self-deceived enthusiast or a crackpot. But such a view calls for modification. In the first place, it is clear that many wise and learned men and highly placed statesmen held him in personal esteem. These include some who are placed by historians at the center of seventeenth-century culture. Before he finally left England he was active in the group of avantgarde intellectuals who shortly afterward brought about the foundation of the Royal Society. While the Westminster Assembly was becoming enfeebled he retained his connection with it, but held a post as librarian of the Library of St. James in London. Out of this experience came his book on *The Librarie Keeper* (1650), a pioneering work of such value that it has been more than once republished in our century. His other work of the same date, *The Reformed School,* takes an important place in the history of educational theory. In Dury these incidental matters show unmistakable flashes of genius.

There is greatness, too, in his constancy and tenacity of purpose. In many statements, he indicates that this was sustained by a steadfast faith so strong as to be almost impervious to temporal disappointment. This made Dury the most indomitable ecumenist in what Baxter called "a contentious dividing age." After the death of King Gustavus and that of the ambassador Spens, who had befriended him and aided him with funds, he wrote to Sir Thomas Roe (November 18, 1632):

> As for my purpose and business, though I have full assurance that if His Majestie had lived he would have used all means to further it, and could to all appearance have brought it to effect, yet I cannot cast off the hopes I have in God because I know that it is his work.

So he works on, involved in a wide and busy correspondence to promote "a holy communion of godly men." [11]

The last phrase is characteristic; it suggests very well Dury's essential aim. His many projects for securing union often exhibit plans of a structured approach to this end by means of synods and conferences crowned by a Europe-wide assembly. But the end in view was not either a previously devised form of church government or the adoption of a comprehensive confession of faith. His concern was for such agreement of Christian minds as would assure ecclesiastical peace and fruitful spiritual fellowship—"a holy communion of godly men." He was not indifferent to theological studies; but he believed that the theologians had often missed the central things in their zest for disputation over peripheral matters. If I may paraphrase the language of a French contemporary of Dury, they had pulled down the roof of charity to prop the walls of dogma. Like Spener and the Pietists, but earlier, he advocated courses of study in "practical theology" to be led by professors more concerned for charity than for narrow definitions. One of the functions of church government, he thought, should be to curb the abusive controversialists. He often expressed his conviction of the primacy of spiritual and not external forces in Christian union. In 1637 he wrote to Lord Forbes:

> For I know that the Communion of Saints (believed in the Creed verbally by many, but practised in effect by very few) . . . is the only instrument which God doth make use of to builde up his Church.[12]

We have noted his advice to the Scots in 1641: "to live together in the Communion of Saints, one toward another." Dury took so seriously the clause "I believe in the Communion of Saints" that he thought it worth trying to reshape the visible church in ways favorable to the realization of that communion. To this end he gave all he had, unembittered by rebuffs and reproaches, with a certain gallantry of devotion.

Some of the leading members of the Westminster Assembly, quite independently of Dury, were advocates of conciliation and unity. This is true of George Gillespie, the brilliant Scot whose early death (1648) cut off a promising career. "His writings," says W. K. Jordan, "are temperate, reasoned and conciliatory. Had he lived he might well have assumed the leadership of the moderate Presbyterian party."[13] Of the same spirit was Stephen Marshall, who in *The Moderate Presbyterian* (1645) sought a way of reconciliation especially with the Independents on the basis of Biblical faith, and condemned all persecution. Thomas Manton in *Meate out of the Eater*

(1647), and a number of others of the party, produced a considerable body of tracts of this type.[14] Instead of the general toleration advocated by some Independents, these men desired the "accommodation of tender consciences" within the one church. In the swift movement of events, their proposals were ineffective.

There are other names of note for their interest in the unity of the church among Scottish and English Presbyterians of the seventeenth century. One of these was James Durham of Glasgow (d. 1658), who did his utmost to heal the strife between the liberal Resolutioners and the exclusive Protesters between which parties the Scottish church was torn as a result of Cromwell's invasion of Scotland and suppression of the Assembly (1651–1653). In his *Treatise of Scandal,* Durham asks his readers to consider whether if all the Reformed churches were asked to judge the matter they would not commend mutual forbearance. Union of the church he calls "a commanded duty," even where defects remain, and schism is condemned by the councils and the Fathers. In his Commentary on Revelation he stresses the idea of the Catholic Church as an integral whole, in language reminiscent of Calvin's. Robert Boyd (1578–1627), having spent his youth in France and at Mornay's invitation been made a professor at Saumur, returned to Scotland on invitation from King James (1615) and became in turn divinity principal of Glasgow and of Edinburgh and minister of Paisley. His Commentary (*Praelectiones*) on Ephesians, not published until 1652, a Latin work of vast learning in historic and contemporary theology, offers a plea for the abandonment of polemics and attaining to "the unity of Faith."

Nor can we exclude from consideration here the celebrated "Aberdeen Doctors," Calvinists and broad churchmen, who held episcopacy tolerable if not essential and were hence unable to subscribe the National Covenant of 1638. Their chief inspirer, Patrick Forbes, was bishop of Aberdeen from 1628 to his death in 1635. In a defense of the ministries of churches of the Reformation, he "joyfully called attention to the Church of England and many other famous Reformed Churches, all agreeing in communion with us and glad to give us the right hand of fellowship." [15] His son, John Forbes of Corse (1593–1648), stands nearer to the company of those who have come to notice in these pages. He was a student of Pareus and a fellow student of Comenius at Heidelberg and of Dury at Sedan under Melville, of whom, like Dury, he was a kinsman. Appointed professor in King's College Aberdeen, he became the author of a work of permanent im-

portance for ecumenical history, his famous *Irenicum* (1629).[16] Though
suggested by the Scottish situation and addressed to Scottish readers,
this work has much wider implications. Forbes looks upon the matters raised by the policy of the Stuart kings as minor by comparison
with the need to preserve continuity with the historic church and
with the churches of the Reformation in Europe. With the triumph
of the Covenanters in 1638 he was in trouble with the authorities.
Finally deprived of his chair, he continued to worship as a Presbyterian, as he did also in Scottish and Dutch churches during two
years of scholarly work in the Netherlands (1644–1646). He and his
colleagues thought of themselves as loyal men of the Kirk, although
the more extreme of their opponents regarded them as traitors.

Preeminent among the Puritans of his time was Richard Baxter
(1615–1691), still well known as a prolific and spirited writer. He was
the foremost among the moderate Presbyterians who after the Cromwellian period, with the failure of Presbyterianism as an exclusive
system for the English church, were disposed to cooperate with others
and to seek unity on a basis of general agreement. While pastor at
Kidderminster he was able to organize for cooperation in discipline
and mutual edification almost all the ministers in Worcestershire,
Presbyterian, Independent, and Episcopal. This association he describes in his *Christian Concord* (1653), the first of a long series of
writings that represent his quest for Christian unity. In all the twenty
volumes of Baxter's *Practical Works* this theme is never lost sight of,
and a number of treatises are specifically given to it. He liked to call
himself a "mere catholic," as one who desired fellowship with all true
Christians, and he called for an approach to dividing issues in a mood
of "learning" as opposed to "disputing." It must be added that on
matters of real concern for him he could dispute as hotly and sarcasti-
cally as any contender; but in general his tone is conciliatory and
imaginatively considerate of others' opinions. While he addressed himself chiefly to the problems of the church in England, he was always
aware of the need for general union, and in 1658 wrote a tract supporting "Mr. John Dury's endeavors after ecclesiastical peace." The
critical years 1658 to 1661 called forth a number of his writings
worthy of mention here. His *Necessary Grounds, Ends and Principles
of a Universal Concord between all Pastors and Churches* (1658)
examines the requisite conditions of unity. It is in three parts: (1) belief; (2) practice; (3) ministry and worship. He condemns here the
modern elaboration of creeds, pointing out that an early Christian

martyr might be rejected by their framers. Discipline is necessary, but must be conducted without censoriousness. In *The True Catholick and Catholick Church Described* (1660), he twits those who "run from room to room to find the house," the true church being in fact the faithful in all the churches, many of whom are in the Roman communion despite the error into which it has fallen. Required articles of belief are sufficiently given in the Creed, the Lord's Prayer, and the Ten Commandments.

In 1661 Presbyterians were invited to the Savoy Conference on equal terms with the bishops but treated as petitioners with no standing. On their behalf Baxter presented a hastily framed "Reformed Liturgy" to be permitted for congregations that favored it instead of the Book of Common Prayer. The document, though of some merit, "was instantly, and without examination, rejected." [17] At this time he also tried without success to obtain consideration for Archbishop James Ussher's project for a compromise polity, the *Reduction of Episcopacy to Synodical Government* (1644), which Baxter now hoped might serve to draw the disputing parties into one comprehensive church. Like his learned friend Ussher, Baxter thought of episcopacy as ideally "a constant but limited presidency" among presbyters, and would have synods associated with bishops in administration, with a moral authority over pastors "for unity and communion sake." In 1669 he published an extended work entitled *The Cure of Church Divisions* in which he so criticized the controversialists as to expose himself to attack by a former friend. Such were the sensitivities of party leaders in that age that the most irenic intentions could not protect a writer from angry condemnation. Baxter himself was not free from venom in advocating peace and goodwill, and he often complained that blows were rained upon him from both sides amid a fray that he had sought to assuage. This happened after he published *Catholic Communion Defended against Both Extremes* (1684), in which John Owen and the Independents were charged with schismatic attitudes and certain Anglicans were also assailed, including Edward Stillingfleet, author of a celebrated *Irenicum* which later embarrassed him. In all this Baxter's aims were lofty and his mind sincere, but he lacked the psychological wisdom that would have made him a sufficiently persuasive writer to bring to life a general movement of moderate and charitable men strong enough in numbers and in learning to snatch the initiative from those for whom a mere difference of opinion justified breach of communion. The title page of his *Defence of the Principles of Love* (1671) contains the ascription "By Richard Baxter, One of the Mourners for a self-dividing and self-afflicting land."

Baxter's thick folio volume *Catholic Theology* (1675) in its prodigiously long subtitle indicates that it was written "chiefly for posterity." In a long life he had found controversies among Protestants "far more about equivocal words than matter," and he had accepted the primary task "to call men . . . to more peaceable thoughts." The task was too great for him, and there were few who offered him help; "therefore," says his biographer, William Orme,

> all due allowance should be made for the mistakes into which he fell. With all his faults and imperfections, he was a man of a truly catholic spirit, who labored hard to heal the wounds that had been inflicted on the church by various means, and for which there seemed no cure.

Orme anticipates a "period of love and union" in which "the services of Baxter as the indefatigable advocate of catholic communion will not be forgotten." [18]

The most conciliatory of the Independents in the Westminster Assembly, Jeremiah Burroughs, was the author of treatises and sermons that have a bearing on our theme, including his *Irenicum to the Lovers of Truth and Peace* (1646), where he deplores the evil condition of things in which "good men cause affliction to good men." But his primary concern was to warn against what he regards as an intolerant system emerging in an alliance of the Presbyterians with the Parliament. Somewhat later John Owen, a learned and cooperative Independent, in his *True Nature of a Gospel Church* (ch. xi) and elsewhere, expounds a high conception of the spiritual union which every particular church holds with the Catholic Church of the Creed. Owen was apparently the chief framer of the Preface to the Savoy Declaration of 1658, which rejects all constraint in religion and calls for "a forbearance and mutual indulgence unto saints of all persuasions" in "matters extra-fundamental, whether of faith or order." This Preface, a somewhat miscellaneous commendation of the Declaration itself, is throughout irenical, if not in a more ample sense ecumenical. He once described the communion of saints thus: "a holy conjunction between all God's people, wrought by the participation of the same spirit, whereby we are all made members of one body whereof Christ is the Head." [19] Unlike Baxter, Owen avoided eucharistic intercommunion with Anglicans. But under the adverse policy of the Stuarts, Presbyterians and Independents alike suffered under great disabilities, and their differing attitudes toward Anglicanism made little practical difference in their actual relations with the established church. This situation led to certain acts of cooperation between them. Even in Cromwell's time, organizations such as that introduced by Baxter in Worcestershire drew the ministers together for the examination and ordination of new ministers in Cumberland and Westmorland and some other counties. As conditions worsened for both denominations after the Restoration, attempts were made to revive this type of association; but no such plan was possible until after the Revolution of 1688. A common fund was provided for the education of ministers in 1690, and in 1691 a mutual covenant was entered into by the two parties in a document called the Heads of Agreement. Baxter lived just long enough to welcome this step. It came as a result of much conference among London ministers, and was apparently chiefly framed by John Howe (1630–1705), an irenical Presbyterian in high repute as a preacher, while Increase Mather was among the Congregationalist negotiators. As early as 1672, Independent and Presbyterian ministers had unreservedly joined in secretly conducted ordinations, and now that Nonconformists were no longer prevented from holding such meetings openly, the agreement provided fully for such cooperation.

But this promising arrangement was soon disrupted over a doctrinal issue, "the alleged antinominianism of Dr. Crisp, a deceased Anglican divine, whose views were favored by leading Congregationalists and rejected by leading Presbyterians." [20] That the Nonconformists should have allowed their "Happy Union" of 1691 to be shattered over the suspected orthodoxy of a minor Anglican writer is ironical enough, and discloses the fragility of the bond between them. In this situation John Howe was the leader of a defeated remnant of the ministers who sought to maintain the Heads of Agreement. They drew up a new supporting agreement on doctrine in 1692, but the debate continued. Howe's late years were spent in puzzled sorrow over the anomaly that Christians neglected the great things on which they were agreed and kept harping on the slight matters on which they differed. His friend Calamy, in an intimate account of Howe which is rather a documented appreciation than a biography, represents him as one of the most gentle yet most constant advocates of a broadly based unity. Since Calamy was himself of the same mind, his work abounds in quotations on this theme from Howe's sermons and other writings. In 1688, representing the Dissenters on the occasion of William III's reception in England, Howe addressed the king on the topic "The Protestant Interest throughout the Christian World." William was favorably impressed: one wonders whether he called to mind the plea of Cornelius Trigland addressed to him in his youth (see above, p. 70). Howe was shocked by the exclusiveness of those churches which practiced closed communion. "The holy table," he wrote in 1693, "is the symbol of communion: and if it be the Lord's it ought to be free to his guests. . . . Who dare invite others, or forbid these?" With reference to his peaceableness and charity Calamy likens him to "that eminent German divine, Martin Bucer." [21]

Such gentle and thoughtful Christians have too often been wounded in the ecclesiastical battlefield. The new rationalistic currents of the eighteenth century brought new occasions of strife and left both denominations of the "Holy Union" in weakness and theological disorder. In that era some of the Presbyterian advocates of unity disregarded the presuppositions of traditional, including Reformed, theology. An example is John Taylor of Norwich (d. 1761), who looked for a coming universal Christianity resting on fresh scholarly study of the Bible in freedom untrammeled by creeds.[22] It was not in such rationalistic latitudinarianism, but in a new evangelicalism on the one hand and in the Tractarian quest of catholicity on the other, that the ecumenical spirit was to be vigorously revived in the British churches.

VII

FRAGMENTATION AND REUNION
OF THE CHURCH OF SCOTLAND

THE STORY of the Reformed Church of Scotland exhibits in one small country the divisive and unitive trends characteristic of Protestantism as a whole. But there the causes of separation were peculiarly in the realm of polity and of state-church relationships rather than of confessional doctrines. The work of the Reformation left a nationally organized church impoverished but well coordinated and functioning for all the people. The civil government was pledged in 1560 to the maintenance of this church, and after some inner conflict about episcopacy the obligation was renewed in 1590 and 1592. The national Reformed church regarded itself not as a new entity but as continuing the pre-Reformation *Ecclesia Scotticana,* and this claim was justified not only by the fact that it gathered to itself virtually the entire living membership of the former organization but also that it held firmly a doctrine of the Holy Catholic Church and was aware of itself as the Catholic Church visible in the realm of Scotland.[1] The reforms of 1560 produced a church polity without bishops, authority being exercised by associated presbyters in synods and assemblies. The government-sponsored effort to place bishops over the presbyterate was the occasion of animated controversy with far-reaching results. This effort took a rather crude form when in 1572 the Earl of Morton, who in that year became regent of Scotland, induced certain ministers to accept appointments to the vacant bishoprics, mainly in order to secure through these accommodating clergymen the incomes from the episcopal properties for the public revenues. The appointees were derisively called "tulchans," from the Gaelic word for a stuffed calfskin used to induce the mother cow to yield her milk. In this and later incidents the very word "bishop" took on

unsavory connotations for many in Scotland, and a polarity was set
up between "bishop" and "presbyter" which became characteristic of
later controversy.[2] Before his death, November 24, 1572, John Knox
had reluctantly consented to the first of these appointments, but with
a grave warning of the peril involved. After 1575, under Andrew Melville's uncompromising leadership of the resistance to King James VI,
the dominant note was that of absolute rejection of prelacy in any
form. In 1580 the General Assembly adopted the Second Book of
Discipline, in which the term "bishop" is mentioned only as identical
with "pastor" or "minister." By 1590 the king had come to terms
with Presbyterianism and addressed the ministers praising in fulsome
terms the presbyterian order of church polity. This attitude was dis-
trusted; but Presbyterianism was fully triumphant in 1592 when an
act was passed by Parliament abolishing all previous acts favorable
to prelacy. James actually believed, however, that episcopacy was an
indispensable safeguard of monarchical government. Accordingly, in
crass violation of the act of 1592, he suppressed the General Assembly,
later permitting it to meet only under close control by his agents, and
proceeded to designate as bishops ten presbyterially ordained ministers. These were not "tulchans" passing their incomes on to the politicians, but were invested in the old episcopal estates and held seats
in the Scottish Parliament. As king of both kingdoms after 1603,
James was resolved to unite the two nations ecclesiastically by the
establishment in Scotland of the episcopal and liturgical features of
Anglicanism. His firm pressure in this direction bore fruit in 1610
when three of the Scottish presbyter-bishops were consecrated by
three English bishops in London. Two years later he obtained the
repeal of the Presbyterian establishment act of 1592. In 1618 he
forced through a manipulated Assembly at Perth a set of articles re-
quiring minor liturgical changes displeasing to the Scots, and the more
unwelcome because of the implication that the Kirk was to have no
spontaneous life but to be helpless under royal absolutism. Between
1618 and 1638 the General Assembly was not permitted to meet. The
churches continued to function with little obvious local change, and
while dissatisfaction ran deep, it might conceivably have been overcome had not Charles I attempted to complete his father's work by
the imposition of a book of Canons and Constitutions (1636) and a
new prayer book that would have abruptly transformed the habitual
worship of Scottish congregations (1637). A wave of resentment now
swept through the land.

Many spontaneously gathered in Edinburgh, where a group of committees ("Tables") promptly prepared the National Covenant and presented it for signatures at Greyfriars Church, February 28, 1638. It was thereafter eagerly signed by many of all ranks throughout the kingdom. It rehearses older official documents of the Kirk, complains of the attempt to supersede them, and solemnly declares: "That with our whole heart we agree and resolve . . . constantly to adhere to and defend the foresaid true religion." In the tide of revolt thus begun bishops fled to England, and, against the king's wish but with his prudent consent, a free Assembly met at Glasgow in November, under the moderatorship of Alexander Henderson, the chief author of the Covenant. When it proceeded against episcopacy the king's commissioner pronounced the Assembly dissolved, but it continued in session until by a series of acts it had restored the presbyterian system, utterly repudiated episcopacy together with the liturgical innovations, and annulled all the acts of assemblies managed by the king since 1606. All accounts show that the Assembly closed in the exultation of victory. In taking the ground that prelacy was subversive of Protestantism it gave evidence that the Kirk had through controversy moved in spirit and outlook from Knox to Melville—a development which, we must admit, involved some loss of Christian charity.

In all this we are unavoidably reminded of the ancient enmity that gave to history Bannockburn and Flodden Field. But now the Stuart fixation with absolute monarchy had aroused strong opposition in England also, and the Presbyterian Scots had allies there. As early as 1586 Peter Wentworth representing the Presbyterian cause had, against Elizabeth I's directives, boldly claimed the right of free speech in Parliament. At the beginning of the Interregnum (1640) many of the Puritans, and a majority in the Long Parliament, were of the Presbyterian persuasion. The Scottish counteroffensive against Anglicanism-by-decree meant a vigorous attempt to presbyterianize the English church. We have already referred to the Westminster Assembly; its history is both too complicated and too familiar to be recited here. We must address ourselves to the story of the Scottish church, and first to its multiple divisions during the two centuries after the crisis of 1638.

The work of the Divines at Westminster was not yet completed when a serious cleavage arose in the Kirk over the "Engagement" negotiated (1648) between King Charles and Alexander Henderson for Scottish aid to the king against Cromwell. The strict Covenanters disbelieved the king's liberal promises to them and denounced the "Engagers." After Cromwell had defeated the Scots at Dunbar and entered Edinburgh a Commission of the General Assembly adopted certain "Resolutions" agreeing to the enlistment "of all fencible persons" to fight the invader. The "Resolutioners" were now condemned by the "Protesters," who wanted an army of Covenanters only, lest the king's religious policy should come back through the army. While dispute was continued, the Assembly, meeting in Edinburgh in July, 1653, was rudely interrupted by an officer and soldiers of Cromwell's army. The members were marched out of the city and commanded to return to their homes. The party names passed out of use, but there remained a tradition of unyielding adherence to the Covenant of 1638 on the one hand and on the other a tendency to regard it as secondary amid changing issues. Charles II, who in 1650 had subscribed the Covenant, proved a ruthless foe of Presbyterianism. In 1661 an act was put through the Scottish Parliament rescinding all legislation since 1633 by which the presbyterian revival had been legalized, and in 1662 Parliament enacted the restoration of "government of the church by archbishops and bishops." Until the Revolution of 1688 the attempt to enforce this change and to silence all opponents was attended by severe measures of repression and cost many lives. Some of the persecuted resorted to armed resistance, without success. A remnant of irreconcilable Covenanters, survivors of much struggle and suffering, continued a detached existence. They protested against the fact that in William III's recognition of the presbyterian order of the Church of Scotland the Covenant was not reaffirmed. Only in 1743 were they strong enough to form a presbytery. After 1690 the General Assembly, sadly diminished in numbers, despite some initial friction with William, resumed its role as the authoritative governing body of the church. William had refused at his coronation to obligate himself to any course of persecution, and in 1712 Parliament withdrew all the civil penalties entailed by excommunication. In Scotland as elsewhere, the eighteenth century was marked by a fairly wide toleration, a condition that made it easier for dissidents to organize secession movements.

Apart from the Covenanters, all laymen until 1706, we might regard as the earliest of these secessions the rise of an independent Episcopal church. It first existed in a few separate congregations where episcopalian ministers remained, and was more adequately organized when in 1712 an act of the united Parliament recognized the "Episcopal Communion" in Scotland. In the same year Parliament restored the pre-Reformation practice of patronage (previously abolished, restored, and again abolished) whereby propertied lay patrons had the right to nominate to the pastorate. The patronage act became the source of great dissatisfaction and much conflict. In it the Church of Scotland paid a high price for the Union of Parliaments of 1707. The Scottish General Assembly from year to year protested the abuses connected with this act, and in some instances local struggles resulted from attempts to settle a pastor selected by a patron against the will of the people. But the dominant part in the Assembly at this period was opposed to pursuing the issue in such a way as to bring on a church-state conflict that might be disastrous. The Scottish Moderates drew their designation from the message of William III to the Assembly of 1690: "Moderation is what religion requires, neighboring churches expect of you, and we recommend to you." The king's chaplain and intimate consultant, William Carstares, later minister of Greyfriars and of St. Giles, Edinburgh, and four times moderator of the Assembly, was the chief founder of the party, although its name was not applied until long after his death. Later in the century the celebrated historian William Robertson was its competent leader. The Moderates were largely affected by the liberal philosophies of the eighteenth century, and were indifferent both to the intense convictions of the Covenanters and to the evangelical fervor of the school of Thomas Boston. Elements from both these sources entered into the so-called First Secession led by Ebenezer Erskine, minister of Stirling, but it sprang largely from indignation against the loss of the free call of the church members under the system of patronage. For a protest made in 1732 Erskine and three other ministers were placed under censure and suspended from the ministry. They explained that they were seceding "from the prevailing party in the church," appealed for a free and faithful Assembly, and regarded themselves as still within the Church of Scotland. They organized as the Associate Presbytery in 1733. They had much sympathy throughout the country, and they stoutly resisted efforts of the Assembly leaders to bring them back into fellowship prior to their final deposition in 1740. One of their grievances was that the Covenant had not been reaffirmed at the Revolutionary settlement. They invited George Whitefield to Scotland; but finding him unwilling to sign the Covenant, they denounced him as a "prelatic hireling." The growing body of seceders, scrupulously conscientious men, divided over the Burgess oath obligating magistrates to "the true religion presently professed within this realm and authorized by the laws thereof." Erskine was with the Burghers, but he and his adherents, including his talented brother Ralph, were excommunicated by the Antiburghers, among whom was Ralph's son John (1747).

In 1752 another secession arose from the same issue. When the parishioners of Inverkeithing rejected a patron's appointee to that parish and ministers of the presbytery of Dunfermline declined to induct him, the General Assembly voted to depose one of the latter as an example. The one deposed was Thomas Gillespie of Carnock, who had studied in Philip Doddridge's Academy at Northampton and felt the influence of English evangelical Nonconformity. The Moderates thought that in disciplining him they were vindicating the rightful authority of the General Assembly as the supreme court of the church. But the popular tide was beginning to run with the secessionists. In 1761 Gillespie and his supporters formed the "Relief Presbytery," finding "relief" from patronage. Gillespie and his friends had little in common with the Erskine secessionists. They were not Covenanters, and were distinctly looking forward to the abolition of patronage and the revival of the church. They took a stand on "free communion," the admission of Christians of any denomination to the Lord's Supper; and they participated actively in the Evangelical Revival soon to gain headway. Both groups of presbyterian seceders found more and more adherents during the latter part of the century, and they annually added to the number of their congregations.

It is necessary to add that the Burgher branch of the First Secession divided in 1799 into Auld Lichts and New Lichts, the former favoring state connection and the covenanting principle, the latter opposing national covenants and state support. A like division of the Antiburghers took place in 1806.[3]

By this time the religious atmosphere in Scotland was changing under the influence of the Evangelical Revival, which had its beginnings in personal experience and preaching missions not planned or directed by church authority, and was from the first affected by similar movements of great significance in America and England. Its first manifestations were at Cambuslang (the "Cambuslang Wark") in 1742 under the ministry of William McCulloch, and it later had the leadership of able and scholarly ministers of Edinburgh and Glasgow. Both Whitefield and Wesley made many preaching tours in Scotland.

The Evangelical party in the General Assembly was increasing although still unable to withstand the Moderates. But no widespread popular movement took place until near the end of the eighteenth century. Following a preaching visit to Perthshire by Charles Simeon of Cambridge in 1796, came the extensive mission of James Alexander Haldane, who had been Simeon's companion. In 1794 both James, an Edinburgh-educated sea captain, and his elder brother Robert, a retired naval officer, had undergone conversion through personal Bible study. Both were to follow notable careers devoted to evangelization and religious enterprises. James Haldane and a group of co-workers brought an awakening message to a great part of Scotland, including the Highlands and Islands, and though he later became a Congregationalist and finally a Baptist, his influence upon the Kirk was of lasting significance. One effect of the revival and of the home and foreign missionary enterprises it engendered was that of escape from the narrow concerns of the denomination and a view of the problems of the church in something of an ecumenical perspective. Robert Haldane's work in Geneva and Montauban instituted the great awakening of Protestantism in Switzerland and southern France. All Scotland felt the force of the movement; it put forth a great effort to evangelize and educate the Gaelic-speaking population of western Scotland and the Hebrides, a task long neglected by the Kirk.[4] As part of a movement affecting nearly all Protestantism, the revival in Scotland served to arouse an awareness of the Protestant world which had been of too little concern for the Scots since the era of the Westminster Assembly. In the new atmosphere the divisive course of Scottish church history began to be reversed. But the patronage problem was actually to become more critical, and the most serious of all the secessions was still to follow, the Disruption of 1843.

The Disruption may be looked upon as a courageous protest on behalf of the advocates of a larger role for the church, against the declining Moderate party who feared to alienate the secular powers. The practice of patronage had become more burdensome and presented an impediment to the newly developing religious interests and activities that were largely an expression of the Evangelical Revival. By 1834 a majority in the General Assembly were Evangelicals. In that year the Assembly passed the Veto Act which declared the right of the parish by vote of its heads of families to reject a patron's appointee. It also authorized in the Chapel Act the recognition as members of presbyteries of ministers in the many new "chapels of ease" that had sprung up, giving these the status of parishes *quoad sacra*—parishes, that is, in church administration though not as units in secular government. Resistance to the operation of these reforming measures naturally led to litigation in the secular courts. The Scottish Court of Session in 1838 and the House of Lords in 1839 made decisions that invalidated the Veto Act, and the Chapel Act was also held contrary to statute law. In 1842 the Assembly adopted a statement briefly known as the Claim of Right, a strongly worded protest against "sentences of the Civil Court in contravention of the Church's liberties." In both houses of Parliament efforts were made by Scottish members to redress the grievances that had prompted the acts of Assembly, but these were summarily defeated. It would seem, indeed, that from a purely legal point of view, the Assembly's anti-intrusion acts were of very questionable authority, although they were consistent with the church's position and expectations in 1690, and had been widely acted upon in local instances since 1834.

During the Ten Years' Conflict (1834–1843) it gradually became evident that no deliverance from the religiously intolerable patronage system could be obtained within the establishment. The period was marked by increasing agitation by way of print and preaching, in which Thomas Chalmers (1780–1847) emerged as the most effective leader of the Evangelicals. Other able leaders of the cause included David Welsh, Edinburgh professor of church history, and Robert Smith Candlish of St. George's, Edinburgh. When the 1843 Assembly met in St. Andrew's Church, Edinburgh, the act of separation was inevitable, but no one knew how many ministers would join in it. Welsh, as retiring moderator, at the opening of the Assembly (May 18) read a protest against the rejection of the Claim of Right, laid the text of the protest on the table, bowed to the Lord High Commissioner, and stepped out of the church, followed by a procession that proved more numerous than had been expected. They marched a mile to Tanfield Hall, where they came to order as a free assembly, and elected Chalmers as moderator. Without hesitation they formally renounced all emoluments and privileges in the establishment. The ministers who signed this deed numbered 451, well over one third of the entire ministry, and they included a greatly disproportionate number of the abler and more earnest of the church's pastors and teachers. The Christian world marveled at their costly testimony to the church's right to be free.[5]

An outside observer of the fragmentation of the Scottish church in

1800 or in 1843 might have assumed the truth of the Englishman's taunt that "presbyterianism is prone to schism as the sparks fly upward." But those who are most familiar with the thoughts and teachings of seceders and Kirkmen see the picture in a different light. There always existed what R. Stuart Louden calls "a deep-seated tradition of the one Kirk in Scotland," together with a realization that this church belonged within the Holy Catholic Church. Those who with deep sorrow took the course of secession from "the church by law established" were not sectarians assured of some saving grace not shared by the conformists. They may have been blameworthy from impatience, and at certain points they may have lacked wisdom, but we may truly say that they left the church because they loved it and could not bear to see its rights invaded by secular interests, and that in general they kept alive the hope of reunion under conditions favorable to its spiritual health.

All the administratively severed branches of the Kirk continued to adhere to its authoritative confessions, including the Westminster Confession, which states the doctrine of the visible church thus:

> The visible church, which is also catholick or universal under the gospel (not confined to one nation as before under the law), consists of all those throughout the world that profess the true religion, together with their children. . . .

On the Communion of Saints it declares that

> saints are bound to maintain an holy fellowship and communion in the worship of God . . . Which communion, as God offereth opportunity, is to be extended to all who in every place call upon the name of the Lord Jesus.

Even where contacts with the wider church were not well maintained, there was no lapse of belief in the Holy Catholic Church, visible as well as invisible. Earnest men of all parties sincerely longed for the unity of the Church of Scotland as one geographically and politically defined province of the worldwide church of Christ. This is true even of an episcopalian such as Archbishop Leighton, who in Charles II's time sought an accommodation that might bring all Scottish Christians together. Seceders frequently testified that they broke communion not with the Church of Scotland but with a misguided party within it. Many of the Relief church regarded that organization not as a separate church but as a separate order within the church, waiting until the Church of Scotland should obtain "relief" from patronage.[6] It was characteristic that a week after the Disruption a learned Original Seceder addressed the Free Church Assembly in the words: "We recognize in your Assembly the representative of the ancient Church of Scotland." Beyond Scotland as well as within it, in a kind of ecumenical chorus spokesmen of many churches expressed their joy on learning of the Scottish renunciation of privilege for the sake of religious conviction. To many it brought a new assurance of the reality of Christianity.[7] Notwithstanding the fact that the established church had been rent in twain, there went abroad from the Disruption among Christians everywhere a sense of common Christian victory in which millions shared and were made more aware of a spiritual bond crossing denominational fences. From the first the Free Church, and notably its first moderator Chalmers, proclaimed the hope of unity in something like twentieth-century terms. Within two months of the event, in celebration of the bicentenary of the Westminster Assembly, Chalmers eloquently declared against that cooperation which shuns corporate union, and gave the slogan, "co-operation now and this with the view, as soon as may be, to incorporation afterwards." [8]

Some beginning of reunion had already appeared in Scotland. The New Licht branches of both the Burghers and the Antiburghers began to think less exclusively of their inherited views of church-state relationships, and drew together. Lay members of congregations in Mid-Calder and East Calder instituted a movement for union of these two main seceder groups. On September 8, 1820, in Bristo Street Church, Edinburgh (where they had separated in 1747), the act of union took place, forming the United Associate Synod of the Secession Church. Entering the union were 139 Burgher and 123 Antiburgher congregations. The assemblage was large and the feeling of gratification intense as all voices were raised in Ps. 147, with its victorious second stanza, "God buildeth up Jerusalem." A small number later split off from this church and ultimately entered what was called the Original Secession Synod, which joined the Free Church in 1852, leaving a minute remnant that still continues. It should be noted that a parallel union had taken place in Nova Scotia in 1817 and in Ireland in 1818.[9]

The secession churches had no great difficulty in maintaining themselves without government aid, and as time passed they began to assert the "voluntary" principle and to regard self-support from the beneficence of the members as highly preferable, or obligatory, for a sound church life. This was not, however, the ideal of the Auld Licht Burghers, and when their minds turned to union it was in the direction of the establishment. In 1839 they reunited with the Church of Scotland, established, the ministers individually applying to presbyteries of that church, having first voted to dissolve their own synod.[10] The leaders of the Disruption too were consciously and outspokenly opposed to the voluntary principle. Chalmers in his address as moderator of the Free Church Assembly of 1843 made this emphatically clear:

> The voluntaries mistake us if they think us voluntaries. Though we quit the establishment, we go out on the establishment principle. We hold by the duty of Government to give of their resources for the maintenance of a gospel ministry. We quit a vitiated establishment, but we would rejoice in returning to a pure one. To express it otherwise, we are advocates for a national recognition and national support of religion, and we are not voluntaries.[11]

Thus there could be in 1843 no immediate expectation of union of the Free Church with the United Seceders. The Free Church expectation and prayer was rather that it might rejoin a reformed and purified establishment; and this hope has been in some sense fulfilled.

Actually a wave of interest in church unity was now setting in, as appears in *Essays on Christian Union* (1845). The contributors were two Free Church ministers, two of the United Secession, one each of the Relief and Reformed Presbyterian churches, and two Congregationalists of whom one was in Birmingham, England. In the first essay Thomas Chalmers declared himself "sanguine of a larger union" than that of the Scottish churches, extending indeed throughout the Christian world. A number of the other essays are less rhetorical but more informing. Several of the contributors show familiarity with a wide range of irenical writings. The book has little by way of practical action to suggest, but it is a timely affirmation of the desirability and possibility of Christian union.

Other unions were soon to follow. The Relief church had at first felt no special attraction to the Erskine seceders with their narrower churchmanship and attachment to the Covenant. But the New Licht had triumphed in the union of 1820, and the United Secession had become, like Gillespie and his brethren, forward-looking and concerned for the people of Scotland. Talks leading to union were first proposed in 1834 by a Relief Synod minister, William Mackelvie,

whose congregation at Balgedie was in Erskine territory, and his approaches were welcomed by local ministers of the United Secession.
Serious negotiations were then begun, but were delayed by the disturbing events of the era and completed only in 1846, in time for
the synods to come together at their May meetings in 1847. Finding
that the Bristo Street Church was too small for the numbers attending, they held the service of union in Tanfield Hall, on invitation of
officials of the Free Church which had taken its separate origin there
four years earlier. The moderator elected was the oldest minister,
Dr. William Kidston, who had been in the union of 1820. With a
sense of continuity, he chose for this larger gathering the psalm
then used, Ps. 147. That evening the hall was packed by lay people,
and an overflow meeting was required to accommodate the eager folk
who came to hear celebrities of both uniting churches. The combined
synod took the name United Presbyterian Church. Of its 518 congregations, 60 of which were in England, only 118 were of the Relief branch. But the spirit of the newly formed church was more in
accord with that of the Relief than with that of the early seceders. In
the basis of union the adoption of the Westminster Confession is accompanied by a disavowal of persecution; members in full communion
alone may vote for office-bearers; voluntary support is enjoined upon
the members, and open communion is approved.[12]

The United Presbyterian Church throughout its span of existence
under that name, 1847–1900, was to be one of the most vigorous units
in Presbyterianism. In numerical strength it stood third, following
the Established and the Free Church in that order. Not only statisti-
cally but also in church ideals the Free Church held the middle position, since it favored state connection while deploring the denatured
existence of the Church of Scotland in that relationship. But in fact
no one of the three main bodies was happy in separation from the
others. It soon became evident that the Free and United Presbyterian
churches were drawing toward each other. The question that divided
them was voluntarism; but as the first-generation leaders passed away
and there appeared little prospect of a change in the establishment,
while the habit of self-support seemed justified by its success, the
Free Church moved nearer to the position of the United Presbyterians
on this issue. In 1863 negotiations for the union of the two churches
were begun, but minorities in both were opposed. In the Free Church,
especially in the Highlands, many still held precious the principle of
establishment and were disinclined to unite with voluntarists. Amid

much uncertainty and some embittered agitation, the negotiations were abandoned in 1873. But the Free Church was now responding to the leadership of Robert Rainy, principal of New College, Edinburgh, who by 1880 so far departed from Chalmers' position as to join forces with John Cairns of the United Presbyterians in a campaign for the disestablishment of the national church. It was due to the currents of English politics that this campaign failed. Both churches were also affected by the work of visiting evangelists (including D. L. Moody, 1874–1879), and both felt a relaxation of the older attachment to the language of the Westminster Confession. This fact is well illustrated for the Free Church by the words of its moderator of Assembly in 1866, Dr. William Wilson, who declared: "No confession of faith can ever be regarded by the Church as a final and permanent document. . . . We lie open always to the teaching of the Divine Spirit, nay we believe in the progressive advancement of the Church into a more perfect knowledge of the truth. . . . It is lawful for the Church to revise her confession . . . but to retain a confession which has ceased to be believed can never be lawful." [13] In 1879 the United Presbyterians and in 1872 the Free Church adopted declaratory acts which attest this increasing disinclination to regard the Confession as final. Both these acts represent a liberalized interpretation of the Westminster Standards, laying emphasis on God's universal love, allowing for a diversity of opinion, disavowing persecution, and asserting the church's right to determine doctrinal issues accordingly.[14]

In 1896 and 1897 the union project was resumed on the initiative of the Free Church. A joint advisory committee was appointed to deal with interchurch cooperation, and another on the terms of a possible corporate union. Skillfully the union committee narrowed down its problem and brought forward the proposal to unite by mutual acceptance without further delay, leaving details of organization and policy, including the form of subscription to the Confession, for later common settlement. Prior to the union, however, each Assembly adopted a short document containing five declarations, of which the first reads:

> The various matters of agreement between the Churches with a view to union are accepted and enacted without prejudice to the inherent liberty of the United Church, as a Church of Christ, to determine and regulate its own constitu-

tion and laws as duty may require, in dependence on the
grace of God and under the guidance of His Word.[15]

The union took place October 31, 1900, in the spacious but un-
ecclesiastical setting of Waverley Market, Edinburgh. The members
of the two assemblies entered in a joint procession which had been
formed at the Castle Terrace. Dr. Walter Ross Taylor of Kelvinside
Free Church of Glasgow who had been a leading figure in the negotiations, as senior moderator, presided until Principal Rainy, then aged
seventy-four, was unanimously elected moderator of the joint Assembly. The name adopted, United Free Church, is a reminder of
the two members of the union; the phrase "of Scotland" used by the
Free Church but not by the United Presbyterian was omitted. Indeed, in view of the wide connections of both churches through missions and emigration, it would have seemed a limiting phrase, and it
might have been taken amiss by the establishment, which it actually
outnumbered. The two churches came together in a strong and
flourishing state of existence. The United Free Church had in 1900
almost half a million members and almost eighteen hundred ministers. Again an irreconcilable minority of Free Churchmen rejected the
union. Asserting that the new organization in its freer attitude to
the Westminster Standards had deserted the Free Church, and that
they themselves were that church, and the legal possessors of all its
properties, they contended for this in the civil courts. The Scottish
courts decided for the United Free Church, but on appeal to the
House of Lords the minority was successful (1904). By a curious in-
version, the Lords upheld the representation that the Claim of Right,
which the House of Commons had cast out in 1842, was an indispensable element in the Free Church constitution. But to invest twenty-
seven ministers and sixteen thousand laymen with these vast and
widely extended properties in Scotland and abroad was clearly an
absurdity. A new act of Parliament was passed in 1905 setting up a
commission to make an equitable settlement of the property, and
ultimately most of what was claimed was legally vested in the United
Free Church. In retrospect the eminent United Free leader Alexander
White looked on the decision of the Lords as "a vitalizing judgment."
It called forth the United Free Church Assembly's act of 1906 which
asserts the church's right "to alter, change, add to or modify her constitution and laws, subordinate standards and formulas, to determine
and declare what these are and to unite with Christian churches despite all legal decisions to the contrary." [16]

As the inheritors of the secessions and the Disruption progressively coalesced into the United Free Church, the desire for a more comprehensive union of Scottish Presbyterianism came more and more to expression. It was voiced as much within the established church as among the others. The Disruption had left the Church of Scotland wounded, and depleted of its best ministers. Some of those remaining sympathized with the objectors to patronage, if not with their revolutionary action. The point was obvious to all Kirkmen that patronage was the major cause of the disaster. The Assembly under new leadership began at once to take measures toward recovery. Ministers were recruited, largely from the schoolmasters' ranks, for the vacant charges. Provision was made to hear objections to presentees from members of the parish; it brought such a volume of complaints that the abolition of patronage again became an issue. In 1869 the Assembly petitioned Parliament for this. The General Assembly of 1870 deplored the evils of division and pledged the church to seek reunion. Gladstone opposed the antipatronage move; but when Disraeli came to power in 1874, a bill was passed declaring that the right of choosing ministers was vested in the congregation under the oversight of the church courts. Patronage was abolished, with compensation to the patrons.

At this time new voices were gaining a hearing in the church courts. Notable among these was Norman MacLeod who with Gaelic fervor and a somewhat liberalized theology called the Church of Scotland to think of itself as the church of the future. His cousin, MacLeod Campbell, had been deposed for heresy (1831) but remained influential, and later Robert Flint, another liberal spirit, divinity professor in Edinburgh (1876–1903), had a large role among those who helped to revive and redirect the Kirk.[17] Despite the loss of membership at the Disruption the number of communicants increased between 1843 and 1908 by 15 percent.[18]

On the whole it was the established church that took the initiative in the negotiations with the United Free Church. A powerful sermon before the Pan-Presbyterian Alliance[19] by Robert Flint in 1877 gave notice of the new approach. The Laymen's League to resist disestablishment and disendowment (1890) advocated the reunion of the three main presbyterian units then in separate existence. In 1894 and 1895 several unofficial conferences were held, and in 1898 the churches adopted a common hymnbook. The Church of Scotland had no delegate at the union assembly of 1900, but in 1901 fraternal greetings were exchanged with the United Presbyterians. From about this time an active interest in union on the part not only of forward-looking ministers but of the people of both churches can be discerned. A Christian Unity Association, formed in 1904, helped to promote the spirit of unity. "Men were at last realizing that the clear-cut pros and cons to which they had been accustomed did not sum up all the truth." [20] The resistant elements were, on the one hand, the demand for disestablishment and, on the other, a diminishing hard core of Kirkmen who held that straying Presbyterians should simply "return to Mother." Some of these were now changing their minds. On the other hand the property decision of the House of Lords in 1904 awakened the disestablishmentarians to the surprising power of government to wound a church without state connection, and their propaganda faded out. Leaders in both churches now began to plot the way ahead. Norman MacLeod, heading a committee of the Church of Scotland and reporting to the General Assembly in May, 1908, proposed an approach to the United Presbyterian Church with a view to "a larger measure of Christian fellowship and cooperation," and that "the way may be prepared for that closer union for which many hearts long and pray." This was accompanied by an impressive statement of the cooperation already practiced. The United Free Church Assembly a week later responded cordially, and in 1909 large committees were appointed by both assemblies to seek union, first examining "the causes that keep the churches apart." These held their first joint meeting November 9, 1909. It is recognized that from this beginning of active negotiations it was John White of the Church of Scotland on whose shoulders the burden of bringing the negotiations to completion chiefly rested. Despite the general approval of union in principle, fears and suspicions lurked in many minds, and numerous objections in detail had to be overcome. Wisely it was decided to seek legislation in Parliament that would guarantee the church's freedom and autonomy and forestall a return of the church-state troubles of the past. The terms of the proposed act were still under discussion when the First World War caused a suspension of the negotiations. The war with its devastating losses left all parties, including the British Parliament, in a mood of concession. Articles of agreement were submitted and adopted by assemblies and presbyteries of both churches in 1918. In them the church to be formed is held to be a part of the Catholic or Universal Church holding a peculiar responsibility "to bring the ordinances of religion to the people of every parish of Scotland," and with power "to legislate and adjudicate finally" in all matters of belief and polity within it. The Westminster Standards are recognized as the church's subordinate standards subject to the past and future interpretations placed upon them "by acts of the General Assembly or by consuetude."

The Church of Scotland Act, approved by the churches, was passed by Parliament virtually without opposition or delay, July 25, 1921. It is the most notable landmark in the modern relations of any established church with the state government. One of its Articles Declaratory reads:

> The Church has the inherent right, free from interference by civil authority, but under the safeguards of deliberate action and legislation provided by the Church itself, to frame or adopt its subordinate standards, to declare the sense in which it understands its Confession of Faith, to modify the forms of expression therein, to formulate other doctrinal statements, and to define the relation thereto of its office-bearers and members, but always in agreement with the Word of God and the fundamental doctrines of the Christian Faith contained in the said Confession, of which agreement the Church shall be sole judge, and with due regard for liberty of opinion in points which do not enter into the substance of the Faith.[21]

Thus on the path to union a momentous principle of church freedom and autonomy was affirmed by church and state alike.

But there remained to be settled a formidable array of issues concerned with property and endowments, a task that involved long and difficult negotiation and called for a second act of Parliament. It was then possible to frame the final plan of union. Opposition on the part of small minorities in both churches was encountered all the way; in the United Free Church it was highly organized and ably led by Rev. James Barr, who gained a seat in Parliament to fight from that position. Even after Parliament passed the needed legislation, in May, 1925, some resistance continued, and there were differences of opinion within the negotiating committees. Even the name of the united church was not obvious to all; but this was settled in 1927 when John White pointed out that the United Free Church had always regarded itself as the true Church of Scotland and hence that name should be acceptable to all. White by firm insistence induced the king's com-

missioner to the Kirk Assembly in 1927, in accordance with the spirit
of the new legislation, to change the formal language previously used
in the closing act of the Assembly to make clear the autonomy of
the Assembly in calling its next meeting. White toured the nation ad-
dressing many audiences and arousing warm support for the union.
The documents of union were referred to the Kirk sessions and
presbyteries and approved by an overwhelming vote (1928). In May,
1929, the decisive action was taken in both assemblies, and on October 2 of that year the long-anticipated act of union took place in
Edinburgh.

The assemblies met previously to finish their separate work, and
on the appointed day formed a combined procession on Bank Street
to move into St. Giles. The weather added something to the drama of
the occasion. The *New York Times* reporter saw a rainbow overarch-
ing the procession; others record a noisy hailstorm during the meeting. Within the cathedral, robed Anglican archbishops and other
visiting dignitaries were prominently seated. The two moderators
signed the uniting act, Alexander Martin for the United Free Church
using the pen with which the separation document had been signed
in 1843. John White was unanimously and with acclaim elected moderator of the united Assembly. In an eloquent address he called to
mind honored personalities in Scottish church history, and significantly
affirmed: "In the forefront of our testimony we claim our part in the
Holy Catholic or Universal Church." [22]

The church thus formed embraces in harmonious union more than
nine tenths of the once-fragmented Presbyterianism of Scotland. It is
at peace with the state, the latter having acknowledged (not granted
or bestowed) its full freedom and the autonomy of its courts. It has
been able to act with new strength and to respond with vigor to the
mounting problems of the twentieth century. It outclasses in strength
and activity all other Scottish churches, and, while not "established"
in the old sense, it takes responsibility for every parish in Scotland.

The reconstituted Church of Scotland draws from its deep past a
concern for the whole people of Scotland. Among the Articles Declaratory of 1921 is the statement, "The Church and the State owe mutual
duties to each other, and acting within their respective spheres may
signally promote each other's welfare." In this spirit the church stresses
the work of the territorially defined parish, and follows a revised program of religious teaching amid the secularizing trend of public education in this century. The well-known development of the Iona Com-

munity since 1938 bears testimony to a strong religious current within the church which, like the Haldane revival, extends far beyond Scotland. Nothing is more characteristic of the ethos of the Church of Scotland than its ecumenical testimony and ecclesiastical fraternalism. This is well illustrated by the Ecumenical Statement put forth by the Assembly, May 25, 1954, in which we read:

> The Church of Scotland, believing in one Holy Catholic and Apostolic Church, and acknowledging one Baptism for the remission of sins, affirms its intention of seeking closer relations with every Church with which it stands in fundamental doctrinal agreement, but from which it is separated in matters of government and the ordering of the ministry.
>
> In its approach to other Churches . . . the Church of Scotland would desire to look beyond the divisions of history to the ultimate fulness and unity of the Church's life in Christ, and to affirm its readiness to consider how the contributions of all such Churches may be embraced within that unity and fulness.[23]

The reintegrated church has undertaken heavy tasks in the changing life of the nation, and its participation in ecumenical matters has been notable. It brings to these tasks a rich heritage together with a new sense of commission as the Church of Scotland, national and free. The Church of Scotland Assembly in 1932 entered into committee discussions with the Church of England, and the Episcopal Church of Scotland joined these talks in 1954. The reports of the conferences indicate large areas of agreement, but no significant progress has been made toward union with the Anglican Church. More promising is the series of conversations with the Congregational Union of Scotland begun in 1959. In 1966 these expanded into multilateral conversations involving six Scottish denominations. These are, with the two just mentioned, The Church of Christ (Disciples), The Episcopal Church, The Methodist Church, and the segment of the United Free Church that declined to enter the union of 1929. These churches have been associated with the "Tell Scotland" movement, instituted by the Church of Scotland, which aims to invigorate Christian faith and life and secure the betterment of social conditions throughout the nation.

The Church of Scotland has also lent encouragement to the union negotiations that have resulted in the formation of a new united church in England and Wales. This union brings together the Congregational

Church of England and Wales and the Presbyterian Church of England to form the United Reformed Church of England and Wales. Although the new church has only about 250,000 members, the union is an event of significance. Discussions toward this result began as early as 1933. A period of planned and active cooperation followed, while negotiations for unification were being instituted. Since 1963, when the two denominations created a joint committee to frame the terms of union, the effort has gone forward, not without difficulties but with steady progress. The act of unification took place at Westminster on October 5, 1972, and was attended by impressive ceremonies. The goodwill of larger churches was dramatically demonstrated by their hospitality on the occasion. The United Reformed Church was formed under a Methodist roof, that of the Central Hall, Westminster, and the organizational meeting was followed in the evening by a great service of thanksgiving which filled Westminster Abbey and in which the Archbishop of Canterbury and the Dean of Westminster warmly participated. The first moderator of the united church, John Huxtable, a former Congregationalist, indicated that the negotiations had been carried on in hope that reached beyond the present act of union to "a larger coming together of Christian communions." [24]

VIII

TRANSPLANTATION TO AMERICA
AND CONSOLIDATION
[Presbyterian, Congregationalist, Reformed]

THE BRITISH COLONIES in North America received the greatest concentration of Europeans in their migration overseas from the seventeenth century. In the process the churches of many countries were thrown together in unfamiliar juxtapositions and new proportions and untried relations with government. Virtually the whole gamut of European varieties of Christianity was transplanted and the American experience even added a few more. Opportunity arose, at the same time, for close association and even merger of churches which in the homeland had no comparable relations.

The largest churches in the American colonies were Reformed, chief among them, of course, the Congregationalists and Presbyterians of British origin. But beside these there were in the colonies appreciable communities of all the major Continental Reformed churches except the Hungarians: Huguenots, Swiss, German, Dutch. These were all minorities, of course, cultural and linguistic enclaves scattered about among the more numerous British settlements. Their coexistence posed the question as to whether there might be a new actualization of the international community of the Reformed in this new colonial society.

The French Reformed never formed an enduring separate community in the American colonies. There were appreciable numbers of Walloons throughout the seventeenth century in Nieuwe Nederland, and as late as 1695 there were nearly three times as many French Reformed as Anglicans in New York. Thousands had crossed the Atlantic in the persecutions of Louis XIV to join the Walloons. But most of the French churches disappeared individually into Anglican,

127

128 ECUMENICAL TESTIMONY

Dutch, or Presbyterian connections, and only scattered isolated relics remained.

The Dutch were the Reformed pioneers in the American colonies, anticipating even the Puritans of Massachusetts Bay. From 1628 a Reformed congregation was worshiping in the Dutch and French languages on Manhattan Island under the civil authority of the Dutch West India Company. When Nieuwe Nederland surrendered to English frigates in 1664 it counted thirteen Dutch Reformed congregations with seven active ministers and about ten thousand members. An Anglican congregation was now assembled, but Anglicans remained a small, although privileged, minority in New York. The Dutch Reformed congregations, by far the largest church in the early eighteenth century in New York, were administered at a distance and ineffectively by the Classis of Amsterdam. There were three times as many congregations as pastors, and some ecclesiastical organization in the colonies competent to ordain ministers was badly needed. In the 1730's the Amsterdam Classis encouraged the New York ministers to plan an association or coetus, but they denied it power to examine ministerial candidates or to touch doctrinal matters.

But the Amsterdam Classis had other American responsibilities also. A second major Continental Reformed immigration came to the colonies from the Palatinate, Württemberg, and German Switzerland. The atrocious scorched-earth campaigns of Louis XIV in the Rhine provinces had driven thousands of refugees into exile in various countries and the War of the Spanish Succession burned over the ruins again. Thirty thousand "Palatines" made their way to England in 1709, begging to be sent to America. By 1730 it was estimated that over half the Germans in Pennsylvania were Reformed. A few ministers were sent out from Zurich and Berne and especially Heidelberg. But in 1728 the Heidelberg Oberkonsistorium, unable to match resources to the need, asked the Synods of North and South Holland to take over the responsibility. The Synods appointed the Classis of Amsterdam to be their agent in ministering to the refugees from the sister German churches. That Classis thus found itself considering the problems at once of the Dutch and German Reformed churches in the American colonies.

At this juncture the Dutch Synods made for the first time a proposal that was to be repeated several times in American history. They suggested that the Dutch and German Reformed churches be joined to the English-speaking Presbyterian Synod, which was already functioning, in one Reformed Church.[1] The overture, however, was premature. It would not be possible to realize any normal church life across the barriers of three different languages. The Dutch were becoming bilingual, but the Germans would not for another century develop sufficient willingness to use English to make such a proposal plausible. Perhaps the kairos came in the 1840's. If the Dutch and German Reformed in the United States had then succeeded in merger, they might have been strong enough together to merge with Presbyterianism on relatively equal terms. An American Reformed church so constituted, with continuing ties to churches in the Netherlands, Germany, and Switzerland, as well as Scotland and Ireland, and with the manifold heritage of liturgy, doctrine, polity that would involve, would have been a richer, more flexible and more catholic church. But the kairos was missed and the Continental Reformed churches in America were relegated to serving dwindling ethnic enclaves, while the Presbyterianism of British provenance was repeatedly threatened by a Scottish provincialism. The sense of an international Reformed community had been strong enough to make itself felt, but not to prevail over divergent nationalities.

Of the Reformed of British origins, the Congregationalists and Presbyterians were most representative. Great attention has been paid by historians to the Puritans of Massachusetts Bay and the various settlements in Connecticut, since the cultural heritage of the New England church-states was to prove the most influential of all the colonies in later history. Apart from Plymouth, which was more separatist and atypical, the Bay settlements were organized by a distinctive strain of churchmen, not at all conspicuous on the English scene, but clearly distinguishable from the Presbyterianism dominant among English Puritans on the eve of the Civil War. These "non-separating Congregationalists" were able to secure commercial charters under which they could organize a large measure of civil as well as ecclesiastical control for their distinctive variety of Puritan churchmanship. Its genius was to combine a Reformed sense of the visible catholic church, and thus recognition of the congregations of the Church of England, with many of the features of separatist independency, especially the requirement of evidences of regeneration from all candidates for church membership.[2] Their chief theologian was William Ames, who taught for years on the Dutch Reformed faculty at Franeker. The internal tensions of this Congregationalist conception of the church left a very unstable legacy. One might say that the Congregationalists sought to be Presbyterian and Separatist at the same time and that history ever since has pushed them to choose one course or the other. In England they were also to be among the pioneers of religious liberty, but in New England the church-state regime was as rigorous as any Old World Presbyterian establishment.

Congregationalists shared with Presbyterian Anglicans in drafting the doctrine and constitutional documents of the Westminster Assembly, fighting chiefly for greater flexibility. The Cambridge Platform and the Savoy Confession were to define more precisely the amendments they desired in the Westminster Standards. The divergence of the two, particularly on church-state relations and religious liberty, were to seem ever less important after 1662, when the restoration of the episcopal state church forced Presbyterians into a posture substantially equivalent to that of the English Independents. In 1690–91, as we have seen (see above, p. 105), the London area ministers of the two groups were able to lay down Heads of Agreement as a basis for cooperation.

The Heads of Agreement were to have a longer and more significant history in New England than in Old England. Increase Mather of Boston had contributed to their formulation on a visit to the mother country in 1690, and like other leading New Englanders, wished to see New England church life developed in a more synodical form. Proposals to this effect were rejected in Massachusetts in 1705, although ministerial associations were established. But in Connecticut the Saybrook Platform three years later set up a loose Presbyterianism, incorporating the text of the Heads of Agreement. The Platform was imposed by legislative decree for the colony, assigning authority over ordinations and dismissals to standing "consociations" in each county. Only regularly installed clergy were supported by the church tax, and congregations who did not yield to the authority of the consociation were liable to the sentence of "non-communion." As Baptist and Anglican dissenters penetrated the colony, they were permitted tax relief, but Presbyterians and Congregationalists were subject to church taxes.[3] The word "Presbyterian" was widely used of themselves by the eighteenth-century Connecticut churchmen.

There had been considerable movement of population from Connecticut southward, to Long Island, lower New York, and New Jersey, and Puritan churches were planted in those areas also. They were established one by one, and it did not much matter at first what their preferences were as to church structure above the congregational level when they were still isolated. When they began to associate, the New

England solution was clearly not available in the Middle Colonies. An itinerant Scottish merchant-preacher named Francis Makemie was apparently the catalyst who assembled seven ministers in Philadelphia to form a presbytery in the interval between the rejection of the Massachusetts Proposals and the adoption of the Saybrook Platform. The makeup of that presbytery of 1706 illustrated the mixed provenance of American Presbyterianism. Most of the people in the constituent congregations (Philadelphia, New Castle, Lewes, Patuxent) were English or New England Puritans, along with three of the ministers. The other four ministers and a minority of the laymen were Scots or Irish. Ten years later, when a synod was erected, of 25 ministers, there were 8 Scots, 7 Irish, 7 New Englanders, 3 Welsh. Thus was launched what was to become the main body of American Presbyterianism, itself something of an achievement in church union from the very beginning. Something like a comity agreement also became apparent in the relations of New England Congregationalism and Middle Colony Presbyterianism. Except for a few purely Scottish groups, Presbyterians settling in New England affiliated with the state churches. Congregationalists moving south or west out of New England, on the other hand, came to attach themselves to presbyteries.

The rapid increase of Scottish and Irish ministers in the Presbyterian Synod is an indication of a massive immigration getting under way from Scotland and Ulster. It was to continue for much of the eighteenth century and indeed into the nineteenth, and to make the Scots and Irish the largest strain in the main body of colonial Presbyterianism, in addition to founding some smaller purely Scottish or Irish Presbyterian bodies. The polarity between English (and New England) Puritanism and Ulstermen was to dominate both the internal history of American Presbyterianism and its relations with Congregationalism until the time of the Civil War.

Virtually all colonial churches, but especially the Congregationalists and the Presbyterians, were profoundly affected by the Great Awakening of the middle generation of the eighteenth century. The ecumenical consequences were momentous. The Awakening was the first religious movement that transcended the diverse peculiarities of place and church. As itinerants circulated and news was relayed, names such as George Whitefield, Gilbert Tennent, Jonathan Edwards, James Davenport became known from Maine to Georgia, and in all denominations. In this way a colony-wide consciousness was kindled in the religious sphere before it appeared politically.

But while the Awakening united many denominations in a common experience and greatly added to the strength of most, it also split the major church bodies along new lines. Like the Puritan movement of a century earlier it opened new avenues for the religious layman. Any converted man might preach the gospel, and many did. Attempts to regulate and control the excitement by church authorities often led only to anticlerical rebellion. In New England the "hireling clergy" and the whole establishment structure came under attack. New Lights sometimes became Separates and Separates, Baptists, in Connecticut. The Presbyterian Old Side expelled the revivalistic New Brunswick group in a schism that lasted from 1741 to 1758. The German Reformed lost the followers of the revivalist Philip William Otterbein in Maryland, the United Brethren. The Dutch split into Coetus and Conferentie. Anglicanism lost its Methodists. Everywhere the energies of the revival seemed to put great strains on the existing dikes and channels.

Some of the schisms were healed, but many were not, as the fires burned low at the end of the generation, and political issues preempted the stage. The Presbyterian reunion was a testimony chiefly to the vitality of the Awakening, since the New Side had grown notably, while the Old Side remained static. The reunion was also a reaffirmation of the flexible doctrinal formula of the Adopting Act of 1729 against the party, chiefly Ulstermen, seeking to impose a rigid subscription. And in a general way the Awakening tended to assimilate Presbyterianism and Congregationalism more closely. In New England the revival was presented as a return to the Congregationalist ecclesiology of a century before, in which church membership was confined to "visible saints," not in the sense of moral achievement as much as a certifiable experience of justifying grace. In the interval the New England churches had subsided into the quasi-Presbyterian practice of the "halfway covenant" and Stoddardeanism. With the Awakening the balance swung back the other way. Not only were Congregational churches again filled with members ready to give an account of their gracious experiences, but so many Presbyterian churches adopted a virtually Congregationalist standard for full membership that the character of American Presbyterianism was significantly changed.

The withdrawal of the Congregationalist Separates usually came over the refusal of the state church to enforce the exclusion of the unconverted with sufficient rigor. This stress on "regenerate" membership, however, made the Separates, in turn, peculiarly vulnerable to the argument for "believer's baptism." Baptist parties arose in many Congregationalist churches and Baptist itinerants systematically fished in Congregationalist pools. The majority of the hundred Separate churches in Connecticut went Baptist, as did great numbers of New Lights in the regular Congregationalist churches.[4] The New England Baptist denomination was transformed in character and greatly enlarged by the Awakening. From a small, predominantly "Arminian," nonevangelistic body, it exploded into a strongly evangelistic Calvinist denomination, next only to the Congregationalists and Presbyterians in size. From 1740 to 1776, in one generation, Baptist congregations grew from 60 to 472. Thus the Baptists profited more from the Awakening than did any other denomination, representing a revivalistic modification of the Reformed tradition, originally Congregationalist in New England, and, to a lesser degree, Presbyterian in the Middle Colonies. At the least, one might say that, under certain pressures, the Reformed tradition was much more liable to development in this direction than either Anglicanism or Lutheranism. Except as regards the radicalization of church and sacraments, the new Baptist denomination was at one with Awakening Congregationalists and Presbyterians in doctrine and worship.

Like the Awakening of the middle generation of the eighteenth century, the political controversies of the last generation brought Congregationalists and Presbyterians closer together. In considerable measure the Revolution was a provincial sequel to the seventeenth-century Civil War, but with the opposite outcome, since the colonies were dominated by those of Puritan sympathies. The conflict aligned the Anglicans and Methodists who supported the duty of passive obedience to the crown against Congregationalists, Presbyterians, and Baptists (with many Anglicans), who maintained the responsibility to hold government under law, even at the price of revolution. Some pacifist groups (Mennonites, Quakers, Moravians) stood aside.

About 1750 the proposal of resident Anglican bishops in the colonies had aroused organized opposition from Congregationalists and Presbyterians. The issue had been foreshadowed in several colonies, such as Massachusetts, New York, and Virginia, where the English authorities had used their political power to aid the Church of England to something like the predominance it enjoyed in England. In much of the colonial situation, however, it had only a little more claim to represent the Christian population than it did in Ireland. Now if bishops were introduced in the colonies, would this mean episcopal judicial privileges and legal and financial impositions on dissenters? For the fifteen years before the battle of Lexington, the controversy over an American episcopate played a significant role in focusing and heightening colonial grievances against the British authorities.[5]

In 1766 the reunited Presbyterian Synod invited the "Presbygational" General Association of Connecticut to a General Convention to concert means of defense against the anticipated Anglican aggression. The Convention, which met at Elizabethtown, declared that no organic unity was intended, but cooperation in spreading the gospel as well as in defending religious liberty. Other Reformed bodies—Presbyterian, Congregationalist, and Dutch Reformed—were also invited, and in England the "Dissenting Deputies" of the old Puritan denominations readily lent valuable support.[6] The meetings were held with regularity for a decade and could not but increase the personal acquaintance and trust of Presbyterian and Congregationalist leaders. There is little evidence at this time of common effort in spreading the gospel; they were almost wholly preoccupied with the defense of religious liberty. But after the revolutionary period the common evangelistic concern would come to the fore.

The success of the American Revolution entailed many new questions of church organization. Churches previously subordinate to European ecclesiastical authorities—at least Protestant churches—now reorganized independently. The larger churches, except for the established Congregationalists, generally altered their perspective and structure to accept a mission to the new nation as a whole. Relations to government, both national and that of the several states, were now reorganized in many ways. These issues were intertwined with the possibility of church mergers.

The church population was predominantly Reformed, with the largest single bodies being the Congregationalists of New England and the Presbyterians of the Middle States and the South. If they were combined, together with the Dutch and German Reformed, there might have been a case for calling such a body the national church. In fact, some, such as Benjamin Franklin, feared that they entertained such an ambition.[7] Perhaps John Livingstone, the leader of the Dutch Reformed, did. But the Presbyterian Synod disclaimed any ambitions to special status with the government. And if the Presbyterians remained disestablished, how could they be merged with state-church Congregationalists?

One or two small mergers did occur, however, on a scale that would occasion no worries over the maintenance of religious liberty for others. There were in the colonies a number of Scottish splinter groups, strictly ethnic in character, unlike the main body of American Presbyterians, and oriented to irrelevant Scottish controversies. The Erskine Secession movement, the Associate Presbytery, was replicated in America, in its Burgher and Antiburgher, Old Light and New Light varieties. A few intransigent Covenanting families were organized in lay "societies," and acquired one or two ministers from Scotland in the eighteenth century. There was a preposterous scene in Octorara, Pennsylvania, in 1744, when Alexander Craighead and his supporters renewed the Solemn League and Covenant with uplifted swords. In 1782 three of these Covenanter congregations were combined with the Associate Presbyteries to form the Associate Reformed Synod, due chiefly to the efforts of John Mason, perhaps the leading Reformed ecumenist of the generation in America. All but two of the ministers entered the union, but unfortunately, as so often happened with attempts to unite the Scottish splinter groups, further immigration from the mother country revived separate covenanting and Antiburgher Associates. The merger of 1782 had expanded two groups to three!

There were negotiations also between the Associate Presbyteries and the main Presbyterian body just before the Revolution. John Witherspoon, president of the College of New Jersey, was active in this enterprise, as also in a possible Presbyterian–Dutch Reformed merger. But in the case of the Scots, at least, the mother synod in Scotland apparently prevented the merger.

After the Revolution, a series of conferences among the three synods of the Dutch, the Associate Reformed, and the Presbyterians were held from 1785 around New York City. These efforts were headed by the three New York pastors John Mason, John Livingstone, and John Rodgers. A regular biennial convention was agreed on and the first held in 1786. The Dutch, Presbyterians, and German Reformed, however, all organized separately on a national basis. A revival of the proposal for merger of the (Dutch) Reformed Church in America and the German Reformed Church foundered on the language question.

One concrete result, however, of the close Reformed relations occurred a generation later, in 1822. The Associate Reformed Church seemed to be in a process of dissolution, as its western and southern synods had separated from the New York and Pennsylvania synods.

The Presbyterian General Assembly proposed organic merger to the latter. The Associate Reformed Presbyterian General Synod and presbyteries split on the question, but most of the Pennsylvania synod merged anyway, while the New York Associate Reformed Presbyterian Synod decided to continue and sued to recover its seminary library from Princeton. John Mason, however, joined the larger body.

After half a generation more, the Associate Reformed Church again undertook discussions with the Associate Synod, which, as we have seen, had been resurrected as a separate denomination again after the union of 1782. A plan of union was tried in 1844–1846 and then again in 1857. This time it was to be consummated, with no significant residues, as the United Presbyterian Church, a body of some 660 congregations and about 55,000 communicants. Representing essentially the legacy of the Erskine Secession from Scotland, with a slight ingredient of Covenanters, this United Church was to be distinguished for its exclusive devotion to metrical psalmnody and closed communion. It was concentrated in Pennsylvania, Ohio, and Illinois.[8]

Just before the turn of the century, meanwhile, had begun what later would be referred to as the Second Great Awakening. From then until the Civil War the rhythm of alternating periods of "revival" and doldrums was central to American Protestant history. A constantly moving and expanding population, with religious institutions chronically inadequate for the need, developed the revival as a characteristic American phenomenon. The consequences for relationships among the churches were much as they had been in the eighteenth century: new schisms on the one hand, and increased assimilation to each other of the denominations most involved.

New England Congregationalism split in the first generation of the nineteenth century, as Connecticut and western Massachusetts churches were caught up in the revival, and the area dominated by Boston reacted negatively and lost many churches to Unitarianism. The divergent tendencies had been evident already in the days of Jonathan Edwards and the first Awakening, and had deepened in the period of the Revolution and constitutional organization. The contrast with English developments is striking, for there it was the Presbyterians who had largely dissolved into Unitarianism in the eighteenth century, while Congregationalism had been much more receptive to the new evangelical tide. The contrast was to prove an enduring one into the twentieth century, when English Congregationalists would often find themselves more at home theologically with American Presbyterians than with American Congregationalists. And in the United States it was the Congregationalism of the Connecticut Valley which was most disposed to cooperate with Presbyterians in the mission across the Hudson River.

The Presbyterians and the Congregationalists struggled manfully to produce ministers to match the hundreds of requests that poured in at the turn of the century, but refused to relax their educational expectations of a college course and a year of theological reading. In practice, to be sure, presbyteries not infrequently waived some of the requirement, but it remained the standard. One undesigned consequence was that these churches lost their numerical predominance to such bodies as Baptists and Methodists, whose educational standards were much less rigorous. The Baptists grew in the Second Awakening as in the first, increasing nearly four times in the generation after the War of 1812. The Congregationalists and the Presbyterians, meanwhile, took on increasingly an upper-class or upper-middle-class character, providing the theological leadership for Protestantism generally and educational leadership in the whole community. A certain specialization of function appeared among the denominations, in which, without perhaps being fully conscious of it, they depended on each other to fill out their several inadequacies. Members came increasingly to move back and forth in response to changing religious needs.

In the Kentucky Revival there was a Presbyterian disruption akin to the Old Side expulsion of the revivalist party in 1741. The synod was largely Scotch-Irish and Old Side, while the Cumberland presbytery was pro-revival and New Side. The issues related to control of ordination and the educational qualifications of ministers and also a protest against the "fatalism" of the Westminster Standards. The result, by 1813, was a distinct Cumberland Presbyterian Church, a schism that was only partially healed a century later.

The movement that produced the Disciples of Christ in the same general frontier area also throws some light on the character of the Reformed tradition. The Disciples were only the largest body of a widespread type. Beside them there were Christians, Churches of God, Churches of Christ, and others who held similar views. The orientation was widely held in Baptist and Presbyterian circles, and the chief leaders of the Disciples, Alexander and Thomas Campbell and Barton Stone, were originally Presbyterians. One might describe it as anticlerical Biblicism, impatient with sectarian divisions, and hoping to "restore unity, peace and purity to the whole Church of God." It was supposed that if one separated all the diverse "human opinions" of the rival Christian traditions from the sole indispensable authority, the New Testament, unity would be achieved on that basis and one might "sink into union with the Body of Christ at large." The principle was "Where the Bible speaks, we speak; where the Bible is silent we are silent." The movement grew rapidly in frontier communities, using a revivalistic technique, but with a strong note of common-sense rationalism and legalism. Among the prescriptions usually found in the New Testament were the independence of each local congregation from higher church authority and baptism by immersion. The leaders expected to win immediate acquiescence in their ecumenical tactic, once it was understood, and it was frustrating to find that the restoration of "New Testament Christianity" did not lead in fact to church unity but only to another denomination. By the time of the Civil War there were about 200,000 Disciples and the movement rivaled the Baptists and the Methodists in its own territory as a popular church.

The challenge of the frontier also produced a new kind of cooperation of Congregationalists and Presbyterians. Almost inadvertently they produced a notable, if regional, church merger. This fusion, which is usually referred to comprehensively and inaccurately as the "Plan of Union," can only be fully understood against the background of the so-called "voluntary societies," and in particular the closely interrelated American Home Missionary Society and American Education Society. Although the pattern of the societies in general came from Great Britain, the mother country did not develop anything comparable to the AHMS and the AES. These societies were church extension organizations. They subsidized the education of ministerial candidates and subsidized ministers in the planting and strengthening of new churches. Neither the Congregationalists nor the Presbyterians had agencies equipped to meet these needs at the beginning, and were grateful for the work of the societies. The result was that the extension of the churches was put into the hands of bodies officially independent of the ecclesiastical structures. The societies were agencies by which (originally) state church Congregationalists and free church Presbyterians could work together unofficially, thus circumventing the barriers of their disparate relations to the state.

A hybrid pattern of church life was agreed upon in the new territories, not exactly like the Congregationalism of either Connecticut or Massachusetts, nor like the old Presbyterianism of colonial New York, New Jersey, or Pennsylvania, but a new, third form of church.

This modified Presbyterianism was startlingly successful and the result was precisely what one would have had with a formal church merger. A crisis then emerged out of this success. Were the founding denominations willing to accommodate themselves to this intermediate form in a complete merger? If not, what would be the status of the hybrid church?

The original cue had been given by the newly constituted General Assembly of the Presbyterian Church in 1790. That Assembly resolved —unanimously—that it was desirous "to strengthen every bond of union between brethren so nearly agreed in doctrine and forms of worship as the members of the Congregational and Presbyterian churches evidently are." The Assembly invited the renewal of the annual joint convention of the decade before the Revolution, although the threat of an Anglican episcopate was a dead letter and the common concern now was the planting of churches in the new territories into which settlers were moving in large numbers. Fraternal delegates were exchanged between the Assembly and the Congregational State Associations, from 1794 with full voting rights. Here were two branches of the Reformed tradition, sharing the doctrinal standards and directory of worship of the Westminster Assembly and the formative influence of the Great Awakening. They had always accorded each other full "pulpit and altar fellowship," to use a Lutheran term, and there was extensive movement back and forth of both ministers and church members. Their differences in polity were no greater than those found among various Reformed churches on the Continent. In 1801 they agreed on a Plan of Union for the home mission field, primarily New York west of the mountains, and the old Northwest Territory. That plan provided in effect for the dual standing of ministers, so that Congregational ministers might serve Presbyterian churches, or vice versa, and a maximum use might be made of the desperately limited resources on the frontier.

The opening of the frontier proceeded with great rapidity, producing the largest migration of population yet seen on the continent, chiefly from Connecticut and western Massachusetts. In the 1820's western New York was the most rapidly growing region in the whole United States. The people in this region responded enthusiastically to the cooperative arrangement of Congregationalism and Presbyterianism, which established itself as the strongest church in the area culturally and socially. There was little concern as between the two traditions.

Congregationalism, however, was a state church in New England

and had no unitive organization outside these establishments. What kind of structure could hold together new congregations on a frontier where there was no state provision for religion? Some kind of synodical organization was evidently called for to perform functions previously carried on by the state. Presbyterianism had just such a structure. A new pattern emerged in 1808 when the Synod of Albany, the comprehensive Presbyterian body for the upstate area, received the Congregationalist Middle Association as a constituent presbytery (or rather as two presbyteries, Onondaga and Cayuga). By this Accommodation Plan and others that followed it, local Congregational churches could, and often did, retain internal government by male communicants rather than a session of elders, and were represented in Presbytery and Synod and General Assembly by elected "committeemen" accorded the status of elders. The arrangement was welcomed by westward-moving New Englanders, and within thirty years from 1808 over 150 Congregational churches were thus incorporated into the Presbyterian structure. By 1822 there were no Congregational organizations left in New York State above the local church. A loose form of Presbyterianism had become the most influential church in New York State.[9]

The agency that supervised the expansion of this hybrid church was the American Home Missionary Society, which drew ministers and funds from both denominations on a voluntary basis and was controlled by neither. Created in 1826 out of the United Domestic Missionary Society of New York, it continued to devote the bulk of its resources to this area. Of the 169 missioners, 120 on the AHMS budget in 1826–27 were assigned to New York, and the staff rapidly expanded. Many or most of its men were trained in New England colleges or seminaries and embodied the new mixed pattern of church. In the first decade of AHMS activity, New York Presbyterianism, including these substantial New England elements, comprehended a third of the whole Presbyterian Church. Three western New York synods—Utica, Geneva, and Genesee—together in 1830 comprised a larger body than the whole Presbyterian Church which had authorized the Plan of Union thirty years before.

But whereas the first generation of the Plan of Union exhibited generally an ecumenical mood and enthusiasm, the tide changed in the 1830's. While New England had been moving westward, substantial immigration had continued from Ireland and Scotland, especially into Pennsylvania. A strong Scotch-Irish wing had been making itself felt increasingly in a very conservative tendency, akin to the Old Side movement of the colonial period. The Irish preferred strict subscription to the flexibility of the colonial Adopting Act; they suspected the Edwardean or Hopkinsian tradition in theology, which had once been established even at Princeton; they desired a centralized ecclesiastical authority over presbyteries like that of the Church of Scotland. For all these reasons they deplored the whole Plan of Union. They intended to remodel American Presbyterianism in quite another direction.

The divergent tendencies polarized into parties, Old School and New School, first in the cities of New York and Philadelphia and then from 1830 in the annual General Assemblies. In 1831 the New School held a majority in the General Assembly for the first time and the Old School began to look around for desperate remedies. Opportunity came six years later when an Old School majority at the Assembly made a compact with the slaveholding South and high-handedly "exscinded" 600 New School churches and 500 ministers, about four ninths of the whole Presbyterian Church.[10] They also ordered the AHMS and the AES to cease operation within Presbyterian bounds. The New School, however, protested the unconstitutionality of the action, and when it was not restored, it consolidated as a separate denomination. It was essentially the modified Presbyterianism of New York State and part of the old Northwest Territory. In that region it had proved the permanent value of the ecumenical venture, but on the national level the Plan of Union had provoked schism.

Tensions also mounted for the New School church on the other side. Congregationalists had increasingly resented the vilification and abuse poured out by Old School writers against everything from New England, and grew ever less inclined to cooperate with any kind of Presbyterian. In the 1840's and 1850's they organized as a separate denomination in Plan of Union territory and appealed to New School churches with New England backgrounds to leave the New School church and become Congregationalists. A significant number did so and the New School church registered little net growth in this period. Congregationalism, on its part, at last organized as a denomination, independent of the state, outside New England, first by state associations in the Midwest and New York, and then finally at a national convention in Albany in 1852. Here the Plan of Union was finally repudiated, leaving a legacy of bitterness to be felt for decades between the two denominations. Congregationalists became more jealous of local independency than before. Presbyterians in the United States were no longer generally to look first toward Congregationalists when they contemplated interdenominational union. Relations between the sister denominations, which had been uniquely close for two centuries, grew markedly more distant.

The voluntary societies, especially the American Home Missionary Society and the American Education Society, also proved to be casualties of the breakup of the Plan of Union. The separate history of the New School church exhibits a slow and regretful retreat from dependence on the voluntary societies, and the gradual development of denominational "boards" to perform the same functions.[11] The same thing had happened with Baptists, Methodists, Episcopalians in the 1830's and 1840's, but New School Presbyterians and Congregationalists, the chief supporters of the voluntary societies from the beginning, were also the last to leave them. In the end the New School Presbyterians formed their own boards and the chief voluntary societies became Congregational boards by the default of everyone else.

By this middle generation of the nineteenth century, however, a new issue had come to dominate both mergers and schisms, Negro slavery. As was observed in passing, the alignment of views over slaveholding played an indispensable role in the Excision of the New School in 1837. Slavery was to be the governing issue in nearly all splits and also reunions of the American Reformed churches for more than a generation to follow. Nothing else posed the meaning of ecumenism more sharply.

Up to the 1830's most of the opposition to slavery in the Presbyterian and Congregational churches was colonizationist. There had been only a few scattered abolitionists. But the British debate over slavery gave the cue to American abolitionism in the 1830's. In the churches the new militants such as Theodore Dwight Weld and the Tappan brothers sought to have discipline enforced on slaveholding, interpreting the latter as a sin against the Eighth Commandment. The peak of the abolitionist effort in the Presbyterian Church came in 1835, and made it clear that denomination-wide discipline was impossible on the issue. It had been left too long to local discretion, and the church was regionally split in its moral attitude. To force the issue meant schism. Was it more ecumenical to maintain administrative unity by diplomatically avoiding the issue, as some denominations were able to do, or to face schism and come up with a much smaller church, like the Quakers or the Free Presbyterians (who split off from the Old School in 1845)? Which unity would be closer to the unity Christ wills for his church? The popular churches with substantial constituency in both North and South split, the Methodists in 1844, the Baptists in 1845, and the Presbyterians variously in 1837, 1845, 1857, 1861, the last two dates marking the main splits of the New School and the Old, respectively. In the Midwest, indeed, the abolitionist issue was also important in the breakup of the Congregational-Presbyterian Plan of Union. The Congregationalists, having no southern constituency, became more militant than the Presbyterians, and congregations tended to sift out on the slavery issue. In the South, by contrast, Presbyterians supplied most of the ammunition for the theological and Biblical defense of slavery, with James Henley Thornwell for the Old School and F. A. Ross for the New.[12]

The Emancipation Proclamations also had an unexpected consequence in healing the Old School–New School schisms in American Presbyterianism. At the time of the firing on Fort Sumter no one would have guessed that such a reconciliation was feasible in any calculable future. The northern Old School and the New School Assemblies did not even exchange fraternal delegates, although each church regularly did so with other less closely related denominations. There was considerable sniping and mutual asperity in the press on both sides. Yet five years later saw a joint committee appointed to explore reunion. Terms were drafted and accepted by presbyteries and assemblies of the northern New School and Old School churches in 1869.[13]

How was it done? The answer seems inescapable—agreement on the moral issue of slavery came to seem more important than the faith and order issues on which Old School and New School had divided thirty years before. Reconciliation was pushed in the North by the antislavery men of the Old School, who were ashamed of the politic silence of the Old School position, and wished to push that church toward the outright condemnation of slavery held from before the War by the northern New School church. This antislavery group captured the Old School church in 1864, and the Assemblies of that year and the next finally took vigorous and explicit action against slavery. In 1866 the Assemblies of the two churches met in St. Louis and set up the joint committee on reunion which was to succeed with its project.

Charles Hodge and Robert Breckenridge tried to revive the Old School doctrinal polemics of the 1830's but no longer found a following. In fact, the Old School Assembly of 1868 explicitly recognized as an acceptable version of Calvinism the very Auburn Declaration which had been found inacceptable in 1838! Evidently Old School theology had significantly changed or else doctrine had not really been as important in 1837 as was claimed at the time. Henry B. Smith of Union Seminary, the leading New School theologian, must be given the largest measure of credit for leadership in the reunion movement. His opening address, as retiring Moderator, at the 1864 General Assembly, "Christian Union and Ecclesiastical Reunion," is probably the most substantial statement of the case.[14]

One should also take into account the enthusiasm generated by the pan-Presbyterian Convention of 1867 in Philadelphia. Its organizer, George H. Stuart, of the Reformed Presbyterians, had revived the old dream of a united American Reformed Church, as first suggested by the Classis of Amsterdam in 1743, and as discussed again in the 1780's and 1840's. This time the German Reformed were not included, perhaps because of their involvement in the Mercersburg movement (see below, pp. 161 f.), but the Dutch and almost all the splinter Scottish bodies were represented along with New School and Old School and the Cumberland Church. In its wider scope the Convention was unsuccessful. Indeed, its leader was repudiated by his own Reformed Synod. But its enthusiasm flowed into the New School–Old School negotiations at the critical moment and contributed to the reunion of 1869–70.

The contention that political ethics overruled faith and order in this whole development is supported by the story on the southern side. There, too, the New School United Synod had been already reconciled in 1864 with the Old School church of the former Confederate states. Thus the main body of American Presbyterians was again divided in two, but no longer on Old School–New School lines, but along the issues over which the Civil War had been fought. And that new division was to endure for more than a century.

The Presbyterian and Congregationalist churches, to be sure, numbered relatively few Negroes, as compared to the Methodists and Baptists. The largest Reformed concentration was in the Cumberland Church, with about 20,000 blacks. After Emancipation the blacks were encouraged to organize separately, with very little help, and the first General Assembly of the Colored Cumberland Church met in 1874. Presbyteries of the other two Presbyterian churches in the South were also generally segregated in the period after 1877, when the Jim Crow system was generally established. By the end of the century the over-whelming majority of American Negroes of all denominations were in segregated churches. Probably the most powerful demonstration of Christian reconciliation and unity in this whole story is the degree of Christian recognition American Africans continued to extend to their exploiters and tormentors.

From the time of the ecclesiastical readjustments related to the Civil War and slavery few merger efforts were successful until after the First World War, when there were important new developments. In the 1890's, to be sure, the proposal to merge the Dutch Reformed (of New York and New Jersey, Michigan and Iowa) with the German Reformed (of Pennsylvania, Maryland, and Ohio) was renewed and reached its high-water mark. The two churches had been intimately related from colonial times and were closely akin. They supplemented each other geographically and their combined resources would enable them to reach out more vigorously beyond ethnic enclaves. But a major difficulty had emerged on the Dutch side. The eastern synods of New York and New Jersey favored the merger, but a new Dutch immigration had given Michigan and Iowa a different flavor. Not only were the ethnic ties more recent and vivid, but the churchmanship of the nineteenth-century immigrants was more separatist. Many in the Reformed Dutch synods of the Midwest felt closer to the separatist Christian Reformed than to any non-Dutch denomination, such as the German and Swiss Reformed. This alignment, thus revealed in the 1890's, was to prove an enduring one. Despite a score or so of merger negotiations with various partners in the nineteenth and twentieth centuries (German Reformed, United Presbyterians, Southern Presbyterians), the Dutch Reformed Church was to be unable to overcome this difficulty.[15]

The Cumberland Presbyterians and the Presbyterians in the United States of America were to be somewhat more successful. When the Presbyterian Church in the U.S.A. adopted interpretations and supplements to the Westminster Confession in 1903, leaders in the Cumberland Church felt that the grounds for their earlier doctrinal protests had been satisfactorily removed. The predestinarian elements of the Westminster Confession had been neutralized and a theological basis for evangelism made explicit. Committees were accordingly put to work by the respective General Assemblies, and a Basis of reunion was drafted and accepted in 1906. About a third of the Cumberland Presbyterians, however, were not reconciled and formed a continuing assembly. Suits were brought in the civil courts to retain denominational property. The old issue of educational requirements for ordination was still important. The black minority in the Presbyterian Church in the U.S.A. also fought in vain against the racial segregation adopted in the reunion. They generally felt, as the former Moderator of the General Assembly, Herrick Johnson, put it, "Better far no union than union at such a cost!" [16] The larger part of the Cumberland Church was thus reunited with the mother church, but there remained a continuing body of about 50,000 and a separate black Cumberland Church.

After the First World War the pace of reunion movements quickened. Two small ethnic minority churches sought broader connections in the 1920's. The Welsh Calvinistic Methodists, a group of about 15,000, had discussed merger with the Presbyterians before the War but without resolution. The conversations were revived in the War and consummated in a union in 1920. Similarly the Hungarian Reformed Church in America, a small community resulting from twentieth-century immigration, was, for the most part, united with the German Reformed in 1924. A few congregations remained outside the union and took again the name of the Hungarian Reformed Church in America in 1958.

There was a succession of attempts in the twentieth century to unite the larger American churches bearing the Presbyterian name, so many, in fact, that the story is very complicated. The historian is hard put to it to explain, on the one hand, the dozens of negotiations undertaken unsuccessfully, and, on the other, success, however limited, when it did come. The amount of effort that has gone into this work is staggering when compared with the results. A successful consummation, by contrast, may seem to be sheer luck, so many and varied are the hazards that must be threaded. Rather than recapitulating an intricate and not very enlightening succession of overtures, committees, negotiations, plans, and votes, it may suffice to attempt some generalizations.

The matter was easiest for the largest body, the Presbyterians U.S.A. They were the most inclusive church anyway and the readiest to accept some diversity. As the largest they could be confident of continuing strength and momentum in a united church, and need not fear being "swallowed up." They had some sense of a historical responsibility to serve as a nucleating center for American Reformed bodies, and after the reunion with the Cumberland Church looked hopefully for further mergers.

The thought of general Presbyterian union was probably hardest for the Southern Presbyterians, the second largest body.[17] They were the heirs of the Presbyterians of the Confederate States and of the legacy of bitterness and defeat. Attempts at conversations in the late nineteenth century had not been successful and the idea of reunion did not attain serious support until after the First World War. It was the Presbyterians of the border states and the southwest, where the two denominations overlapped, who raised the question ever more insistently, while the spokesmen from the Deep South felt little sympathy for it.

In 1936 the Southern Presbyterian General Assembly set up a Permanent Committee on Cooperation and Union with instructions to explore possibilities with other Presbyterian bodies. Conversations with Presbyterians U.S.A. followed and by the outbreak of the Second World War in 1939, the tide seemed to have turned. Debate was animated, led by rival church journals, especially the *Presbyterian Outlook* and the *Presbyterian Journal*, and opinion crystallized in opposing organizations. But the rising generation seemed increasingly ready to look to reunion. With time on their side, the reunion party agreed in 1948 to a five-year moratorium in negotiations.

During the moratorium of 1948–1953 the third Presbyterian body, the United Presbyterians, entered the picture. The United Presbyterians, originally created by a merger (see above, p. 136), had been more inclined to church union, generally speaking, than the Southern Presbyterians. They had initiated conversations with several other Reformed bodies in the nineteenth century who shared their insistence on confining sung praise to psalms. They had repeatedly wooed the Covenanters, the southern synod of the Associate Reformed Presbyterians, and even tried the Dutch Christian Reformed denomination. In the twentieth century, however, their conversations were rather with larger bodies, such as the Presbyterians U.S.A., the Southern Presbyterians, or the Dutch Reformed, the last of which was about their own size. In all these cases, the United Presbyterians were faced with the likelihood of having to permit the use of some hymns, and this decision did not come easily. The United Presbyterians rejected overtures from each of the larger Presbyterian bodies in the first half of the century. They would have united with the Dutch Reformed in a plan sent to the lower judicatories in 1949, but that was defeated by the Dutch.[18]

It was at this juncture that a Three-Way Plan to bring together the United Presbyterians, the Southern Presbyterians, and the Presbyterians U.S.A. was broached. The thought was, in part, that the psychological difficulties of the disparity in size might be partly overcome with two smaller bodies and one larger one. The plan was originally devised in 1951 and redrawn in 1953. It was approved in 1954 by the Assemblies and sent down to the presbyteries. Unfortunately there the voting coincided with the peak of southern resentment against the Supreme Court decision of 1954 on school integration. The southern presbyteries rejected the plan, by 43 to 42 with one tie, and brought to defeat an effort of nearly twenty years' duration. The outcome also indicated that reconciliation of northern and southern Presbyterians might well involve, as it had in the cases of Cumberland reunion, and the Methodist reunion, an incorporation of racial segregation into the church structure. This problem, to be sure, was rapidly ceasing to be a southern problem as the migration of Negroes from the South increasingly forced the whole nation and its churches to acknowledge their racism.

The positive residue of the rejected plan of 1953 was its revision as a two-way merger of the remaining parties, the United Presbyterians and the Presbyterians U.S.A. The United Presbyterians had declined previous proposals from the Presbyterians U.S.A. as well as a score or so other schemes of merger at various times. But now, after these failures, and after the southerners withdrew, they had accumulated enough merger momentum to agree to unite with the Presbyterians U.S.A. The merged church adopted their familiar title, and all now became "United Presbyterians." The union was consummated in 1958 at Pittsburgh.

There was also a strong ecumenical current in this generation among the Congregationalists, the closest kin to Presbyterian churches in England and the United States, and indeed throughout the Commonwealth countries. The repudiation of the American Plan of Union and Accommodation plans had left resentments and scars on both sides. These differences were heightened by the divergent responses of the two communities to late nineteenth-century theological liberalism and Biblical criticism. Both, to be sure, had their heresy cases (Andover, Chicago Theological Seminary, the American Board of Commissioners for Foreign Missions, as well as Union and Lane Seminaries), but the Presbyterians were clearly more conservative. Congregationalists were confirmed in their suspicions of the Presbyterian machinery of courts as a threat to conscience and the freedom of the spirit. But as Presbyterianism fought off successfully the fundamentalist attempt to capture the denomination in the 1920's, and as Congregationalism also was influenced by Continental theology, the two families again came closer in the United States. Merger conversations were undertaken in England also, although both churches were discouraged by their twentieth-century losses in that country.

After the First World War the American Congregationalists were one of the major American denominations most disposed to ecclesiastical cooperation and merger. At the same time they were among those most influenced by liberal theology, and were thus impatient with church traditions, except their tradition of religious liberty and congregational independence. Conversations for consolidation were carried on with two smaller bodies in the 1920's. The Evangelical Protestant Church of North America, the first of these, was a group of about 6,000 German Swiss immigrants of the nineteenth century who were ready to affiliate with a major American denomination with a wider mission. They were incorporated into the Congregational National Council in 1925. The second body was the Christian Church (General Convention), a largely rural Midwestern group of more than 100,000 members akin to the Disciples of Christ. The Christians were locally independent, negative toward confessions of faith, and while they practiced baptism by immersion, were not insistent on it. They too were merged into what became officially the "Congregational Christian Churches" in 1931.[19] Both of these mergers were consolidations for more effective work, and neither involved serious reconsideration or reordering by the much larger Congregational body.

But the Congregationalists wished to continue, not only as a united, but a uniting fellowship. In looking about for a partner toward the end of the 1930's, they came upon the Evangelical and Reformed Church. It was less a matter of affinity or of long association than that these were the two denominations most disposed to merger in principle who were not otherwise engaged. They knew little of each other and were so distributed geographically as to have limited contact. The one was in background English Puritan, the other Swiss and German; the one predominantly suburban upper-middle-class business and professional people, the other with a substantial rural constituency and more lower-middle-class in the cities. And the Evangelical and Reformed denomination acknowledged certain confessional standards unfamiliar to Congregationalists, the Augsburg and Helvetic Confessions and the Heidelberg Catechism, and maintained a loosely presbyterian form of government. One might have expected the Evangelical and Reformed to enter conversations with the Presbyterians rather than the Congregationalists, and perhaps they would have if the Presbyterians had not at that time been engaged in other conversations. On the other hand, it was easier for Congregationalists to come to terms with such a loose synodical structure than it would be for them to deal with one of the larger Presbyterian bodies.

Official conversations began in 1937 and eventuated a decade later in a Basis of Union predominantly Congregationalist in character. The Basis was approved by the Evangelical and Reformed, but the Congregationalist Christians ran into trouble. A determined minority, some conservative evangelicals and others very liberal in theology, joined forces on a program of congregational autonomy. To placate them the majority adopted certain "Interpretations" of the agreed Basis, which, of course, sent the whole matter back for a second vote by the Evangelical and Reformed. In 1949 both bodies seemed at length in agreement on the revised basis, but the merger was held up by a lawsuit in the civil courts, the *Cadman Memorial Congregational Society* v. *Helen Kenyon*. As with the Scottish churches in 1904–05, the case raised some fundamental issues of church and state relations. The first judge denied the Congregationalist Christian General Council the right to effect the merger, but the judgment was reversed by the Appellate Division in 1952 and again by the Supreme Court of Appeals in 1953. The first General Synod of the United Church of Christ convened in 1957, representing over two million members. Two separatist splinter groups remained outside. A statement of faith and a constitution for the United Church were adopted in 1959 and 1963.[20]

The United Church of Christ was often said to be a church merger across distinct forms of polity. American Congregationalism, however, had never consistently maintained congregational autonomy. In colonial days the Congregationalist civil magistrate had exercised coercive authority over local congregations on behalf of the whole fellowship, and a variety of associations and consociations, up to the national council, had later functioned with limited but significant representative powers. With real congregational autonomy it is impossible to have a denomination at all, to say nothing of a merger, and American Congregationalism as a whole clearly intended to be at least a denomination. The merger constituting the United Church of Christ marked a slight shift in the scope of binding engagements which local congregations of Congregationalist background acknowledged to each other. In this area there was no such clear issue as with diocesan episcopacy;

it was, rather, a matter of moving a notch or two one way or the other on a graduated scale of organizational patterns. And it was argued more on grounds of efficiency or of types of democratic government than theological principle. The significant differences in this merger were really social, cultural, perhaps liturgical, rather than matters of church order.

Congregationalists and Presbyterians also drew together on a world level. There had been a series of international Congregational conferences since 1891, stimulated in part by the World Reformed Alliance and other world denominational gatherings. There were not many of them, only three before the First World War and two more before the Second, and there was no continuing structure; these were simply occasions for the exchange of information and for fellowship. And the Congregationalist fellowship was, apart from mission churches, virtually confined to the English-speaking world. At the Boston Council of 1920, for example, the British Isles and the United States divided between them three fourths of the delegate assignments, and of the remaining quarter over half were assigned to Canada and Australasia. The American Congregationalists and those of England and Wales, in fact, were the only two large bodies in the fellowship and the Council has had difficulty in finding any suitable place to meet outside the United States and the British Isles.[21]

This geographical and cultural location has influenced the self-understanding of Congregationalism, which has been polemically determined within the generically Reformed theological context of British churches, Anglican, Presbyterian, and Baptist. "Congregationalism has no doctrinal peculiarities," said Robert William Dale, the chairman of the first international council. What he meant was that Congregationalism distinguished itself from Anglicanism on matters of church organization and the separation of church and state but not in the central understanding of the gospel. Similarly, American Congregationalism in the twentieth century prided itself on its relative theological freedom, as contrasted with the Presbyterians and their heresy trials, but it was the *same* doctrinal tradition to which the Congregationalists now sat looser than the Presbyterians. So long as they remained largely insulated from contact with Lutherans, Greek Orthodox, and Roman Catholic Christians, Congregationalists were more impressed with their minor distinctions from Episcopalians and Presbyterians than with the common ground they shared with these traditions.

Even in the United States, to be sure, there were problems of self-definition in terms merely of congregational polity. The largest churches of congregationalist polity in the United States were those of the Southern Baptist Convention and the Missouri Synod Lutherans. In each case there were matters other than those of formal polity which were important in defining these communities as something quite different from Congregationalists. But the Congregationalists were much less ready to declare what they were, apart from polity, than either the Baptists or the Lutherans. English Congregationalists such as Fairbairn, Forsyth, Whale, Manning, Micklem, and Jenkins might understand Congregationalism as "decentralized Calvinism," but this was not congenial to many American Congregationalists.

The problem of self-definition became crucial for the International Congregational Council after the founding of the World Council of Churches. The ICC was organized as a continuing body in 1949, and invited by the Central Committee of the WCC to be represented in the WCC as one of the "world confessional organizations." As such it began to establish connections with free churches in Lutheran Scandinavia, such as the Swedish Mission Covenant, and other small free churches on the Continent. The Dutch Remonstrants were one such body who were genuine kin as liberal Reformed churches. The tendency, however, of this line of development, was to become an association of miscellaneous and disparate free churches with no substantive common platform.

Congregational churches were also increasingly involved with merger negotiations at the home base. They were considering or had effected union in the twentieth century with Presbyterians in England, Canada, Australia, New Zealand, and the United States, and in some of these also with Methodists. Congregationalists were to become constituent elements with Presbyterians in all the major united churches of the century—the South India United Church, the Kyodan of Japan, the Church of Christ in China, the United Church of the Philippines, the United Church of Canada. The International Congregational Council was coming to have a constituency overlapping that of the World Reformed Alliance in ever increasing degree. Negotiations for merger began in 1960.

The uniting General Council of the World Alliance of Reformed Churches (Presbyterian and Congregational) took place in Nairobi, Kenya, in 1970. It was said that it was the first merger of world church families, and the first to cross types of polity. But one could also argue that it was essentially a Reformed consolidation and that the diversities were minor variations. After all, there were already churches of congregational type, such as the Swiss, in the World Reformed Alliance, and there had been a strain of Presbyterianism in American Congregationalism, at least, throughout its history. And both Congregationalists and Presbyterians had shown a steady, if sometimes contested, disposition to church union for the sake of more effective mission.

One need only glance over the list of United States members of the Western Section of the World Reformed Alliance in 1970 to see how long a road still must be traveled for a single American Reformed Church. Apart from a number of small bodies, several of which were unlikely to consider any merger, the larger churches such as the United Presbyterians, Southern Presbyterians, Dutch Reformed, and United Church of Christ continued their separate ways. By contrast the more numerous Methodists had already been unified, and the Lutherans were perhaps nearer unity than the Reformed. The recurrent attempts to unite most or all Reformed bodies had not met with much more success than those to unite all evangelical churches (and there had been several of both). There had been several substantial achievements in church union, but also a number of unexpected new divisions, and it was hard to see any such national pattern of consolidation as might be observed, for example, north of the border in Canada. In the United States, Christian unity by consolidation of denominational families was a slow, erratic, and painful method, needing supplementation by councils and federations and by associations of individual Christians.

IX

REFORMED–LUTHERAN RELATIONS:
UNION IN CONFESSING THE GOSPEL?

ON THE EUROPEAN CONTINENT, as contrasted with the English-speaking world, the traditional partner in Reformed ecumenical discussion has been for centuries the sister church of the Reformation, Lutheranism. Lutheranism is the largest of all Protestant bodies, chiefly concentrated in Germany and Scandinavia. Its absence in Great Britain has had a perceptible effect upon the character of British theology and religion. In the United States there is a very substantial Lutheran community of eight million or so, but it is only in the last generation that Lutheranism has engaged with other American churches in religious activity and discussion. In Europe, however, there have been significant Lutheran-Reformed church unions as well as much conversation. The mergers were largely achieved in the general reconstruction after the Napoleonic Wars and the Peace of Vienna in various German states, all of them, in fact, in which there were substantial numbers of both traditions. Before, during, and after these ecclesiastical unions, however, there was on the Continent, and especially in Germany, an extensive network of voluntary societies, evangelistic and charitable, enlisting individual Christians of both confessions and many states. Both of these forms of ecumenical expression will be briefly surveyed, and we may conclude with the new phase of Lutheran-Reformed relations which has been brought about by the revolutionary consequences of the World Wars of the twentieth century.

Many factors converged to make a Lutheran-Reformed merger plausible in Germany at the beginning of the nineteenth century. The strongest currents of church life at the end of the old century, pietism and rationalism, each tended to minimize the importance of the old issues of controversy. The differences were still there, to be sure, but to large numbers they no longer seemed such as to require the denial of church fellowship. The shared experiences of the War of Liberation and the rising tide of German nationalism contributed to the desire for unity also in the church. And then the end of the wars meant that the map must be redrawn and the administration of the churches as well as the states must be reorganized. Prussia, for example, which had been cut in half by Napoleon, was now given extensive new territories, making it, after Austria, by far the largest German state, and the leading Protestant state of Europe. Some sort of consolidation into a Prussian Protestant church seemed to be desirable for many reasons.

But how should it be done? The matter had been discussed in print even during the Napoleonic period. Three advocates of church union won particular attention: the church historian of Göttingen, Gottlieb J. Planck; the court preacher Bishop F. S. G. Sack; and the preacher and theologian of Berlin, Friedrich Schleiermacher.[1] Schleiermacher had been commissioned by Minister Karl vom Stein to draft a church constitution for Prussia that would utilize the presbyteries and synods of the Westphalian churches as a model. Where such organs of self-government were lacking, the churches could be unified only by government action. Sack, to be sure, suggested that the pastors could be gathered in assembly and asked to vote on behalf of the churches.

In the event, the initiative for action came from the Prussian king, Frederick William III. The king inherited the traditional Hohenzollern desire to unite more closely his own Reformed heritage with the Lutheranism of most of his subjects. He was unusually devout personally, and was pained at his inability to receive communion with Queen Louise, a Mecklenburg Lutheran. In September, 1817, he issued a summons calling on Lutherans and Reformed to become one united church. To inaugurate the union he suggested that common services of Holy Communion should mark the ceremonies commemorating the centennial of Luther's Ninety-five Theses. The court and garrison congregations were united forthwith as models.

The initial response to the royal summons was enthusiastic in the capital, and in the western provinces where the two churches had some knowledge of each other. In many areas church buildings could not contain the crowds at the joint communions, as in Berlin's Trinity Church, where Schleiermacher and Marheineke served each other. A synod of Berlin ministers proposed that the formulas at the distribution of the bread and wine be confined to the language of Jesus, and that both interpretations of the Eucharistic presence be acknowledged as permissible. The chairman of the ecclesiastical commission proposed a complete synodical structure in all sixteen provinces of Prussia, along the lines of Schleiermacher's plan, which would be able to authorize and carry through the union. Steps were taken to organize the congregations, and provincial synods were summoned for 1818.

But just at this point the critical difficulty emerged. The king, and his minister Altenstein, took fright at the prospect of a presbyterian or synodical form of church government. Prussia, after all, was an absolute monarchy, accustomed to arbitrary personal rule by divine right such as had not been known in the English-speaking world since the Stuarts of the seventeenth century. There is more than a little similarity, in fact, between the church merger of Frederick William III and the attempts in Scotland of James I and Charles II to assimilate Presbyterianism into an Anglican episcopacy and liturgy (see pp. 108–110). In both cases the kings found presbyterian government in the church painfully suggestive of constitutional and representative government in the state, and opposed it in the interests of divine right monarchy. The mergers that resulted were then imposed by government without permitting the churches to work the matter out themselves. In Prussia the synods were no longer convened after 1818 and the king put the merger through by royal decree as "supreme bishop" of the church. By a revolution from above, the king carried royal absolutism in the church to a degree never previously known in Germany. The history of the union must be pursued, not in the acts of various church bodies, but in a series of *Kabinettsordern*.

The device utilized by the king, as with the English Tudors, was a prescribed uniform liturgy. Frederick William was a nontheologically-minded layman for whom ceremonial and liturgical formalities were very important. He was impressed by the pomp and circumstance of Anglican and Roman Catholic worship. As early as 1811 he had concerned himself with proposals for a standard clerical garb. An amateur liturgiologist, he had the librarians collect the old Reformation liturgies for him, and in 1820 personally compiled a new liturgy. In 1821 it was sent to all army chaplains, and the following year to all Protestant ministers in Prussia. It was largely modeled on the old Brandenburg-Nürnberg liturgy of 1540 and utilized many medieval usages which had come to be considered distinctively "Lutheran" as contrasted to the Reformed: railed altars, vestments, candles, crucifixes, kneelings, the sign of the cross. Long sermons, on the other hand, which the king considered the chief offense of the existing services, were curtailed; free prayer was eliminated; and choirs took over most of the singing from the congregations. Bread was to be used instead of wafers at communion, and the formulas at distribution were confined to the words of Jesus. Despite the provisions of the *Landrecht* that congregations might determine their own worship, the king claimed the right to prescribe liturgy and denied that it affected doctrine or conscience.

To the king's dismay the overwhelming majority of the clergy raised objections to his handiwork and an extended debate ensued, keeping all Prussia preoccupied with liturgy for a decade or more. There were hundreds of pamphlets for and against the union and the liturgy. The boldest and most persistent opponent of the royal liturgy was Schleiermacher, the greatest theologian of his generation. He contested both substantive matters in the proposed liturgy and the royal right to prescribe it, and it was not his fault that he was not judicially prosecuted. He must be given credit for awakening again some minimal sense of the proper independence and self-determination of the church. From 1824 the king yielded to the extent of permitting some local variations and this became the general solution from 1829, when Schleiermacher at last came to terms. The variants were such that really not much uniformity was left, but the principle of royal control of the Protestant church in worship was made good.

In the course of the controversy the king had established a new unified Prussian church in which the monarchy exercised power over its internal life in a way unknown to the old absolutism. A structure of general superintendents or bishops culminated in the Oberkirchenrat and the king as supreme bishop. This was parallel to the civil administration of the church under the *Landrecht,* with consistories and the Kultusministerium, and independent of it, since it was conceived as ecclesiastical administration. It gave the king a direct channel of control of the church apart from synods, or even the *Landrecht,* and justified Schleiermacher's description, the "court church." The price of this capture of the church by the monarchy was to be the alienation of both the educated and the masses. Individual kings might be convinced Christians, but the administration of a religiously pluralistic nineteenth-century state must be neutral or indifferent, as was illustrated from the beginning by the case of Altenstein, the minister of Frederick William III. There was thus a profound falsity in the relation of church and state, from which the church suffered severely.

Thus the United Evangelical Church of Prussia came into being, no doubt the most important merger of the Reformed church in the nineteenth century, and perhaps the most important merger of any sort. The result was the largest single Protestant church in Europe. But was it really a church? It was defined like the Church of England, not confessionally but administratively and liturgically. The union purported to rest on the ancient Catholic creeds and the Lutheran and Reformed confessions "as harmoniously received." But what of those who could not receive Lutheran and Reformed doctrine as harmonious? The most intransigent of these were some in formerly Saxon territories in Silesia, now incorporated into Prussia. Saxon Lutheranism took some pride in being the Lutheran mother church, and had long been bitterly anti-Reformed. Court preacher Ammon of Dresden, the Saxon capital, compiled pages and pages of "fundamental" doctrinal issues on which Lutheranism and Calvinism were irreconcilable. Harms of Kiel and Tittmann of Leipzig feared that Lutheran consciences would be violated by the union. Professor J. G. Scheibel of Breslau was leader of the Silesian Lutherans who considered Calvinists heathen and anti-Christian. But Berlin would not budge. Several Old Lutheran pastors were jailed and Scheibel fled. The Silesian protesters were not even allowed to emigrate until after Frederick William IV succeeded in 1840. Then they led an antiunionistic migration to the United States and Australia.

There was resistance on the Reformed side too, apart from Schleiermacher in Berlin. As with the Lutherans, it was located in the newly assimilated territories, in this case the Rhinelands. The Rhinelands Reformed, much influenced by pietism, had little sympathy for formal liturgy and were jealous of their presbyterian self-government. They were generally predisposed to merger, but disliked the method used in this one. They held out into the 1830's and finally accepted the union in 1835 with a variant liturgical option and a compromise form of church government. In that system, presbytery was associated, to be sure as a junior partner, with a state-appointed consistory. Even this much self-government had been preserved only at the price of accepting the king's liturgy. Elberfeld, under the leadership of Gottfried D. Krummacher, refused to enter the union, insisting on the self-determination of the church and the importance of ties with the Reformed of Holland, France, Great Britain, and America.

King Frederick William IV, who succeeded in 1840, was even more insistent than his father on a "Christian" monarchy. He would have liked to establish a full episcopal hierarchy for Prussia, with an archbishop at Magdeburg, and "succession" from Canterbury and Uppsala.

But there was little interest in, or sympathy for, such a project in the church. When a general synod was permitted in 1846, the old request for presbyteries and synods was voiced again, along with desires for a new ordination formula. The court would accept neither and dissolved the synod.

The revived confessionalism of the 1830's and 1840's, meanwhile, especially among Lutherans, was putting new pressure on the union. Some wished to interpret the union in effect as a federation rather than a church. After the revolution of 1848 and the related constitutional changes, the status of the merger was defined again in two *Kabinettsordern* of 1852 and 1853. It was stipulated, on the one hand, that the two confessions must be maintained and protected within the union, and that, on occasion, the members of the Oberkirchenrat should meet and vote separately as Lutherans and as Reformed. The union was to be maintained, on the other hand, as a church, and in fact was so, under the new German Empire from 1871. Partly from the stimulus of the World Reformed Alliance from 1875, a movement developed to draw together the Reformed communities of Germany, both within and without the United Churches. Some felt that the effect of the unions had been simply to absorb the Reformed minority without perceptible influence or contribution. A "Reformierte Bund" was organized at Marburg in 1884 and gradually built a fellowship of congregations and individuals. It did not, however, become a major force in German church life nor threaten the union churches. They were to endure also through the tribulations of the Nazi period in the twentieth century.

In half a dozen of the smaller German states and in the United States the Lutheran-Reformed merger was carried out in a healthier way than in Prussia. Here synods were able to act on behalf of the churches, as in Nassau, the Rhine Palatinate, Baden. In some cases the confessional question was treated explicitly. East of Germany in the Austro-Hungarian Empire a Lutheran-Reformed union was also proposed in Hungary in the 1840's, but without success, save for a joint theological faculty in Budapest. In Austria, a small Evangelical Church of the Augsburg and Helvetic Confessions was constituted somewhat later, in 1891, but more as a federation than a church.

In Pennsylvania the union movement was closely followed in Lutheran and German Reformed circles, and attempts were made to emulate it in the 1820's and 1830's.[2] There was a high proportion of *Simultan-kirchen,* in which the same building was jointly owned and used, usually on alternate Sundays, by Lutheran and Reformed congregations. The *Gemeinschaftliches Gesangbuch* dominated both churches for a generation. A German college was jointly conducted at Lancaster, and for a time it was hoped that a union could be organized. This failed in the early 1820's, but for fifteen years or so the Lutheran and Reformed synods, which exchanged voting delegates, considered proposals for ecclesiastical merger. After 1830, however, denominational consciousness was heightened on both sides, and the desire to assimilate the new immigrants in the Mississippi Valley tended to strengthen denominationalism in the East.

The Lutheran-Reformed union was more successful in the Midwest. It grew spontaneously out of the outlook dominant in the post-Napoleonic War German migration to the Mississippi Valley. The religious orientation of the most effective ministers of the movement was the interconfessional pietism of the Basel and Barmen missionary societies. Perhaps the largest section came from Württemberg, which had not experienced the controversy over "unionism." Others were from the Rhine provinces especially. In America one could watch the religious tendencies which largely initiated the union in Prussia, but here they were not manipulated by government.

The union-minded immigrants were pushed to organize by the efforts to sort them out for the confessions separately. There were some attempts at church extension by both Lutherans and Reformed of the East Coast, although some, like the Reformed Rauch, opposed denominational canvassing among them. But the westerners were not generally disposed to sort themselves out again as Lutheran and Reformed. When the doctrinaire Old Lutherans of the Saxon migration arrived in Missouri in 1840, however, this put the evangelicals under such pressure that they organized in defense. To the Saxons the Reformed were "children of Satan" and they insisted dogmatically on exclusively scholastic Lutheran formulations on all theological issues. The German Evangelical Conference of the West was organized in 1840 in defense against the denominationalist militants.

The core of the organizing pastors were Basel and Barmen missionaries, who were following the interconfessional tradition of their home societies. By 1850, for example, eleven members of the Conference were Basel men, six were from Bremen, three from Barmen. In contrast to the Saxon Old Lutherans, few of them were university-trained academics; they had, rather, received the practical and Biblical education of the mission schools. They were not antitraditionalist, however, and intended to stand on the Reformation confessions, to the disgust of the German freethinkers of the West. When they drew up their confessional paragraph in 1848 they listed the Augsburg Confession, the most catholic of the Lutheran confessions, and then instead of some of the extended polemical confessions, two catechisms in which personal faith was more prominent, Luther's and the Heidelberg Catechism.[3] The relatively simple Württemberg liturgy was widely used. Thus their association was a more integrated union than that of Prussia. A delegate of the Evangelical Conference was sent to the Bremen Kirchentag in 1852 and relations with the Prussian Inner Mission were cordial.

Before leaving the Prussian church union and its American reverberations we should note in a parenthesis how it became the channel through which a new dimension was brought into Reformed ecumenics, that of a positive relation to Roman Catholicism. Some Lutheran romantics had objected to the merger with the Reformed because it would preclude or at least delay union of Lutheranism with Roman Catholicism. In fact, however, it appeared that the union of Lutheranism with the Reformed opened to some of the latter a new vision of ecumenical relations with Rome.

There was no such development in the Evangelical Church of Prussia generally, to be sure, but a current of opinion with this tendency did have notable support at the court of Frederick William IV in the 1840's. Here one found an interesting parallel to the "branch theory" of Catholicism maintained in England by the Tractarians. In the Prussian version the Church Catholic lived in Roman Catholic, Eastern Orthodox, and Evangelical "branches." These also represented the three great divisions of Christian civilization, as found in the Holy Alliance and Metternichian politics. The tendency of this line of thought was to interpret "evangelical catholicism" in a traditionalist and conservative fashion, and to emphasize the Lutheran component of the Prussian union.

The consequences for Reformed ecumenics arose from the transplantation from this high church milieu of a young theology teacher, Philip Schaff, to the militantly anti-Roman Protestantism of the United States. To maintain, as Schaff then did at the German Reformed Seminary in Mercersburg, that medieval Catholicism had nurtured the true gospel, and had given birth to the Reformation out of its deepest religious impulses, scandalized Reformed churchmen who were accustomed to think of the Middle Ages as a period of apostasy

and Antichrist.[4] To aspire to eventual reunion of Protestantism and
Roman Catholicism, as Schaff also did, made his historical errors seem
a present danger. Schaff was actually tried for heresy. But with the
support of his colleague John Nevin he survived the trial and the
two men captured the leadership of the German Reformed Church in
America. Nevin was an erstwhile Princeton Presbyterian and a formidable polemic theologian, who carried the argument far beyond the
German-American churches to challenge the whole Presbyterian and
Reformed community in the United States. Nevin and Schaff challenged American Presbyterian, Reformed, Congregational churches
to come to terms with the "churchly" sides of the Reformed tradition,
which would, of course, bring them within speaking distance of European Lutheranism and Roman Catholicism. The Puritan and pietist
movement, it was argued, had left the Reformed churches with a prevailingly memorialist view of the Lord's Supper, and with low views
and careless practice with regard to baptism. But the Reformed confessions and theologians of the sixteenth and seventeenth centuries
had occupied quite different ground. The classical statements of the
Reformed heritage on the visible church also bore witness against
the extreme individualism of the nineteenth-century churches. The
appeal to "private judgment" was shown to be something more recent
and more simplistic than the Reformation appeal to Scripture, and a
reformulation of a Reformed understanding of tradition was demanded. Concretely, the traditions of corporate prayer and devotion
were cultivated in a liturgical movement which brought the Mercersburg emphasis home to the laity. Presbyterians, Congregationalists,
Dutch Reformed, Baptists, American Lutherans generally recoiled in
shock and outrage. It took some decades before the ecumenical perspectives of the theologians of the Mercersburg Seminary were generally acceptable in American Protestantism. But especially in the person of Philip Schaff, who moved after the Civil War to Union Theological Seminary in New York, these ideas were widely disseminated
in Presbyterian and Reformed circles, and more widely still in the
Evangelical Alliance and World Alliance of Reformed and Presbyterian Churches.

From this parenthesis on ecumenical relations with Roman Catholicism we must return to our central theme of Lutheran and Reformed
ecumenics. While considering ecclesiastical mergers in Europe and
the United States we have caught glimpses of another major form of
ecumenical activity, that of the interconfessional voluntary societies,

such as the Basel and Barmen missionary societies, or the Kirchentag and Innere Mission. The nature and work of these societies also must be surveyed. These societies generally expressed the kind of pietistic fraternalism that had been voiced in the correspondence of Francke in Halle with Cotton Mather in Massachusetts, or in Zinzendorf's overtures to the Cardinal de Noailles, and exemplified in Whitefield's readiness to cooperate with evangelicals of several denominations.

With Zinzendorf's reorganization of the Unitas Fratrum, the old pre-Reformation Hussite church, a new kind of pietist ecumenism had emerged. Not only did the Moravians feel sympathy for awakened souls, lovers of Jesus, in other denominations, they provided an interconfessional organization for them. This was a novel form of church life, expressed in the theory of "tropes." In Zinzendorf's conception the true church of Jesus Christ existed in several manifestations or tropes, Lutheran, Reformed, Anglican. All these forms were valid and enduring. He did not intend to proselytize from any of these traditions, but hoped to nurture better Lutheran, Reformed, or Anglican Christians by the religious fellowship of the Unitas Fratrum.[5] The Unitas was, in effect, an ecumenical missionary religious order superimposed upon ecclesiastical Protestantism and maintaining its fellowship chiefly by a common devotional discipline.

The conception was not developed all at once, and was not readily understood or accepted by others. It developed, obviously, out of the practical exigencies of the refugee Hussites, seeking to maintain their identity as a church and at the same time to claim the status of a pietist community within a regular parish of the state church of Lutheran Saxony, or later of the Reformed church in the Rhinelands. In William Penn's German-speaking enclave of Pennsylvania, again, Zinzendorf found an ecumenical enterprise after his own heart in the Associated Brethren of the Skippack in the 1730's. They attempted to organize a synod of the Pennsylvania Congregation of God in the Spirit in a series of gatherings in Germantown in 1741. After the fourth meeting, all withdrew but the Lutheran, Reformed, and Moravian contingents. To Zinzendorf this association was reminiscent of the Consensus of Sendomir, but to most others the status of the Congregation of God in the Spirit was not clear. After Zinzendorf's return to Europe, the Congregation did not long endure. Some ministers tried to maintain double standing, but Reformed congregations, e.g., increasingly refused to accept ministers from the Unitas, and thus forced the latter to accept the status of a rival denomination. On the Continent of Europe, on the other hand, the interconfessional network of societies nurtured by the Unitas endured and flourished. Such Moravian cells were often to prove seed-plots for the Awakenings of the early nineteenth century, in Scandinavia, Switzerland, and many German states.

The Moravian network was also the model of perhaps the most significant ecumenical institution of the first half of the nineteenth century, the interdenominational evangelical voluntary society. The most notable transitional formation was the Basel-based Deutsche Christentums Gesellschaft, founded by J. A. Urlsperger a decade before the French Revolution. The German Christian Fellowship quickly established groups in London and Amsterdam as well as in numerous German and Swiss cities, deliberately crossing ecclesiastical as well as national lines in its ecumenical and missionary thrust. It was essentially a society of Lutheran and Reformed pietists. It also fathered other organizations around specific functions, the Basel Missionary Society, the Bible and Tract Societies, with the same interconfessional character. C. F. A. Steinkopf was the secretary of the German Christian Fellowship. At the turn of the century he moved to London as chaplain and there played a notable role in the development of even more extensive societies on the same model in the English-speaking world. He was the "foreign secretary" of the British and Foreign Bible Society as well as of the Religious Tract Society and an ecumenical agent and liaison figure of first rank. The further development of these British evangelical societies must be pursued later. Here we note the leaven of the Unitas and later interconfessional pietistic societies in strengthening the mutual trust and friendship especially of the Lutheran and Reformed.

The Basel Missionary Society (1815) was the first of half a dozen pietist and interconfessional missionary societies founded in Germany and Switzerland in the two decades after the Napoleonic Wars. The Berlin Society followed in 1824, and then in 1828 the Rhenish Society was constituted out of a local auxiliary to the Basel Society. The North German (later Bremen) Society dates from 1836. These were the largest, and drew funds and personnel from Lutheran and Reformed alike. They were not merely German in their support, either, but enjoyed Swiss, Dutch, Scandinavian, Hungarian participation. Similarly in France, the comparable Paris missionary society, Bible Society, and Sunday School society drew on Lutheran as well as Reformed contributors. With reference to the American Midwest we have had occasion to observe the work of the kindred societies supplying missionaries for that frontier. When the movement of exclusive confessionalism gained ground among Lutherans in the middle generation of the century, tribute was paid to the interconfessional missionary societies by imitating them.

The Innere Mission and Kirchentag should also be considered in this connection, although their original purpose was something different. The Wittenberg Kirchentag of 1848 was a Protestant response to the many proposals and movements of that revolutionary year. In the mind of its most influential leader, J. H. Wichern, the Kirchentag aimed at the union of German Protestantism and the religious renewal of the nation. In the event the ecumenical achievement was much more modest. The Innere Mission was called into existence as a cooperative organization of German Protestant benevolent agencies, and the Kirchentag was continued as a sort of promotional device, comparable to the annual festivals of the foreign missions agencies, at such centers as Basel and Hermannsburg.

Both Kirchentag and Innere Mission were strongly nationalistic. Wichern viewed them as comparable to the Evangelical Alliance, reading something akin to his own nationalism into that body and supposing that it was an English enterprise. Even as a German institution, however, the Innere Mission won something less than universal support. The central committee was dominated by dignitaries of the Prussian Union church, although the structure was formally separate. But those who suspected or disliked Prussia on either political or theological grounds tended to hold the Innere Mission at arm's length. To the strict Lutherans of Hanover, Bavaria, and Saxony, for example, it represented "Unionism" and Prussian leadership, and, as in the case of foreign missions, they preferred to establish comparable safely Lutheran agencies. With all such limitations, however, the Innere Mission constituted into the twentieth century a very comprehensive network of the most devoted and ecumenical Protestants of Germany, both Lutheran and Reformed.

The nineteenth-century patterns of church life which we have been analyzing were radically disrupted by the World Wars of the twentieth century. One interesting new church emerged with the new Czechoslovak Republic in 1918 out of the dissolution of the old Austro-Hungarian Empire. This church represents a unique fusion of Lutheran and Reformed ingredients on the soil of a Bohemian Protestant consciousness. As such it revived the character of Bohemia at the turn of the seventeenth century, when strong Lutheran and Reformed elements were mingled with an indigenous reform movement dating from John Huss. At that time, of course, the country was 95 percent Protestant.

This unique form of Protestantism had been all but exterminated in the violent Counter-Reformation oppression of the seventeenth and eighteenth centuries. When Emperor Joseph II at last granted some limited toleration in 1781 the reconstitution of the old Bohemian church was not permitted. Protestants were allowed, if they wished, to attach themselves to one of the two confessions legally recognized in the Holy Roman Empire, the Augsburg or the Second Helvetic Confessions, although these were not widely known to Czech evangelicals. No other confession was permitted until the fall of the Hapsburgs in 1918. Denied theological schools or a religious press, the Czech Protestants had had to import German or Slovak Lutherans or Magyar or Swiss Reformed ministers.

The five hundredth anniversary of Huss was celebrated in 1915 during the War and kindled hope of reviving the Bohemian religious heritage. An assembly of delegates of the 120 Czech-speaking evangelical congregations (34,000 Augsburg Confession, 126,000 Helvetic Confession) unanimously voted in 1918 to reconstitute the Evangelical Church of the Bohemian Brethren. The church claimed the Bohemian Confession of 1575 and the Confession of the Brethren of 1662, as well as the Lutheran and the Reformed confessions which they had been using. There was certainly a powerful ingredient of nationalism in this development, but in sharp contrast to the Prussian Union of a century earlier, there was no political manipulation involved. The precise sense in which the several confessions were to be related to each other, or were individually or collectively authoritative, remained to be defined, presumably by the new Huss Theological Faculty, but this was a problem common to all confessional churches. In half a generation the church doubled in size, adding 100,000 formerly classified as Roman Catholic. It was still a diaspora church, lacking means to provide religious facilities to many of its people more than occasionally. And after the Second World War, of course, it would have to deal with a Marxist state as well as Roman Catholic pressures. But among other things, it represented an effective fusion of the legacies of the two great branches of the Reformation, the Lutheran and the Reformed.[6]

A new phase of Lutheran-Reformed relations generally began to manifest itself in the 1930's. The struggle of the church against Nazi heresy drew hitherto distant Christians together, in many cases, and made some themes of traditional debate seem relatively academic. The joint production of the Barmen Confession of 1934 is the most dramatic instance of this cooperation. This background of common struggle was a necessary precondition also for the new Roman Catholic–Protestant relations associated with the name of Pope John and Vatican II, but it was at least as important for a new warmth of Lutheran-Reformed relations. At about the same time, the two great sister churches of the Reformation were discovering each other again in the great ecumenical conferences from Stockholm, Lausanne, Jerusalem, Oxford, Edinburgh, Madras, to Amsterdam and its successors after the War. Geographically largely separated from each other, it took the ecumenical debates of the conferences to make the leaders of these churches aware again of the deep community of doctrine and ethos they shared as compared with free church or spiritualist views on the one side or catholic institutionalism on the other. By the end of the 1950's Lutheran-Reformed conversations were under way in nearly every country where both churches were present.

The Faith and Order Conference at Lund, Sweden, in 1952, supplied occasion for explorations on the part of Church of Scotland representatives of Church of Sweden attitudes toward pulpit fellowship and intercommunion. Archbishop Brilioth's reply that no obstacles existed encouraged the Scots to widen their inquiries. The Church of Norway reported in 1953 that "our attitude . . . is like yours" and the next year similar assurances were received from the Church of Denmark and the Church of Finland.

Mutual recognition among such national churches was not likely, to be sure, to result in extensive practical consequences. But in such countries as France, Germany, the Netherlands, Lutheran and Reformed churches were to be found on the same ground, or at least as neighbors. From these countries came more complicated replies to the Church of Scotland. In Germany, where the Union churches and several others were ready to extend mutual recognition, some ten Lutheran territorial churches were prepared for "limited intercommunion" as a matter of "economy," but not for full intercommunion.[7]

In the Netherlands, on the other hand, steps were being taken toward more definite grounds of church fellowship. For a century or more there had been interchange of pulpits and mutual accessibility to the Lord's Table as between the small Dutch Lutheran churches and the Nederlandse Hervormde Kerk. The two churches were also akin in worship practices, the Lutherans accustomed to a simple order like that of some South German liturgies. After the Second World War it was agreed to try to clarify the meaning of this de facto inter-communion theologically. The new Biblical theology and the eucharistic revival promised fresh understandings. Conversations were undertaken which resulted in a Consensus in 1956.

This joint statement specified some ten points of agreement and disagreement in the teaching of the two churches on the Lord's Supper. Unanimity was registered on six issues, while differences remained on four, concerning specifically church discipline, the manner of Christ's presence at the communion, and the *manducatio impiorum*. The points of agreement seemed so much more central and essential than the issues of difference that it was agreed to try to strengthen fellowship at the Lord's Table, while continuing discussion on the open questions within church fellowship. The one essential, it was agreed, was that "Jesus Christ alone, present in his church in word and sacrament, stands in the center." [8]

A similar undertaking was being pursued at the same time by a commission of Lutheran and Reformed theologians assembled by the Evangelical Church in Germany. In view of widespread de facto inter-communion and the intermixture of confessional communities brought about by the movements of population in Germany, a fresh attempt at eucharistic theology was indicated. New currents of Biblical theology and exegesis and modern historical perspectives on the Reformation and confessional eras alike gave promise of a fresh approach to hackneyed arguments. The result was a much discussed document, the "Arnoldshain Theses" of 1957.[9]

The theses were significant in that each side rejected certain formulations as no longer useful, and both agreed in the identification of Biblical themes which had not been brought forward in the sixteenth-century formulations. The results were not universally accepted, to be sure. The United Evangelical Lutheran Church of Germany in particular appointed a commission that requested further clarification on several points. But some new degree of ecumenical understanding had clearly been achieved.

In France, as in the Netherlands, church fellowship of Lutherans and Reformed was general practice. The bulk of French Lutherans are in Alsace, where the Napoleonic concordat with the state is still in force, in contrast to the rest of France. There is one Reformed "district" in Alsace, and sixteen elsewhere; while the Lutherans have seven dioceses in Alsace and two elsewhere. The distinctive development in France was the adoption in 1962 of a common Ordination Service for these four churches, which could serve as the instrument of mutual recognition of ministries.[10]

These several ecumenical approaches in various parts of Europe were brought into a Continental focus in the 1960's at the instance of the Lutheran World Federation, the World Reformed Alliance, and Faith and Order. Before we survey those further conversations, however, some important events in the United States should be noticed.

Lutheran-Reformed theological conversations in the United States were very late in developing. Although Lutheranism had been represented in the American colonies from the beginning, it was throughout American history largely isolated by language and culture from other churches. The pattern of immigration was such that through most of the nineteenth century and into the twentieth the Lutheran community was dominated by recent arrivals insistent on maintaining German or Scandinavian cultural identity and Lutheranism as a symbol of it. Lutherans, like Roman Catholics, generally felt themselves to be alien in "American" culture and society until after the First World War. Only in that generation between Wars, with the virtual cessation of mass immigration, did these two religious communities come to regard themselves as rooted in America, and to play a role in its intellectual life in any way comparable to their massive numbers. Only in that generation were genuine Christian alternatives presented to Anglo-Saxon Protestantism in the wider forum of the society.

A further Lutheran-Reformed consolidation occurred, meanwhile, within the community of German culture in America, that between the German Reformed Church and the Evangelicals in 1934. The Evangelicals, as we have seen, were in origin irenically oriented pietists. They had moved only gradually from a pastors' conference to ecclesiastical structure, developing delegated membership in the "Evangelical Synod of North America" only in 1880. The German Reformed, in contrast, had long maintained a presbyterian system of graded courts with General Synod, particular synods, and classes. In the 1920's these two denominations discussed a three-way plan of union with the United Brethren. When the last withdrew, the Evangelical Synod and the Reformed Church agreed on union with surprising ease in 1933. The first General Synod of the Evangelical and Reformed Church, representing 675,000 members, met in 1934. A constitution was not settled until 1940, but the common German heritage and a prevailing pietist outlook, especially in the Midwest, facilitated the merger. The united church was to give American Protestantism its most distinguished early twentieth-century theologians, Reinhold and Richard Niebuhr, who came out of the Evangelical Synod in the Midwest.

The main body of American Lutherans, meanwhile, was still barricaded behind the "Galesburg Rule," originally adopted by the Lutheran General Council in 1875:

> The rule, which accords with the Word of God and with the confessions of our Church, is: Lutheran pulpits are for Lutheran ministers only; Lutheran altars are for Lutheran communicants only.[11]

The rule had been adopted at the insistence of newer immigrants, who disapproved of the occasional pulpit and altar fellowship practiced by some Lutheran groups more assimilated to the society about them. Theological implications had not been carefully weighed; the rule was more a device to brace the walls around the cultural enclaves. Controversy was fierce as to whether exceptions might be permitted, and the Wisconsin Synod withdrew in 1888 over what it regarded as excessive looseness in enforcement. But by the 1930's, and especially after the Second World War, American Lutheranism was ready to take a more theological approach to the question.

Official conversations were authorized in 1961 by the appropriate sections of the Lutheran World Federation and the World Reformed Alliance. Organized in 1962, the exchanges continued for the next four years. Position papers and summary agreements were presented in book form in 1966, with the title *Marburg Revisited: A Reexamination of Lutheran and Reformed Traditions*.[12] The themes treated included confessions and confessional subscription, ethics and moral law, Christology and the Lord's Supper, with greatest attention, as might be expected, to the mode of the eucharistic presence. The participants discovered that their respective views of each other were in part inherited caricatures. In other instances apparent differences were now seen to be complementary rather than contradictory. For the rest,

> we regard none of these remaining differences to be of sufficient consequence to prevent fellowship. We have recognized in each other's teaching a common understanding of the Gos-

pel and have concluded that the issues which divided the two
major branches of the Reformation can no longer be regarded
as constituting obstacles to mutual understanding and fellowship. . . .

As a result of our studies and discussions we see no insuperable obstacles to pulpit and altar fellowship and, therefore,
we recommend to our parent bodies that they encourage their
constituent churches to enter into discussions looking forward
to intercommunion and the fuller recognition of one another's ministries. . . .

Intercommunion between churches . . . is not only permissible but demanded whenever there is agreement in the
gospel. Such agreement means proclamation of the same gospel as the good news of God's reconciling work in Christ
rather than uniformity in theological formulation.[13]

At almost the same time as the American conversations, a comparable series was conducted at Bad Schauenberg, Switzerland, from
1963 to 1967, for Europe as a whole. One year after *Marburg Revisited,* the Bad Schauenberg report appeared, "Lutheran and Reformed Churches in Europe on the Way to One Another." [14] It was
accompanied by theses on "The Word of God—The Presence of God,"
"The Law," and "Confessions." [15] Through these test cases the work-
ing party considered that it had shown that the inherited doctrinal
differences could be overcome and that there was genuine prospect
in the foreseeable future of a common theological declaration and
complete pulpit and altar fellowship. Important differences would
still remain in matters of church organizations, worship, and national
culture as well as doctrine, but were these the kinds of differences
that have to be lived out in separate churches? The meaning and
authority of all confessional statements had changed vastly as churches
had come to find themselves minorities within a secularized culture
and required to redefine themselves and their message in the light of
new questions. In both churches it had come to be widely doubted
whether a comprehensive confession was any longer possible.

On the basis of the clarification of doctrinal issues achieved in the
Bad Schauenberg conferences, a conference of official delegates of
sixty churches assembled at Leuenberg, Switzerland (1969-70), to consider what specific manifestation of church fellowship was indicated
for the Reformed and Lutheran churches of Europe.

It was observed that "already the majority of Lutheran and Reformed Christians in Europe live in such close fellowship that for them the sense of separation has largely disappeared." [16] These churches had, "in special measure, a duty to realize church fellowship together" because of their common historical origin, and as now facing together "a new task of reconciliation in a disunited, threatened world." Such church fellowship must include the elimination of actual divisions, the granting of full fellowship in word and sacraments, the greatest possible degree of shared activity in the inner life of the church, in witness, and in service to the world. What such fellowship might mean in terms of organizational merger would have to be considered case by case in the several countries. It should not entail an enforced conformity in worship, church order, forms of service or of proclamation. And a living process of theological debate should be encouraged on the agreed dogmatic canon that Jesus is the only mediator of salvation.

The instrument proposed to effectuate this fellowship would be a concordat or agreement that, on the basis of a common understanding of the gospel,

> the doctrinal condemnations contained in the confessional documents no longer apply to the contemporary position of the signatory churches. . . .
>
> The signatory churches acknowledge one another as churches of Jesus Christ inasmuch as they accord one another pulpit and table fellowship. This includes mutual recognition of ordination and permission for intercelebration. By this declaration church fellowship is achieved.[17]

The various churches had this declaration before them for action in 1972. Since many were already practicing such church fellowship, it was anticipated that a substantial number would subscribe to the concordat. This whole method of approaching church union was characteristic of churches with a confessional heritage from the Reformation and a strong sense of the continuing responsibility to confess their understanding of the gospel.

X

THE EVANGELICAL ALLIANCE: THE ECUMENISM OF THE VOLUNTARY SOCIETIES

THE FIRST significant worldwide ecumenical agency (essentially Protestant, to be sure) was the Evangelical Alliance, organized in 1846. The Evangelical Alliance was only one of a number of societies engaging individual Christians in cooperative work across ecclesiastical lines. We have already had occasion to remark on missionary societies, Bible societies, tract societies from an ecumenical perspective. Collectively these societies were the most important and successful type of unity endeavor in the first three fourths of the nineteenth century.[1] As that agency among them explicitly concerned with Christian unity, the Evangelical Alliance can serve as representative of this type of ecumenism.

The Alliance had a far wider outreach than merely the Reformed churches, but those churches formed its base. It began with the British Reformed churches, first of all the Presbyterians and Congregationalists, and embodied conceptions predominant in those churches at that time. The denominational representation at the organizing conference in London in 1846 tells the story. The largest bodies were not, as one might have expected, Anglicans and Methodists. The largest contingent was composed of 215 Presbyterians, followed by 181 Congregationalists. These two together comprehended nearly half the whole body, and their combined representatives on the Select Committee, which organized the conference, constituted a majority of that body. Of the American delegation, Presbyterians alone were nearly half the total.

This distribution of denominational representation is confirmed by an examination of the individuals and groups that had taken the lead in bringing the conference to pass. The major initial impetus came from the English Congregationalists. The Congregational Union of England and Wales had formally approved efforts for an evangelical union at its regular meeting in 1842, and for the year following, its secretaries served as staff in the preliminary steps leading to a mass meeting at Exeter Hall in June, 1843. No other denomination was so formally and generally committed to the project.

But this English Congregationalist leadership was also an embarrassment. Independents were in lively debate with Anglicans over a variety of legal disabilities and oppressions as well as the whole principle of church establishment. They were engaged also in polemics with Baptists about infant baptism, with Wesleyans about predestination and perfectionism. How to get an Archimedean point of leverage outside the English balance of ecclesiastical forces? "Who was to be the world's convener?" [2]

Two further developments were crucial. First was the Disruption in the Church of Scotland in the summer of 1843. This siphoned off the bulk of the evangelical strength of the Church of Scotland into a new Free Church, an event that enlisted the active sympathy of evangelicals in many countries of Europe and America, and, paradoxically perhaps, became a major ecumenical impetus. Fidelity to God as the ground of unity, it often appears, has more attractive power ecumenically than the maintenance of merely institutional bonds.

The Free Church was not, like the English Congregationalists, committed to the separation of church and state as an abstract theory, but as being in fact disestablished, its members were open to cordial relations with English nonconformists as they had not been able to be when they were still members of the Church of Scotland. The basic axis on which the Alliance structure was erected was thus the alliance of the Congregational Union of England and Wales with the Free Church of Scotland, two Reformed bodies that had not existed as such fifteen years before. The Alliance was largely cemented at the Bicentennial of the Westminster Assembly in 1843, at which Congregationalist as well as Presbyterian representatives were welcome. John Henderson, who was to become the chief "angel" of the first stages of the Alliance, was captured for the project at the Bicentennial. The overture that actually launched the preparations for the Evangelical Alliance meeting was a call issued by representatives of eight Scottish churches.

Beside the English Congregationalist initiative and the developments in Scotland connected with the Bicentennial of the Westminster

Confession and the Disruption, the Alliance received a significant impetus from the controversy over the endowment of Maynooth. Maynooth was the seminary for Irish Roman Catholic priests which the British Parliament had inherited from the Irish Parliament in 1801 as a client institution. It had received grants of money many times before Peel's government proposed in 1845 to make the grant permanent, increase it about threefold, and accompany it with a substantial sum to remodel the buildings. The proposal was generally seen as establishing the principle of endowing the Roman Catholic Church concurrently with the Anglican. The opposition which rapidly developed was composed of two camps, those Anglicans and others who held that a Protestant nation should not support Catholicism, and those increasingly militant opponents of all state churches who were winning ever-wider support among Independents and Baptists. The government, apparently, was simply seeking Irish support, without regard for constitutional principle.

An Exeter Hall public meeting in March established a Central Anti-Maynooth Committee which met daily for months and coordinated a campaign of circulars, petitions, speeches, local and provincial meetings, climaxing in a great conference from April 30 to May 3, of over one thousand delegates. Observing this response, many were led to urge a less politically and polemically oriented association of the whole Protestant community. So it was with the able chairman of the Central Anti-Maynooth Committee, Sir Culling Smith, treasurer of the London Missionary Society. The CAMC sent a delegation as such to the Liverpool meeting that autumn which planned the London Conference of 1846 of the Evangelical Alliance. There was a substantial carry-over both of personnel and of organizational pattern from the political organization to the ecumenical one.[3]

The state church–free church issue remained tense. The Anti-Maynooth Conference had actually split off a rump assembly, called the Crosby Hall Conference, of supporters, chiefly Baptist, of the Anti-State Church Association (formed in 1844). The London Conference of the Evangelical Alliance never split on this issue, but it was never out of the minds of the participants. The membership of the conference was probably divided about evenly between supporters of establishment (especially Anglicans, Methodists, Church of Scotland Presbyterians) and its opponents (especially Congregationalists and Baptists, and generally the Americans). The state churches, from this perspective, were seriously underrepresented. Of the 216 members of the preparatory Liverpool Conference only twenty were from the Church of England and none from the Church of Scotland. In London the next year these two churches had little more than token representation. Some sixty Nonconformist churches of the London area invited delegates to preach; only six or seven Church 'of England parishes did so. All the bishops and the great majority of the Anglican clergy, including many of the evangelical wing, held aloof from the Evangelical Alliance movement. Similarly for years the state churches of Germany, the Netherlands, Scandinavia, Switzerland were to be cautious about the Evangelical Alliance. The ecumenical conception which it embodied was not naturally congenial to churches identified with an old-regime establishment. Expressions of suspicion or open hostility to the Alliance from High Anglicans, Lutherans, or even some Reformed churchmen were not infrequent. In the meetings there was always danger of open controversy between the prevalent anti-establishment party and the minority spokesmen of establishment. (Such an anti-state-church speech occasioned the most awkward crisis of the New York Conference in 1873.) The dominant thrust in the Alliance was that of a Christianity which sat free to the state and was intensely missionary in outlook. It was no accident that the chief activity of the Alliance, after sponsoring ecumenical and missionary conferences, and exchanging information, was to be that of a watchdog of religious liberty.

It is true that the organizing conference of the Evangelical Alliance in 1846 owed something in its structure as well as personnel to the Anti-Maynooth Conference of the preceding year. But really both exemplified a pattern that had been established over the past half-century, that of the evangelistic or benevolent voluntary Christian society. The organizers of the Alliance made frequent references to the London Missionary Society, the Religious Tract Society, the British and Foreign Bible Society as their precedents and models. Through these societies there had arisen since the 1790's a new extraparochial, extraecclesiastical ecumenical structure of Christian service. The societies cooperated and overlapped in various ways, both at home and abroad, and were directed, in Great Britain as in the United States, by an interlocking directorate of agents and philanthropists. There had been evangelical societies from the days of Baxter, Spener, and Mather, but the scale had been different. Apparently it was the adoption of new business methods from the 1790's, of governing boards, hired executives, great numbers of stockholders, assembled annually to hear reports, both at great central assemblies and also in local auxiliaries, which made something new of these societies. In the early nineteenth century there emerged what has been called in its American manifestation the "benevolent empire." The organizers of the Evangelical Alliance were to a large degree men who were already in the habit of regular cooperation through this structure of extradenominational church life. Although it did not at once achieve this status in the United States, the Alliance may be fairly viewed as the explicitly ecumenical agency of the benevolent empire of voluntary societies. In that sense it was not so much a pioneering enterprise as the articulation of what had been going on for a generation and a half and was in fact already in decline, or at least in process of transformation into something different.

How this kind of ecumenism operated can be illustrated from the case of the (London) Missionary Society of 1795. The drafter of its basic principles was the Scottish Independent, David Bogue. The Society's design, he wrote, was "not to send Presbyterianism, Independency, Episcopacy, or any other form of Church Order and Government (about which there may be differences of opinion among serious persons) but the glorious gospel of the blessed God." [4] It would be left for future converts "to assume for themselves such form of Church Government as to them shall appear most agreeable to the Word of God." The central polity issues on which the definitive schisms of English Protestantism had occurred in 1662 were thus assigned to the nonessentials. One could hold the sum of saving knowledge under independency, presbyterianism, or episcopacy.

The London Missionary Society, to be sure, like its American imitator, the American Board of Commissioners for Foreign Missions, was unable to sustain its union or undenominational character. Scots and Irish Presbyterians and Calvinistic Methodists held on for a time with the Congregationalists, but such Anglican Evangelicals as John Venn and Charles Simeon, while grateful for the London Missionary Society, could not join it. They could hope to enlist Anglican support for missions only if they avoided any such association with Nonconformists. So they converted the evangelical Eclectic Society into the Church Missionary Society in 1799. Even so they won only bare toleration from the bishops. Even in the 1840's most Anglicans disliked evangelicals.

Evangelicalism, and with it the missionary and the cooperative thrust, had better success among Independents and Baptists. The denominational structures of these bodies, in fact, developed precisely out of the missionary organizations. The annual meetings of the

Baptist Missionary Society and the London Missionary Society were at first the *only* general convocations of the respective denominations, in each case, and the Congregational and Baptist Unions arose out of these annual missionary assemblies. It was the missionary spirit which made one body of these traditions as they had never been before.

But despite the apparent rivalry of the several societies, the missionary spirit, as the Congregationalist lay theologian Conder wrote, "has done more to promote a catholic intercommunion of different sects than all the forms of concord, or plans of comprehension, that ever were devised." [5] From as early as 1819 the "secretaries" of the chief London-based societies (at first the Baptist Missionary Society, the London Missionary Society, the Church Missionary Society, and the Wesleyan Methodist Missionary Society) were meeting monthly. Within the next decade or so, similar conferences of missionaries of these and other societies were meeting in the chief cities of India— Calcutta, Bombay, Madras. And when returned missionaries spoke in Great Britain in the local auxiliaries they would be heard eagerly by an interdenominational audience. It is these local auxiliaries especially which must be evaluated for a true assessment of the ecumenical impact of the missionary enterprise. Secretaries and treasurers and board members of these several missionary societies were then, in turn, conspicuous at the organization meeting of the Evangelical Alliance.

Some further dimensions of evangelical ecumenism came to light in connection with the production of religious literature. The idea of a religious tract society was proposed in 1799 at the annual meeting of the London Missionary Society. George Burder, foreign secretary of the LMS, and editor of the *Evangelical Magazine,* was founder, and the merchant-prince Reyner, whose partner Hardcastle was treasurer of the LMS, became treasurer of the Religious Tract Society. The first sermon for the new society was preached by David Bogue, and he drafted the first tract with its basic principles. There were to be no sectarian "shibboleths," no polemics, nothing to commend any one denomination or to throw odium on any. But every tract must give some account of the sinner's way to salvation, of justification by faith and regeneration by the Holy Spirit. It was felt that "all the saving truths" of orthodox Protestantism could be so conveyed, and reference was specifically made to Salnard's *Harmony of Confessions* (see above, pp. 36 f.).

In pursuit of these principles writers were found from "every denomination of believers." Matters of church polity were avoided, also the differences over baptism, and the issues over election and perfection which divided Methodists and "Calvinists." The devotional writings of Bunyan and Doddridge were reproduced, and hymns, addresses, narratives from varied sources. Sometimes exception was taken: Hannah More objected to some publications and Rowland Hill emended a tract to avoid offending Anglicans. But on the whole the procedure worked smoothly and the Society labored to provide edifying literature for the thousands of new readers emerging from the spreading Sunday schools.

In the United States the American Tract Society (for adults) and the American Sunday School Union (for children) followed similar editorial policies. The latter organization developed an interdenominational committee designed to censor out anything offensive to evangelicals of any denomination. Perhaps the most influential work published by the American Sunday School Union was Charles Hodge's *Way of Life,* which undertook to state the evangelical common core. There is nothing in it on polity or baptism, nor on election or imputation. Hodge treats the authority of the Bible, sin, atonement, justification, faith, repentance, holy living. This was apparently enough for salvation, but as Hodge's position in the schism of Old School and New School makes clear, it was far from enough to make an acceptable fellow Presbyterian! In Massachusetts, on the other hand, it became quickly apparent that the evangelical catholicity of the American Sunday School Union textbook list could not satisfy the Unitarians, and Horace Mann was able to pin the label "sectarian" on evangelicalism in general without having it equally assigned to Unitarianism.

A meeting of the Religious Tract Society in 1802 discussed the need for Bibles, and at the 1803 meeting rules and plans were drafted for what was to become the Bible Society. The new Bible Society won the patronage of the "Clapham Sect." Until 1831 most meetings were held at Free Masons' Hall; thereafter they were held at Exeter Hall. Henry Thornton was made treasurer. John Owen, chaplain to the Bishop of London, who made the motion for organization, was himself incredulous to see the different denominations cooperating. He was especially astonished at the presence of Quakers, which Reyner had arranged. This widened the net of evangelical "union" farther than any of the previous societies. To Owen it seemed a new era in Christendom to be

> surrounded by a multitude of Christians whose doctrinal and
> ritual differences had for ages kept them asunder, and who

had been taught to regard each other with a sort of pious estrangement, or rather of consecrated hostility.[6]

The structure was carefully arranged. There were to be thirty-six committee members, all laymen. Fifteen would be Church of England, fifteen other Englishmen, and six resident foreigners. Three secretaries were chosen: an Anglican, Owen; a Nonconformist, Hughes; and a Continental, Steinkoff. Clergy could be voting members. The appeal was to all who "regard the Scriptures as the proper standard of faith." They were to be distributed "without note or comment" and only the authorized translation should be used. On that basis Owen won the support of Bishop Porteous of London, and soon there were four episcopal vice-presidents. Thus the "necessary preeminence" of the Church of England was secured and the British and Foreign Bible Society quickly became the wealthiest and largest of the members of the British benevolent empire.

This constitutional structure was carried back to the parent organization, the Religious Tract Society, in 1816. The committee was reorganized to give Anglicans as many seats as all dissenters together, thus assuring them of a predominant voice.[7] There were to be those, such as the editor of the *Christian Observer,* who urged that the Evangelical Alliance should be organized on the same principles, with due regard to "those subordinations of society which God has ordained." [8]

The strength of the British and Foreign Bible Society system lay in the auxiliaries (176 by 1816), which were soon found in every shire in England. The wealthiest of these was the Norfolk Auxiliary, whose leading figure was the Quaker banker Joseph John Gurney. For a quarter of a century Gurney annually entertained thirty or more members of the Norfolk Bible Society at Earlham Hall—High Church, Low Church, Baptist, Lutheran, Quaker. Similarly Hardcastle had for years nurtured the interdenominational fellowship of the Religious Tract Society at his estate, Hatcham House. Not all the shire auxiliaries had such commodious resources for ecumenical fellowship, but the reconciling influence of their gatherings was often remarked.

The uncommented Scriptures evoked some favorable response even among Roman Catholics, so that the evangelical ecumenical network touched Roman Catholicism positively in a few cases. Some priests participated actively in its work, for example, in South America. But the Vatican reaction was negative, in 1816 in certain local regulations,

and then in a general encyclical of Leo XII in 1824. This was renewed in 1829 by Pius VIII and again in 1844 by Gregory XVI. The
last encyclical, condemning Bible societies, was translated by Sir Culling
Eardley Smith and published by the Christian Alliance in the United
States.[9]

There were also Protestants who found the Bible alone inadequate.
Professor Herbert Marsh of Cambridge contended that the Bible
Society was likely to lead to the dissolution of the Church of England
and John Henry Newman tried to sabotage it. First the American
Baptists and then the English Baptist Union protested against the
Society's refusal to translate *baptizo* as "dip" or "immerse." They felt
constrained to organize a Baptist Bible Translation Society to make
that emendation. Its secretary, Edward Steane, surprisingly enough,
was to become one of the chief architects of the Evangelical Alliance
six years later.

We might continue, for example, with the Education Societies and
the Anti-Slavery Society, but this must suffice to outline the ecumenical character of the voluntary society system. By the time the Evangelical Alliance was launched in 1846 several of the societies were arranging their fifty-year jubilees and were in the second or third generation of their leading personnel. Taken together they represented a
major new development of church structure and activity quite outside the canonical units of congregations and associations or parishes
and dioceses. Here was a fervently evangelical but extradenominational British Israel, channeling the energies of tens of thousands of
devoted Christians. The Evangelical Alliance became another manifestation of the same movement, hoping to manifest explicitly the
Christian unity that was already there, to maintain it against Protestant divisiveness within and against "Roman aggression" and the new
infidelity of Owenism and Ludwig Feuerbach and the Chartists without.

Exactly what was this new confederation? Some, like Thomas
Chalmers and Robert Smith Candlish of the Free Church of Scotland,
had hoped for ultimate corporate union. But the debate over the
doctrinal basis made it abundantly clear to all that ecclesiastical
merger was not in the cards in hand. The conference unanimously
resolved that:

> This Alliance is not to be considered as an alliance of de-
> nominations, or branches of the church, but of individual
> Christians, each acting on his own responsibility.

That in this Alliance . . . no compromise of the views of any member, or sanction of those of others, on the points where they differ, is either required or expected.

That it is not contemplated that this Alliance should assume and aim at the character of a new ecclesiastical organization, claiming and exercising the functions of a Christian Church.[10]

The conception of the ecumenical goal was also adopted unanimously.

The Church of the Living God . . . is one church, never having lost, and being incapable of losing, its essential unity. Not, therefore, to create that unity, but to confess it, is the design . . .

That this conference . . . feel constrained to deplore its existing divisions, and to express their deep sense of sinfulness in the alienation of affection by which they have been attended, and of the manifold evils which have resulted therefrom.[11]

A code of ecumenical behavior was adopted, whereby each member would strive to promote in his own communion a spirit of repentance and humiliation for its peculiar sins, and to use double forbearance with others, and where constrained to assert controverted views, would aim to avoid all insinuations, personalities, or irritating allusions. Similarly, none would suppose that only those were sincere friends of Christian union who joined this Alliance, and all would offer special prayers for all merely nominal Christians holding those errors which the basis of union was designed to exclude, as well as Jews and Gentiles throughout the world. It was agreed to urge on all ministers and religious writers to record the serious purpose to watch more against sins of the heart or the tongue or the pen against other denominations.

The definition of a doctrinal basis required no less than five days of debate at the London Conference. A text had been drafted at Liverpool, apparently by Candlish, which with two or three amendments eventually won approval. It was a curious document, not exactly a confession of faith, but an index of topics to be included in one, yet without pretensions to comprehensiveness, adequacy, or logical sequence. Some nine articles were at length adopted, referring to, but not defining, "what are usually supposed to be evangelical views" with regard to such topics as Scripture, private judgment, Trinity in Unity, depravity, incarnation, atonement, reign of Christ, justification by faith, conversion and sanctification, final judgment with eternal blessedness and punishment, the divine institution of the ministry, and the perpetual obligation of baptism and the Lord's Supper.

It was noted with some regret that the Quakers were ruled out by the articles on the ministry and sacraments, and the conference voted to acknowledge as Christian brethren Quakers and others who adhered to the basis otherwise and who manifested in their lives the fruits of righteousness. Many had come to respect deeply the piety of such men as Gurney, but they were unwilling to accept for the Alliance the embargo on common worship to which the Bible Society had found it necessary to submit to keep its Quaker membership.

It was the Americans especially who had pushed the article on eternal blessedness and punishment, wishing to rule out the universalism which was then occasioning controversy in the States and undercutting hellfire revivalism. The small European contingent (6 percent) did not vote against the doctrinal basis, but was not at all happy with it, anticipating that it would be a handicap to the Alliance on the Continent. Eight years later the French and French-Swiss Branch adopted a shorter and more coherent statement, which was published as the basis for the Alliance world conferences at Paris in 1855 and at Geneva in 1861. The French branch was ready to admit to membership

all Christians, who, wishing to live in brotherly love, express the desire to confess with her, conformably to the Scriptures inspired of God, their common faith in a Saving God: in the Father who loved them and justified them by grace, through faith in his Son; in the Son, who redeemed them by his expiatory sacrifice; and in the Holy Spirit, author of their rebirth and their sanctification, one God only, eternally blessed, to whose glory they desire to devote their lives.[12]

And when the American branch of the Alliance was reactivated in 1865, in the study of Philip Schaff in New York City, the nine articles of 1846 were preceded and subordinated by the following preamble, which almost certainly reflects Schaff's views:

We propose no new creed; but, taking broad, historical, and evangelical catholic ground, we solemnly reaffirm and

profess our faith in all the doctrines of the inspired Word of
God, and the consensus of doctrines as held by all true Christians from the beginning.[13]

The second great debate of the 1846 conference, after that on the
Basis, concerned Negro slavery as it affected church discipline and
church fellowship. Great Britain had outlawed slavery in 1834, culminating a vigorous abolitionist propaganda of a sort regarded as
extreme in the United States. The Congregationalist and Baptist
unions, rejoicing in the abolition, had delivered themselves in 1835
and 1836 of "affectionate remonstrances" and "fraternal expostulation"
on this subject to the American churches (Baptist, Congregationalist,
and Presbyterian) with whom they were in correspondence, for continuing to condone slavery. In 1844 the Congregational Union had
written that no American fraternal delegates would be received who
were apologists for slavery. The Scots Presbyterians considered an
overture on American slavery the same year, and two years later debated whether they could maintain fraternal correspondence with
the American Presbyterian General Assembly while it continued to
countenance slavery. Abolitionist sentiment permeated the British
constituency of the Alliance in 1845 and 1846, as was evident from
the resolution of the Birmingham Aggregate Committee on March
31, 1846, "that invitations for the London Conference ought not to be
sent to individuals, who, whether by their own fault or otherwise, may
be in the unhappy position of holding their fellow-men as slaves." [14]
The British were more willing to welcome a slave than a slaveholder,
and the Alliance would never have gotten off the ground in Great
Britain if it had countenanced slaveholding by Christians.

The American delegates who arrived that summer were startled
by the intensity and rigor of British church opinion on this subject.
Only one of them, the Presbyterian Dr. T. Smyth of Charleston, who
admitted to owning nine slaves, would defend the system as such,
and he was quickly made aware that he was not welcome in Great
Britain. Several of the American delegates were actively opposed to
slavery and had paid more of a price for their convictions than their
British critics, few of whom had done more than make rhetorical
demonstrations before sympathetic audiences. But the American national denominations were able to keep their unity only by tolerating
slaveholding in the southern regions. The prevailing American
church tactic was to temporize and hope something could be accomplished by "colonization" in Africa. The Americans were taken aback

by the Birmingham resolution and pointed out that this position should have been announced before delegations from America were solicited, not after plans had been made. That resolution seemed to commit them to disfellowship their slaveholding sections. To try to coerce Americans would embarrass them in their struggle at home, since they would be represented as yielding to foreign pressures.

The slavery controversy was also tangled up with the question of the constitutional structure of the Alliance. The Liverpool planners had thought in terms simply of a British organization, with perhaps overseas affiliates. But the Americans as a group supported the more ambitious proposal of Samuel Schmucker, of a genuinely worldwide ecumenical body. They carried the London Conference with them at first, until the controversy over slaveholding as a test of fellowship emerged. Then they were forced back to a federative structure with each branch free to set its own terms of discipline. The Americans, however, were served notice that unless they did purge their churches of the slavery taint, their branch would be disavowed by the mother branch in Great Britain. Thus it was not a "faith and order" issue, but slavery, which, in 1846, proved to be "the insurmountable barrier to oecumenical union." [15] The Evangelical Alliance, wrote its chairman, Sir Culling Eardley Smith, "sacrificed to its sense of duty in the matter of slavery, the cherished idea of an immediate, numerous, mutually responsible Ecumenical membership." [16]

For nearly thirty years more the transatlantic ecumenical bond was tenuous, and the Evangelical Alliance barely existed in the United States. The American churches were regarded in Great Britain much as the Reformed Church of South Africa is often viewed in ecumenical opinion in the mid-twentieth century, as living in open and unrepentant sin. The American delegates met in New York in May, 1847, and attempted to organize an American branch, with their own way of handling the slavery issue. At the next world conference of the Alliance, at the time of the 1851 Exposition in London, Robert Baird was almost the only American delegate. He expressed in an address an American testiness with the continual criticism from England, and noted an increasing alienation. As he wrote the editor of the *Presbyterian*,[17] "things were getting to such a pass that no American could even attend their religious anniversaries without being insulted." In fact, the Evangelical Alliance was never to amount to much in the United States until after the Civil War had ended slavery. Then the American churches entered the evangelical ecumene with a rush.

The Evangelical Alliance had scarcely planted a foothold in German territory, on the other side, when all central Europe exploded in the Revolution of 1848. Out of this excitement was born a sister organization, the German Kirchentag, which in a measure made the Alliance seem unnecessary in Germany and impeded its growth there. On the other hand, the Kirchentag was suffused with the nationalist enthusiasm of those years, and in no way matched the international scope of the Alliance. The gathering at Wittenberg was a defensive move in part, as against the anticlerical persecutions expected from the revolutionaries. It also expressed the hope of many Protestants for some kind of union of the many territorial churches into which German Protestantism was divided. The resultant fellowship and mutual recognition among Lutherans, United, Reformed, Moravians, and others was a "strangely novel spectacle." Doctrinally the Kirchentag rested on the Bible interpreted by the catholic creeds and Reformation confessions, especially the Augsburg Confession understood as open to a Reformed interpretation on Article X. The strict Lutherans and the rationalist left wing stood aside.

The prophetic voice at Wittenberg was that of J. H. Wichern, the greatest German churchman of the century. He presented an ecumenical vision of a Christian rebirth of church and nation in which the lay priesthood would find its expression in the Christian charity of voluntary organizations, and a genuine people's church would be created. In fact, however, ecclesiastical union was not effected, nor a people's church, nor was the alienation of the proletariat overcome. The churches remained captive to the monarchy and patriarchal social order, and the enduring product of Wichern's campaign was the cooperative structure of the Inner Mission, comparable to some of the evangelistic and philanthropic societies of the English-speaking world. The related annual gatherings of the Kirchentag provided, in Schaff's judgment, "by far the largest and most respectable representation of evangelical Christianity" in Germany.[18]

The realities of the ecclesiastical situation had thus compelled both the Evangelical Alliance and the Kirchentag to abandon hopes of church union and settle for the association of individuals. Any union of churches in Europe must build on existing state churches in which the ultimate authority was the civil ruler. Would one enter into ecumenical conversations with the heads of state, who were, on occasion, professed infidels or notorious profligates?[19] And if one turned to the community of the faithful, he found that everyone was baptized and confirmed as a matter of social etiquette, whether genuinely devout or an unblushing unbeliever. A significant portion of the clergy and professors of theology, again, were personally indifferent, satisfied to fulfill their obligations as civil servants. Philip Schaff, who had grown up in the Continental system, had in the 1850's come to believe that such indiscrimination was a greater evil than sectarianism. The only convincing ecumenical program was that of the Alliance, "union on the basis of religious liberty," even if it meant placing "all evangelical confessions and sects on a perfectly civil and religious equality, so that the distinction between Church and sect disappears altogether." [20] Schaff questioned the desirability of a confederation of churches such as churches then were in Europe, feeling that "the mission of Protestantism, for the present at least," lay rather in the free association of individual Christians.[21]

Apart from its periodic conferences, regional and ecumenical, the journal *Evangelical Christendom* with its news of the Christian world, and its schedule of prayer for unity, the Alliance was chiefly active in defense of religious liberty, seeking to focus moral and diplomatic influence where it would do the most good. The largest number of cases of persecution came, as one might expect, from Roman Catholic countries, but by no means all. It was the republican and largely Protestant Swiss who began the series with a vindictive persecution of a religious minority in Vaud in the very year of the London Conference. In 1849 it was the ex-priest Dr. Achilli in Rome, then two years later several Florentine Protestants. Most notorious was the case of the Madiai, sentenced to the galleys for five years for reading the Bible. But the memorials went to the Sultan of the Ottoman Empire about the time of the Crimean War, and again twenty years later, and to the Shah of Persia over the Nestorians in 1861. Most famous of all were probably the Spanish cases of the 1860's, but representations went twice to the Czar of Russia, as well as to Francis Joseph I of Austria, to the Japanese in 1872. Sir Culling Smith usually organized and led the deputation and presented the memorials. Philip Schaff was elected spokesman of the international delegation to the Russian czar, appealing for cessation of the attempt to force Baltic Lutherans into the Orthodox State Church.

This kind of activity, however, did not commend the Alliance to the state churches of the Continent. Few of them espoused religious liberty without substantial qualifications. The Alliance found itself making representations to the governments of Sweden and several German states on behalf of the Baptists and to the Swiss for the

Salvation Army. The Dutch and many German churches tended to identify the Alliance with Baptist proselyting. The Continental Protestants who did associate freely with the Alliance tended to be the minority free churches of France and French Switzerland, or the small minorities in Belgium, Spain, Italy. The larger Reformed state churches in the Netherlands, France, and Switzerland were dominated most of the time by a rationalist bureaucracy which had little theological sympathy with the Alliance; and where the conservatives were in power in Germany, they were often confessional Lutherans hostile to anything Reformed or "unionistic." There was almost no contact with the Bohemian or Magyar Protestants in the Austrian Empire. The whole outlook of the Alliance seemed alien to most Continental Protestants and its significance there never approached that reached in the English-speaking world.

The relation of religious liberty to ecumenism received perhaps its fullest airing when the Alliance first met in a Lutheran country. The initial proposal of a Stockholm conference evoked opposition from the Swedish state church. Ten bishops signed a circular against it and no bishop, pastor, or theological professor would sign an invitation. They did not want to admit "dissenters" into Sweden. Even the *American Lutheran* remarked that the Alliance "suffered itself to be used as a tool for breaking into people's houses." [22] After all, the Alliance had had occasion to make protestations to Sweden in the interests of religious liberty, and the Swedes remembered.

So barely four months before the projected meeting, in April, 1884, invitations were sent out for Copenhagen instead of Stockholm. But Denmark had little more tradition of toleration than Sweden and the friends of the Alliance there were few and far between. The great majority of the Lutheran clergy were hostile or indifferent, "partly from exclusiveness and bigotry, partly from ignorance of the nature and aim of the E.A." [23] But the conference opened without incident; four of the seven Danish bishops put in an appearance, as did even the royal family.

Under these circumstances a discussion of the relation of religious liberty to ecumenism called for some wisdom and tact. Schaff himself united these traits with courage in a notable address (September 2, 1884) on the "Discord and Concord of Christendom, or Denominational Variety and Christian Unity." Nearly all the main divisions of Christendom, he declared, had been guilty of intolerance or exclusiveness, some of actual persecution and proscriptive legislation. Such actions demeaned Christ. Most churches now had come to repudiate the theory and practice of coercion in religion. "The problem of mutual recognition and Christian union" was receiving increased attention in connection with religious liberty, "and is slowly but surely approaching a solution which can only be effected on the basis of freedom." "Experience teaches," Schaff continued, "that most of those countries which recognize and tolerate but one organized form of Christianity are most backward in spiritual life and energy. . . . Denominationalism or Confessionalism . . . is not the best state of the Church, but it is far better than a dead or tyrannical and monotonous uniformity." [24]

Schaff was no doctrinaire on the point. "I regard it one of the most difficult problems of Church government and statesmanship," he wrote, "to define the exact limits of religious toleration, i.e., not simply the liberty of conscience, which no despot can deny, but the liberty of public worship with the right of proselyting, in those countries which still hold to the principle of some official connection of the government with the Christian religion and national Church establishment. This problem, I believe, cannot be solved abstractly by theory, but only practically and gradually by the irresistible course of events. . . . There are questions which are too knotty for philosophy and theology." [25]

The enthusiastic reception of this address startled Schaff. He had looked for no very cordial response, but received more thanks and congratulations than ever in his life before. "Thus," he reported, "I have been permitted before scholars and princes to bear my testimony against the divisions and distractions of Christendom, and for Christian union on the basis of religious liberty. This is the idea and aim of the Alliance." [26]

The American branch of the Alliance signalized its effective advent into the world organization after the Civil War by inviting the Amsterdam Assembly in 1867 to hold its next world conference in New York City in 1870. The American central committee was composed predominantly of New Yorkers, several of them Presbyterians connected with Union Theological Seminary. Professor H. B. Smith, the leading theologian of the New School Presbyterian Church, was assigned to make the arrangements, and when he fell ill Philip Schaff inherited the task. Virtually single-handedly he selected the European delegates, made up the roster of speakers, and assigned themes. For what turned out to be four years he carried the whole burden of administrative correspondence.

The date had to be twice postponed. At the urgency of the British, the Americans first scheduled the conference for 1869. Then in February of that year the British reported that it was too soon, so the Americans recalled the invitations and moved it to 1870. Arrangements had been made for several hundred and then the Franco-Prussian War broke out. After some protests Schaff sent out word in August of a second postponement. But since some delegates were already on the way, some meeting had to be arranged for them in September of 1870.

After the war the Executive Committee began preparations again in 1872. Schaff was sent to Europe and attended the General Synod of the French Reformed Church that year, the first legal synod since the revocation of the Edict of Nantes. When the Synod agreed to send delegates to New York, even if there were to be Germans there, Schaff felt the conference had been saved. But when he tried to reactivate his old list of speakers and delegates he found that he had lost a great part of them. So off he went to Europe again in 1873 on a last whirlwind tour to do much of his work all over again. When during the Council in September Schaff entertained over a hundred foreign delegates in his home, one can imagine that he felt an almost proprietary interest. Four years' labor, he recorded, "was abundantly rewarded," as he looked back on "the most important chapter of my life." [27] New York was the greatest of the "evangelical ecumenical councils" [28] of the Alliance, in considerable measure a Protestant counterpart to Vatican I.

This is not to say that Schaff was representative of the outlook of the American branch of the Alliance, or the British. Few others seem to have had the scope of his ecumenical vision. Most were wholly unaware of the Orthodox and effectually ruled out Roman Catholicism as unchristian, looking for no more than pan-Protestant irenics at most. But they listened to Schaff and heard him out; they permitted him an unprecedented breadth in his invitations to New York. Who else would have thought of inviting the Old Catholics to an Evangelical Alliance meeting? The speakers at the New York conference on the theme of Christian union were sensational in their caution, as is illustrated by the fact that the only one who got so definite as to talk of mutual recognition of denominations was Charles Hodge of Princeton. Schaff's own ecumenical strategy, however, while under the circumstances accepting the pattern of voluntary association of individuals in the Evangelical Alliance or the Kirchentag, looked also to confederations of churches as such, including the Roman Catholic and Orthodox.

Schaff was to continue as foreign corresponding secretary until 1874 and then again from 1876 to 1888. He attended all the successive General Councils of the Alliance: at Basel, 1879; Copenhagen, 1884; Florence, 1891; and finally Chicago, 1893. At all of these he read papers of substance, usually the most important paper by any American delegate. It seems fair to say that for nearly a quarter of a century Schaff was the key figure in the international Alliance, the most significant ecumenical organization of the time.[29]

The New York Conference of 1873 seems to have been the high-water mark of Evangelical Alliance history. In the 1880's ecumenical leadership seemed to be passing to other hands, among them those of the World Alliance of Reformed Churches. One often hears the explanation that the theology of the Basis became antiquated and an obstacle. That is no doubt true, but one could say the same for the 1840 theology of the Congregationalists, Presbyterians, or Episcopalians. Why could not the Alliance rework its theology as they did? Is not the explanation perhaps as much institutional as theological? The Alliance, we have argued, was the ecumenical expression of the voluntary society system. But the system was already in decline when the Alliance was born in 1846. It was being cannibalized by the churches, who were thus creating their own denominational missionary and publishing agencies, even Bible societies. The voluntary undenominational societies were being replaced by the denominational "boards." But at the same time the churches thus incorporated the evangelical functions and concerns which had shaped the ecumenical drive. The consequence was that the reconstituted church structures assimilated also evangelical ecumenism. By the end of the century the center of ecumenical attention had passed to the relations among churches and their "boards."

The Evangelical Alliance, and more generally the whole system of interdenominational voluntary societies, was also the appropriate ecumenical form for the early-nineteenth-century relation of states and churches. One could expect little official ecumenical action from churches controlled by civil authority. Both in England and the United States, voluntary societies proved to be the most effective way of bridging the difficult gap between state churches and free churches. In Germany the societies brought about effective, if unofficial, co-operation across the frontiers of the numerous Landeskirchen, sometimes of different confessions.

From the time of the French Revolution a great transformation of the millennial Constantinian union of church and state was in progress, as the European governments made ever clearer their inner emancipation from Christian convictions and norms. The anomaly of the administration of churches by such governments grew ever more painful and helps to explain the epidemic of church-state conflicts in the 1830's and 1840's in most countries with Reformed churches. Gradually governments were persuaded to concede more independence to their churches, and in turn to open to them possibilities of interchurch relations. Thus the accelerated ecumenical pace of the nineteenth and twentieth centuries was in large measure the counterpart of the process of secularization of the state. Voluntary societies continued to be significant thereafter in ecumenical life, especially such institutions as the Y.M.C.A. and the Student Christian Movement; but in the more recent period, churches as such have taken over the leadership in ecumenical work.

XI

THE WORLD ALLIANCE OF REFORMED AND PRESBYTERIAN CHURCHES

IN A SENSE one may say that the conception of the World Reformed Alliance[1] was as old as that of the Evangelical Alliance, and that the two were complementary and interrelated from the beginning. There was a very substantial overlapping of personnel throughout. The organizing nucleus of the Evangelical Alliance was composed of the British Reformed, specifically the Free Church of Scotland and the English Congregationalists. The Scots, especially, hoped originally for a confederation of *churches,* but gave this up in order to find a basis to include Baptists, Methodists, and others. But the hope remained. When Professor James McCosh of Belfast bore a message from the Council of the British branch to the United States in 1866, to urge an American branch, he also had letters from his church to the evangelical Presbyterian bodies in the States. And it was during the Evangelical Alliance meeting in New York in 1873 that a large meeting of Reformed and Presbyterian delegates decided to try to organize a world league of Reformed church bodies. All the founding members of the World Reformed Alliance were already members of the Evangelical Alliance and committed to that broader but unofficial basis of Christian union. The three most influential founders were James McCosh, Philip Schaff, William Garden Blaikie.

The organizing committee met at London in 1873. From the first planning meetings Schaff was a faithful attendant at every sitting of the World Reformed Alliance except the General Council held in Toronto the year before he died. In 1875 Schaff formulated to I. A. Dorner his conception of its role as follows:

> We have the Christian union of individual believers in the Evangelical Alliance and now this is a confederation of

193

churches of all Presbyterian and Reformed bodies. The last
step would be organic union in one body, which will hardly
appear till the millennium. But, in the meantime, the Lutheran churches should have a Lutheran alliance, and the
Episcopalians, Methodists and other ecclesiastical families
should have their alliances. In this way the problem of union
would be simplified.[2]

This last suggestion was in fact largely realized before Schaff's
death. The World Reformed Alliance became the model of a series
of world denominational alliances: Anglican, Methodist, Congregational, Lutheran. (The Anglicans date their Lambeth Conferences
from 1867, but this was an ad hoc consultation occasioned largely by
the Colenso affair. The conception of a continuing consultation on a
regular schedule was first developed by the Reformed Alliance.) And
at least in the case of the Reformed, the world confessional structure
was from the beginning set in the context of expectation of a wider
union.

When the first council of the World Reformed Alliance met in
Edinburgh in 1877, Schaff was commissioned to pick and invite dele-
gates from the Continent and the Near East as he had done for the
New York Evangelical Alliance conference three years before.

"The chief difficulty in the way," Schaff had written, "is to secure
official delegates from the various National and State Churches." [3]
It was the old problem he had remarked on twenty years before with
regard to the organization of the German Kirchentag (see above,
p. 186). How could one relate ecumenically Christian groups without
effective standards, discipline, or internal organization? These Continental state churches were legally unable to act without government
authorization, and the governments were not interested in ecumenical
ventures. Furthermore, the churches were unable to define and maintain a platform or purpose. In the churches of Zwingli and Calvin
the old confessions had been abolished and almost anything could be
preached. The Swiss politicians who administered church affairs considered that the pulpit should be adjusted to the various shades of
belief or unbelief in the population generally. In 1872 the French
government had permitted the first Protestant synod to meet in generations, but then would not permit its decisions to be carried out.

The Edinburgh Council, accordingly, had two choices. Either it
excluded these Continental churches altogether, or it should invite

from them individual evangelical leaders just as the Evangelical Alliance had done. This was not in accordance with the Constitution of 1875, but a strict enforcement of that Constitution would leave them with an Anglo-American Alliance deprived of a Continental contribution. Schaff, accordingly, urged that the Constitution be compromised in this fashion. It was just not possible in the 1870's to effect an ecumenical relation among official church bodies even among the Reformed alone. The World Alliance, consequently, was not strictly, although it was primarily, a league of *churches*. And for France, Switzerland, the Netherlands, Belgium, Italy, the delegations to the World Reformed Alliance and to the Evangelical Alliance were essentially the same people.

Schaff's hope of the Reformed and similar confederations was that they might address directly the faith and order issues which were beyond the scope of the Evangelical Alliance. After all, his chair at Union Seminary was in "Symbolics," which he defined as "comparative dogmatics," pointing the way to future harmony.[4] His favorite lifelong ecumenical project was planning for a doctrinal consensus, both of the Reformed and, consequently, of evangelical catholicism at large.

"The Consensus of Evangelical Protestant Christendom," he wrote, "waits yet for its proper expression." The nine articles of the Evangelical Alliance had served a good practical purpose, but something better might be hoped from a general conference after mature deliberation and cooperation of all the branch Alliances. Before that, however, each of the great leading families "should simplify their symbols and set forth what they consider essential for all Christians to believe. Then they might come together and compare notes. Such movements are in progress." [5]

The London sessions planning the Constitution of the World Reformed Alliance had based it on an undefined consensus of Reformed doctrine. "It will be," wrote Schaff, "one of the most important tasks of a future Presbyterian Council to formulate this consensus. The difficulty is not so great as might be imagined, for there is really a very remarkable agreement between the Helvetic, Gallican, Belgic, English, Scotch and other Reformed Confessions of the sixteenth and seventeenth centuries in all essential articles of faith." [6] This project was to be Schaff's characteristic concern for the next fifteen years in the World Reformed Alliance.

The most notable paper delivered at the first Council of the World

Reformed Alliance in Edinburgh, July 4, 1877, was by Philip Schaff, entitled "The Consensus of the Reformed Confessions, as related to the present state of evangelical theology." [7] Schaff began with the famous interchange between Calvin and Cranmer on a doctrinal consensus and then swiftly outlined the chief Reformed confessions and their consensus as a kind of Salnard brought up to date.

But what was the status in the nineteenth century of these Reformation documents after the successive movements of eighteenth-century rationalism and the nineteenth-century evangelical revival? Schaff noted five main modifications:

1. The Scriptural norm of authority remained, although there was considerable modification in conceptions of the *mode* of inspiration.
2. In its polemic standpoint modern theology was less anti-Roman than opposed to unbelief. It was less focused, consequently, on soteriology and more on the doctrine of God and especially of Christ.
3. Sectarian bigotry was losing its hold and all theology was more catholic and irenic.
4. High Calvinism was generally abandoned. The canons of Dort could not be passed by any Continental synod today.
5. Religious liberty had become generally acknowledged in contrast to the sixteenth century. Christian debate henceforth must be on the basis of freedom and civil equality.

Specifically, what should the Alliance do in this new situation about the "consensus of Reformed doctrine"? They might just leave the question open, but it would probably be forced upon them sooner or later. If they did define it, should they simply accept a historical summary of the classical statements? Or should they adopt a list of loci, like the nine points of the Evangelical Alliance? Or, and this was obviously Schaff's hope, should they proceed to "a new ecumenical Reformed confession," a testimony of living faith in the nineteenth century and a bond of union? It should simplify Reformed doctrine in fraternal spirit to other evangelical churches.

But Schaff confessed he had grave doubts as to whether the time was ripe. It was very dubious whether the traditionalist Americans could find common ground with the individualistic and liberal Continental churches. A confession, moreover, was not to be concocted in the study, it was an act of faith and fervor in times of deep religious testing.

The discussion was extensive and ended, as one might predict, with a committee on confessions, with Dr. Schaff to be chairman. The Committee was to investigate the confessional status of the member churches, the standards they acknowledged and the terms of subscription they exacted. This material was collected and reported to the next Council, which met in Philadelphia in 1880.

Philadelphia postponed action four years more until Belfast, and on the eve of the Belfast Council in 1884 Schaff's hopes came to grief as the Committee on the Consensus Creed for the Reformed Churches met in Edinburgh. Schaff spoke for the project on the floor of the Belfast Council, but it was defeated by the joined votes of the traditionalist and liberal wings, who opposed it for different reasons. But something of the same nature was nailed down in the great debate over the admission of the Cumberland Presbyterians which marked this Council. Some American Southern Presbyterians, in particular, opposed the admission of the Cumberlanders because of the changes the latter had made in the Westminster Confession in expunging its "fatalism." Philip Schaff was an influential voice in winning admission for the "semi-Arminianism" of the Cumberlanders, a decision which implied that high predestinarianism was not essential to the definition of the Reformed consensus held by the Alliance.

Schaff's pressure toward filing down the rougher edges of inherited polemics was felt a year later in the Presbyterian General Assembly. In a debate over the validity of Roman Catholic baptism it was Schaff's amendment which carried. It was to the effect that, while corrupt, the Roman Catholic Church was still a branch of the visible church of Christ and its baptism was valid and could not be repeated. Similarly in the Evangelical Alliance Council at Florence, Italy, in 1891, Schaff came out against antipopery: "For more than 300 years Protestants of the radical type have been abusing the pope as Anti-Christ, papists as idolaters, and the Church of Rome as the great apostasy and as the synagogue of Satan. Is this courteous? Is it charitable? Is it Christian?" With regard to Roman Catholicism, he urged: "We do not pray for her destruction—God forbid!—but for her reformation. . . . We cannot expect or wish Italy to become Protestant, but we do hope and pray that she may become evangelical and Christian in the best sense of the term." [8] Italy ought not to break with her Catholic tradition and import a foreign religion, but to renew and purify her Catholicism. Schaff had maintained this ecumenical openness to Roman Catholicism for five decades. In his *History of the Apostolic Church* (1853), he had written: "The deeper . . . tendency of the time is thus towards . . . a higher union of Protestantism and Catholicism, in their pure forms, freed from their respective errors and infirmities. We might indulge the hope that a union, or at least a friendly approach of the two greatest principles of church history, and of the pious portions of the two most hostile sections of Christendom, will precede the second coming of our Lord, and the perfection of his Kingdom, when there shall be one fold and one shepherd." [9]

The movement for revision of the Westminster Confession, which arose in the American Presbyterian Church in 1889 and spread so rapidly, revived Schaff's hopes which had been discouraged at Belfast five years before. It promised not only to eliminate the doctrine of preterition and the antipopery clauses from the old confession but also to form "a new, shorter, more scriptural and popular creed, that shall express in an irenic, evangelical and catholic spirit, the living faith of the present age rather than the faith of the seventeenth century." [10]

Schaff's famous colleague Charles Briggs undoubtedly spoke for both men when he wrote:

> We should use our utmost endeavors to construct a new consensus creed that will better express Christian faith than the old creeds. The Alliance of Presbyterian Churches is approaching this problem with some degree of hopefulness of ultimate success. When each of the great alliances of Christian denominations has reduced its symbols to consensus creeds, it will be easier to frame a consensus creed in which all may unite.[11]

When Schaff delivered his swan song, "The Reunion of Christendom," at the Chicago Parliament of Religion in 1893,[12] he again expressed the hope and expectation of a brief Reformed Consensus creed. He noted that the Methodists, Congregationalists, and Episcopalians had now all organized world federations also. He could still speculate on the reunion of the "entire Catholic Church," Greek and Roman, with Protestantism. It would require restatement of all the controverted issues and neutralization of the mutual anathemas and curses. To the end, thus, he kept his hope and faith in the possibilities of doctrinal resolution of faith and order issues and an approach to the problem which accepted the centrality of these issues.

"God has owned and blessed these several denominations and uses them. . . . True union can only be built on the historic basis of mutual recognition of the peculiar gifts of God which he has bestowed upon the various branches of his Church, and the work which they have done and are still doing in the world.

"The denominations must lay down their exclusiveness, their vanity and pride. They must cease to imagine and to boast that they have the monopoly of truth. . . . Romanists must learn to recognize genuine Christian life and power outside of the papacy. Episcopalians must acknowledge the validity of non-Episcopalian orders. Lutherans must concede to the Reformed that they have the real sacrament, although they cannot accept the notion of a corporeal presence or oral manducation. Calvinists must not so hold divine sovereignty as to deny human responsibility, and Arminians must not teach human freedom to the exclusion of the all-controlling purpose of the Almighty. Baptists must allow other modes of baptism than by immersion." [13]

Schaff's argument was harmonistic, that the aspects of truth in the several traditions were all complementary, and that the incompatible items were "idols" and better dropped. But how many of those who would fault him for eclecticism had opened themselves as honestly to the evident actuality of God's work through other apparently incommensurable traditions?

There was also a negative or purgative function for critical history. All the contending orthodoxies would in time have to make their peace with critical history. The church had in the past learned with some agony to come to terms with Aristotle, Copernicus, evolution; it had given up in most cases the theory of persecution, of witchcraft. Favorite texts such as the Donation of Constantine and the pseudo-Isidorian decretals, or one or another Biblical proof text had been rendered incapable of settling or even furthering ecclesiastical polemics. Similar changes in historical judgment might in the future substantially change the ecumenical situation. What a change had there been in Schaff's lifetime since Neander in Protestant history of the medieval papacy, and in Catholic treatments of the Reformers, culminating in Doellinger on Luther or Kampschulte on Calvin! And it was Schaff's expressed hope in developing the American church history series that such a series of studies in comparative denominationalism would help to bring all closer together. Impartial history would find no ideal church in any age, but the footprints of Christ on every age and every church.

With this hope in the influence of historical study and the relativizations implied, there went some shift in eschatological thought. Schaff still utilized the language of organism, of a theocratic totality, in his later years, but no longer as a paradigm for practical action. It was now an image of the transfigured future of the Lord's Return, which was not continuous simply with the conditions of our historical struggle. Applied improperly to the historical situation, as he had realized in the 1850's, it might easily become the ideology of political reaction.

The ecumenical calling was rather to recognize, maintain, or promote unity in the midst of ecclesiastical diversity so far as truth and conscience would permit. The basis of that unity was at hand in the living union of the faithful men with Christ and the communion of saints deriving from it. One could only belong to the church catholic through one of these several traditions, but each within his tradition could recognize the others generously and live in hope of new creative possibilities.

Schaff's project of a consensus creed for the Reformed churches was revived a full generation later after the First World War. There was a lively and instructive debate at the Cardiff General Council of the World Reformed Alliance in 1925 as to whether such a creed were feasible or desirable. The most extensive and provocative statement (the full text would have taken over two hours!) came from a young Swiss theologian from the University of Göttingen, named Karl Barth, and marked his debut before the Alliance.

Barth's cautions did not dissuade the Council from appointing a committee to prepare a draft for the next Council, but the report of that Committee at Boston four years later recommended that the matter be dropped. Theological diversity within the Council seemed greater, if anything, than in the 1880's. Some preferred a brief affirmation of faith of more liturgical than doctrinal character.

Barth's conception of a creed was something distinct from either a hymn or a consensus. For him a creed was an act of desperation or Christian compulsion. "There are things you may and can do only when you must. . . ." [14] A creed should be presented only when a church had something important and definite to say in God's name about God's revelation and will for his church. Barth asked the Cardiff fathers whether they really were under any such compulsion.

Only nine years later, however, the Barmen Confession of 1934 was to illustrate his conception. To be sure, the Barmen Confession was not a statement of Reformed doctrine; it was more nearly a union declaration for Reformed, United, and Lutheran Christians in the face of Nazi Christianity. But it was to become one of the great historic confessions and to win official acknowledgment by many churches, not only in Germany but as far afield as the American Presbyterians. It is unlikely that any balanced consensus platform could have won comparable authority in the Reformed churches as a reminder of the ground of their unity.

Apart from faith and order issues, it was generally agreed that the chief interest of the Alliance, and its greatest success, in the forty years up to the First World War, was in missionary cooperation. These decades saw the climax of the foreign missions enthusiasm in Western churches and nowhere more so than among the Reformed and Presbyterians. Meetings of synods and assemblies without a program on missions were unusual. At the Washington Council in 1899 self-congratulations were expressed:

> The Presbyterian Churches of the new and the old world are doing a larger amount of Foreign Mission work, and reaping a more abundant and a more satisfactory missionary harvest, than any other of the great sections into which the followers of Christ are divided. It is computed that the Presbyterian Churches contribute about one-fourth of the entire sum (£2 000 000) raised . . . , the Episcopalian Churches contributing about one-sixth, while the other denominations, Methodists, Baptist, etc., contribute smaller fractions.[15]

The Reformed missions leaders also knew themselves to be the chief promoters of cooperation and unity in missions.[16] This was their most characteristic ecumenical expression in these years. In this they inherited and developed further the work begun by the Evangelical Alliance. Others approached ecumenism in other ways, as the Anglicans, for example, sought administrative unity along the lines of the Lambeth Quadrilateral, and gave the major impetus to Lausanne and the Faith and Order movement. But it was the Reformed who were the backbone of the movement which consolidated after Edinburgh 1910 into the International Missionary Council.

In this general orientation of the Presbyterian and Reformed churches the Alliance was able to play a significant role. This had been intended from the beginning. The overture to the Irish General Assembly of 1873, which was then picked up by the General Assembly of the Presbyterian U.S.A. Church, requested the opening of correspondence

> with other churches holding by the Westminster Confession of faith, with the view of bringing about an Ecumenical Council of such churches, to consider subjects of common interest to all, and especially to promote harmony of action in the mission at home and abroad.[17]

Other objectives stood beside "harmony of action in the mission field" when the Constitution of the Alliance was finally drafted, but no others won more support in the decades that followed. A committee on cooperation in foreign missions was at once established, with North American and British sections. It was to gather information as to fields occupied, methods used, possibilities of cooperation or consolidation, and to report to the next Council. This was generally agreed, but few realized the dimensions of the assignment.

Elaborate reports were submitted by both subcommittees to the Council at Philadelphia in 1880. There was now a much clearer idea of the problems, as, for example, that there "should continue to be four native churches in India ruled by four churches in Scotland, and probably as many more ruled by separate American churches; not to speak of an Indian-English Presbyterian Church, an Indian-Welsh Presbyterian Church, etc." Or, again, in the New Hebrides, "is the native church to continue to be governed from five centers, geographically so far apart from each other as Scotland, Canada, Australia, New Zealand, Otago and Southland?" [18]

The issues were focused especially on two matters: first, the division of territory in comity agreements, and second, the internal reorganization of young churches to constitute a single native church out of the fragments of several foreign churches on the same territory. Most attention was given in the 1880's to the second matter.

The great missionary conventions, of 1854, 1868, 1878, 1888, 1900, 1910, in all of which the Presbyterians and Reformed carried at least their share, were by constitution, at least until the last, largely precluded from *doing* anything. They overflowed with rhetoric and enthusiasm and passed into history. The Alliance was for a decade or so the only agency in a position to focus debate and push toward common policy. As was said in 1888:

> The central, impartial position of the Alliance, and its representative character, enabled it to do what has been done and with a promptness and decision which could have been reached in no other way. . . . It will ultimately lead to the cooperation of nearly all Protestant bodies in the definite purpose to raise up . . . in each heathen land, a native church.[19]

One might argue that it was in part the very size of the Presbyterian and Reformed investment in missions which pushed them to ecumenism. Throughout the whole period it was a commonplace that the initiative and conviction about unity came from the mission field, from the missionaries themselves. The more missionaries, the more ecumenists. The Alliance then became a forum, wherein the views and proposals of the workers on the field achieved extended resonance among the home churches.

Among missionaries all through this period, the prevailing conception of missionary policy was that of Rufus Anderson, the missionary statesman of the American Board of Commissioners for Foreign Missions. The goal of missions, it was held, was to produce in each country, a self-supporting, self-governing, self-propagating church. This conception was rarely, if ever, challenged in Alliance circles. The debates were on preliminary steps and on timing.

The missionaries had already accomplished much before the Alliance was launched in 1877. Probably the most important contribution of the Councils of Edinburgh (1877), Philadelphia (1880), and Belfast (1884), in this connection, was the wide publicity given to ecumenical activities already under way in various mission fields. By the end of the 1880's the Alliance had visibly shifted its views on missionary policy as a result.

At the beginning of the decade the prevailing patterns of Presbyterian missions precluded effective unity on the mission field. Wherever missionaries organized a "native" presbytery, that presbytery was integrated as a constituent part of a home synod. Thus the presbyteries of North Laos and Siam belonged to the Synod of New York (U.S.A.), and in Bombay one might find fragments of various Scottish and Irish Presbyterian churches. Needless to say, the representation in the home synod was extremely irregular and ineffective, but it was sufficient to tie the hands of the native presbytery in meeting the needs of its own situation.

The American Southern Presbyterians had advanced beyond this practice in an ecumenical direction. The goal conceived by their spokesman Leighton Wilson was one native presbytery in any given area, to which the converts of all Presbyterian missions in the area should be sent. The missionaries, however, were not to belong to the native presbytery. They were conceived as evangelists, fundamentally itinerants, and would maintain ecclesiastical connections only with the sending churches.

This last feature, however, did not commend itself to other Presbyterian bodies and prevented merger, e.g., with Presbyterians U.S.A. in areas such as Mexico and Ningpo. The more general opinion was that it was wiser to associate missionaries with the presbyteries, either as full members, or at least as advisory assessors. And by the time of the first meeting of the Alliance there was some experience with this pattern.

The most famous instance was from south China. In general the enormous Chinese Empire was not the most auspicious territory for missionary union. Diversity of language, added to the vast population and the distances, made effective consolidation unlikely. But something unique had occurred in the immense area in the south where the Amoy dialect was spoken. The missions there of the American Reformed Dutch and the English Presbyterians had worked in close harmony from the beginning. In 1862 they had on their own initiative set up a joint Presbytery of Amoy (or Presbytery of Chang-Chew and Chin-Chew) in which American, English, and Chinese ministers were jointly enrolled. The English Presbyterians accepted the arrangement, but the Reformed Church of America General Synod sent out instructions to its missionaries to form a separate Classis of Amoy as a part of the Synod of Albany. The missionaries, however, refused to break up the union presbytery and one of them, G. M. Tallmadge, succeeded in persuading the General Synod to reverse its ruling in 1863. Thereafter the American Reformed Dutch were to maintain a pioneering leadership in missionary ecumenism.

The Presbytery of Amoy grew and prospered as an independent Chinese Presbyterian church aided by two different Western bodies. Originally there were three American, two English, and seven or eight Chinese members. Two decades later there were about the same number of Westerners, but nearly thirty Chinese. The church developed its own financing, missions, even a confession of faith. To be sure, the missionaries were not subject to discipline save from home, and retained control of missionary funds. To that extent the system was hierarchical rather than presbyterian.

The island of Trinidad in the West Indies saw a comparable development. Initiated in 1863 also, it lapsed for a time and then was revived in 1872. A Presbyterian Church of Trinidad was constituted of two ministers of the Scottish United Presbyterian Church, two Canadian Presbyterian missionaries to the Hindu immigrants, and a minister of the Portuguese Free Church among the refugees from Madeira. In this case the Canadian and United Church authorities had concurred. The missionaries here were subordinated to presbytery, but with a right of appeal to the supreme court of the home church.[20]

Japan provided a third instance of an independent national Presbyterian church out of diverse elements. After consultations in the early 1870's, the Union Church of Christ in Japan was constituted in 1876 by the three missions of the American Presbyterians (U.S.A.), the American Reformed Dutch, and the Scottish United Presbyterians. Four years later the church was divided into three presbyteries under a General Assembly. By 1885 there were forty-four congregations and a union theological seminary in Tokyo. By 1888 the American German Reformed, the Southern Presbyterians, the Women's Missionary Union of America, the Cumberland Presbyterians, and the American Congregationalists were considering merger in the Church of Christ, involving in all some two thirds of Japanese Protestantism. In blocking this development, Joseph Neesima was to prove that not all opposition to merger came from the West, but the unitive movement in Japan was still strong. It was noted that the various branches of the Methodist and Anglican churches in Japan were drawing together also in the late 1880's, a development not conspicuous elsewhere.[21] The Japanese converts, often of samurai class, were not willing to accept a lower caste status in their own church, and self-government came early.

In the New Hebrides, where Alexander Duff had, with amazingly bad judgment, proposed a union Alliance mission, a united church was out of the question. The missionaries of eight different missions from Scotland, Canada, Australia, and New Zealand scattered on sixteen islands gathered annually for conference and cooperated extensively. But they had had to translate the Bible into nine languages and there was no prospect of a single church. The missions council, however, exercised most of the supervisory functions of the missions together as a single body.[22]

In the *Proceedings* of the Edinburgh Council of the Alliance (1877) the fullest documentation of missionary consolidation was that of the "Presbyterian Alliance of India." The Synod of North India (Presbyterian U.S.A.) had mooted the subject of organic Presbyterian union in India in the 1860's, and a scheme was elaborated in 1871 at a conference in Allahabad, drawing 144 ministers and missionaries from the Church of Scotland, the Presbyterians U.S.A., the American Reformed Dutch, the Scots Free Church, and the American Reformed Presbyterians. When this was found impracticable, the General Missionary Conference at Allahabad in 1872 voted for a consociation at once, without regard to organic union. This became in 1875 officially the Presbyterian Alliance of India, involving some eight varieties.

Various schemes of consolidation were advocated in the Alliance. Chamberlain of Arcot campaigned for years for a full presbyterian structure over the whole subcontinent, with synods, for example, in Bengal, Madras, Bombay, the Punjab, the North-West Provinces. But distances, expense, the variety of languages made this impracticable. The Alliance missionaries also appealed to their home churches to let them handle at least some categories of discipline, since effective discipline on Indian problems from Great Britain or the United States was not possible. But few of the home churches were willing to yield such authority. Frustrated in this effort also, the Alliance, which continued to meet triennially, turned to local consolidations and cooperation in institutional work, colleges, hospitals, publications. We shall return to developments along these lines.

These five instances of spontaneous Reformed consolidation on mission fields must suffice. They undoubtedly played the major role in persuading the Alliance churches to move from the older pattern of missionary presbyteries integrated into Western churches. A definite policy was enunciated, first by the British section in 1886, and then finally by the Alliance as a whole in 1888 after polling the several churches:

> It is desirable that Churches organized under Presbyterian order, and holding the Reformed faith, should be placed under a Presbytery within territorial boundaries suitable for effective government, and that such Presbytery, wherever constituted, should, as far as practicable, include all the Presbyterian Churches within the bounds, by whatever branches of the European or American churches originated.[23]

The Council added to its resolutions about Presbyterian consolidation "its earnest hope that all Evangelical churches in each foreign field may ultimately unite in one, and that, wherever incorporation is not yet practicable, cooperation be increasingly sought." [24]

It was up to the several churches, of course, to implement the principles thus laid down, and there was at least some vigorous action. The General Assembly of the Presbyterian Church U.S.A., for example, acted in 1887 to discourage the formation of further missionary presbyteries in connection with itself and strongly urged the dissolution of existing presbyteries of this sort into union presbyteries wherever feasible. The London Council of the Alliance received a report of the application of the new principles from that church:

> Japan and Syria have already realized it. In Brazil and Mexico the Presbyterians of the Northern and Southern Churches, both encouraged by their respective General Assemblies, have begun to move in the matter with unanimity and enthusiasm; and the Missions in China are expecting to follow their example in the Synod to be held in August next. In Persia, Siam, Laos, Korea, West Africa, Colombia, Chile, Guatemala, our Missions are so isolated from other Presbyterian bodies, that this question does not affect them. When the China Missions have taken their stand, only India will be left out, and India was the first to call for organic union.[25]

Another significant merger, this time of Irish Presbyterian and Scots Free Church missionaries in 1890, produced an independent presbytery in Manchuria. This was a particularly happy consolidation, although it was shortly to undergo the successive fires of the Boxer Rebellion and the Russo-Japanese War.

In all these reorganizations the most difficult question was the relation of the missionary to the young presbytery. Missionaries were rarely ready to expose themselves to full discipline by the native presbytery. And what of finances? The presbytery was usually given authority over "spiritual" matters, except those involving money. As a rule the missionary body retained control of finances from the West and decided when and to what extent self-government was indicated. This kind of feudal or hierarchical structure was greatly influenced by the enormous disparity of living standards in most missionary areas. "Even the plainest type of living for a missionary," it was observed, "is, in the eyes of the heathen, the highest and most worldly of self-indulgent luxury."[26] This disparity made it very difficult to testify convincingly to the poor Christ. It also corroded relations within the

Christian community. The Glasgow Council, for example, deliberated as to how to discourage Christian converts from coming to the West for education, "and especially from expecting to be commissioned on the regular missionary basis, even if so educated." [27]

Before we pass to another subject, it should be noticed parenthetically that in its work for Presbyterian mission consolidation the Alliance considered only English-speaking missions. The missionary statistics of the London Council in 1888 recorded figures for Indonesia (classified under "Burmah, etc.") which put those for India, China, Japan far in the shade. One could discover that half a dozen Dutch societies were operating there on at least half a dozen islands, but no information was given of the cooperative agencies and activities of these bodies either at home or in the Indies. Similarly the statistics disclosed that the Rhenish and Barmen societies between them employed more missionaries in the field than the largest single church of the Alliance, the Presbyterian U.S.A. But there was no discussion of their operation. In fact, after their résumé the Committee asked the Council whether they should not be instructed to inquire into the missionary work of the Continental Reformed churches.[28] At this stage the ecumenical missionary work of the Alliance was confined to the English-speaking ambit. The German, Swiss, Hungarian, Dutch, French work was still to be involved.

For English-speaking Presbyterianism, the work was virtually done by the First World War. The North American section of the Alliance in 1912 recorded with gratitude "the fact that with the exception of two points [northern Syria and southern China] affecting less than a dozen ordained missionaries [of the Synod of the Reformed Presbyterian Church], organic union of the Churches in the mission world has already been effected in all places where two or more of the Churches represented in this section are conducting foreign mission work." [29]

The roll of the last prewar Council, at Aberdeen in 1913, shows something of the results of the effort to create unified independent Reformed churches out of missions. On the roll were the Presbyterian Church of India, the Church of Christ in Japan, the Church of Christ in Korea, the Presbyterian Church of South Africa, the Presbyterian Church of Brazil, the Presbyterian Church of Mexico, the Presbyterian Church of Jamaica, the Synod of Formosa, the Missionary Synod of New Hebrides. The Council hoped for an undivided Presbyterian church in every field. "With regard to other Missions [than Reformed]," it was remarked, "a number of cases may be noted in which united effort has been found possible." [30]

In the last decade of the century Reformed ecumenism turned in a new direction, to "comity." Most of the practicable consolidations on the field had been effected, and for a time the formation of new independent merged churches slowed down. Having clarified policy for themselves, Presbyterian and Reformed ecumenists turned attention to relations outside the Reformed family. It had been the Presbyterian Duff, after all, who had first persuaded the American denominations to lay down some comity principles in 1842. At the end of the 1890's the Washington Council heard that the Presbyterian Churches had been among the foremost "in the more recent advances along the same line." "We are glad to report that Presbyterians, who have sometimes been called narrow, have generally been in the van of all movements toward friendly recognition and cooperation." [31]

The problem of comity was of course inseparable from the question of "essentials" in faith and order. Comity was hardly feasible without substantial mutual recognition. Throughout the period up to the First World War such recognition was generally lacking between Reformed churches, on the one hand, and Roman Catholic, Orthodox Catholic, and Anglo-Catholic churches on the other. The Alliance frequently heard complaints about high Anglican aggressions, and the Reformed were generally viewed as intruders by Roman and Orthodox Catholics claiming whole states as their territory. There does not seem to have been much trouble either with sectarian bodies or with Lutherans, at least as compared to later twentieth-century developments. The bulk of the comity arrangements were with related Anglo-American denominations whose kinship was earlier indicated by their common interest in the Evangelical Alliance. As was recorded in the minutes of the Western Section Executive Commission in 1905:

> The Churches of our Reformed Alliance have long been familiar with the idea (of cooperation and union in mission) and with the splendid results of cooperation on the part of the different members of their Great Family; but now, in these glad days, the Baptist, the Methodist, and the Congregationalist Churches are overturing to the Presbyterian and Reformed Churches for cooperation.[32]

The journey of the secretary of the Alliance, Dr. George Mathews, to South Africa in 1894, was an interesting episode dramatizing some of the aspects of comity. Because of his official and neutral position, the secretary found himself willy-nilly, almost pushed into the position of a comity arbitrator. The Zambesi Industrial Mission had moved in on the Church of Scotland Mission at Blantyre and the Wesleyan Missionary South African Conference had committed, he felt, a "great breach of comity" in relation to the Swiss Romande mission near Delagoa Bay. American Methodists gave offense at Rajputana; the United Presbyterians of the U.S.A. wrote about breaches of comity by the General Synod of the Reformed Presbyterians at Roorki, and the Syrian Evangelical Church petitioned against the aggressions of the Mission of the Archbishop of Canterbury.[33] An arbitrator, however, could do nothing unless both parties bound themselves, and in most cases nothing could be done outside the Reformed family.

The Toronto Council of the Alliance (1892), at the instigation of Dr. F. F. Ellinwood of the Presbyterian U.S.A. Board, authorized a new and fruitful line of activity. The Council recommended that representatives of the various Presbyterian and Reformed mission boards of North America be convened for conference, as was done, in January of 1893. But on the following day a second suggestion was carried out, that representatives of *all* Protestant missions and boards of the continent be assembled. This meeting was repeated the next year and the resultant Foreign Missions Conference became a regular annual affair, coordinating North American Protestant missions as comparable bodies in Great Britain and the Continent were already doing. Over twenty different organizations were represented, including Presbyterian and Reformed, Methodist, Baptist, Episcopalian, and Lutheran bodies.

The Alliance committee was thus in effect enlarged into the Foreign Missions Conference, in which Alliance members took "a large part." [34] The ecumenical interest and effort of Alliance representatives increased, but found its expression in this broader operation. The Alliance committee ceased to meet separately, finding few matters to tend to which were not of interest to all Protestant missionary organizations.[35]

The Foreign Missions Conference was then the agency through which Ellinwood, again, was the chief organizer of the Ecumenical Council of 1900 in New York. Ellinwood had largely organized the preceding London Missionary Conference of 1888, which was by far the largest held up to that time, assembling some 1,500 delegates from 140 missionary societies. The New York Conference, of course, outdid even its predecessor. The effect of both was to enlist widespread interest and enthusiasm, which was channeled with increasing effectiveness by the planning bodies, such as the Foreign Missions Conference, and the Central Committee which came out of the New York Ecumenical Conference. In 1900 the Executive Commission of the Western Section of the Alliance recorded in their minutes that the Ecumenical Missionary Conference was "a practical result of the work of our Alliance." [36]

Another evidence of the conscious effort of the Reformed to conduct their missionary work in a larger-than-Reformed context is given by the Presbyterian Church U.S.A., the largest church in the Alliance. The General Assembly of that church declared in 1900:

> The object of the foreign missionary enterprise is not to perpetuate on the mission field the denominational distinctions of Christendom, but to build up on Scriptural lines, and according to Scriptural principles and methods, the Kingdom of our Lord Jesus Christ.[37]

Thus the basic principles of the London Missionary Society, adopted a century and five years earlier (see above, p. 177), were reaffirmed, but now, not by an interdenominational society, but by a denomination, a church. Early in the century Presbyterian denominations as such had often seemed suspicious of such bodies as the London Missionary Society and the American Board of Commissioners for Foreign Missions and had felt it important that Presbyterianism be propagated. Now, having taken the mission really seriously, they had been converted themselves to the more ecumenical stance. The church had captured and divided up the missionary structure, but in the process the missionary concern had permeated and changed the church.

There had been numerous earlier declarations of sympathy for younger national churches incorporating Reformed and Presbyterians with others, but this definition of 1900 was still a significant landmark. Its thrust was to be felt in the following decades in Japan, China, India, Korea, the Philippines, and elsewhere.

India was the scene of what was to become the most notable mission church consolidation of the first three quarters of the new century. The American Reformed Dutch mission at Arcot issued an invitation in 1900 to the two Scottish missions in neighboring Madras, those of the Free Church and the Church of Scotland, to consider union. When the plan was submitted to the home authorities, the first two approved but the Church of Scotland delayed. It was determined to go ahead, and in 1902 the Synod of South India was constituted, with Jacob Chamberlain, who had campaigned forty years for Indian Reformed union, its first moderator. Some thirty-three congregations were grouped in two classes or presbyteries, in a constitution largely based on that of the Church of Christ in Japan. There was a short confession of eleven articles.

This local merger in the Madras region was generally thought of as an element only in a larger union to come. Stimulated by it the Presbyterian Alliance revived from a decade of inaction and again worked out a plan for a unified national Presbyterian Church. Responses from the home churches were considered at an Allahabad conference in 1903 and the next year the Presbyterian Church of India held its first General Assembly. The strains of this structure were great, however, since it had to function in nine languages and was spread thinly over a teeming subcontinent. In 1907 there were only 125 congregations.

In Madras Presidency meanwhile, the Synod of South India had entered into local negotiations with two Congregationalist communities, the missions of the American Board of Commissioners for Foreign Missions in Madura and Ceylon and those of the London Missionary Society. The General Assembly of 1907 encouraged this movement and released cordially over a quarter of its constituency to enter this regional merger, which was, to be sure, still generically Reformed. The South India United Church was thus constituted in 1908 with about 24,000 communicants and 140,000 adherents. Conversations had also been held with the Lutherans and the Society for the Propagation of the Gospel. Further consolidation in India was to follow this regional interdenominational pattern, rather than that of national denominational bodies. In South India the Reformed ingredient was relatively small in the total Christian community, but it had taken a lead in consolidation, first of the Presbyterian and Congregationalist bodies separately, and then in their combination into the South India United Church, which was prepared thus for the meeting at Tranquebar in 1919 which projected a united Church of South India.

In China in these years there were similar or even greater barriers to the consolidation of an effective national Reformed body. The 1908 Plan for the Presbyterian Church of Christ in China, making six synods of eight missions—Presbyterian U.S.A., Presbyterian U.S., Reformed Church in America, English, Irish, Canadian Presbyterians, the Church of Scotland, and the United Free Church of Scotland—had to be deferred. Meanwhile the China Centenary Conference at Shanghai in 1907 approved of a federal union of various denominations, with Provincial Councils meeting once in two years, and a National Representative Council to be held every five.[38] But the most tangible results of the movement were the various projects of institutional cooperation, as at the Nanking Christian University (Presbyterian U.S.A., Disciples, Methodists), the Union Seminary at Canton (Presbyterian U.S.A., Canadian and New Zealand Presbyterians, and perhaps English and American Congregationalists and United Brethren), the Union Christian University in Chentu, West China (American Baptist, Methodist Episcopal, Canadian Methodist, Friends), Peking University (Presbyterian U.S.A., LMS, ABCFM), the Shantung Protestant University (Presbyterian U.S.A., English Baptist), and cooperation in secondary schools, as at Peking, or at Changsha in Hunan Province.

The climax of this movement of cooperation and union in missions, in the era before the World Wars began, was the World Missionary Conference of 1910 in the Edinburgh Assembly Hall of the United Free Church of Scotland. The conference was originally planned as a great demonstration like the preceding decennial missionary conferences of London, 1888, and New York, 1900. But, under the influence of the regional conferences held in Madras in 1902 and Shanghai in 1907, it took on a different character, that of a consultation, with carefully prepared study materials, of official delegates of the societies, and thus, indirectly, of the churches.

The study volumes prepared in 1908 and 1909 constituted the most comprehensive assessment yet made of the total Protestant missionary enterprise. In the Report of Commission VIII, *Cooperation and the Promotion of Unity*, it was observed that "the greatest progress in the direction of union has been made by the bodies professing the Presbyterian polity." [39] More space was allotted to Presbyterian and Reformed unions than to all the rest together—Anglicans, Methodists, Lutherans, Congregationalists, Baptists. The instances cited were those of the Church of Christ in Japan, the earlier union presbyteries of Amoy and Manchuria in China, and the attempts then in process to organize a Presbyterian Church of Christ in China in six synods, the successive union attempts we have noted for India, culminating in the South India United Church of 1907 and the Presbyterian Church of India (1904), the Union Presbyterian Church in Korea (1907), and the New Hebrides Presbyterian Mission Synod. It was also observed that Presbyterian and Reformed bodies were participants in the two notable attempts at union across denominational lines, the South India United Church of 1907 and the federation of missions projected in Kenya in 1909.

The Reformed Alliance could view the Edinburgh Conference with some justification as the natural culmination of an ecumenical enterprise it had been pursuing for decades. The chief architect of the conference, and the man who, with John R. Mott, guided it so skillfully, was the missionary statesman of the United Free Church, J. H. Oldham. Oldham served as a full-time secretary of the international planning committee, and was, "more than any one other, the spirit . . . at the back of that great Conference, not merely in respect of its organization and its methods, but also of its ideals, its aspirations, and its hopes." [40]

The Edinburgh Conference was the initial impetus from which, in the era of World Wars, were to emerge both the World Council of Churches and the International Missionary Council, the two most important institutional expressions of the ecumenical movement. In that new era, as we shall see, the whole missionary enterprise was to face new questions. But each generation has its own ecumenical task and the work of unity in missions before the Wars deserves recognition for what it was in its own time.

XII

REUNION
ON THE HISTORIC EPISCOPATE?

A NEW PHASE in Reformed ecumenical outreach manifested itself toward the end of the nineteenth century and largely dominated the first two generations of the twentieth century. Relations had been closest on the Continent with the Lutherans and in the English-speaking world with the Congregationalists. Now, for the first time since the seventeenth century, Reformed churches engaged in serious discussions with Anglicans, and a new set of issues, primarily those related to the "historic episcopate," came to occupy center stage. These issues were in considerable measure also points of disagreement between the Reformed churches and the Roman Catholic and Eastern Orthodox, and the Anglicans often presented themselves in the discussions as spokesmen for the whole "Catholic" tradition. Toward the end of the period the hitherto reticent larger churches increasingly entered into dialogue on their own account and the conversations widened from the English-speaking world to the whole ecumenical arena.

It is an interesting historical question why the Reformed churches became so preoccupied with a range of questions relatively peripheral to their own priorities. They had not regarded episcopacy as a very crucial matter one way or the other. Why the new preoccupation with it?

Certain negative factors seem clear. Much of the hostility to episcopacy had come from its association with political power. As churches were more and more widely disestablished and bishops ceased to be addressed "My Lord," there might be more disposition among the Reformed to consider possible religious uses of the office. At the same time there was a general blurring of doctrinal and liturgical distinctions. In many areas, as in the United States, laymen and clergy alike moved back and forth across denominational lines in large numbers. Theological partisanship, e.g., as between Arminianism and Calvinism, could no longer be identified denominationally. It was agreed, for example, that no serious doctrinal issues any longer divided Presbyterians and Methodists in the United States. The United Church of Canada, which was centrally a Methodist-Presbyterian merger, established the point.[1] Similarly the old battles over "free" and "liturgical" worship were ever less denominationally demarcated. Nearly all the important issues except orders and organization now cut *across* denominations, which meant that the denomination as such was taking on a new character, less confessional in nature.

Another distinctive feature of this phase of ecumenical discussion in relation to the Reformed tradition is that most of the debate was carried by the Anglicans or, at the end, the Roman Catholics. It was largely an *internal* debate for them while the Reformed stood by in relative passivity. Perhaps one should say that the Reformed case was really being carried by the older Reformed tradition of classical Anglicanism, locked in struggle with the neo-Anglican concepts which had gained such strength since the Tractarians. In general the "bridge" character of Anglicanism manifested itself only in theology; when it came to action the Anglican church was chronically immobilized and with one notable exception, hung suspended on dead center. But its theologians were more generally sophisticated than those of any other church in the issues which defined their internal debate.

The story best begins with a surprising overture from the Anglican communion in the ninth decade of the nineteenth century, the so-called Chicago-Lambeth Quadrilateral. The Quadrilateral was a set of four bases for ecumenical discussion proposed first by the Protestant Episcopal General Convention of 1886 in Chicago to a number of other church bodies with a view to possible church union. Two years later the bishops of the worldwide Anglican communion met at Lambeth Palace, and adopted the four bases, with minor revisions, making them the official platform of the Anglican communion. The conversations and debates to follow for two generations were to clarify the meaning of the Quadrilateral and especially of its fourth basis, the "historic episcopate."

The American Episcopalians had appointed a committee in 1886 to confer with other churches on this platform. The committee opened correspondence with two Lutheran bodies, the Unitas Fratrum, and the two larger bodies of American Presbyterians. Of these, however,

only the Presbyterians U.S.A. took up the invitation seriously. The
General Assembly of 1887 welcomed the Episcopalian overture, appointed a committee for conference, and gave it certain principles as
guidelines.

In an exchange of letters in 1888 it became clear that the American
Presbyterians were ready to accept the first three principles of the
Quadrilateral as a basis of negotiation. They would have preferred
more precise language at various points. As the overture from the
Presbytery of New York suggested, they would have wished an acknowledgment of the Scriptures, the first point, not only as the revealed
Word of God, but also as the supreme and only infallible norm.[2] They
would prefer to insist, secondly, on baptism and the Lord's Supper,
as the only dominical sacraments, and as understanding their grace to
be the work of the Holy Spirit and not of the minister. They were
not sure, thirdly, that the Nicene Creed was "sufficient" theology for
a united church, but did not anticipate difficulty in doctrine "especially since the doctrinal symbols of the two churches, viz: the Thirty-
Nine Articles, and the Thirty-Three Chapters of our Confession of
Faith, embody the same Calvinistic system of doctrine, and the two
churches, as far as their doctrinal standards are concerned, are one." [3]
(The two Lutheran bodies corresponding, it may be noted, had both
suggested that discussion proceed on the basis of the Augsburg Confession.)

With regard to the "historic episcopate locally adapted," the fourth
pillar, the Presbyterian committee was ready to accept that also in
their understanding of it:

> The Presbyterian Church holds and always has held firmly
> to what we believe to be the genuinely historic Episcopate
> as this is set forth in the New Testament and in the practice
> of the early church so far as it did not swerve from apostolic
> models and directions. It finds the Presbyter-bishop in all
> ages of the Church, in unbroken succession until the present
> day.[4]

As an English Presbyterian had observed in relation to the Lambeth
overture,

> we are an Episcopal Church. It is an absolute delusion to
> suppose that the difference of the relations lies in the institu-
> tion of Episcopacy; the difference lies in Prelacy. For my own

part, I would not belong to a Church where all men were not under a sort of superintendence. We exercise superintendence.[5]

Did these interpretations come within the scope of what the Quadrilateral might consider local adaptations of the "historic episcopate"? The Episcopalian committee replied that their only authoritative definition of the three orders of ministry was in the preface to their ordinal and that that formulation was intended as "a statement of what is historic, what is evident unto all, and not at all as dogmatic article of faith." Reassured thus that they were not required to concur in the statement of the ordinal, the Presbyterians declared their readiness to recommend negotiation on the basis of the Quadrilateral. They stated their understanding that the "adaptation" of the historic episcopate fell, not in the sphere of doctrine, but in that of discipline, and that for both churches concerned, disciplinary matters were open to alteration in accordance with agreeableness to Scripture, expediency in given circumstances, the practice of the early Christians.

The Presbyterians were not insisting on their own form of episcopate.

> We can unite with those who think bishops to be a superior order of the clergy, provided we are ourselves not asked to abandon our conscientious conviction that bishops as instituted by the apostles are not of superior rank, but that all who are ordained to the ministry by the laying on of the hands of the Presbytery and are entrusted with the care and oversight of souls are bishops.[6]

But while thus clarifying the sense in which they were willing to use the Quadrilateral as a basis of ecumenical negotiation, the Presbyterians repeatedly pressed on the Episcopalians the guidelines they considered essential from their side, especially one laid down by the 1887 General Assembly:

> Mutual recognition and reciprocity between the different bodies who profess the true religion is the first and essential step toward practical church unity.[7]

The Episcopalian committee was unable, however, to give a positive assurance on this point. To them recognition and reciprocity were possible consequences of negotiation, but evidently not its presupposition. And when the Presbyterians pushed the issue practically in 1893 by suggesting the exchange of pulpits, this too was rejected. The Presbyterian committee consequently recommended to the Assembly in 1894 that the correspondence be suspended until the General Convention should be able to accord such recognition. This at last produced the clarification which the Presbyterians had been seeking for seven years. Such a recognition, they were at last informed, was "inconsistent with, and indeed subversive of the purpose and spirit" of the fourth Lambeth proposition.[8] Evidently the Presbyterian understanding of the "historic episcopate locally adapted" was not, after all, acceptable, and the Episcopalian proposal meant that they did not recognize the Presbyterian ministry. Negotiations, in the Episcopalian conception, were to deal with the question of how Presbyterian deficiencies might be repaired. This no longer interested the Presbyterians.

All this interchange, it was acknowledged on both sides, took place in a sociological vacuum. Presbyterians and Episcopalians generally dwelt in separate camps. At their conference in 1892 the committee members noted "the unhappy attitude in which the members of the two churches now stand toward each other: their almost complete isolation, the almost utter absence of that personal intercourse and mutual recognition and Christian fellowship and hearty cooperation which ought to obtain between them as brethren in Christ."[9] Within the committee it seemed to be agreed that negotiations should not be pressed until the people of the two churches had had occasion to become better acquainted. But how should they become better acquainted if even the exchange of pulpits was debarred?

The first testing of the Chicago-Lambeth Quadrilateral, and specifically its fourth point, had made clear that the Episcopalian understanding of "historic episcopate locally adapted" was considerably more restricted than it seemed. Certain passages of the history, such as the origins in the first century, and certain local adaptations, were not to be admitted. (Even the Anglican adaptations, on the other hand, were inadmissibly deviant from the perspective of Pope Leo XIII. In 1896, the year when the Presbyterian-Episcopalian correspondence was published, the Pope pronounced that "Ordinations carried out according to the Anglican rite have been and are absolutely null and utterly void.")

The next significant testing of the Quadrilateral came a decade later from the side of an American Reformed Church, in this case the

Congregationalists. Newman Smyth, the pastor of Center Church, New Haven, published in 1908 a work called *Passing Protestantism and Coming Catholicism*. He had become excited with the ecumenical possibilities of a historical outlook when applied to Roman Catholicism and identified the Episcopal Church as the destined mediator between Roman Catholicism and Protestantism in such a future convergence. The Episcopalian bishop of Connecticut invited Smyth to address his clergy on the calling of their church in the situation. Bishop Brewster also sent a copy of the book to the Archbishop of Canterbury on the eve of the 1908 Lambeth Conference, and there is some evidence it may have contributed to the 1908 Lambeth resolution advocating conferences with other communions. The first official reply to this Lambeth suggestion came that same year from the Congregationalist General Conference of Connecticut and in 1910 the Congregationalist National Council adopted a resolution in response to Lambeth.

Smyth's notion was to push episcopacy as a constitutional structure, without any specific theological doctrine about it. This could be done without denying the ordinations of nonepiscopalian churches. Such churches might be permitted freedom of rites and much of their own polity, while still adopting the "historic episcopate." In all this Smyth was largely dependent on his personal friend William Reed Huntington, the original inspirer of the Quadrilateral. His own contribution was simply his convinced adherence to these conceptions as a Congregationalist and the tireless campaign he maintained in their behalf for more than a decade. His influence was greater, perhaps, in Great Britain and India than in the United States, where he was rather a lonely Don Quixote.

The Episcopalians were nearly as skeptical of the ecumenical tendency as the Congregationalists before the World War. They had refused to join the new Federal Council of Churches in 1908, and indeed refused repeatedly until 1940. The Church of England, similarly, was brought to participate in the Edinburgh World Conference of 1910 only at the last minute and with many reservations. And after the Edinburgh Conference of 1910 it took the conviction and eloquence of Bishop Charles Henry Brent to persuade the General Convention of the American Episcopalians to approve his plan to summon a world conference on faith and order. That same year Smyth persuaded the Congregational National Council to set up a committee to respond to the Lambeth overture, and from that time all his ecumeni-

cal labors were directed with an eye to the faith and order conference
to come. He was chairman of the American deputation of 1913 to the
British Free Churches which paved the way for the meeting in 1914 of
the Church of England with the Church of Scotland and the free
churches. We must return to these wartime consultations of the British
churches later.

Back in the States, Smyth pressed vigorously for a series of specific
proposals which might be expected to give the cause a bit of momentum. With all of them he was frustrated by Episcopalian inertia.
The first prospect was to secure approval for the proposal for the
joint conduct of much of the parish programs of two congregations
in Lenox, Massachusetts, one Congregational and the other Episcopalian, as desired by the two ministers in the town. Then in 1917
Smyth issued an "Appeal to All Our Fellow-Believers" calling for
joint or supplementary consecrations or ordinations of military chaplains so that they would be able to perform their ministries in the
name of more than their own individual denominations. The House
of Bishops refused to consider the proposal in 1918.

The last effort fared a little better. A private conference at General
Seminary in 1919 on the subject of supplementary ordination produced some "Proposals for an Approach Towards Unity." Smyth's
scholarly coadjutor in the conversations was the Yale church historian,
Williston Walker. The Proposals were about to go down in the House
of Bishops that year when they were rescued by Brent. A committee
was appointed to continue the conversations and certain constitutional adjustments were voted to implement the proposals if they
should be adopted. In the further course of events "Canon 36" was
accepted by the General Convention of 1922, although only with revisions already rejected by the Congregationalists in the negotiations.
The canon was intended to enable a minister to hold double standing, but was so hedged about with procedural difficulties as to be
practically inoperative.[10] For a decade Smyth had struggled to get
from the Protestant Episcopal Church some tangible step toward
church unity on the basis of the Quadrilateral and failed. Did the
"historic episcopate locally adapted" have any specifiable meaning
short of simple absorption into the ministry of the existing Episcopal
denomination? The Presbyterians were to explore the question again
with regard to a concordat on supplementary ordination a quarter of
a century later, but with the same result.

Newman Smyth's readiness for the historic episcopate as a Reformed churchman was to be significant also in the South India United Church (see above, p. 212). That church, it will be recalled, was predominantly Congregationalist in origins, both English (London Missionary Society) and American, together with the (Dutch) Reformed Church in America mission and the Scottish Presbyterians. The British Independents were cautious in the matter, but the Americans, in particular Sherwood Eddy, J. S. Chandler, and J. P. Jones, joined by Dr. Wyckoff of the Reformed Church in America, were ready to consider seriously some modified episcopacy as a basis of a larger union with Anglicanism in South India. The writings of Newman Smyth and Charles Briggs influenced them.

It was Sherwood Eddy more than any other single figure who fathered the Church of South India. The fundamental concept was that of a merger of the South India United Church and the Anglican church on the basis of the historic episcopate apart from any doctrinal interpretation of it and without questioning the order of the SIUC. Eddy, still full of enthusiasm from the Edinburgh Conference of 1910, assembled ten men for a meeting of three days at Bishop Henry Whitehead's house in Madras that same year.[11] Although "a life-long Congregationalist and an independent of independents," Eddy, like Smyth, pinned his hopes for organic union on "a simple, modified, constitutional episcopacy on the primitive model," associated with a mutual recognition of ministries. South Indian Anglicanism was dominantly evangelical, the fruit of Church Missionary Society missions, and before that of Lutheran non-episcopal missionaries, so that such conceptions won a hearing on the Anglican side also. Many other contributory streams flowed into the decisive meeting at Tranquebar in 1919 and the shaping of its "Indian Manifesto," but the basic conceptions were still those of the Madras meeting of 1910 and Eddy's consequent article of June, 1911, on "A National Church for India." It was his persuasive powers, more than those of any other, which carried the idea with the missionaries of the SIUC. With the rising pressure of Indian nationalism behind them, they were to have far greater success in India than in the United States. Tranquebar 1919 publicly launched the merger proposal and for three decades and more it was to be debated around the world.

That such a program would not have smooth sailing on the Anglican side was made dramatically conspicuous by a crisis in another Church Missionary Society mission field just before the First World War. In British East Africa the Lambeth encouragement of ecumenical

ventures in 1908 was followed by a series of missionary conferences
for the next five years. At Nairobi in 1909 a series of resolutions were
drawn up proposing a federation of the several missions involved
(CMS, Church of Scotland, Wesleyans, and Africa Inland Mission)
with the ultimate goal of a self-governing, self-supporting, self-ex-
tending Kenyan Church. The program was based on the Quadrilateral, but since agreement had not been achieved on the point of
the historic episcopate, the proposal was put in the form of a "federation." In 1913 a conference was held at Kikuyu to implement the
Nairobi resolutions of four years before. The agenda included such
matters as comity arrangements, mutual recognition of each other's
members and discipline, and a partially open communion. The conference was concluded with a communion service in the Church of
Scotland church, conducted by the Anglican bishop of Mombasa,
at which the Presbyterian Norman Maclean preached, and in which
all were invited to communicate.[12]

The Kikuyu Conference and especially the communion service
evoked a violent reaction from the Anglo-Catholic Bishop of neighboring Zanzibar, Frank Weston. Weston wrote to the Archbishop of
Canterbury, formally charging his fellow bishops "with the grievous
faults of propagating heresy and committing schism."

In the ensuing debate three particular grounds of offense were
cited by the Anglo-Catholics. In order of ascending importance they
were, first, the exchange of pulpits, second, admission of unconfirmed
communicants at Anglican communions, third, reception of communion by Anglicans at the hands of non-Anglican ministers. The
Archbishop of Canterbury avoided a formal heresy trial and passed
the matters in dispute to a Central Consultative Body, which held
hearings and gave him its recommendations. At Easter, 1915, while
the World War was in process, the Archbishop released his own pronouncement on the basis of the consultation's recommendations. Interchange of pulpits under episcopal authorization was not objec-
tionable, but the Archbishop advised "at present" against such services as the closing communion service held at Kikuyu.

Newman Smyth's American delegation to the British free churches
on behalf of the proposed faith and order world conference arrived
in England just as the Kikuyu row hit the newspapers. Despite the
Anglo-Catholic counterattack, however, an unprecedented series of
conferences between Anglicans and free churchmen in England occurred during and immediately after the War. Smyth's enthusiasm

for episcopacy was matched by others from backgrounds even more militant for local independency, such as his colleague on the American deputation, the Disciple Peter Ainslie, and the English Baptist, J. H. Shakespeare, chairman of the British Free Church Council in the war period. The conferences of 1916–1918 came out generally for a "constitutional" episcopate with no reordination as a basis for church merger. This was essentially Eddy's program at the time in South India and the two sets of conversations moved ahead on parallel lines and with significant mutual influence.[13] The catastrophe of the War and the enormous struggle for order and peace which loomed ahead drove the churchmen to measure more carefully the price of their patterns of segregation.

The convergence of the Indian and the British projects of union on the Lambeth formula was manifested in the "Appeal to All Christian People" [14] published by the Lambeth Bishops in 1920. The chief draughtsmen of the Appeal was Bishop William Palmer of Bombay, who was also to be the chief theological architect in shaping the vision of "Tranquebar 1919" into a concrete ecclesiastical program for a united church in South India. He brought the urgency of the mission field back to Great Britain, and the result was a statement that marked the high-water mark of Anglican-nonepiscopal relations.

The bishops acknowledged God's will for visible fellowship among Christians and frankly confessed their share in the guilt which had contributed to the actual rupture of fellowship. They reformulated the four points of the Quadrilateral as essential ingredients of the visible unity of the church, claiming that the Episcopate was the one means of securing a ministry acknowledged by every part of the church.

> It is not that we call in question for a moment the spiritual reality of the ministries of those Communions which do not possess the Episcopate. On the contrary, we thankfully acknowledge that these ministries have been manifestly blessed and owned by the Holy Spirit as effective means of grace.

The bishops urged, nevertheless, that the Episcopate was and would be "the best instrument for maintaining the unity and continuity of the Church." They desired that the office "should be everywhere exercised in a representative and constitutional manner." They were persuaded that, terms of union having been satisfactorily adjusted, their own bishops and clergy would willingly accept from authorities of other communions "a form of commission or recognition which would commend our ministry to their congregations." Similarly they hoped ministers who had not received it would accept a commission through episcopal ordination to be able to minister in episcopalian congregations. "In so acting no one of us could possibly be taken to repudiate his past ministry. . . . We shall be publicly and formally seeking additional recognition of a new call to wider service in a re-united Church, and imploring for ourselves God's grace and strength to fulfil the same."

In response to the Lambeth "Appeal" the Federal Council of Evangelical Free Churches of England set up a committee, with the Congregationalist W. B. Selbie as chairman, and the Presbyterian P. Carnegie Simpson as convener of the drafting committee, which produced a report of some twenty pages in May, 1921.[15] The Free Church comment acknowledged the generous intent of the Anglican Appeal and confessed that the concern of free churchmen over the evils of disunion had often been too slight. They were ready to cooperate with Anglicans in social and civic work, in worship, and indeed held the Lord's Table open to them as to other fellow Christians. They welcomed the Lambeth recognition of nonepiscopal ministries as "effective" but inquired whether that meant that these churches were already in Anglican judgment parts of the visible church of Christ. And were those churches which responded to the Appeal expected to constrict the terms of their sacramental communion to those currently maintained by Anglicans, and cut themselves off from their former company of fellow communicants?

Again, there were ambiguities with regard to episcopal ordination. The free churchmen held that no one form of polity for the church had been laid down by the Lord, and they consequently maintained an open mind toward episcopal order as toward any other. But what was intended by episcopal "ordination" in the proposed scheme of mutual ministerial recognition? Ordination, by definition, is given once for all. If the word was used strictly, then what was being proposed was in fact *reordination,* presupposing a denial of the previous ordination and ministry. If what was meant was an extension of license to exercise one's ordination in certain situations, then why not use more precise language?

The concluding theme of the report was to be stressed again by Carnegie Simpson in a later report that year for the 11th Council of the World Reformed Alliance meeting in Pittsburgh. Was not God showing a way to visible unity, he asked, in common mission and service, in the interchange of pulpits and in sharing at the Lord's Table? [16]

A joint conference of Anglicans and free churchmen met from 1921 to 1925 to elucidate the meaning of the Appeal and related questions. The recognition that nonepiscopal ministries were "real" and "effective," it was made clear, did not mean that they were "sufficient in authority" or that they were not, "in varying degrees irregular or defective." The Anglicans felt bound to their 1660 Ordinal, at least by the practical threat of schism from their Anglo-Catholic wing, and because of their relations with Old Catholics and Eastern Orthodox Churches. As to ordination, schemes of deliberate ambiguity were proposed, or a conditional ordination ("If you have not hitherto been truly ordained," etc.). The English free churchmen preferred an "extended commissioning." [17] There was still clearly much room for disagreement on any specific proposal in the West.[18] But while difficulties seemed to mount in these countries, developments were moving ahead in India.

The initial reaction in India to the Lambeth pronouncements had been disappointment; they seemed to mark a retreat from the position adopted at Tranquebar on intercommunion and against reordination. But the consulting committees went back to work, driven by the conviction, as Bishop Palmer put it, that if they broke off negotiations, the Indians would settle it one way or the other. There was considerable discussion of a proposal made by the Congregationalist historian, Vernon Bartlet. Bartlet's idea was that of a common service of mutual commissioning to extended ranges of ministry. The objection was that the same prayer would be offered with varying intentions; for some it would be actual ordination in fact, for others not.

Still another alternative procedure was set forth in 1926 at Trichinoply by Bishop Palmer, one which was in the event to be adopted. This was the idea of an "Interim" (originally of fifty years) of an avowedly transitional character. All ministers of all uniting churches would be acknowledged from the beginning, but no individual congregation would have to accept the ministrations of a minister about whom they had conscientious scruples. This kind of arrangement was not wholly strange to Anglicans, who were accustomed to situations where the clergy of an Evangelical diocese were never invited to minister in a neighboring Anglo-Catholic diocese, and vice versa. During the interim the uniting church would maintain relations with all its related overseas churches, but all ministers accepted for service must be episcopally ordained. To cope with the difficult cases which were obviously likely under such arrangements, a resolution was adopted, which came to be known as the "Pledge."

> They therefore pledge themselves and fully trust each other that in the united church no arrangements with regard to churches, congregations or ministers will knowingly be made, either generally or in particular cases, which would offend the conscientious convictions of any persons directly concerned, or which would hinder the development of complete unity within the church or imperil its subsequent progress towards union with other churches.[19]

The Pledge and the Interim were to constitute the distinctive elements in the Scheme of Union of 1929 which emerged as the specific proposal for South Indian merger. They were to endure through six successive editions and survive in the final plan of 1941.

The negotiations were greatly helped by the internal reorganization of the Anglican communion. In 1927 the Church of South India, Burma, and Ceylon was set off as an autonomous self-governing body, independent of British government connections and able to function as a "free church." In these years also the Anglican church was developing parish, synodical, and provincial councils of laity to participate in church government, thus increasingly resembling the polity of the South India United Church.

The Scheme of Union of 1929 was the main preoccupation at the Lambeth Conference of Anglican bishops in 1930. The Anglican communion, it was decided, would be unable to grant recognition to the proposed church, at least in its formative Interim. This was to remain essentially the Anglican position, even after the actual consummation of the union in 1947. Anglicanism had great difficulty in coming to terms with the one successful effort to actualize the Quadrilateral.

Lesslie Newbigin, the only former Presbyterian who was elected a bishop in the new church, published in 1948 the *Reunion of the Church,* probably the most searching theological interpretation of the merger. Newbigin's argument focused on the local congregation and why it is important that there be but one Christian congregation in the locality. Only so, he contended, is the missionary responsibility made inescapable; if there is only one Christian congregation, what is not done by it will not be done. Similarly one congregation cannot evade the responsibility of transcending and reconciling all the sociological and personal rivalries and hostilities of the community.

In the effort to be faithful to both these responsibilities a congregation will constantly be forced to seek the basis of its unity and the source of its authority.

> In this situation it has been easy to remember the truth, which is often disastrously obscured in a situation where a number of small congregations exist together in one locality, that the Church is not primarily an association constituted by the agreement of its members on a number of points of belief and practice, but simply humanity reconstituted by its redemption and regeneration in Christ. . . . It is not possible to continue steadily testifying to men that the one thing that matters to them is their relation to Christ and at the same time steadily to maintain that many of the things on which Christians differ matter so much that even the common bond of redemption in Christ is not big enough to transcend them.[20]

In the years after the South Indian Scheme of Union of 1929 that Indian model was very influential, both in the West and among certain "younger" churches, as in North India, Ceylon, and Iran. The attempts to emulate South India in the United States and Great Britain, which we may consider first, were less successful.

Bishop Brent, the shaper and mover of the Lausanne Conference, wished to push on after that conference to specific merger negotiations in the United States. The Episcopalian General Convention of 1928 passed his resolution proposing a meeting with the two main Methodist and the two main Presbyterian bodies. At the meeting, however, the southern churches in each of these cases were absent. In 1931 the Lutherans also were invited to the conversations. But in the following years both Lutherans and Methodists decided that consolidation of their own internal divisions should take priority over interconfessional discussions. The Presbyterians, however, although they had not yet healed their own Civil War disruption, remained in conversation with the Episcopalians as they had in 1887. What followed was a curious reenactment of the conversations of 1887–1894.

The Episcopalian General Convention of 1937 took the initiative with a resolution proposed to the Presbyterians that they "hereby formally declare their purpose to achieve organic union between their respective churches." The Presbyterian General Assembly of 1938 passed the same resolution and a commission was put to work. Bishop Parsons and Henry Sloane Coffin were to be the chief representatives of their respective churches.

One product of the commission was a proposed concordat, somewhat akin to that of 1919–1923 between the Episcopalians and Congregationalists, whereby in certain specified cases ministers might be authorized to function on behalf of both churches. The conception was that the authorization should take the form of "supplemental ordination" or "extension of ordination," since in a state of schism all ordinations were limited as the ordaining body was limited. A second proposal, of joint ordination of some or all ministers, was also explored. Both devices were included in the final *Proposed Basis of Union,* according to which presbyters would be associated with bishops in ordination, and it was agreed to maintain the continuity of the episcopate. At the initial consummation of union, ministers of both churches were to receive supplemental ordination by the formula:

> The ministry of the Word and Sacraments which thou hast already received is hereby recognized; and the grace and authority of Holy Orders as conferred by this Church are now added.[21]

This notion of supplemental ordination was taken up by the Anglican Church in India in 1944. This seemed to them preferable to the Interim Period which had been worked out in their negotiations. The Archbishop of Canterbury advised that this was easier for Anglicans, and the Lower House of the Canterbury Convocation also associated itself with this method. The Church of Scotland representatives also welcomed it for South India. But in South India the Independents blocked it in the Joint Committee.[22] In the United States it was rather the Anglo-Catholics who succeeded in shelving the whole *Proposed Basis* by threatening schism. The Episcopalian General Convention of 1946 did not dare to put the report to a vote, fearing possible schism and lawsuits. As before, the Episcopalians had both initiated and terminated the conversations.

Whether the *Proposed Basis* would have been sustained by the Presbyterian General Assembly and presbyteries was never tested. But the indications were that in the interests of church union a substantial body of American Presbyterians would have committed themselves to accepting and maintaining the historic episcopate in a constitutional form as of the *bene esse* of the church.

Another proposal of the joint commission had been the recommendation that where church facilities of one's own denomination were lacking, Anglicans and Presbyterians should be recommended to use each other's services. This recommendation had again been dropped on the Episcopalian side. It was the old difficulty; it was generally agreed that fuller intercourse of the two churches was essential for any union, but strict Episcopal discipline did not permit such intercourse. The Episcopalians wanted advance commitment to their positions before exposing their people to other ideas.

In Great Britain, meanwhile, parallel conversations were under way, involving the Church of England and the Church of Scotland, and, at times as observers, and at times as participants, the Presbyterian Church in England and the Episcopal Church in Scotland. In a first round in 1932–1934 a joint statement of agreements was achieved along with some proposals of things to be done together, such as interchanging pulpits and occasional intercommunions. Then after the Second World War came another round in 1949–1951, partly occasioned by the proposal of the Archbishop of Canterbury, in his "Step Forward in Church Relations," that such churches as the Scots Presbyterians should "take episcopacy into their systems." And finally the Second Assembly of the World Council of Churches at Evanston in 1954 signaled another stage which produced a unanimous joint report in 1957, called *Relations Between Anglicans and Presbyterian Churches,* or more popularly in Scotland, the "Bishops' Report." The central proposal, which was the basis for that nickname, was that of instituting in the Church of Scotland "bishops-in-presbytery." The Church of England, meanwhile, would make provision for more adequate lay participation on the several levels of ecclesiastical administration. The goal was full intercommunion between two continuing national churches, not organic merger.

This proposal evoked a limited degree of interest in England, but nothing compared to the widespread and vehement debate in Scotland. Even before the General Assembly of 1957 had received the report and transmitted it to the presbyteries for consideration, the newspapers generally were featuring it. Nationalist grievances made themselves felt, more among marginal members than those normally active in the church, and revived the historical Scottish apprehension of bishops as agents of political aggression from south of the border and threats to the spiritual independence of the church. This general climate had already made the success of the proposals problematical in Scotland when the 1958 Lambeth Conference of Anglican bishops issued a report that pulled the rug from under the Scottish advocates of bishops-in-presbytery. The Lambeth Committee expressed the opinion that while the spiritual effectiveness of Presbyterian ministerial orders "ought not to be implicitly or explicitly questioned," nevertheless "Anglicans conscientiously hold that the celebrant of the Eucharist should have been ordained by a bishop standing in the historical succession, and generally believe it to be their duty to bear witness to this principle by receiving Holy Communion only from those who have thus been ordained." [23] After that the Scottish General Assembly of 1959 could only register the general judgment in the Church of Scotland that the joint report was unacceptable, and attempt to arrange continuing conversations with the more modest goal of "a single united national church." The Scottish Committee on Inter-Church Relations recommended that the General Assembly express the view that "the next step towards greater unity between the Anglican and Presbyterian Churches lies in the recognition of one another as true members of the Church Catholic and of their ministries as valid and regular ministries of that Church." [24]

The joint committee in Great Britain had been spurred on by the success of the Church of South India, which seemed to demonstrate the possibility of episcopalian-presbyterian reconciliation. But even there problems of interchurch recognition remained. The Lambeth Conference had found itself unable to accord full recognition to the Church of South India. Would it be able to accord full intercommunion with a Church of Scotland which had incorporated bishops-in-presbytery, unless perhaps that church in turn cut off its intercommunion with other Presbyterian and Reformed churches which lacked such officers?

Schemes of church merger in North India, Ceylon, and Iran, meanwhile, were largely shaped by that of South India, save that to avoid the embarrassing transitional generation they all turned instead to devices of mutual commissioning-or-ordination. Discussions had begun in North India in 1929, and official negotiation was undertaken after Indian independence, in 1951. Four revisions of the plan were seen in the 1950's and 1960's, the last winning approval from six of the seven churches involved, all but the American-related Methodists.

The new Church of North India was launched in November, 1970, drawing together Baptists, Brethren, Disciples, Anglicans, Methodists (of British and Australian connections), and the United Church of North India (Presbyterian and Congregationalist). Representatives of the ministries of the several churches commissioned and authorized each other mutually and bishops-elect were installed and consecrated. Thus there came to be a church in North India about half the size of that in South India, but even more comprehensive ecclesiastically, in that it included Baptists and Disciples and the issue they pose to churches using infant baptism.

The ambiguity of the procedure distressed some. In 1961, for example, the Anglican Convocation of Canterbury proposed that the Ceylon plan be recognized by Anglicans if it were clear that reordination was intended. In general Anglicanism seemed to have progressively retreated from the ecumenical openness of 1920.

An attempt was made in the 1960's to emulate rather directly the growing union in North India, in the United States. It was launched unexpectedly by Eugene Carson Blake, the Stated Clerk of The United Presbyterian Church in the U.S.A., in a sermon preached in the San Francisco cathedral church of the Episcopalians in 1960. Speaking as a minister and apart from his official capacity, Blake proposed "to the Protestant Episcopal Church that it together with the United Presbyterian Church . . . invite the Methodist Church and the United Church of Christ to form with us a plan of church union both catholic and reformed." [25] The four denominations mentioned all rose to the challenge and officially designated representatives to a Consultation on Church Union in 1962. The consultation gathered representatives annually thereafter for several years, acquiring other participants up to a total of ten denominations at one time, together with "observers" from still more, including, from 1964, the Roman Catholics.

To satisfy the "catholics," Blake had proposed substantially the Quadrilateral. To satisfy the "reformed," he stipulated constitutional or "democratic" church government, diversity in doctrine and worship, and the principle of continuing reformation under the Word known in Scripture. On the crux of ordination Dr. Blake urged a joint commissioning service of all ministers by ordaining representatives of all participating churches, as in the Ceylon proposal. In Bishop James A. Pike's language, "We must let everyone lay hands on everyone else, and then let the Holy Spirit sort out who has done

what to whom." [26] Father Tavard raised the question whether a
church so constituted would be *either* catholic or reformed, apparently feeling that someone beside the Holy Spirit should be able to
tell when it was one or both.[27]

Principles of Church Union had been published in 1966. They
evoked criticism especially from Episcopalians, although the provisions
for the "historic episcopate" were the most carefully worked out aspect of the proposal. In 1968 it was decided to develop a draft plan,
and it was produced in 1970.

By that time, however, the focus of interest had somewhat shifted
from the traditional conundrums of ministerial orders to the aspiration for local unions which would effectively engage the laity. The
Consultation came up with a scheme to break up and recombine congregations in new structures called parishes. This feature, however,
did not win general lay support and the plan ran into trouble. The
revolt came unexpectedly from the United Presbyterian General Assembly of 1972, which voted to withdraw from the Consultation. The
vote was clearly a judgment on the plan in part, as was made clear
by the vote of the next Assembly to return to the Consultation. It also
reflected the widespread battle fatigue over the endless ecclesiastical
"restructuring," and distrust of the judgment and accountability of denominational and interdenominational bureaucracy. In the face of
such criticism COCU undertook to change its program to a less focused
process of consultation on church union.

Of far greater ecumenical significance than the COCU venture was
the stunning revolution in Roman Catholic–Protestant relations initiated by Pope John XXIII and the Second Vatican Council. If ecumenical achievement is to be measured by the depth of estrangement reconciled, by the intensity of the scandal which is purged, then
the relation with Roman Catholics is probably the most important
ecumenical challenge to Reformed Christians. The hostility, resentment, fear, suspicion on both sides in virtually every area where the
two churches were neighbors was previously the most conspicuous
denial before the world of the atoning power of the gospel. In these
respects a miracle occurred in the decade after 1962, signifying a
startling gain in the integrity of personal and corporate Christian life
for hundreds of thousands, Protestant and Roman Catholic.

In several ways the ecumenical opening at Vatican II was reminiscent of Lambeth 1920 and its "Appeal." There was the same
newly vivid sense of the community in Christ of all baptized, the

same willingness to confess a share in the guilt of schism, the same acknowledgment of the ecclesial reality in some form and degree of other churches, ministries and sacraments, the same eagerness for dialogue, but on a much greater scale.

In the conversations which followed over episcopacy and ministry there were great similarities and, indeed, many of the principles and arguments were equally applicable, *mutatis mutandis,* to primacy and to the historic episcopate. The Roman Catholic conversations, however, were broader, and involved some themes of special interest to the Reformed, as the stress on the Word read and preached, and unity in obedience and service to humanity, which had not generally figured in discussions with Anglicans. Formal bilateral conversations between Roman Catholics and Reformed and Presbyterian churches were instituted in the United States and on a world level. They have published some results and in general seem to have been able to formulate their differences *within* more basic agreements, which is a significant advance. The prevailing attitude of the Reformed churches in these relations is indicated by the declaration of the General Council of the World Reformed Alliance in 1964:

> We further urge the Churches to be alert to explore, with other Reformed churches and those of other traditions, the possibility of closer fellowship, joint action, or union; . . . to keep before them and all their people the truth that the wholeness of the Church must be made manifest in every local community. . . . We believe that the Roman Catholic and Reformed Churches are prepared to reassess and alter traditions in the light of deeper understanding of the Scripture, and call upon the Roman Catholic Church to continue with us such study and self-examination.[28]

XIII

PRESBYTERIANISM AND CHURCH UNION IN CANADA, AUSTRALIA, AND NEW ZEALAND

WITH THE EXPANSION of the British dominions in the modern era, Presbyterians, chiefly of Scottish origin, migrated in large numbers from their homeland to settle in distant localities and presently to take their part in newly formed communities and congregations. In addition to the Scottish migrations, and in most instances earlier, were the settlements of Dutch Reformed people in New York, New England, Nova Scotia, South Africa, and Indonesia, as well as the thwarted attempts of Admiral Coligny and others to establish colonies of French Protestants in Brazil, South Carolina, Florida, Tadoussac on the St. Lawrence, and Acadia.

In November, 1603, Henry IV of France commissioned a Protestant nobleman of Saintonge, Pierre du Guast, Sieur de Monts, an experienced seaman and explorer, as his "lieutenant general" to establish French settlements in "La Cadie, Canada, and other parts of New France." In his broad instructions, De Monts was to Christianize the natives and to set up the agencies of government for all inhabitants. The resulting settlement at Port Royal (Annapolis Royal, Nova Scotia), of which the Protestant lawyer Marc Lescarbot left a fascinating account,[1] was abandoned in 1607 under pressure from rival French interests, and having been revived was finally extinguished by the privateer Samuel Argall in an expedition based on Virginia (1613). It was under the authority of De Monts that Samuel de Champlain founded Quebec in 1608. There was no restriction on religious liberty in New France before the death of Henry IV in 1610, and the trade of the colonies was controlled by Huguenots. But in the 1620's under Richelieu the era of tolerance ended and from 1627 trade and settlement in New France were forbidden to

Protestants. The capture of Quebec for Britain by David Kirk of Dieppe and his brothers in 1629 was a mere interruption of the exclusive system. The colony was restored to France by treaty, and in 1633 Champlain returned as governor. Protestantism in any organized form was extinguished in the St. Lawrence settlements. Nevertheless from time to time a few individual Huguenots entered until 1685 when the Edict of Nantes was revoked by Louis XIV. Acadia, however, several times fell to the English and was recovered by France prior to the Treaty of Utrecht (1713) which made it finally a British possession as "Nova Scotia." A number of energetic Huguenot leaders participated in the government under both flags, and the French settlers in Nova Scotia were largely Protestants. Many of these entered the province from New York and New England. The Germans who came to America from the Palatinate in the eighteenth century were accompanied by numerous French-speaking Protestants from both France and Switzerland. "Some hundreds of these," says Dr. Ian F. Mackinnon, "chiefly from the neighborhood of Montbéliard, joined the German emigrants to Halifax and became a most valuable addition to the Protestant population of the province." A congregation was formed at Lunenberg consisting of Dutch and German-speaking immigrants who settled there in 1753. Unable to obtain a pastor from the homelands, this community elected one of its trusted laymen and applied to Presbyterian and Congregational ministers in Halifax for his ordination. Thus it came about that in the Dissenters' Meeting-House in Halifax, July 3, 1770, Bruin Romcas Comingoe received presbyterial ordination and entered on a fruitful pastorate of no less than fifty years.[2]

Scottish Presbyterianism entered Canada during the era of secessions from the Church of Scotland. But the divisions were soon felt to be meaningless in the actualities of the new land where the Kirk had no establishment and no patronage. A certain urgency in the spiritual needs of the settlers made it imperative to abandon the spirit of contention and move toward Presbyterian unity. In Nova Scotia although the Church of England for a time enjoyed the rank of an established church, Protestants dissenting from that church, "of what denomination soever," were not only free to worship and build "meeting-houses" but also exempted from Anglican church rates. In the Protestant Dissenters' Meeting-House erected in Halifax (1749), Presbyterians from Ireland and Scotland worshiped with Congregationalists from New England. The congregation during the early decades of its history sometimes suffered from internal discord. In 1787 its officers formally asked the Church of Scotland to select for it a pastor. Andrew Brown, an able Edinburgh graduate, was appointed. He bore a warm recommendation from the eminent leaders William Robertson and Hugh Blair, as a good preacher "of such liberal sentiments as to render him acceptable to persons of every denomination among you." Mr. Brown served the congregation well for eight years. The Dissenters' Meeting-House ultimately became St. Matthew's Church.

Scottish migration to Nova Scotia and Prince Edward Island was already beginning, and after 1783 the Highlanders became a leading population factor. The majority of these immigrants belonged to branches of the First Secession commonly called Burghers and Antiburghers.[3] But the Burgess oath, the cause of their division, had no bearing on their new situation. The Burgher Presbytery of Truro was formed in 1786 by ministers previously sent by the Scottish Burgher Synod. The Antiburgher Presbytery of Pictou was organized in 1795, but its ministers were already in fraternal intercourse with the Burgher group. In 1817 the two Presbyteries came together to form the Presbyterian Church of Nova Scotia. This was a year before the corresponding union of seceders in Scotland.

From New York State, Dutch Reformed Church missionaries followed the settlement of Germans and others north of Lake Ontario. The mission was active from 1795 to 1819, but the congregations founded by its ministers were absorbed into the Presbytery of the Canadas. Founded in 1818, this presbytery stemmed from the Burgher branch of the Scottish seceders. In 1831 it was expanded into a synod. In that year the Church of Scotland ministers in the Canadas organized the Presbyterian Church of Canada in connection with the Church of Scotland, in a synod and four presbyteries. A notable step toward unity was taken in 1840 when these two synods were united under the name of the latter. The "connection" with the Church of Scotland was an affirmation of spiritual fraternity and was in no sense administrative. But progress toward unity was interrupted by the formation in 1834 of a missionary branch of the Scottish United Seceders among new settlers in Western Ontario, and again by the effects of the Scottish Disruption of 1843.[4] The "Free" churches that were formed as a consequence of the Disruption in Ontario, New Brunswick, and Nova Scotia promptly entered into negotiations for union with the units of secession origin. In Nova Scotia these were united in 1860 as the Presbyterian Church of the Lower Provinces of

238   ECUMENICAL TESTIMONY

British North America, and in Ontario and Quebec the Canada Presbyterian Church, composed of like elements, emerged in 1861.[5] Nova
Scotia and Prince Edward Island had a synod connected with the
Church of Scotland, and New Brunswick had another; but in 1868
they were united in the Synod of the Maritime Provinces. This union
reduced to four the churches still to be joined for the completion of
Presbyterian union in the Dominion.

The expectation of this was already widely held. By 1860 *The Presbyterian Witness,* published in Halifax and then ably edited by Robert
Murray, advocated a General Assembly for "the British Provinces."
He and other far-seeing churchmen in the various segments of Presbyterianism were already giving expression to hopes not only of the
consolidation of these units but of a coming "accord among all God's
people." Professor James Ross of Truro at the uniting service of 1860
exclaimed: "We accept what has been done as a token of further
union. . . . When the spirit of union begins to move, who will set
bounds to its influence?" And at the Canadian union of 1861 William
Ormiston voiced a prayer that the spirit of union might prevail in all
the churches.

A new sense of Canadian nationality was in the making and was
strongly shared by Presbyterians. The Confederation of four provinces
under the name Dominion of Canada, achieved in 1867, encouraged
the hope of unity in the church. The Intercolonial Railway, even before its completion in 1876, made possible convenient intercourse between the provinces. In 1872 George Monro Grant, minister of St.
Matthew's, Halifax, accompanied an engineering expedition to the
Pacific Coast. His account of this in a vivid book, *Ocean to Ocean,*
widened the range of thinking for Canadians. The vast expanses he
described were soon to become parts of the Dominion.[6] In each of the
churches there were men to match the opportunity of the time. The
generation was blessed by a gifted and devoted company of ecumen-
ically-minded churchmen whose task it was to guide the several parts
of Canadian Presbyterianism toward unification.[7] In view of the tide
of events, their task cannot be said to have been particularly difficult.
Yet there were other than geographic hindrances to be overcome. In
the synods of Church of Scotland connection there existed a presupposition, not shared by those of secession origin, of obligations to the
church on the part of the political government. But in the Canadian
situation after 1854 this issue was hardly more than academic, and it
was not much agitated in public disputation. On various grounds,

however, minority opposition was vocal in each of the negotiating churches. There were a few persistent individual opponents, and local points of continued resistance; but these were insufficient to halt the movement.[8]

Definite negotiations began from a letter written by William Ormiston, moderator of the Canada Presbyterian Synod, to the moderator of the Kirk-connected synod, which was read in a meeting of the latter, June 5, 1869. The proposal was for a Joint Committee to consist of three ministers and three laymen from each of the four synods concerned. (Of these the Canada Presbyterian Synod became a General Assembly in 1870.) All four courts considered and approved the plan and sent their representatives to the first meeting of the Joint Committee under John Cook's chairmanship, September 28, 1870. This meeting drafted a basis of union, which though later enlarged was not to be otherwise greatly altered. The church-state issue was put to rest by inserting in the preamble a statement, proposed by the Canada Presbyterian Church, that the united church would be "independent of all others in its jurisdiction, and under authority to Christ alone, the Head of His Church and Head over all things to His Church." The three articles that follow affirm the authority of Scripture, the Westminster Confession and Catechisms (full liberty of conscience in matters of religion being explicitly guarded), and the Westminster documents on church government and public worship. Attached to the Basis are eight "Accompanying Resolutions." Notable in these is declaration of "Christian affection toward the whole Church of God" and the desire for intercourse with its branches as opportunity offers. The process of voting on the Basis in presbyteries and sessions consumed some time. For different reasons, some twenty-five congregations declined to enter the union; most of these soon afterward reversed their decision and were admitted to the appropriate presbyteries. Enabling legislation by the provinces and final action by the several synods were completed shortly before the date set for the consummation of union, June 15, 1875.

On that day the 560 commissioners to the supreme courts of the four churches, having been in session in Montreal, in a mingled procession entered Victoria Hall, a capacious building used as a rink, where a great assemblage had gathered. After a service of worship, in which the One Hundredth Psalm, "All people that on earth do dwell," was sung with feeling, the Basis of Union was read, and subscribed by the retiring moderators. Senior among these was Peter George

McGregor of the Synod of the Lower Provinces (son of James McGregor, the eminent missionary founder in the Maritimes), who now pronounced the four churches to be united as The Presbyterian Church in Canada. Dr. John Cook, a venerable and impressive personality, was elected moderator of the newly formed Assembly. His opening address contained a prophetic forecast of a wider union yet to be achieved:

> Far larger union is, I trust, in store for the churches of Christ even in Canada, than that which we effect this day. This is but a small step to the union which Our Lord's intercessory prayer seems to contemplate. . . . I look for a union in the future before which the present—blessed and auspicious though we justly count it—shall appear slight and insignificant. May God hasten it in his time.[9]

The Presbyterian Church in Canada at once exhibited a strong internal life and entered upon an era of active service within and beyond the Dominion. A flowing tide of immigration, populating the Western provinces and territories, challenged the church's energies and offered a limitless field of expansion. The foreign missionary activities of the tributary churches were coordinated and greatly increased. Many of the missionaries attained distinction in the lands to which they went, especially for their contributions to elementary and college education, and to medical services and the founding of hospitals. In these enterprises they were characteristically in full cooperation with personnel of other denominations, a relationship which in turn helped to promote an ecumenical spirit in the home church. Conditions in Western Canada also called for interdenominational cooperation. Dr. Samuel Dwight Chown tells the (possibly apocryphal) story of a Doukhobor who, seeing four churches on the public square of a prairie town, asked of each, "Is this a Jesus church?" Receiving affirmative answers from each, he then asked, "Why four?" The argument against the multiplication of weak local charges was both religious and economic. It was pointed out that religion appeared as the one divisive factor in otherwise unified communities, and the separation was costly in funds that might be more usefully bestowed. The most rapidly growing of other denominations was the Methodist Church, which formed a nationwide union in 1884. In 1889 a measure of comity was introduced whereby Methodists and Presbyterians agreed that neither would set up a mission charge where the other already had begun one. This was followed by the agreed withdrawal of one mission pastor wherever two were unprofitably stationed in small charges. Congregational home missions, fewer in number, soon participated in the plan. In 1911 a fuller scheme of cooperation, "in the interests of the Kingdom of God in Canada," was negotiated, by which the overlapping of dependent charges was to be eliminated, new districts were to be entered by common agreement, and work among foreign-language immigrants was to be conducted jointly. Anglicans and Baptists, without any unfriendliness, chose not to participate in this agreement.

Organization to guide these local arrangements gradually took form. In Alberta the synod's Committee on Home Missions and Social Service together with a similar Methodist agency became a joint provincial Committee on Cooperation under which district committees served. These met with representatives of charges in which readjustments were proposed and made decisions on the information presented. It was convenient for the success of this method that Methodism in Canada had adopted a polity which in many respects matched that of Presbyterianism, district and conference corresponding to presbytery and synod. Moreover, the two denominations, as they faced in common the issues of the time, were growing more alike in their Christian life and social concerns. Actually in the formation of union congregations in this way extremely little opposition was encountered. By 1922 no fewer than three thousand "local unions," comprised within more than one thousand pastoral charges, chiefly in the Western provinces and northern Ontario, had been organized, many of them from the first in definite expectation of the general union to which the denominations concerned were irrevocably committed. The hope of this outcome, indeed, gave reality to the plan of cooperation, which merely in itself had serious ecclesiastical limitations. There was a recognized inconsistency in a policy of uniting small charges while leaving those in populous centers to continue their competitive existence. However, in a good many instances the local union took place on the initiative of the local people, who after due process of voting obtained the approval of the appropriate denominational committees. It should be noted that the theological schools of all three denominations helped to direct the minds of ministers in training toward church unity. Cooperation in theological training was increasingly practiced from about 1900. This involved interchange of teachers and interdenominational mingling of students. In Montreal and Vancouver, Anglicans participated in such programs.[10]

The history of the formation of the United Church of Canada does not begin, as often assumed, within the twentieth century. The notion of "a far larger union" voiced by Dr. Cook in 1875 and by many others in that era, remained, it is true, for more than a decade vague and formless. Hopes of union then took the direction indicated by the so-called Lambeth Quadrilateral of 1888, which had really been promulgated by the 1886 Chicago Convention of the Episcopal Church and was based upon a proposal of William Reed Huntington in a work of 1870. Canadian Anglicans began to stir up discussion of Protestant union, and in 1885 the Anglican Provincial Synod of Canada appointed a committee to confer with the Methodist and Presbyterian churches. Following the favorable response of the Methodists, the Presbyterian General Assembly appointed a committee for union discussion, and an earnest and friendly conference was held in Toronto in April, 1889. But the fourth clause in the Quadrilateral, on "the historic episcopate," presented difficulties that seemed insuperable, and, despite the wishes of Principal William Caven of Knox College, Toronto, no further conversations were held in this context. Nevertheless the Assembly on hearing a report of the conference reappointed and enlarged the committee on union (1890).

But Presbyterians were beginning to look more directly toward the Methodist and Congregational churches. In a discourse entitled "The Church of Canada, Can Such a Thing Be?" George Monro Grant in 1890 wrote: "The Presbyterian and Methodist Churches are nearly ready for corporate union," and in 1893 he declared: "It is wrong to blame Baptist views of Baptism and Anglican views of the episcopate for our divisions. Until the churches that are at one on these points unite it is a waste of time to talk to others about union." [11] Thus the course ultimately followed was clearly anticipated in some minds well before the turn of the century. In 1893 the Assembly appointed a new and carefully representative committee on union, and this committee was annually reappointed until 1901. Its work was, however, not very fruitful. In 1895 it was asked to confer with a corresponding Methodist committee on a federal union that had been proposed by the Methodist General Conference. The project was to frame an overall plan for "dependent charges." In the ensuing conversations it became apparent that no federal union could be the goal for the churches concerned, but that a corporate union must be sought. The

Canadian Society of Christian Union, founded in 1898 by Presbyterians and Anglicans and participated in by others, helped to arouse a desire for union by exposing the wastefulness of denominationalism in small communities, but failed to lead to a consensus on major issues. At this time discussions in the press helped to make familiar the idea of that triple union which was later to be achieved. Without abandoning the desire for wider, even total, Christian union, ministers and people began to envision the first practical step for Canada in this direction as the corporate union of Congregationalists, Methodists, and Presbyterians.

Although the year 1902 does not mark the first interdenominational approach to church union in Canada, it dates the inception of those specific negotiations that were to bring together three denominations in 1925. It appears that the voices of interchurch delegates played no small part in bringing on the first steps. At the 1902 Assembly a delegate from the Congregational Council expressed his expectation of forthcoming union of his denomination with the Presbyterians, and the moderator gave a cordial reply. Principal William Patrick, a brilliant and outspoken newcomer from Scotland to Winnipeg, was quick to sense the opportunity before the Canadian churches. As a member of the Presbyterian delegation to the Methodist General Conference held in Winnipeg in September, 1902, he made a rousing appeal for Methodist and Presbyterian unity. This utterance was made, as Dr. Patrick was careful to say, solely on his own initiative; but those who heard it were aware that it was well backed by Presbyterian opinion. Two days later the Conference declared "in no spirit of exclusiveness toward others not named" that it would favor a movement for organic union with the Presbyterian and Congregational churches. In 1903 the Assembly received this declaration favorably, and in that year the Congregational Council unanimously decided to begin negotiations for union with the other two. As a result a preliminary conference of representatives of the three churches was brought about in April, 1904. At this meeting the aged Principal Caven, in a speech long remembered, "poured out his soul on behalf of union," pointing to the existing agreement in essentials of belief and polity.

The way was now cleared for effective negotiation. When the large Joint Committee met in December, 1904, its chairman, Caven, had passed from the earthly scene; but it went forward in accordance with his hopes. Subcommittees were set up on doctrine, polity, ministry, administration, and law. These reported a year later to the Joint

Committee. This cooperation between the Joint Committee and the special sections continued fruitfully until 1908, when the Basis of Union was drafted. Its doctrinal statement, mainly prepared in 1905, made large use of two documents of Presbyterian but not of Canadian origin. These were the Articles of Faith adopted by the English Presbyterians in 1890 and the Brief Statement of the Reformed Faith approved by the General Assembly of the Presbyterian Church in the U.S.A. in 1902. In 1906 the Anglican and Baptist churches were invited to send delegates to participate in the Joint Committee. The graciously worded replies from each of these denominations were affirmations of positions irreconcilable with those of the Committee and with the Basis of Union; and no delegates were sent. Apparently nobody then thought of the more recent practice of sending nonparticipating observers.

Although at crucial points Presbyterians had taken the initiative in the approach to union, it was chiefly among Presbyterians that opposition now began to arise. When in 1910, in accord with the Barrier Act, the Assembly sent the Basis of Union to the presbyteries, a considerable minority voted to oppose it. An anonymous pamphlet appeared protesting against the union and presenting anew the alternative of federation with a central committee to determine the affiliation of rural and village charges. Of 67 presbyteries, 50 voted for the Basis, some of these however, with sizable minorities. In 1911 Assembly sent the matter to the local churches, dividing the issue into that of the union in general and that of the Basis itself. Perhaps surprisingly, the majority favoring the Basis was a little larger than that for union: of elders 70 percent, communicants 74, and adherents 73. While the Methodists and Congregationalists awaited the final action of the Presbyterians, the Assembly, hoping for "practically unanimous action," again consulted the presbyteries and people. The Basis, now slightly amended, was presented in 1915 and the vote showed no marked change; presbyteries were more favorable, elders and people less so. Agitation against the union was intensified during the War. From 1916 an agency calling itself the Presbyterian Church Association labored, in a nationwide campaign of speech and print, to consolidate and increase the opposition. There then existed no corresponding office or organization for the promotion of the Union. Yet most of the trusted leaders of the church from coast to coast in true succession to their predecessors of the days of Grant and Caven were fully committed to the union, and the percentage of opponents was not greatly changed by propaganda.

By this time the First World War was at its height, and many Canadian youth and ministers were in some branch of the service. The Assembly of 1916 resolved by a vote of 496 to 90 to proceed with the union but to delay final action until "the first Assembly following the first year after the close of the War," the necessary legislation to be prepared in the meanwhile. Not until 1921, however, did the Assembly find opportunity to resume the issue. The opponents of union had now become highly organized and vocal. The doctrinal Basis of Union, though drawn largely from Presbyterian documents, was denounced as a denial of traditional Presbyterianism. In a writ filed in the Ontario courts it was stated that the Assembly had no authority to enter a union or to alter the standards of the church so as to omit such distinctive doctrines of Presbyterianism as that God has "eternally predestined a fixed number . . . to eternal life" and "decreed others to eternal death." The Assembly of 1923 rejected after discussion a new proposal for cooperation and reaffirmed union by 444 to 92. In that year somewhat belatedly the Joint Committee established a bureau of literature and information. The legislation placed before the provincial parliament was opposed by many legislators who disclosed an unexpected solicitude for what they assumed to be the Presbyterian Church. In 1924 the Assembly, fortified by a new decisive endorsement on the part of the presbyteries, firmly proceeded on its course and by a vote of 426 to 96 requested the federal Parliament to enact appropriate legislation. An informed exposition of church autonomy in relation to the state by the leader of the Opposition, Arthur Meighen, was instrumental in securing an overwhelmingly favorable vote, and the United Church of Canada Act became law, July 19, 1924. As in the case of the Scottish union of 1900, the nonconcurrents claimed all the property held by the church. The Act provided for a commission, consisting of three from each side and three chosen by these six, to determine an equitable division.

In the final vote by congregations, which took place after the union, those entering the United Church from all three denominations numbered 8,691 while 8 Congregational and 784 Presbyterian congregations chose to remain out of it. A disproportionate number of the larger congregations were within this Presbyterian minority. In the end the nonconcurrents numbered 30.18 percent of the Presbyterian membership with about 25 percent of the ministers. This minority claimed, and finally obtained, the right to use the old name "Presbyterian Church in Canada." Despite the cleavage, the Presbyterians entering the union constituted nearly half the membership of

246ECUMENICAL TESTIMONY

the United Church. All foreign mission units of the Presbyterian Church, and all but 17 of its 328 foreign missionaries, at once attached themselves to the United Church, and their work continued without dislocation in the new relationship.

At this time Newfoundland was a crown colony politically independent of Canada. Its people were predominantly Methodist, and Presbyterianism was confined to nine charges. These were, however, within the Presbyterian Church in Canada, being connected with the Presbytery of Halifax, and in accord with the policy of the church were in cooperation with the Methodists. By far the largest and most influential of the congregations was St. Andrew's in the capital city of St. John's. In successive votes St. Andrew's twice changed its alignment and finally declined to enter the union, while recommending that five of the smaller charges join the United Church, and itself making substantial contributions to the latter's benevolent funds. By agreement with the Union Committee in Toronto, final decision and legislation in Newfoundland were somewhat delayed. There was also prearranged agreement with the Methodists regarding the legislation enacted in 1926, by which Newfoundland Methodism's attachment to the United Church was confirmed. In the same year the nonconcurring Presbyterians were made a part of the Presbytery of Cape Breton and Newfoundland then formed by the Presbyterian Assembly. Cooperation in education was effected in 1924, and in 1964 resulted in the complete amalgamation of educational agencies, Presbyterians being represented on the United Church School Board of St. John's.[12]

The formal inauguration of the United Church of Canada took place in the Mutual Street Arena, Toronto, June 10, 1925. A solemn and elaborate order of service helped to make the occasion one of glad celebration, reverence, and deep emotion. The crowning experience came in the administration of the Lord's Supper to the thousands who filled the Arena. It was the part of Samuel Dwight Chown, the Methodist Superintendent, to declare the consenting churches "one communion within the Body of Christ," and the General Council of the United Church of Canada was constituted with prayer. In a later session Dr. George Campbell Pidgeon, a stalwart Presbyterian leader of that era, was unanimously elected moderator of the General Council.[13] Dr. Pidgeon died, an honored veteran in his hundredth year, in June, 1971.

The doctrinal articles of the Basis present a typical early-twentieth-century statement of Protestant belief, stripped of seventeenth-century scholastic terminology and without specific reference to historic documents of the assenting denominations. Of its twenty articles, fourteen are taken with minor changes from the Brief Statement of the Reformed Faith adopted by the Assembly of the Presbyterian Church in the U.S.A. in 1902.[14] Article III, "Of the Divine Purpose," reads:

> We believe that the eternal, wise, holy and loving purpose of God so embraces all events that while the freedom of man is not taken away, nor is God the author of sin, yet in His providence He makes all things work together in the fulfillment of His sovereign design and the manifestation of His glory.

Article VII, "Of the Grace of God," affirms that God in Christ "freely offers His all-sufficient salvation to all men." Article XV, "Of the Church," with a typical Reformed definition of the Holy Catholic Church cites certain activities proper to the visible church, including "the universal proclamation of the Gospel." Article XVIII, in an echo of the Westminster Confession XVI, 2, enjoins Christians "to live in fellowship with their brethren, which fellowship is to be extended, as God gives opportunity, to all who in every place call upon the name of the Lord Jesus." [15] This implies the United Church's commitment to the pursuit of "far larger union" and its involvement in the ecumenical revival of this century.

The constitutional structure of the United Church of Canada is typically conciliar, with stratified elective governing bodies. There is a recognizable resemblance to the polities of the Reformed churches of France and Scotland and of the Presbyterian churches of the United States. Above the "session" of the pastoral charge are ranged in order the Presbytery, the Conference, and the General Council. The respective duties of these courts are spelled out in detail. "The liberty of the pastoral charge" within its sphere is assured, and the duties of its session and committee of stewards are defined. Ministers are examined and ordained by authority of the Conference after recommendation by presbyteries. The Conference appoints annually a Settlement Committee to secure a settled pastor without interruption in every charge. This does not preclude the call of ministers by the congregation. Difficulty was experienced in the transfer of ministers from one conference to another until this was expedited by the creation of a Transfer Committee under the General Council. In worship no abrupt change was required, but in 1932 a book of worship was issued, the product of thoughtful and scholarly labor, which has been gradually brought into use in the congregations and has won high praise in other churches.

The Statement of Faith in twelve articles adopted in 1940 makes no substantial change in the church's professed faith. In it the principle is stressed that all members of the Holy Catholic Church in every age are one in Christ. The United Church has from the first been deeply engaged in remedial social work, but this has not been given an adequate theological basis. Taking his cue from a *Christian Century* editorial, Randolph Carleton Chalmers, a secretary of the church, in 1945 discussed the critical need for a reinvigoration of theology that would affirm and expound "the moral and spiritual authority of the Word of God." [16] It is characteristic of Canada that it has attracted or produced theological scholars rather than theologians. While the theological stance of the United Church of Canada resembles in general that of The United Presbyterian Church in the U.S.A., it has no document comparable in weight and range to the latter's Confession of 1967. But through a trying era of history it has taken a leading place in the religious life of Canada, and on census returns its percentage of growth has been surpassed only by Roman Catholicism. It has attained an almost complete coalescence of the parent denominations and as an active member of the world organizations of each of these, and of the World Council of Churches, it participates in the whole ecumenical enterprise.[17] Within Canada itself, as Bishop Neill has observed, it continually reaches out to other communions "in the hope that, whereas this Union is a great achievement in itself, to later ages it may present itself as only a step forward in the development of a great and truly Catholic Church of Canada." [18] It has already been joined by a number of detached congregations that had their beginnings under other auspices. In 1945–1948 a plan was drawn up for union with the Canada Conference of the Evangelical United Brethren, but negotiations were then discontinued. They were resumed in 1964 and completed in 1967. This union, which adds sixty-one congregations to the United Church, was consummated in Kitchener, Ontario, January 10, 1968.

There have been many evidences of progress toward reconciliation with the minority Presbyterian Church of 1925, including cooperation in home mission planning and in various local undertakings, and in recent years discussions on doctrine. Conversations looking toward union with the Anglican Church of Canada were several times begun and halted before 1958; since then they have advanced to a decisive stage. First a Joint Committee on Christian Unity and the Church Universal was created to guide the negotiations. It consisted of ten members from each of the two churches plus an ex-officio member from each. This body issued in 1965 *The Principles of Union Between the Anglican Church of Canada and the United Church of Canada*. This condensed but sufficiently explicit statement deals with "faith and order," including sacraments and ministry, and in a section on "organizational unity" approves the threefold ministry of bishops, presbyters, and deacons. After the adoption of this document by the Anglicans (1965) and the United Church (1966), the Christian Church in Canada, a small denomination affiliated with American, Australian, and other Disciples of Christ, became a third party to the conversations (1969) and accepted the *Principles*. In 1966 and 1967 the two churches then negotiating created a fuller organization for union in the General Commission on Church Union with five special commissions reporting to it. From their efforts came *The Plan of Union—First Draft*, issued in February, 1971. In the modesty and tentativeness of its language this document is rather novel among official statements. This is a feature of Section III, "A Declaration of Faith," much of which is written in a tone of inquiry rather than pronouncement. Yet the Plan decides some issues quite unambiguously. In Section V, "Constitution and By-laws," we read: "The ordained ministry shall consist of bishops, presbyters and deacons, and shall be open to both men and women."

The name tentatively adopted for the new communion is The Church of Christ in Canada. Its organization has been worked out in ample detail. The units in the structure are to be: the pastoral zone, with a local council; the bishop, with a conference to cooperate with him in securing pastoral oversight; and the region with a regional synod. At the outset the country will be divided into sixteen regions. The structure, which is soundly conciliar in its series of representative governing bodies, culminates in the National Assembly in which lay representatives are to constitute a majority. If the new church comes into being without serious numerical loss by schism, it will have well over three million members. Meanwhile a great deal of planned cooperation between the present denominations goes on. Several stages must still be passed before final commitment to the union by all concerned can be reached, and no hasty action is to be looked for. Whatever the outcome of the present plan, it seems most unlikely that the churches concerned can ever revert to their former mutual detachment.[19]

Halfway around the world from Canada, the islands of Australasia saw the rise of colonies that were to become important parts of the British Commonwealth. Australia, though neglected by the Dutch who in the 1640's had made landings on its western and southern shores, was repeatedly visited by Captain James Cook in the 1770's. It was not until 1788 that the first immigrants, consisting of convicts and soldiers to the number of more than 1,000, were sent to form a settlement on Botany Bay. From this unpromising beginning the flourishing colony of New South Wales arose. It was rescued from disorder in the regime of Governor Lachlan Macquarie (1807–1820), who brought out with him a regiment of Highlanders. Through the nineteenth century, while the interior was explored and population expanded, Australia's government was in separate political units. Efforts toward political consolidation were delayed by the reluctance of New South Wales. But the negotiations were finally successful, and in 1901 the six colonies, which were now spread over the main island and Tasmania, formed the Commonwealth of Australia, with a federal parliament of limited powers, a supreme court, and a governor-general.[20]

Immigration to Australia was prevailingly from the British Isles, and included a due proportion of Scottish and other Presbyterians. A community of Scots arrived at the Hawkesbury River, north of Sydney, in 1802, and soon built a stone church. They used the services of a catechist until they could secure a minister from the Church of Scotland. The subsequent story of Presbyterianism in Australia contains chapters of conflict as well as of reunion effort. The brilliant and impetuous John Dunmore Lang, who came to Sydney in 1823, was a great promoter and at times a divider of the church. Having founded a number of preaching centers, he visited Scotland and brought ordained ministers to man them. As a result the Presbytery of New South Wales was founded in 1832. But becoming incensed by the passing of a law, supported by some of his ministerial colleagues, to bring the Presbyterian churches under a measure of state control, and by the refusal of the Presbytery to admit as members certain ministers whom he had more recently brought from Scotland, he withdrew from the Presbytery and with these newcomers formed, without higher authority, a new body under the name Synod of New South Wales. Sanction for the Synod was later obtained in Scotland, and in 1840 it was again in union with the Presbytery under the changed title "Synod of Australia in connection with the Church of Scotland." Lang now visited America to study the American way of supporting churches and colleges without government aid. Returning, he presented proposals and pursued courses of action that caused trouble in the Synod, and in 1842 he was deposed for arbitrary conduct, to lead another small schism that was in the end reconciled with the Synod in 1860. In 1843 he was elected to the New South Wales legislative council, where he long took the lead in opposing the state establishment and endowment of churches. If his ability and sincerity had been matched by a cooperative spirit, his service to the Australian church might have been greatly enhanced.[21]

Meanwhile Presbyterian ministers were active among the Scots settlers in Victoria, where James Clow, a former East India Company chaplain in broken health, began work at Melbourne in 1837. James Forbes, an Aberdeen man who followed Clow in 1840, was one of those secured for Australia by Dr. Lang, but was a man of different disposition, who cherished fellowship with his brethren in Presbyterian and other churches, radiated spirituality and unworldliness, and looked for the future emergence of a church for all Australians. Questions related to the Scottish Disruption now began to disturb the Australian churches. The Presbytery of Melbourne was constituted by authority of the Synod of Australia in 1842, with Forbes as its first moderator. In 1844 he was instrumental in bringing the Synod to affirm its support of the nonintrusion principle of the Free Church, which, it was recalled, had been asserted by the Church of Scotland itself in the Veto Act of 1834.[22] The Synod did not, however, formally ally itself with the Free Church. In 1846, without receding from its position on nonintrusion, it voted to retain "connection with the Church of Scotland." Heated correspondence from both parties in Scotland aroused partisan feeling in Australia. A minority separated to form the Synod of Eastern Australia, and Forbes and his colleagues in 1847 established in Victoria the Free Church Synod of Australia Felix. Ministers of the Relief church began work in the Melbourne area during the 1840's, and, becoming attached to the United Presbyterian Church in consequence of the union of 1847, formed in 1850 a United Presbyterian Synod.

In 1851 Australia Felix was politically severed from New South Wales and became the colony of Victoria. This event was immediately followed by an extraordinary gold rush, by which the population of

the colony was in five years multiplied by four. The Free Church of
Scotland did its utmost to meet the need by sending many able ministers, and their labors were rewarded in the founding and growth of
churches. The leaders, among them Dr. Adam Cairns, who arrived in
1852, and Irving Hetherington, who had succeeded Mr. Forbes in the
Scots Church, Melbourne, in 1851, soon began to look toward a union
with the United Presbyterians. It was the latter, however, who first
proposed such a union. In a letter read in the Free Church Synod of
1853 they invited the Synod to appoint a committee to negotiate with
a committee of their own United Presbyterian Synod. But the Free
Synod was embarrassed by the fact that it had just approved the policy
of accepting donations of sites for churches from the government, a
course which involved a principle known to be unacceptable to the
other body. Action was accordingly postponed. Presently Mr. Hetherington and others raised the wider proposal for a union to include
the Presbyterians of the Church of Scotland connection. The concept
of a general Presbyterian union within each state soon prevailed. In
1859 the Presbyterian units in Victoria came together to form the
Presbyterian Church of Victoria. A few of both the United Presbyterian and the Free Church ministers held aloof until state aid was
wholly withdrawn in 1870. In 1865 the above-mentioned synods of
Australia, of Eastern Australia, and of New South Wales united, constituting the General Synod of the Presbyterian Church of New South
Wales. In South Australia, Presbyterian union was completed in the
same year; in Tasmania it was delayed until 1896.[23] In all these unions
the Westminster Standards were retained. In Victoria, following a heresy incident of 1883, the General Assembly adopted a Declaratory Act
on the decrees of God, infant salvation, the days of Creation, and other
topics in modern discussion. No embarrassing differences existed to prevent the general union of the Australian Presbyterian churches. Conferences held in Sydney and Melbourne led to the plan for a federal
union and this was achieved in the formation of the Federal Assembly
in 1886. This body, more consultative than legislative, through its
meetings held successively in the different state capitals of New South
Wales, Victoria, South Australia, Queensland, and Tasmania, promoted the national unification of the church. During the 1890's proposals for a nationwide union were advanced, discussed, amended,
and finally adopted. In 1901, the year that saw the beginning of the
Commonwealth of Australia, the General Assembly of the Presbyterian
Church of Australia also came into being. In the new national Pres-

byterian organization the Assembly holds supreme authority in all essential decisions such as those relating to doctrine, worship, missions, and the training and admission of ministers. The Westminster Confession was again affirmed, with a declaratory act interpreting doctrinal points in modern discussion.[24]

From its beginning the nationally constituted Presbyterian Church held in expectation the rise of a united evangelical church of Australia. At once a committee was charged with the task of framing principles that might be accepted as essential for such a union. For some years (1905–1912) there were discussions with the Church of England in Australia with a view to federation, but, partly because that church lacked autonomy in Australia, this effort failed. From 1919 there has been cooperation in ministerial education with Methodists and Congregationalists, led by the combined theological faculty of Sydney. During the years of the First World War, Methodists, Congregationalists, and Presbyterians together prepared a scheme of corporate union, which went to the congregations of the three churches for a vote in 1918. In 1919 cooperation among the three in ministerial education was inaugurated, led by the combined theological faculty of Sydney. All three voted favorably on the union proposal, but with considerable opposition, and this was largest among Presbyterians. Amended proposals in 1922 were rejected in the state assemblies and never reached the presbyteries or congregations. The 1924 General Assembly, in view of divided opinion in the church, decided against immediate action. Only in 1942 was the project resumed by the Assembly, in a resolution that authorized "exploratory conferences with the Methodist and Congregationalist and/or other churches." A joint conference in December, 1942, projected a federal union with joint departmental boards, corporate union being still ultimately in view. Negotiations on this basis went on hesitantly until 1951, when they were regretfully discontinued by the Assembly. The other churches halted action, still hoping for Presbyterian participation. The 1954 Assembly reopened the issue of corporate union and asked for a new vote. This proved surprisingly affirmative, and interchurch negotiations were resumed in 1956, committees being appointed by each church.

A Basis of Union was framed by the conveners of these committees and circulated for comment and revision. In revised form it reached the Assembly in 1957, and was hotly debated. A Joint Commission consisting of seven from each church now entered upon intense work.

In 1959 it produced a report entitled *The Faith of the Church*. This contains a well thought out declaration of the place of the received creeds and confessions, and an exposition of "the new awareness of the Church" in the present age. It proceeds to indicate (Part II) where the church's faith is to be found, noting not only the Scripture and the ancient creeds but Reformation documents, the Scots Confession, Westminster Confession, Savoy Declaration, "affirmations of the Evangelical Revival," and Wesley's sermons. This is followed by a brief confession, evidently based on the Apostles' Creed. A second report, on *The Church: Its Nature, Functions and Ordering*, embodying much historical research, came from the Commission in 1963, together with its "Proposed Basis of Union." From the three denominations suggestions for alterations have been returned to the Commission and acted upon by the church authorities.

It was intended that the Uniting Church have a threefold ministry of bishops, presbyters, and deacons, the office of bishop being defined in constitutionally restricted terms. In this connection a concordat was proposed with the Church of South India, and bishops of that church were to be invited to join in the consecration of the first bishops of the Australian church at its formation. Objections to this plan prevailed, however. The Joint Commission was charged to revise the Basis in the light of criticism from each of the church authorities in time for their 1970 meetings. A revised Basis appeared in March, 1970, and this document was again altered slightly in 1971. An "Interim Constitution" has been in preparation for use in the Uniting Church until as one body it can determine its own permanent plan of government. The Congregationalists voted in 1973 to join the union; and, after an indecisive vote in 1972, Presbyterian communicants voted a second time in 1973, with a strong majority of congregations favoring union. The Presbyterian General Assembly and the Methodist General Conference delayed until 1974 a decision on whether to join in the formation of a new church body to be named "The Uniting Church of Australia." The churches concerned are, in their present titles, the Congregational Union of Australia, the Methodist Church of Australia, and the Presbyterian Church of Australia. From an early date the General Synod of the Church of England in Australia sent observers to the Commission's meetings, and in 1966 the Synod entered into active negotiations, though without any understanding that the union of the other three would be delayed for the inclusion of the Anglicans. The expectation is that after the Uniting

Church is formed negotiations with the General Synod will continue. The Churches of Christ (Disciples) have also sent observers to the Commission on Union, but prospects of their joining the Uniting Church seem more remote. There are feelers out toward the now united Australian Lutherans, but no purposeful negotiations in that sector have begun.[25]

Although Captain Cook made a landing in New Zealand in 1769, permanent settlement there began only in the 1830's. The first Presbyterian services were held by John MacFarlane of the Church of Scotland at Wellington in 1840. In the subsequent decades the Free Church was more active, and the Presbytery of Wellington, formed in 1857, adopted Free Church standards. Meanwhile Scottish settlements had been made in Otago and Canterbury in the South Island. The shipload of Scots who reached Otago in April, 1848, had been to some extent selected for personal qualities, and most of them belonged to the Free Church. They were under the direction of Captain William Cargill, a descendant of leading Covenanters, and Thomas Burns, nephew of Scotland's poet, a resourceful and devoted minister. They called their settlement Dunedin, the name of Edinburgh in Celtic times. A presbytery was formed at Otago in 1854, the earliest in New Zealand. The district of Canterbury received its first settlers, chiefly Anglicans, in 1850. Many Scots soon followed. They erected Presbyterian church and school buildings at Christchurch, and in 1856 obtained a minister. On the initiative of the Otago Presbytery negotiations for Presbyterian unity for the whole colony were instituted, and in 1861 a conference was held at Dunedin which framed a basis of union affirming the Westminster Standards and proposing a General Assembly and three synods. However, a convocation of representatives at Aukland in 1862 voted to qualify acceptance of the Westminster worship and discipline by the phrase "only in so far as they are applicable to the circumstances of this church." The Otago Presbytery viewed this qualification with alarm as ominous of possible radical changes to come. The convocation further startled the conservatives when it recklessly proceeded to constitute itself the General Assembly of the Presbyterian Church of New Zealand, and authorized some changes in worship. The Otago Presbytery severed connections with the newly formed Assembly, and the Synod of Otago and Southland was formed, unifying the South Island churches.

Other occasions of disagreement loomed up. There was apprehen-

sion in the South Island regarding the school and church properties
in case of union; and positions diverged regarding marriage with a
deceased wife's sister, permitted under the law. In 1871 approaches
from the northern church resulted in fresh negotiations, but the
voting that resulted showed a strong minority still in opposition.
A renewal of the proposal in 1881 brought the same result. In 1893,
however, the Synod of Otago and Southland reopened negotiations
in a more conciliatory spirit. Opponents still found arguments against
union, including that of the forbidding distances between outlying
parts of the islands. But finally the cause of union prevailed and in
October, 1901, the Presbyterian Church of New Zealand was solemnly
reconstituted so as to comprehend all New Zealanders of that communion, and organized under a General Assembly.[26]

The New Zealand Presbyterian Church entered on a period of
growth and consolidation. Friendly relations with other Protestants
were maintained, but efforts toward corporate union with them
were not begun until three decades later. An overture to the General
Assembly in 1930 led to the appointment of a committee to explore
the possibility of union with the Methodist and Congregational
churches. The committee's report encouraged the Assembly to issue
a ballot on the proposal in 1932, but the result was disappointing to
the unionists. The proposal was renewed by the Methodists in 1939,
and the Assembly agreed to enter conversations, as did also the Congregationalists. A ballot was now taken in all three churches, and
the response was favorable in them all. After further study a joint
standing committee to seek terms of union was set up in 1951, with
its headquarters in Melbourne. Other denominations of the New
Zealand Council of Churches were invited to participate, but of these
only the Associate Churches of Christ (Disciples), and later the Anglicans, entered the discussions. The drafting of a declaration of faith
was undertaken in 1956. Successive drafts have been published. The
participation of the Anglican General Synod led to some reconsideration of the statement, especially with regard to the ministry, and a
process of revision followed. On May 10, 1967, the five churches
through their representatives, in Wellington Cathedral, publicly
adopted an act of commitment to union. In September, 1969, a Plan
for Union was issued; it was widely discussed and underwent revision in 1971. Of late years some elements of opposition to the union
have arisen. Professor Lloyd Geering, a Presbyterian and a unionist,
alarmed some Episcopalians and others by his modernistic interpre-

tation of the resurrection of Christ and his opinion went unrebuked by the Joint Commission on Church Union. There exists also an Association of Continuing Presbyterians whose objections to the Plan are mainly with respect to church structure and an alleged trend toward ultimate union with Rome.[27]

A referendum to the congregations completed in September, 1972, has resulted favorably in each of the five negotiating churches, the largest majority (86 percent) being registered by the Methodists with the Presbyterians next (70 percent).[28] While the Anglicans are constitutionally unable to join the union before the meeting of their General Synod in 1974, the other four churches may if they so decide proceed to unite when their general ruling bodies next meet, creating the new "Church of Christ of New Zealand." According to the Plan for Union the ministers of all the participating churches will have full ministerial status, women who are now ministers being included. Whether women are to be ordained to the presbyterate in the new polity is left for decision after the union. The ministry will consist of bishops, presbyters, and deacons, each with clearly defined functions. The diaconate is to be open to persons of secular occupation and of both sexes. The conciliar organs of government are the National Assembly, Diocesan Synod, and Parish Council, and in all of these laymen will participate. Elders elected for a four-year term are to be representatives in the Parish Councils. We recognize here a typical conciliar organization though with some original features.[29]

It is evident that in the young nations of the British Commonwealth the Presbyterian churches have everywhere, during the past hundred years, moved toward ecumenical unity. In each instance the stages have been essentially the same. The first task was to bring together the recently separated units of Presbyterianism within a limited area, province or state. This has been followed by the formation of a national Presbyterian church with a General Assembly and subordinate courts coordinating its whole work. It would be easy at this distance of time to underestimate the difficulties encountered before the latter of these two stages could be reached. In many countries, including the United States, Presbyterianism is far from being unified today. But where this important step had been taken, there arose in each case a zest for wider unity, followed by a patient effort to seek this through fraternal conference with other Christian churches as opportunity might arise. The third stage may be studied in the formation of the United Church of Canada and in other instances of unions in which the participants were all nonepiscopal. This stage has been reached only at the cost of considerable labor and persuasion lasting over some decades.

The fourth stage, already successfully passed in South India, requires the crossing of the Great Divide between episcopal and nonepiscopal polities; and this is a matter of greater difficulty. Conditions in lands populated by non-Europeans such as India, where Christianity is a modern importation, favored a more rapid coalescence of the two types of churches than was possible in the Commonwealth countries of British population. In these, live memories of inveterate antagonism with respect to the orders of ministry were brought from the motherland. It is significant that these inherited antagonisms are being rapidly dissolved in our generation; and of this the projected unions in Canada, Australia, and New Zealand offer strong evidence.

It is also noteworthy that amid many actual or proposed kinds of ministerial service designed to meet new conditions, the historic orders of bishop, presbyter, and deacon retain their positions in the structure and government of the new united churches. The desire for a ministry that shall be accredited by spiritual and intellectual fitness and pastoral efficiency, rather than by one or another line of ecclesiastical succession, is proving consistent with the retention of the traditional threefold ministry, with new safeguards against any entrenched immobility or abuse of power. What is recognized as needful is not some (necessarily untrustworthy) genealogical chart of succession in the ministry, but what an Australian document has called "succession from Christ" with reference to faith and devotion.

In the changing atmosphere of interchurch relations Presbyterian and Reformed Christians do well to remember that when many of our religious forbears assailed the episcopate their antagonism was generated by its involvement in a politico-ecclesiastical system which they felt to be oppressive, rather than by the mere issue of the existence of bishops. In general, episcopacy has not been totally rejected by the spokesmen of Reformed opinion, and the bishop-theologians of the patristic era have been highly respected in Reformed circles from Calvin down.

XIV

CHURCH COUNCILS
AND FEDERATIONS

THE THRUST for visible unity of Christ's disciples has manifested itself in many forms in the history of Christianity, but those of the twentieth century have been sufficiently conspicuous and distinctive to win the popular title "the ecumenical movement." The nineteenth-century pattern of nondenominational voluntary societies has continued, and there has been a marked increase of mergers and church unions. But what is usually thought of as most representative of the ecumenical movement is a great new network of interdenominational and international church agencies, especially of councils and federations, which began even before the turn of the century, but was greatly expanded and solidified in the First World War and its aftermath. Characteristic are the British Free Church Council, the Swiss Federation of Churches, the Federal Council of the Churches of Christ in America, to cite some of the pioneers in the West, the numerous national councils of younger churches, especially as organized by John R. Mott just before the First World War, and most comprehensive and representative of all, the World Council of Churches since 1948. Of such councils and federations there are hundreds, probably thousands. We may suspect that they reflect certain characteristics of the social and political configurations of the twentieth century.

There seems little need to retell the history of the organization and development of the World Council of Churches, which has been surveyed in some detail in the two volumes of *A History of the Ecumenical Movement,* 1517–1948, edited by Ruth Rouse and Stephen Charles Neill, and 1948–1968 by Harold E. Fey, as well as by a large number of popular summaries and interpretations. This is surely the most widely known chapter of general ecumenical history. Similarly the story of the American Federal Council and National Council of Churches, which is the largest and most influential of the national or regional councils, has been made well known by the account of J. Hutchinson and Samuel Cavert's two solid volumes.[1] There are national and regional councils all around the world of similar character, which have come into being in the twentieth century and mostly since the First World War. It will be possible to illustrate only Reformed attitudes and contributions to a select sample of these organizations. Then for the period since the Second World War and the consolidation of the World Council of Churches we may survey some instances of general shift of ecumenical concern from ecclesiastical to ethical and social alienation within the Christian community.

If we review in turn the chief tributary movements that flowed into the World Council, the last to merge was the oldest and most important, the International Missionary Council. The IMC was the most comprehensive and significant ecumenical organization on the world level for the period between World Wars. It had been created as an enduring interchurch body in the reconstruction period after the First World War in 1921 by the continuation committee of the Edinburgh World Missionary Conference of 1910. The members in the West of the IMC were the missionary societies, but on the field it was rather a matter of churches and councils of churches. As the latter multiplied over the decades the IMC became the comprehensive ecumenical structure of the "younger churches," including in its purview both "life and work" and "faith and order" concerns, among others. The World Council, on the other hand, was at the time of the fusion of the two organizations, essentially the ecumenical structure for the churches of the Atlantic community.

Reformed participation in the International Missionary Council was extensive. As we have seen, the Reformed churches had taken the lead in cooperative and ecumenical work on the mission field in the period culminating in the World Missionary Conference of 1910. Joseph Oldham, a Scot and one-time Student Christian Movement secretary, was the chief planner, along with John R. Mott, of Edinburgh 1910. It was he who organized the preparatory studies and established a basic pattern for the later world ecumenical conferences. After the Council of 1910 Mott and Oldham continued as chairman and secretary, first of the continuation committee, and then of the IMC itself, when the latter was finally launched at Lake Mohonk in 1921.

Oldham remained secretary until 1934, when he was loaned by the IMC to organize the Oxford Conference on Life and Work of 1937. Of that conference he was to be the chief architect. He had been joined in the 1920's by A. L. Warnshuis, who ran the American office of the IMC, and William Paton, another Scottish Presbyterian who had served with K. T. Paul as one of the two first secretaries of the National Christian Council of India. A Congregationalist missionary from Japan, J. Merle Davis, joined the IMC staff as a research secretary and organized several very useful studies of the economic basis of missions and churches, especially the volume, *The Economic Basis of the Church,* prepared for the Tambaram Conference of 1938. Another major contribution to thought about missions was the study volume commissioned by the IMC for the same conference, Hendrik Kraemer's *Christian Message in a Non-Christian World.* It may be significant that of the six IMC officers mentioned, all were Reformed save the Methodist Mott. After the Second World War such Reformed thinkers on missions as John Mackay and Lesslie Newbigin maintained the tradition within the new joint structure. We may suspect also that an analysis of financial contributions to the ecumenical missionary agencies would show that the Reformed had met at least their share of the costs. This was a dimension of ecumenical activity particularly congenial to the Reformed churches.

The ecumenical task in missions, however, was made vastly more difficult by the rapidly multiplying crises in at least Protestant missions which had become unmistakable from the 1930's. The established missionary agencies were cooperating indeed, but the churches seemed to be losing conviction about their faith. Missionary zeal seemed to have passed to another sociological and intellectual level where ecumenism had not penetrated. There was an explosion of new uncooperative missionary societies after the Second World War, chiefly in North America, which actually outdistanced the cooperative agencies in the number of missionaries sent abroad. Over one hundred new societies entered the field between 1940 and 1960 from North America alone. They were generally evangelistic free lances, uninformed and unconcerned about existing work in the field or the total scope of the missionary undertaking. During and after the Second World War, for example, Hong Kong acquired sixty-three societies, Taiwan seventy-six. Thirty-two new agencies streamed into the Philippines. Forty were at work in Germany, eighteen in the United Kingdom, nineteen in Switzerland. Most of these congregated in areas where churches and missions had long been at work but did not cooperate with them, and had little conscience about proselyting, so that some thousands of new missionaries did not add very many new converts to the total Christian community.[2] The new societies were also often less than tactful about the culture and politics of the host countries and fueled the nationalist hostility to missions in general. The cooperative missions, on the other hand, had so far committed themselves to institutional enterprises, medical or educational, that they had few resources left for evangelistic work.

The second major tributary movement to the eventual World Council was Life and Work. It produced the first of the world ecumenical conferences after the First World War, in Stockholm in 1925, and another even more famous twelve years later, in Oxford. The central intent was to bring the churches to more effective common action in political and social areas where they were sufficiently agreed. Most of the British and American denominations had acquired "social service" commissions or unions in the half generation before the World War. In Great Britain they federated in 1911 into an Inter-denominational Conference of Social Service Unions. The ICSSU coordinated research and education and conducted the solid study which was to make the 1924 Conference on Christian Politics, Economics, and Citizenship the most mature and competent preparation for the world conference at Stockholm. COPEC, in fact, achieved a higher level than Stockholm itself in most matters.

In the United States, similarly, this goal of cooperative social action was the central motive in the organization of the Federal Council of Churches in 1908, and the first Commission of the new Council was that on the Church and Social Service (headed, incidentally, by the Presbyterian Charles Stelzle). Some kind of inclusive structure was clearly needed if the churches were to interest themselves in social policy and seek to affect governments. It was touch and go for half a dozen years whether the new organization would survive, but the necessity for a joint agency of the churches during the War made the Council indispensable and ensured a tenfold expansion of its budget.

In assessing the contributions of the several traditions to Life and Work, one cannot make too much of individual names. The dominant figure of the Stockholm Conference was Archbishop Nathan Söderblom of Sweden, and perhaps the single most representative spokesman of the American "social gospel" was the Baptist Walter

Rauschenbusch, but the Baptists and the Lutherans would surely rank low on the list of denominations effectively engaged in cooperative social action.

In the United States the Congregationalists had probably produced the largest number of social gospel leaders, such as Washington Gladden, Josiah Strong, George Herron, Graham Taylor. The Congregationalist Elias Sanford did more than anyone else to lay the groundwork for the Federal Council of Churches. The Congregationalist Charles Macfarland was the first general secretary, to be followed by the Presbyterians Samuel Cavert as secretary and Roswell Barnes as associate. After the Congregationalists, Episcopalians would probably rank second in number of social gospel leaders. One suspects that ethical tradition may have had less to do with extent of denominational participation than the relative degree of urbanization and the educational level of the ministry. In England, Bishop William Temple, chairman of the Conference on Christian Politics, Economics, and Citizenship, was surely the dominant individual figure, and the Church of England brought more accumulated experience of dealing with the problems of industrialism than any other denomination. But there was also significant free church participation, from Quakers, Congregationalists, Presbyterians, Methodists. The attempt was made to organize an American COPEC also, with the Presbyterian William Adams Brown as chairman. This did not prove practicable, but Brown was made chairman of the program committee of the Stockholm Conference, and steered his committee through four preparatory sessions. Much of the administrative business, meanwhile, was being carried by the Congregationalist Henry Atkinson, as organizing secretary.

One may speculate, to be sure, about the relative effectiveness of the social programs of the privileged, such as the Anglican bishops, or the American social gospelers, as compared to the effects of Christianity, however politically and socially unsophisticated, on the underprivileged, perhaps Methodist miners in England, or Lutheran or Roman Catholic factory workers in the United States. And there may have been some unfinished ecumenical business as between the two sociological strata. But recognition should be given for the interdenominational cooperation in social education and action of the Reformed in due proportion to their numbers.

At Stockholm the social problems of industrialization were less urgent than international hostilities. Söderblom's personal interest for some years had been that of international reconciliation. As a neutral with close ties to each of France and Germany he had a strategic advantage. His chief foreign support came from Macfarland and the American Federal Council. The Americans, to be sure, were no longer neutral, but they had entered the War late and had not accumulated such a depth of bitterness as the French and Belgians, or even the British. The thesis of Germany's "sole" guilt for the War was the shibboleth. In 1920 the French declared that they would participate with Germans in a conference only if the Germans acknowledged such sole guilt. Another meeting at Zurich in 1923 nearly broke up over the issue. When the Conference actually met at Stockholm in 1925 it was not at all certain that all parties would remain throughout. The Germans were refusing to attend meetings of the International Missionary Council as late as the Jerusalem Conference of 1928, a full decade after the Armistice. The most impressive ecumenical achievement of Stockholm, in the judgment of participants, was the fact that the Conference held together and realized the actuality of reconciliation in Christ, most vividly in the concluding communion in the Uppsala cathedral.

As the Faith and Order movement in its early years was supported financially by the Episcopalian J. P. Morgan, so Life and Work was aided by the Presbyterian Andrew Carnegie. Carnegie had generously endowed the Church Peace Union, which in turn subsidized the World Alliance for Promoting International Friendship through the Churches. That organization was, in Adolf Keller's phrase, a "mother" to the Life and Work movement into the 1930's. Henry Atkinson, the Congregationalist, was secretary through the 1920's of both the World Alliance and Life and Work. Atkinson worked on for four years after Stockholm with the continuation committee until the Universal Christian Council for Life and Work was finally launched, just as the economic depression was making itself felt. Atkinson was made secretary and Adolf Keller associate, so the staff was Reformed. But with the financial restrictions there were no meetings from 1932 to 1934.

Before turning to Faith and Order, which is to be classified with Life and Work and the International Missionary Council as a tributary to the World Council, we should give some consideration to the ecumenical aspects of interchurch aid and relief. In the era of two World Wars the need was monumental, and the hundreds and thousands of contributions made for the practical needs of fellow Christians may represent more of ecumenical reality than some world conferences. In terms of budget and staff such interchurch aid was easily the most extensive of all ecumenical programs.

The neutral and Reformed Swiss seemed appointed by history to play a major role in relief work at the end of the First World War, and they rose to the occasion. The Swiss Church Conference was reorganized in 1920 into the Swiss Church Federation, with Adolf Keller as its executive secretary. They promptly set up a general collection for the suffering churches in their neighboring states, France, Germany, and the former Austro-Hungarian Empire. But they also saw the need for a universal relief action, both to increase supplies and to coordinate the many diverse and overlapping initiatives.

Such a concerted program was urged the next year at the 1921 Assembly of the World Reformed Alliance, in Pittsburgh. With no less than thirteen European delegates pleading the urgency of the crisis, the situation of the Continental churches was put before the Alliance as never before. Arrangements were made to coordinate American, Canadian, and British contributions for the Continental churches through the treasurer of the Alliance, so as to avoid inequitable distribution of supplies. It was natural for church families to seek to aid their own; Lutherans, Methodists, and Baptists were doing so. But there was also danger of injustice and feelings of jealousy or of denominational rivalry, to say nothing of the use of relief supplies for denominational invasion and proselyting.

The Swiss Federation and the American Federal Council convened a so-called Bethesda Conference at Copenhagen the following August, to try to work out a common policy. The Federal Council had had some experience since 1918 with a commission for relief of Belgian and French churches. The largest number at Copenhagen were Lutherans; about a quarter were Reformed. Here it was possible to get an overview of what was being done by the several American denominations and the Federal Council, by the Scottish churches, the Scandinavians, the Dutch, the Swiss. It was also possible to take the measure of the need. "For days the Conference listened to heart-rending accounts of loss, disaster and misery . . . what with churches in ruins, missionary and philanthropic work paralyzed for lack of funds, the difficulty of printing religious literature, the compulsory closing of schools and colleges, the ill-treatment of minorities in not a few lands, the threatened starvation of pastors and their families, the general depreciation of the currency, and a host of other evils." [3] Protestantism was fighting for its very survival in some fourteen countries, most desperately in Austria, Estonia, Hungary, Latvia, Lithuania, Poland, Rumania, Yugoslavia, France, Germany, Czechoslovakia.

The Conference voted to establish the first international and interdenominational agency for interchurch aid, the Central Bureau, with Keller as General Secretary and an executive committee headed by Dean Herold. Many denominations already had their own agencies, the Lutherans being the largest, and the chief support of the ecumenical program in the next few years was to be the Reformed churches of America, Scotland, and Europe. The international committee met regularly in various countries and served as a very useful clearinghouse for all. The American Federal Council opened a special liaison office with the Geneva Bureau. Keller reported on interchurch aid regularly at the meetings of the World Reformed Alliance.

After seven years of work a second general conference was held at Basel in 1929 to evaluate the operation. Over ninety delegates from twenty-three countries surveyed the situation and voted to continue for five years more. It was observed that spiritual and moral support had proved very important along with the practical aid, and that a new sense of Protestant solidarity was perceptible in some quarters. But the work soon passed beyond Protestant frontiers. Help was needed for Jewish refugees from 1933 and, in time, "for the Assyrian Nestorian Church (exiled and finally settled along the borders of Kurdistan and Syria), Russian Orthodox bodies (especially for the Russian Orthodox Academy in Paris), Armenians on the Lebanon and in Marseilles, and even for Christians in China." [4]

The great depression reduced contributions by 30 percent to 40 percent and by more than 70 percent from the United States. Even so, by early 1937, a total of £600,000 had been distributed by the Central Bureau from the beginning of the enterprise. Perhaps as much more had actually been given to needs made known to helping churches through the clearinghouse of the Bureau. The whole made an impressive demonstration of Christian fellowship and interchurch solidarity.

At the end of the war in 1945 the Central Bureau was merged into the new Department of Reconstruction and Inter-Church Aid of the World Council (in process of formation). Thus an ecumenical enterprise which had largely arisen out of Reformed initiative was taken over bodily by the new World Council of Churches. Even under those auspices it was to be led chiefly by Reformed churchmen, such as Hutchison Cockburn, Robert Mackie, and Leslie Cooke. But an operation that consisted in 1945 of one man and a secretary had in 1965 a budget 50 percent larger than the general budget of the World Council, and maintained a quarter of the staff in Geneva and some two hundred elsewhere.

We need give little space to the remaining tributary to the World Council, the Faith and Order movement. In its early years, as we have seen, this was largely directed by an Anglican aspiration to unity through administrative amalgamation. It probably generated less Reformed enthusiasm than any of the three various tributaries previously surveyed, but the Reformed played an active and proportional part at the organizing conference at Lausanne in 1927. After all, they were the hosts in Reformed Switzerland and about a quarter of the delegates were Reformed.

In the 1930's the overlapping and competition of various specialized ecumenical agencies, such as Life and Work, the World Alliance for Promoting International Friendship, Faith and Order, led many to think of merger into something like Söderblom's "league of churches." The conference at Archbishop Temple's home in 1933 which launched the program was suggested by the Presbyterian William Adams Brown, and he drafted the preliminary document. Over half the ten men gathered were Reformed: Brown and Cavert from Life and Work, Oldham and Paton from the International Missionary Council, Henriod from the World Alliance, and Visser 't Hooft of the World Student Christian Federation. Two years later they met again at Princeton Seminary and decided on an enlarged meeting of thirty-five for London in 1937. There a definite plan was drafted of a merger of Life and Work and Faith and Order, to be presented to the two conferences to meet later that year at Oxford and Edinburgh. The name "World Council of Churches" was Cavert's suggestion, and evidently the American Federal Council served in some ways as a model. Both the Oxford and Edinburgh assemblies voted favorably on the proposal in 1937 and a planning body met at Utrecht in 1938 to work it out. Again the Reformed played a significant role in the critical debate of 1938. The Provisional Committee (which was to function considerably longer than originally expected) had, with Visser 't Hooft, Paton, and Leiper, a vigorous Reformed staff. The formation of a Council of Churches meant the divorce of Life and Work from the World Alliance for Promoting International Friendship Through the Churches (which included many individuals, and not only Christians), but to most it seemed worth that sacrifice.

The Oxford Conference of 1937 already in some respects foreshadowed what was to become a dominant feature of World Council life after the Second World War. The preparations for that Conference on "Church, Community and State" were colored by the challenge of Nazi totalitarianism to the Christian community, faith, and ethics. In contrast to Stockholm, only twelve years before, where the focus had been on the civil duties of the individual Christian, it was seen at Oxford that the question was whether the church could survive as a historical community with its own ethos. The great church struggle over "German Christianity" had split the churches of Germany at a deeper level than confessional distinctions of Lutheran, Reformed, United Churchmen, even those between Protestants and Roman Catholics. The ecumenical implications were not at once apparent, but these polarizations were to endure for years after the War in German church life. Something similar took place in Korea and Japan. In the face of the new political religions of the twentieth century the ecumenical task was being redefined, with new alienations and new fraternizations.

The Second World War, which delayed the consolidation of the World Council, did not weaken it. The two parallel ecumenical structures of the "older" churches (World Council in process of formation) and the "younger" ones (International Missionary Council) both came through the war stronger than before. They performed indispensable functions and additional churches steadily applied for membership. Contacts were maintained from Geneva with Christians in occupied lands; cooperative plans for reconstruction were prepared against the time of peace; responsibilities were taken up for the support of "orphaned missions."

Enough has been said, it is hoped, to show the general character and extent of Reformed participation in the tributary streams of the World Council of Churches. As in the heading of church mergers, the Reformed have generally done more than their share in this kind of activity, as measured by their contribution of personnel, of funds, of general institutional support, and of theological clarification and direction. One might continue to document the point from the history of the World Council in the 1950's and 1960's, or of various regional and national councils of churches. This whole style of work is natural to the Reformed, who are accustomed to church action in committees and representative assemblies. And the Reformed have been willing to pay. In 1969, for example, two American churches, the United Methodists and the United Presbyterians, together contributed over half the total U.S. giving to the World Council of Churches. The Methodists contributed $185,000, the Presbyterians, between a quarter and a third of their number, contributed $157,000. Then came the Episcopalians with $80,000, United Church of Christ $60,000, and Lutheran Church in America, $58,000.[5]

The consolidation of the World Council of Churches at the end of the Second World War raised a question, however, as to the further functions of world denominational bodies, such as the World Reformed Alliance, the Lutheran World Federation, the Methodist World Council. There were half a dozen of them then; now the number has more than doubled. The largest, the Lutheran World Federation, is one year older than the World Council, but has come to overshadow the latter, with a staff of one thousand, an annual budget of thirteen million dollars, duplicating on a larger scale many of the functions of the World Council. It was not accidental that the World Reformed Alliance, in contrast, has refused to organize interchurch aid confessionally, and has held down its organization to a staff of half a dozen and an annual budget of $100,000. Reformed funds and men have rather been directed into ecumenical agencies, so that many Presbyterian and Reformed congregations are aware of World Council activities who do not know that there is a World Reformed Alliance.

The World Reformed Alliance has attempted to restrain denominational imperialism on the world level. In 1949 and again in 1951 at Basel the Executive Committee formally declared that the Alliance was not designed to promote world Presbyterianism as an end in itself. "The Alliance would never desire," it was said in 1951, "to be a party to preventing the incorporation of one of its member churches into a wider ecclesiastical relationship when the interests of the Christian cause clearly indicated that such a consummation was desirable." [6] The Committee was keenly aware, through its ties to the International Missionary Council, of the financial pressures among the younger churches being exercised by world confessionalism against the consolidation of regional and national churches.

Three years later, at the time of the Evanston World Council and the Princeton Council of the Alliance, no other world church family had yet made a comparable statement to that at Basel. But several Reformed spokesmen, especially John Mackay and Henri d'Espine, vigorously reaffirmed the principle. The Reformed Alliance Executive committee took the initiative again after Evanston in arranging a conference of the heads of the several international denominational bodies. The representatives first met in 1957 at Geneva, and have continued to meet annually.

The younger churches, especially in Asia, were increasingly resentful of what they considered to be sectarian imperialism. The East Asia Conference of Churches at Bangalore requested a consultation on the subject, and one was held in Geneva in 1963. But the younger church representatives felt excluded by gatherings of Westerners in the West and requested another meeting in Asia. Another EACC meeting at Bangkok in 1964 issued a forthright declaration. They wished the world denominations to find other channels of interchurch aid. "We believe it is vital that the help given by confessional bodies to churches of the same family in Asia should be within the framework of the total ecumenical operation." Similarly they appealed to these bodies not to plan specialized denominational world meetings but to support ecumenical programs on issues common to all Asian Christians. And they called on Asian churches to "resist the temptation to maintain theological positions simply in order to be in good standing with their parent churches." [7] Specific recommendations were addressed to the Anglicans, Lutherans, and Methodists, but significantly not to the Reformed. With the resurgence of denominationalism, the old nineteenth-century struggle for comity was joined again, now on a world level. Would the entry of the Orthodox, and conceivably the Roman Catholics, into the World Council, convert that body into a federation of world denominational families? The invitations to Protestant bodies to send observers to the Vatican Council in the 1960's similarly were directed through the world denominational bodies. Many factors seemed to be furthering a new denominationalism on a world level. The Reformed have led the fight against this tendency.

In relation to the Oxford Conference of 1937 on Church, Community, and State we noticed a phenomenon which was to become increasingly conspicuous after the Second World War. In Germany and Korea, we observed, the classifications of Christians in accord with the attitude they had taken to totalitarian pressure proved to be more deeply felt and more determinative of church life than the inherited confessional and denominational categories. So it was to be with regard to other political and social issues in the next generation. As in the middle generation of the nineteenth century in the United States, schism and merger, alienation and fraternity within the church were governed more by social and political ethics (in this case in relation to race) than by faith and order. Increasingly in the 1950's and overwhelmingly in the 1960's, ecumenical conferences were dominated by racial and international politics. Ecumenical progress, or lack of it, was being measured by a new yardstick.

Perhaps it was in part the penalty of institutional success. After the Second World War the World Council had become part of the ecclesiastical establishment and inherited responsibility for the political, social, and economic establishment as well. The more inclusive the organization, the more tensions it incorporated. The nearer it came to being a genuinely "world" council, the more certainly it would fall heir to the woes and hostilities of the world.

Churches of the Reformed tradition supply a particularly useful test case of the ecumenical task from this point of view. Of the major Protestant bodies the Lutherans have the highest statistics, but the Reformed, who are second to the Lutherans, are more widely spread. They have no one great concentration, like Lutheran Germany and Scandinavia, but are of all the great bodies, save the Roman Catholics, the most evenly and widely distributed. Not as strong in Europe as Lutherans, they are yet there far stronger than Anglicans, Methodists, Baptists, Congregationalists, who are virtually confined to the English-speaking world and its missionary extensions. They are just big enough and sufficiently widespread to incorporate every major divisive force and face every notable threat to Christianity. In this sense they might well be considered the most representative Protestant community, the best sampling of peoples, cultures, languages, continents. At the São Paulo General Council (1959) of the World Reformed Alliance, for example, official documents had to be prepared in English, French, German, Dutch, Hungarian, Spanish, and Portuguese, and in part in some other languages. Over a third of the constituency was to be found in Europe and the British Isles, but there were six million in Asia, especially Indonesia, Korea, India, China, Japan, the Philippines; also four and one half million in Africa, especially the Republic of South Africa; a million in Latin America, chiefly Brazil and Mexico; over a million in Australia and New Zealand. The United States and Canada about equaled the totals of Asia, Africa, Latin America, and Australia. In terms of church bodies, the majority were now from the Third World.

Conditions and problems were enormously different in Marxist Czechoslovakia and Hungary, for example, or in North Korea and China, from what they were in Scotland or Canada. It was again a very different story in areas of Roman Catholic pressure and persecution, in Spain, Spanish Guinea, Colombia, Italy, Mexico. There were large Reformed communities in Indonesia, a predominantly Muslim country, or small ones in Egypt and Pakistan. The Reformed were involved in the most tense situations of racial conflict, as in the Republic of South Africa, Kenya, and the United States. The meaning of the ecumenical vocation also varied radically from one of these situations to another. There were few if any major challenges to ecumenism in this generation not effective somewhere in the Reformed family. We may look briefly at three challenges to Christian unity which have been conspicuous in the 1950's and 1960's: the effect on the churches of the cold war between the communist world and the world of economic liberalism, the effect of the rising tensions between the impoverished Third World and the affluent industrialized societies, and the effect of racial antagonisms, typically in South Africa and the United States. For each of these we can readily find representatives within the Reformed community.

First of all, we shall discuss the ecumenical effects of the communist-noncommunist alienation.

There was a much higher proportion of Christians in the "free world," of course, but across the Iron and Bamboo Curtains there were still significant Christian communities in communist societies. On the European continent the largest Reformed bodies of this sort were the Hungarian Reformed, of Slovakia, Yugoslavia, and Rumania, as well as Hungary proper, and the United Church of the Czech Brethren. In these two churches were to be found the most articulate and vigorous European spokesmen for communism on Christian grounds. They were sharply opposed to those who, like Cardinal Mindzenty, identified Christianity with inherited feudal privilege, and communism with the devil. That was the usual attitude of the refugee, and that was the way most Westerners expected Christians in the communist world to behave.

Perhaps more than any other Josef Hromadka kept the debate before the ecumenical world, maintaining his contacts both with the World Council and the World Alliance of Reformed Churches and nurturing the fellowship of Christians in Czechoslovakia, Hungary, Poland, and the U.S.S.R. The issue was posed at the very foundation of the World Council at Amsterdam in 1948, when Hromadka and John Foster Dulles, both Reformed, debated the proper relation of the faith to the communist movement. Hromadka had left Princeton in 1947 for his motherland on the eve of the revolution, there to join the Czech church in its endeavor to bear its witness in a communist society. As dean of the Huss Theological Faculty in Prague he was to live under great pressures for the next decade, maintaining a communist political commitment together with an unquestionable devotion to Jesus Christ. Bishop Albert Berecsky of Hungary held to much the same line.

But were the contacts with the noncommunist world really serious ecumenical dialogue, or only formal courtesy? The difficulty was vividly defined at the Lund Conference in 1952. Hromadka there faced an overwhelmingly anticommunist audience. He knew, he told them, that he was being discounted in advance more profoundly than if he had been venturing some Christological heresies. Those might have been tolerated or overlooked, but a convinced communist could not expect such leniency. What were divergencies on church-state relations, or even the Catholic-Evangelical polarity compared to communism as an ecumenical problem? [8] And if a Hromadka, with all his personal friendships in the West to build on, could not really communicate with Western theologians, what hope was there of real interchange when the Orthodox spokesmen from the U.S.S.R. should participate in World Council conferences and committees? And there was the same problem for those who sought to move in the other direction. Hromadka's Christian Peace Conference became a kind of counterpart to the World Council in communist countries. A scattering of Western churchmen attended meetings of the Peace Conference, but found themselves marked men, outside the axioms of the discussion.

Of all the major communist countries the alienation of Christians from those of the West was greatest in China, and the rupture of ties and communications most complete. China had been the greatest mission field of the Christian world. At the Tambaram International Missionary Council Conference of 1938 (originally set for Hangchow) the Chinese delegation was by general consent the strongest. But within a year of the establishment of the People's Republic (1949) the Korean War aroused such feeling against the West that missions were virtually eliminated. When the Central Committee of the World Council of Churches identified the North Koreans as aggressors, Dr. T. C. Chao, one of the presidents of the World Council, resigned in protest, and the Chinese member churches withdrew.

As elsewhere in the communist world the church was required to support government policy publicly as the condition of being permitted to operate. From the spring of 1951 the government required that the churches purge themselves by the technique of public denunciation, which was well calculated to effect a psychological rupture of personal ties. The churches of the National Council and especially the United Church of Christ, which had the closest ties to Reformed churches in the West, were expected to demonstrate their rejection of foreign mission boards and their imperialist policies.

There was less response in China thereafter than in most Marxist lands to occasional opportunities for contact with Christians outside. Some evidence is available both of evangelistic action and of moves for church unity within China, but building a new church in China evidently seemed more urgent than restoring ties with the churches of the World Council or the International Missionary Council. The Christian Peace Conference, however, was an international ecumenical movement which could evoke some warmth among Chinese Christians. In 1961 Bishop K. H. Ting attended a meeting of the Conference in Prague and expressed his gratitude for the possibility of establishing ties with the Christians in the Soviet Union.[9] Even after the communist Orthodox had generally joined the World Council of Churches, the Chinese did not relax their hostility to the World Council and Western churches generally.

By the early 1960's, at least, it was no longer clear that the cold war axis of U.S.S.R.–U.S.A. and its ideological manifestations was the dominating tension in the world, although it was still a very significant factor. The World Council of Churches' Geneva Conference on Church and Society in 1966 seemed rather persuaded that the polarity of East and West was less significant than that of North and South, that between the overpopulated underdeveloped South (Latin America, Africa, Asia) and the industrialized northern hemisphere, whether in the state socialist form or in the mixed economy. In the dependent economies the Amsterdam formula of a "responsible society" did not seem very relevant, and the conception of "development" was ambiguous. In Africa and Latin America, especially, the "theology of liberation" struck many themes familiar in the work of black theologians in America. How close could the church come to justifying violent revolution against oppression?

As Presbyterian Ulster is probably the most scandalous instance of Protestant–Roman Catholic relations, so Reformed South Africa seems to be the extreme case of ecumenical failure over the color line. "In South Africa," writes B. J. Marais, "all our ecumenical contact and thinking is overshadowed by the colour problem." [10]

The Dutch Reformed are the key to the situation. There are other denominations involved, Anglicans, Roman Catholics, Presbyterians, but they are all less numerous, less influential, less deeply rooted in the history of the country. The intimate link of nationality and religion of the Dutch Reformed in South Africa is almost unique. These Reformed now regard separation of the races as a solemn duty, the condition of man's dignity as a child of God. They did not at first permit such a bar in the church, where racial segregation was first permitted by a synod in 1857. The deliberate policy of nurturing a separate missionary church among the Bantu dates from 1880. But the very vigorous missions of the last hundred years have brought it about that the large majority of Christians in South Africa are black. All now identify white Christianity and apartheid. In the 1930's and 1940's one even found widespread efforts to justify apartheid Scripturally, with reference to the tower of Babel, Noah's sons, and the Israelite ban on intermarriage. In 1951 the Reformed Dutch Church of the Transvaal took the position that separation of races was obligatory under Scripture. The existence of such theological opinion in the twentieth century dramatizes the intellectual and social isolation of the South African Reformed. The Nationalist Party, which came to power with Malan in 1948, consisted mainly of members of these Afrikaans Reformed churches.

The situation has been greatly exacerbated by the industrial development of the country. When separation of races meant division of territory between two largely rural societies, it was one thing. But industrialization brought mass migration of the Bantu as laborers to the white cities—from 900,000 in 1939 to three million in 1957. The blacks were allowed to work there, but not to establish residence. Instead an enormous system of migrant labor was established, destroying the Bantu family by keeping husbands and wives apart for months at a time. The so-called "pass system" was a device to enforce these residency regulations. A demonstration against it at Sharpeville in 1960 led to a massacre of over five thousand blacks. The whole country was put under martial law for four months.

The Sharpeville massacre led to an overture from the World Council of Churches. A decade earlier W. A. Visser 't Hooft, the General Secretary of the WCC, had visited South Africa in the endeavor to keep open channels for ecumenical contact. Visser 't Hooft, of course, was personally both Dutch and Reformed. Similarly, Dr. Marcel Pradervand had visited on behalf of the World Reformed Alliance, in 1953. Now an American Presbyterian was sent, Robert Bilheimer, who was able to arrange a consultation of South African church representatives with a deputation from the World Council. After great difficulties the consultation was actually held, in December at Cottesloe near Johannesburg. Some eighty people, a quarter of them nonwhite, remained in conference for a week. They were able to issue a joint statement, of which every paragraph was acceptable to 80 percent of the consultation. The Nederduitse Hervormde Kerk representatives disagreed with the statement generally and supported the government action. But the consensus of the rest was dramatic news. Along with specifics concerning political rights, land-owning, mixed marriages, job reservations, a basic theological claim was made. "No one who believes in Jesus Christ may be excluded from any Church on the grounds of his colour or race. The spiritual unity among all men who are in Christ must find visible expression in acts of common worship and witness, and in fellowship and consultation on matters of common concern." [11] Some of the Cottesloe delegates, however, found the unity achieved at the consultation repudiated in their own churches. Three of the Dutch Reformed Churches refused to accept the Cottesloe agreements and withdrew from the World Council of Churches.

The effect on the mission to the African of these developments was, as one would expect, disastrous. A significant number, as in many other areas of Africa, turned to Islam, as relatively free of such prejudice. Others moved back to animism or into semi-Christian cults. And hundreds of independent churches sprang up, which held themselves separate from the white man's church. About a third of the Christian Bantu, some 1,600,000, are in separatist churches, and the proportion is growing rapidly. Whether any links can be maintained with white churches is problematical, to say nothing of reconciliation. As Alan Paton puts it, "The white Christian inhabitants of Africa have it in their power to bring missionary work to an end, not by withholding their gifts, but by withholding their love." [12]

As with South Africa, and much of the rest of the Third World, the United States has witnessed in the last generation acute controversy over race and a growing tendency to separatism on racial lines within Christianity. Race relations were the major preoccupation of many American church assemblies in the 1960's, and together with the worldwide rebellion against white imperialism, they dominated such World Council gatherings as New Delhi (1961), Geneva (1966), and Uppsala (1968).

Again as in South Africa and in much of the Third World, industrialization and urbanization have revolutionized the character of the

American Negro community. As late as 1940 two thirds of American blacks still lived in the states of the old Confederacy, where their prevailing status had been changed at Emancipation from that of slaves to sharecroppers and peons. But a great migration out had begun in the First World War, which swelled to a flood tide in the Second World War. From 1940 to 1960 the black population outside the South nearly tripled, and concentrated in the cities of the North: New York, Chicago, Philadelphia, Detroit, Baltimore, Cleveland, Pittsburgh, Los Angeles. Surrounded there by the evidences of affluence, the mood of the black ghetto oscillates between rage and despairing apathy.

The civil rights agitations which came to dominate the press began in 1954. As late as the elections of 1952 there had been little attention given to the subject. But in *Brown* v. *Board of Education,* the Supreme Court decided that racially segregated education did not come within the equal protection of the law as provided by the Constitution. The states and school boards of the nation were put on notice to end such segregation with all deliberate speed. The struggle for compliance was long and sometimes violent. But several hundred school districts gave up racially segregated classes.

The idea was contagious. At the end of 1955 a black woman declined to move back in a bus in Montgomery, Alabama. Out of the resulting controversy emerged the greatest leader of the movement, the twenty-seven-year-old pastor of a Montgomery Baptist Church, Martin Luther King, Jr. King organized a black boycott of the Montgomery bus system, and a year later enforced segregation in buses was ruled unconstitutional. King's method was disconcerting. He preached against hate and the use of violence. He wanted to appeal to the conscience of the oppressor and in the end be reconciled to him. He gathered a group of largely black Baptist ministers in the Southern Christian Leadership Conference (SCLC), which was to provide the central thrust for years.

In 1960 some college students in Greensboro, North Carolina, began the lunch counter sit-ins in response to the rebuff, "We do not serve Negroes." In six months Woolworth's capitulated, and by the end of the year hundreds more in other cities. Freedom rides followed, as civil rights defenders tested segregation in buses, trains, terminals. On the whole, sit-ins and freedom rides were successful. Carried chiefly by college students and other young people, they opened restaurants, hotels, theaters, as well as public transportation facilities. Black and white students risking injury, careers, even life itself in nonviolent resistance won some grudging respect even from their persecutors. It was some evidence of shift in public opinion that in the election campaign of that year both parties were suddenly for desegregation.

The movement caught up widespread church participation in 1963. That was the year of the Birmingham riots, when news photographs went all around the world of police brutality. That was the year when the defenders of white superiority set off a bomb in a Sunday school class and killed four little girls. Many who walked from Selma marveled at the venom they encountered. America, and the American churches, were shocked to recognize the underlying savage passions of the racial system. There was a surge of sympathetic participation which brought nuns, rabbis, seminarians, black and white, to march past spitting rednecks and police sadists. Eugene Carson Blake, the United Presbyterian Stated Clerk, was arrested that year in a demonstration outside Baltimore. And it was a sound judgment that invited Martin Luther King, Jr., to deliver the opening sermon at the Uppsala Assembly of the World Council of Churches in 1968. Who else bore more adequate witness to the ecumenical dream of visible unity of Christ's disciples where it was denied? King did not speak at Uppsala because he was murdered in Memphis.

But King was already in trouble. He was losing black support to Stokely Carmichael and Rap Brown and Malcolm X. The ghetto riots in Newark and Detroit in 1967 were the worst yet. Adam Clayton Powell talked of Martin "Loser" King, and Malcolm X called him "the chump." Protest marches and devices which had worked well in the South did not make for solutions in the great northern cities such as Chicago, where housing, employment, schooling were enormously complicated matters. And King was two or three years ahead in insisting on the connection of civil rights and black interests with the "immoral war" in Vietnam. Few of his advisers agreed with him and the mass of blacks never were deeply stirred about Vietnam. He was sacrificing administration support at the same time as the backlash began to show in election returns. Perhaps the best thing King could do for his cause was die for it.

The black churches, too, became increasingly separatist. In 1967 and 1968 there were black caucuses in half a dozen of the "white" denominations. A "black ecumenicity" emerged, interested in drawing together all black churches. Should the black minorities in the Presbyterian, Congregationalist, and similar "white" denominations pull out and help to form a new black consolidation? The movement cut across several attempts to unite denominations, such as the reunion of Presbyterians North and South, or the Consultation on Church Union (COCU). James Cone, the young black theologian, applauded the walkout of black Methodists from the communion service celebrating the new United Methodist Church. To many black churchmen racial concerns were far more important than denominational ones. The old Federal Council program of a racially integrated church and a racially integrated society was repudiated widely. What did it mean? The large majority of both blacks and whites worshiped separately, always had, and liked it that way. And since residential segregation was increasing, how could one expect to desegregate either schools or churches? The real question was rather whether the white churches could maintain any meaningful contact at all with the blacks.

In all this denominations and confessional traditions counted for little among either blacks or whites. The great bulk of American black church members, to be sure, are either Methodist or Baptist; no other denomination has a large proportion. About 90 percent of all Negro Christians belonged to solidly black denominations at the end of the Second World War, and most of those in "white" denominations were in exceptional black congregations within those denominations.[13] But the question of how one dealt with racial discrimination cut horizontally across all the churches. To many, Christian integrity and credibility were at stake in the racial, colonialist, national relations within the total Christian society.

A characteristic of twentieth-century history has been the suddenness with which new factors have emerged and radically changed the ecumenical situation. The First World War surprised the "Christian world," and left a gulf between Christians on the two sides that was scarcely bridged firmly a decade later. The Bolshevik revolution, and later the Nazi conquest of Germany, radically and enduringly drew lines within the church in each case. So with the communist capture of China, the cold war, the rebellion against white domination in the Third World. Should we not be prepared for new and unexpected forces of division to rupture Christian fellowship? Ecumenism seems a permanent dimension of Christian obedience, but always vulnerable to new dangers and threats. Achievements are fragmentary only, and far from final, harbingers and earnests of a fulfillment that lies in God's hand.

XV

THE
PRESBYTERIAN-REFORMED TRADITION
AND THE COMING GREAT CHURCH

THE READER of this book has now shared with its authors something of the story of ecumenical concern and effort in the history of one widely extended and diversified branch of the Christian Church in the modern world. In this record we become well aware that a desire for Christian unity has been a characteristic element of the Reformed tradition, attested as it is through the centuries by many writings and projects put forth by typical leaders. No claim is made that in this feature the Reformed churches were unique; but it is recorded that they were not indifferent to the problem of church division, and that with some frequency responsible spokesmen among them devised and advocated proposals for reunion. Almost invariably it is evident that such proposals were thought of as offering steps in the direction of wider union, leading ultimately to the complete integration of the church throughout the world. The efforts of these leaders and writers have not been fruitless, but have helped to prepare the way for many united churches already formed or today held in expectation. Our book must end while progress continues in various aspects of ecumenicity, mainly in directions that are in accord with the projects and ideas we have here explored. It is thus not a history of a completed phase of church existence. The entire ecumenical movement as it goes on apace continues to enlist the active participation of churches of the Reformed-Presbyterian family. In many areas of the world these churches are in conference with others with a view to unitive action on a small or great scale. The large results already attained in this are minor in comparison with the unions projected.

In the swiftly changing world about us in these times we do well to revere the tradition in which we have been reared. But this loyalty to tradition does not make us denominationalists. It does not imply a misplaced reverence for the forms and names that are badges not of Christianity but of its segmented parts. Surely there is nothing in church order or organization that was fixed unchangeably in the first, the fifth, or the sixteenth century or any other past era. We are as free to change church government in response to conditions as our predecessors were from the time of the appointment of the seven ministrants in Acts, ch. 6; and this is a liberty that has often been taken. Some changes in terminology and structure always accompany the union of two or more churches; and new types of ministry are required today. To arrange such changes advantageously, prejudices must be laid aside and the realities of future needs treated as paramount. It is hard for some church members to take a forward look, especially where a certain ecclesiastical comfort is experienced. An economically unencumbered local church, living on terms of guarded courtesy with other denominational units in its own community and in good standing with its denominational headquarters, may not easily be induced to undertake the tasks that are involved in seeking unity. That process would require some revision of these painless relationships, and some laborious committee work as well as the abandonment of prejudice and inertia; and to some all this may seem too large a price to pay. But despite lethargy and resistance, and some fresh expressions of sectarianism, the movement to close the Christian ranks gains momentum with the passing years.

The Coming Great Church is the haunting title of a book written by Canon Theodore O. Wedel of Washington Cathedral and published in 1945. From the basis of the Chicago-Lambeth Quadrilateral, Canon Wedel with generous churchmanship presents his conception of a future worldwide Christian communion. This book helped to quicken anticipations of the shaping of the general union of Christians implied in its title. Numerous writers since his time have addressed themselves to the prospect of future unity and suggested features of the church of all peoples which they see emerging. We may mention Douglas Horton's *Toward an Undivided Church* (1967), Robert McAfee Brown's *The Ecumenical Revolution* (1967), and *Tomorrow's Church* by Peter Day (1969). Samuel McCrea Cavert, in the concluding chapter of his *Church Cooperation and Unity in America* (1970), realistically indicates the retarding factor of a denominational spirit of self-sufficiency that is now modified, but not replaced, by "an increasing emphasis on ecumenical mission." In recent discussions the proposals for reunion are often associated with the concept of world mission as the prime objective of the enlarging church. This is the theme of Henry Pitney Van Dusen's striking book *One Great Ground of Hope* (1961).

Amid the unforeseen political revisions, social upheavals, and scientific achievements of our era religious interests are given relatively little attention. The voices heard in religious broadcasts are hardly representative of church opinion as a whole, or of ecumenical Christian thinking. To many observers Christianity seems to be in retreat. In the past it could be assumed that Christianity had the approval of society, even of those by whom it was not consistently practiced. This assumption is no longer valid. Connection with or profession of Christianity, or indeed of any religion, has little to do with one's social acceptance. Men everywhere are less than formerly committed to any particular church or religion, and many are ready to cast off as outworn the culture and restraint of religion altogether. While religiously motivated agencies, in great profusion, seek to relieve the woes and mitigate the evils of the world, new forms of wickedness lay hold of humanity, and we are confronted by mounting danger from the behavior of desperate men. The Christian Church is still capable of effective response to this adverse environment. But if it is to play a redemptive role it cannot continue to exhibit itself in disorderly division and in mutually exclusive worshiping camps, and of this its people are becoming more aware. Not only in faithfulness to the example of our far-seeing union-seeking forebears, but in reaffirmation of the original Christian principles of brotherly love and communion in Christ, we must accept together our mission to mankind. The course we take must lie toward the integration of the Christian people in a fellowship wide enough to embrace them all. Nothing less than this was the conscious ideal of our predecessors in the Reformed tradition.

Ecumenism is indeed a multiple movement. The later chapters of this book show in impressive variety the participation in it of the Presbyterian and Reformed churches. Its abundant manifestations have offered a problem to sociologists. Some of these have regarded it as an effort by church officials to rescue from extinction churches enfeebled by a prevailing indifference to religion, and as without grass-roots support from the lay members. But when James R. Kelly in 1968 put this judgment to the test in the New England middle-

class community of Lexington, Massachusetts, he was led to pro-
nounce it "speculative rather than empirical." His statistics, too detailed to be recited here, show that Roman Catholics, Protestants of
various denominations, and Jews of that community are alike interested in and on the whole favorable to ecumenism and church union.
Those of this persuasion, too, are more than others aware of their
church's teachings, and, especially the Catholics, more involved in
church activities. Those favoring ecumenism also typically approved
participation of their church in ameliorative social causes. (Articles
in *Journal of Ecumenical Studies,* Winter, 1971, 1–9, and Spring,
1972, 341–351.) One must not generalize too confidently on so limited
an inquiry; but to students of the history of ecumenical literature it
offers no surprises. It is "Christians in earnest" who are alike healers
of church schisms and concerned benefactors of society. Peace and
justice and human brotherhood are by them quite naturally associated
with the communion of saints. '

Official plans and programs to effect unity are always in themselves
insufficient. What is essential is not a product of promotional devices.
The tide of ecumenical achievement will come in only with the rise of
spiritual forces that cannot be set in motion by committees. This
element is not absent, but it is not yet in full vigor. Too many mis-
take the ecumenical movement for mere interchurch politics, while
in its essence it is a revival of elemental Christianity whose Founder
never thought of originating a multiplicity of sects. While we await
a strengthening of the spiritual bonds that should unite us firmly,
we may well take courage from the conditions that today make mutual
understanding among churches so much easier to gain than in former
times. We have entered an era of ready communication in which
misconceptions and alienations tend to be checked by the availability
of information, and thus aided we have passed from an era of mutual
denunciation to a new stage of friendly dialogue and mutual inquiry.

It is a very meaningful thing that we Christians, for the first time
since the fifth century, share a common world of thought. We are all
instantly affected by the same poignant events and potent ideas. The
rallying force exercised by charismatic personalities is sure to be felt
promptly round the world. Apart from certain anti-intellectual groups,
we share a common scholarship in theology and history. The Christian
world has never been so sensitive to new impulses wherever these arise
in all its parts, or so responsive to interchurch overtures and gestures
of goodwill, as during the last quarter century. In a pontificate of six

years John XXIII was able to awaken in countless millions throughout the world a profound response to his brotherly spirit. His reception at the Vatican of an Eastern Orthodox Patriarch, an Archbishop of Canterbury, and a Moderator of the Church of Scotland well betokened the new posture of relations among great historic churches that is one of the impressive phenomena of our time. On a narrower scene, the French Protestant community of Taizé seeks to direct its converts from irreligion into active membership in the neighboring Roman Catholic churches. Within memory it was usual for Protestants and Roman Catholics to keep a social distance from one another and to denounce one another's religious beliefs. There came a period of occasional conference on terms of studied tolerance. But in a degree hardly imaginable a generation ago we have come to trust and confide in one another. A set of essays by Max Thurian and others, *Vers L'Intercommunion* (1970), indicates a rising movement toward sharing in communion by Protestants and Catholics in France. In Britain, Canada, and the United States joint services of prayer, open to attendance by all Christians of a community, are not infrequent, and marriages from time to time occur in which priests and ministers officiate together.

Most modern denominations took their rise in controversy in course of which a strong sense of superiority was generated on both sides. Long after the issues then debated have ceased to be of interest, the feeling of superiority tends to survive and it may even find fresh expression in a discussion of some ecumenical proposal. "We left those people behind a century ago; why should we be tied up with them again?" It can hardly be questioned that this attitude, like racial intolerance, is no longer so widespread as it was. An outstanding fact of denominational statistics is the large number of members who have changed denominations. In most cases this is due to circumstances of residence or marriage, and not to a change of central convictions. Such changes seem almost always to take place without reproach on the part of the families or congregations concerned and to be accepted as blameless adjustments to a new life situation. The equality of denominations seems to be unquestioned. It may be argued that such an attitude is one of indifference; but the persons concerned are not so indifferent as to drift out of the church altogether and in some cases that can be cited they are among the most active church workers. The phenomenon seems to point instead to a new warmth of acceptance between denominations that is prophetic of future reunion.

Such facts as these are indicative of a creeping ecumenism, independent of formal conferences or councils and largely without documentary record, that is gradually changing the spirit of the churches. The progress of the ecumenical movement is not to be measured by the completion on schedule of this or that particular project for unitive action. It came as a disappointment to ecumenists that in 1972 the General Assembly of The United Presbyterian Church in the U.S.A. voted to discontinue connection with the Consultation on Church Union. Many of those voting for this action did so in the hope that it would hasten the unification of American Presbyterianism in itself, rather than with a desire to delay a wider union. But a quiet change took place in the thought of the church before the 1973 meeting of the Assembly. By a majority almost twice that of the 1972 vote, the 1973 Assembly decided to renew the church's membership in the Consultation. This is surely a notable triumph of the comprehensive ecumenism in which a wide range of denominations confer and negotiate. Even if the Consultation had broken down, it would have served an important educative purpose and advanced the ecumenical cause. Its adoption of the name "Uniting" rather than "United" (church) has helped to lay an enduring emphasis on the requirement that union projects should never take such form as to preclude or handicap further steps toward the total reintegration of the church of Christ. We may be confident that in all major steps toward reunion the Presbyterian and Reformed churches will continue to play a significant part.

In the Reformed tradition the quest of unity has been a very real element even though in the minds of many of the members it has often yielded place to more immediate and sometimes controversial issues. The *Form of Presbyterian Church Government* of 1644 holds in view "synodical assemblies . . . national and oecumenical." At the union exercises in which the Presbyterian Church in Canada was formed in 1875, John Cook drew "round after round of applause" for an address in which, warning against an undue reverence for the seventeenth-century doctrinal statements, he anticipated "a far larger union" in accordance with "our Lord's intercessory prayer." Not different was the constant message both of Philip Schaff and of Charles Briggs, as clearly appears in Chapter XI above. These eminent forerunners of the present ecumenical movement were sometimes confronted with suspicion and resistance, and there are still many in the Presbyterian ranks to whom their ideas are uncongenial. Yet they

stood in succession to a long line of Reformed and Presbyterian churchmen, and they have been followed by countless others. Bishop Lesslie
Newbigin, Pastor Marc Boegner, William Visser 't Hooft, Henry Pitney
Van Dusen, and Eugene Carson Blake, all nurtured in Presbyterian or
Reformed churches, are prominent in this company. A worldwide
church "Catholic, Evangelical and Reformed" has in effect been the
pattern in the minds of our predecessors as they appear in this book.
This pattern was set by Calvin when he enjoined his readers to
keep themselves in "brotherly agreement with all God's children,"
and in the letters and personal conferences by which he sought to
combat "sacrilegious schism." It accords with the plea of Francis
Junius that we "cultivate the communion of saints" and with his firm
resolve: "If you tear the brotherhood to pieces, I will do my best to
build it up again." In the nineteenth century Philip Schaff well
exemplified the Reformed ecumenical tradition when he looked for "a
higher union of Protestantism and Catholicism in their pure forms,
freed of their respective errors and infirmities." The prophets have
spoken. Our century may yet see their message prevail.

In our greatly troubled world, menaced by secular divisive forces,
it is one great source of hope that an upsurge of mutual goodwill and
trust has made itself apparent among the churches, offering new possibilities of cooperation and union. The ecumenical testimony is likely
to become more convincing, the ecumenical scene more lively, with
the passing years.

NOTES

INTRODUCTION

1. Augsburg Confession, Part I, Art. XXII.
2. Notably in Ruth Rouse and Stephen C. Neill (eds.), *A History of the Ecumenical Movement, 1517–1948* (London: S.P.C.K.; Philadelphia: The Westminster Press, 1954; now also in a German edition). There are fifteen contributors, several of whom have inserted contributions from other scholars.

Chapter I
CALVIN AS AN ECUMENICAL CHURCHMAN

1. This title was used in an article published in *Church History* XXXIII (1963), 3–15. This chapter, however, has little resemblance to the article but is a product of fresh thought and study. Only a few sentences have been repeated, together with a number of the quotations from Calvin. I am grateful to the editors of *Church History* for permission to use these excerpts.
2. Letter of May 2, 1564. The aged Farel upon receiving it made the journey from Neuchâtel to Geneva for a last visit with Calvin.
3. John Calvin, *Institutes of the Christian Religion* IV. i. 10. Quotations from the *Institutes* are in the translation of Ford Lewis Battles in The Library of Christian Classics, Vols. XX and XXI (London: SCM Press, Ltd.; Philadelphia: The Westminster Press, 1960).
4. *Institutes* IV. i. 3.
5. The Latin text of the *Responsio ad Sadoleti epistolam* (1539), preceded by Sadoleto's letter which provoked it, is edited by Peter Barth in P. Barth and Wilhelm Niesel *Johannis Calvini Opera Selecta*, Vol. I (Munich, 1926), this passage on p. 466. The translation used is from J. K. S. Reid, *Calvin: Theological Treatises*, The Library of Christian Classics, Vol. XXII (London: SCM Press, Ltd.; Philadelphia: The Westminster Press, 1954), p. 231. John C. Olin, in *A Reformation Debate: Sadoleto's Letter to the Genevans and Calvin's Reply* (Harper & Row, Publishers, Inc., 1966), has used Henry Beveridge's translation (1845) of both letters.
6. Commentary on Isaiah, Isa. 44:7.

NOTES

7. *Institutes* IV. i. 3.
8. *Institutes* IV. i. 2.
9. *Institutes* III. iv. 6, referring to James 5:16.
10. *Institutes* IV. i. 16–17.
11. Willem Nijenhuis, *Calvinus Oecumenicus: Calvijn en de Eenheid in het Licht van zijn Briefwisseling* (The Hague, 1958). Most of the letters used by Dr. Nijenhuis are available in English in *The Letters of John Calvin,* compiled by Jules Bonnet, 4 vols. (Philadelphia, 1858). (The earlier 2-volume set reaches only to the year 1557.) Nijenhuis provides citations of the originals; I have here in most instances given dates only, for the guidance of readers who may use different editions.
12. John T. McNeill, *Unitive Protestantism: The Ecumenical Spirit and Its Persistent Expression* (John Knox Press, 1964), pp. 184 f., from *Calvini Opera* XXXIX, 28 f. Cf. Nijenhuis, *op. cit.,* pp. 105 f.
13. William A. Curtis, *History of Creeds and Confessions of Faith* (Edinburgh, 1911), pp. 205 f. Cf. Emile Doumergue, *Jean Calvin—Les Hommes et les choses de son temps,* 7 vols. (Lausanne, 1899–1927), Vol. VI, pp. 80 f., 527; McNeill, *Unitive Protestantism,* pp. 196–198. Rouse and Neill, *op. cit.,* pp. 51 f. The text of the Consensus of Zurich is in H. A. Niemeyer, *Collectio confessionum in ecclesiis reformatis publicatarum* (Leipzig, 1840), pp. 191–217, and in *Calvini Opera* VII, 689–748. For interpretations that accord to Bullinger a more positive role than appears above, see Philip Schaff, *The Creeds of Christendom,* 3 vols., 4th ed. (New York, 1919), Vol. I, pp. 471–473, and A. Bouvier, *Henri Bullinger, réformateur et conseiller oecuménique* (Neuchâtel and Paris, 1940), Part I, Ch. IV.
14. Cf. Jaroslav Pelikan, *Obedient Rebels* (Harper & Row, Publishers, Inc., 1964), p. 40.
15. *Institutes* IV. i. 12–13.
16. *Consilium admodum paternum Pauli III pontifici Romani datum imperatori in Belgis per cardinalem Franciscum, pontificis nepotem, pro Lutheranis, anno 1540, et Eusebii Pamphili ejusdem consilii pia et salutaris explicatio. Calvini Opera* V, 467–508. (A Pious and Wholesome Explanation of Pope Paul III's Advice to the Emperor.) Cf. Doumergue, *op. cit.,* Vol. II, pp. 589 ff.
17. Barth and Niesel, *op. cit.,* I, 489; tr. by Reid, *op. cit.,* p. 256.
18. *Last Admonition to Joachim Westphal,* tr. by Henry Beveridge, *Calvin's Tracts* II (Edinburgh, 1849), Vol. II, pp. 493 f.
19. *Institutes* IV. iii. 15; IV. iv. 1–4; IV. v. 11. His admiring references to church fathers who were faithful bishops are extremely numerous. See also Jacques Pannier, *Calvin et l'épiscopat* (Strassburg and Paris, 1927); Geddes MacGregor, *Corpus Christi: The Nature of the Church According to the Reformed Tradition* (The Westminster Press, 1958), pp. 197–211; McNeill, "The Doctrine of the Ministry in Reformed Theology," *Church History* XII (1943), 77–97.
20. John Strype, *Life of Matthew Parker* (Oxford, 1812–1824), Vol. I, pp. 138 ff.; V. J. K. Brook, *A Life of Archbishop Parker* (Oxford University Press, 1962); McNeill, *Unitive Protestantism,* pp. 213 f.

Chapter II
BEZA'S ECUMENICAL INTERESTS AND THE "HARMONY OF CONFESSIONS"

1. The document is in *Calvini Opera* XVI, 2628. See the unpublished dissertation by Donald H. MacVicar, "William Farel, Reformer of the Swiss Romand" (Union Theological Seminary, 1954), pp. 192 ff.; McNeill, *Unitive Protestantism*, pp. 204–207.

2. A. Ruchat, *Histoire de la Réformation de la Suisse*, 7 vols. (Paris, 1835–1838), Vol. VI, pp. 217 f.; Henry Martin Baird, *Theodore Beza, The Counsellor of the French Reformation* (New York, 1899), Chs. II, III.

3. P. Schaff, *Creeds of Christendom*, Vol. I, pp. 288 f.

4. For the Colloquy of Poissy, consult: *Correspondance de Théodore de Bèze*, recueillé par Hippolyte Aubert (published by Fernand Aubert et Henri Malan, Geneva, 1962), Vol. II, pp. 134–207; Henry Martin Baird, *The Rise of the Huguenots of France* (New York, 1879), Vol. I, pp. 493–541; Baird, *Theodore Beza* (New York, 1899; reprinted 1970), pp. 153–187; Johann Wilhelm Baum, *Theodor Beza* (Leipzig, 1843–1852), Vol. II, p. 199 and Appendix; Benjamin F. Paist, *Peter Martyr and the Colloquy of Poissy*, reprinted from the *Princeton Theological Review* XX (1922); Joseph C. McLelland, *The Visible Words of God: An Exposition of the Sacramental Theology of Peter Martyr Vermigli A.D. 1500–1562* (Edinburgh: Oliver & Boyd, Ltd., 1957), pp. 61–64 and Appendix C.

5. Theodore Beza, *De pace Christianarum ecclesiarum constituenda, consilium pii & moderati cuiusdam viri. Ad Sacram Caesaream Maiestatem, et Rom. Imperij Status Augustae congregatos* (Geneva, 1566). (Film copy in the library of the Foundation for Reformation Research, St. Louis.)

6. Letter of Beza to Bullinger, Sept. 3, 1566, and letter of Bullinger to Beza, Aug. 3, 1567. *The Zurich Letters*, edited for the Parker Society, Second Series (Cambridge, 1845), pp. 127 ff., 154 ff.

7. Sir George Paule was comptroller of Whitgift's household. His *Life of John Whitgift, Archbishop of Canterbury* is reprinted from the 1699 edition in Christopher Wordsworth, *Ecclesiastical Biography, or Lives of Eminent Men connected with the History of Religion in England*, 4 vols. I have used the 4th edition (London, 1853), where the *Life* is in Vol. III, pp. 554–629; see esp. p. 607.

8. See especially Robert Stupperich, *Melanchthon*, tr. by Robert H. Fischer (The Westminster Press, 1965), pp. 139–145.

9. *Calvini Opera* XLV, 92; McNeill, *Unitive Protestantism*, p. 208.

10. Theodore G. Tappert (ed.), *The Book of Concord: The Confessions of the Evangelical Lutheran Church* (Muhlenberg Press, 1959). P. Schaff, *Creeds of Christendom*, gives the *Epitome* only, Vol. III, pp. 92–180. The entire *Formula Concordiae* consisting of *Epitome* and *Solida Declaratio* is textually edited in *Die Bekenntnisschriften der Evangelisch-Lutherischen Kirche* (Augsburg Confession, Commemorative Edition) (Göttingen, 1930), pp. 735–1100. See especially Art. VII of the *Epitome*.

11. Wolfgang Menzel, *History of Germany*, tr. by Mrs. George Horrocks, 3 vols. (London, 1853), Vol. II, pp. 284 f.; John C. L. Gieseler, *A Text-Book of Church History*, tr. and ed. by Henry B. Smith (New York, 1876), Vol. IV,

pp. 440–493; Emile G. Léonard, *Histoire générale du protestantisme* (Paris, 1961), Vol. II, pp. 21–30.

12. See below, p. 42.

13. Jean Aymon, *Tous les synodes nationaux des Eglises Réformées de France*, 2 vols. (La Haye, 1710), Vol. I, pp. 131–133, 274; somewhat freely translated in John Quick, *Synodicon in Gallia Reformata, or, Acts, Decisions, Decrees and Canons of . . . National Councils of the Reformed Churches in France*, 2 vols. (London, 1962), Vol. I, pp. 120 f.; Vol. II, p. 297; Raoul Patry, *Philippe du Plessis-Mornay, un Huguenot homme d'état* (Paris, 1933), pp. 306 f., 412 f.

14. See P. F. Geisendorf, *Théodore de Bèze* (Geneva and Paris, 1949), Chs. XI, XII.

15. Peter Hall, *The Harmony of the Protestant Confessions*. Tr. from the Latin. (London, 1842.)

16. Henry Martin Baird, *The Huguenots and Henry of Navarre* (New York, 1886), Vol. I, p. 401; Baird, *Theodore Beza*, pp. 285 ff.; Lods Armand, "Les Actes de colloque de Montbéliard," *Bulletin de la Société de l'Histoire du Protestantisme Français*, XLVI (1897), 194–215.

17. Robert Dean Linder, *The Political Ideals of Pierre Viret* (Geneva, 1964), pp. 44, 49, 68–73, 170 f., 177. How serious the issue of church government became in the French church may be understood from Robert M. Kingdon's well-documented work, *Geneva and the Consolidation of the French Protestant Movement, 1564–1572* (The University of Wisconsin Press, 1967).

Chapter III
FRENCH AND SWISS REFORMED PROPONENTS OF PROTESTANT UNITY

1. Noted above, p. 36.

2. Henry Martin Baird, *History of the Huguenot Emigration to America* (New York, 1885), Vol. I, pp. 21–77.

3. Quoted in John Viénot, *Histoire de la Réforme française des origines à l'Edit de Nantes* (Paris, 1926), p. 375.

4. Patry, *Philippe du Plessis-Mornay, un Huguenot homme d'état*, p. 21.

5. See Paul T. Fuhrmann, "Philip Mornay and the Huguenot Challenge to Absolutism," in George L. Hunt (ed.), *Calvinism and the Political Order* (The Westminster Press, 1965), Ch. 3.

6. Philip Mornay, *Traité de l'Eglise* (edition of 1600), pp. 335 f., quoted in Patry, *op. cit.*, pp. 289 f.

7. Above, p. 36.

8. Aymon, *op. cit.*, Vol. I, pp. 167, 170; Quick, *op. cit.*, Vol. I, p. 151; Patry, *op. cit.*, p. 287. It was this synod that first officially adopted for the French Reformed church the seal of the burning bush to be used on official letters (canon xxi). Cf. George David Henderson, *The Burning Bush: Studies in Scottish Church History* (Edinburgh: St. Andrew Press, 1957), Ch. I.

9. Malcolm Wallace, *Life of Sir Philip Sidney* (Cambridge University Press, 1915), pp. 175, 183.

10. Lucien Rimbault, *Pierre du Moulin 1568–1658, un pasteur classique à l'âge classique* (Paris, 1966), pp. 71–79, 235–238. Rimbault corrects the

statement in Rouse and Neill, *op. cit.*, pp. 65 f., that the twenty-one articles there described were "adopted" at Tonneins. Aymon included them in the Acts of the Synod, *op. cit.*, Vol. II, pp. 38–64. This document (pp. 57–62) is there entitled *Expédients que l'on propose pour réunir les églises chrétiennes qui ont secoué le joug du pape.* I am indebted to Professor Richard Stauffer of the Faculté Protestante, Paris, for calling my attention to Rimbault's informing study.

11. Patry, *op. cit.*, pp. 439 ff.; Jacques Pannier, "Scots in Saumur in the Seventeenth Century," *Records of the Scottish Church History Society* V (1935), 140–143; Margarite Guignet (Mrs. W. D. Campbell), "Mark Duncan, Professor at Saumur 1606–1640," *Records of the Scottish Church History Society* V (1935), 73–80. On Duncan's work in Saumur, see also Joseph Prost, *La Philosophie à l'académie protestante de Saumur* (Paris, 1907), pp. 11–16, 38.

12. Richard Stauffer, *Un Précurseur française de l'oecuménisme, Moise Amyraut* (Paris, 1962).

13. Aymon, *op. cit.*, Vol. II, pp. 500 f.; Stauffer, *op. cit.*, pp. 17 f.

14. Cf. Stauffer, *op. cit.*, pp. 15 f.

15. The two treatises are closely related, as their titles indicate: *De secessione ab ecclesia romana deque ratione pacis inter evangelicos in religionis negotio constituendae disputatio* (Saumur, 1649); ειρηνικον, *sive de ratione pacis in religionis negotio inter evangelicos constituendae consilium* (Saumur, 1662). In what follows here I am indebted to Stauffer's examination of Amyraut's ecumenical thought, *op. cit.*, pp. 25–51, where both works are drawn upon and many theological points are handled that are omitted here.

16. J. Minton Batten, *John Dury, Advocate of Christian Reunion* (The University of Chicago Press, 1944), pp. 40 f. Batten thinks du Moulin wrote the letter under Dury's influence.

17. See Léonard, *op. cit.*, Vol. II, pp. 74 f.; Rouse and Neill, *op. cit.*, pp. 38 f.

18. The much-discussed passage is in Vincent's *Commonitorium* ii. 3. An English translation with introduction and notes is found in *Early Medieval Theology*, The Library of Christian Classics, Vol. IX, ed. by George E. McCracken in collaboration with Allen Cabaniss (London: SCM Press, Ltd.; Philadelphia: The Westminster Press, 1957), pp. 23–89; this passage p. 38. The use of Vincent's formula in the Protestant era is summarized by Dr. McCracken, pp. 30–35. See also Rouse and Neill, *op. cit.*, pp. 76 f.; Mark Pattison, *Isaac Casaubon, 1559–1614* (London, 1875), pp. 327–346; L. J. Nazelle, *Isaac Casaubon, sa vie et son temps* (Paris, 1897). For renewed interest in Cassander's *Consultatio* on the part of Hugo Grotius, see below, pp. 66 f.

19. See above, p. 47, and below, p. 81.

20. Benedict Pictet, *Dissertationis de consensu et dissensu inter Reformatos et Augustanae confessionis fratres vindiciae adversus animadversiones quas edidit Lutheranus* (Geneva, 1700), pp. 18, 70.

21. Stauffer has fully examined the treatise and the controversy to which it gave rise. It appeared anonymously, having been given to a printer by Tanneguy Lèfevre, a friend of D'Huisseau, and published without the author's knowledge or consent. Stauffer rejects the view of Alfred Soman ("Arminianism in France," *Journal of the History of Ideas* XXXI [1967], 597–600) that D'Huisseau wrote under the influence of Arminius, and regards

La Réunion as a product of the theologically relaxed climate of Saumur where Mornay and Cameron had encouraged a boldly liberal trend. Richard Stauffer, "Une Ouverture oecuménique contestée: 'La Réunion de Christianisme,' " *XVII Siècle*, No. 76–77 (1967), 23–37, and Stauffer's extended study, *L'Affaire D'Huisseau. Une Controverse protestante au sujet de la réunion des chrétiens* (1670–1671) (Paris, 1969).

22. Pierre Jurieu, *De pace inter protestantes ineunda consultatio sive disquisitio circa quaestiones de gratia quae remorantur unionem protestantium utriusque confessionis Augustanae et reformatae* (Utrecht, 1688).

23. Guy Howard Dodge, *The Political Theory of the Huguenots of the Dispersion, with Special Reference to the Thought and Influence of Pierre Jurieu* (Columbia University Press, 1947), pp. 216 f.

24. Jean Alphonse Turretin, *Nubes testium pro moderato et pacifico de rebus theologicis judicio et instituenda inter Protestantes concordia* (Frankfort, 1720). It was translated into English anonymously under the title *Discourse concerning Fundamental Articles in Religion* (London, 1720). Cf. Rouse and Neill, *op. cit.*, pp. 105–109; McNeill, *Unitive Protestantism*, pp. 294 ff.; Norman Sykes, *William Wake, Archbishop of Canterbury, 1657–1737*, 2 vols. (Cambridge: At the University Press, 1957), Vol. II, pp. 27–87.

25. Petrus Ryhinerus, *Samuelis Werenfelsii opuscula theologica, philosophica et philologica*. Editio nova et emendata, 3 vols. (Basel, 1782), I, xxv, xxxiv.

26. Samuel Werenfels, *Cogitationes generales de ratione uniendi ecclesias protestantes quae vulgo Lutheranorum et Reformatorum nominibus distingui solent*, in *Werenfelsii opuscula* II, 61–80. Cf. Martin Schmidt, in Rouse and Neill, *op. cit.*, pp. 106–109; Léonard, *op. cit.*, Vol. III, pp. 52 f.

27. Jean Jacques von Almen, *L'Eglise et ses fonctions d'après Jean Frédéric Ostervald* (Neuchâtel and Paris, 1949), Ch. 4, esp. pp. 45–49; Sykes, *William Wake*, Vol. II, pp. 27–32; Norman Sykes, *From Sheldon to Secker, Aspects of English Church History, 1660–1768*, pp. 137 f.; Rouse and Neill, *op. cit., loc. cit.*

28. Philip Adam Brucker, *Pensées sur la réunion des églises protestantes*. (Copy in the Library of Hartford Seminary.) On this little-known writer, see *Nouvelle Biographie universelle*, Vol. VIII, "Brucker, Philip Adam."

29. For valuable generalizations on Reformed pietism, see James Tanis, *A Mirror That Flattereth Not: A Study of the Life and Theology of Theodorus Jacobus Frelinghausen* (The Hague, 1967), pp. 1–8. For Spener's classic in English, see Theodore G. Tappert (ed.), *Pia Desideria by Philip Jacob Spener* (Fortress Press, 1964).

30. Martin Schmidt, in Rouse and Neill, *op. cit.*, pp. 117 f.

31. Margaret Maxwell, "The Division in the Ranks of Protestants in Eighteenth Century France," *Church History* XXVII (1958), 107–123.

Chapter IV
IRENICAL TREATISES BY GERMAN AND DUTCH REFORMED WRITERS

1. The best account in English of the origin of the Heidelberg Reformed movement is by Bard Thompson in *Essays on the Heidelberg Catechism* (United Church Press, 1963), Chs. 1 and 2. The quotation is from p. 22. See

also the English version of the catechism in Thomas F. Torrance (ed. and tr.), *The School of Faith: The Catechisms of the Reformed Church* (London: James Clarke & Company, Ltd.; New York: Harper & Brothers, 1959), pp. 69–96.

2. Torrance, *op. cit.*, p. 67.

3. John Dickie, "The Reformed Conception of the Church," *Quarterly Register of the Alliance of Reformed Churches* XI (1924), 745 f.

4. Maurice G. Hansen, *The Reformed Church of the Netherlands* (New York, 1884), p. 118.

5. Hansen, *op. cit.*, p. 120.

6. Léonard, *op. cit.*, Vol. II, p. 75.

7. Steuart A. Pears, *The Correspondence of Sir Philip Sidney and Hubert Languet now First Collected and Translated* (London, 1845); Fulke Greville, *The Life of the Renowned Sir Philip Sidney; with the True Interest of England as it then Stood in Relation to all Forrain Princes* . . . (Oxford, 1907; original 1652); Malcolm W. Wallace, *Life of Sir Philip Sidney* (Cambridge, 1915); Mona Wilson, *Sir Philip Sidney* (London, 1931). It was some years after Sidney's death that Gifford became reconciled to Aylmer and a moderate defender of Anglicanism against Henry Barrow. See especially Leland H. Carlson (ed.), *The Writings of Henry Barrow*, 2 vols. (London: George Allen & Unwin, 1962, 1966).

8. Francis Junius, *Eirenicum de pace ecclesiae Catholicae inter Christianos, quamvis diversos sententiis, religiose procuranda, colenda atque continenda; in Psalmos Davidis cxxii & cxxxiii meditatio* (Geneva, 1593).

9. The *Eirenicum* is found in Franciscus Junius, *Opera theologica* (Geneva, 1613), I, 677–762. An excellent modern edition is by Abraham Kuyper, *D. Francisci Junii opuscula theologica selecta* (Amsterdam and Edinburgh, 1882), pp. 293–494. A brief summary in German is given by Otto Ritschl in *Das orthodoxe Luthertum in Gegensatz zu der reformierten Theologie und in Auseinandersetzung mit dem Synkretismus* (Band IV of *Das orthodoxe Luthertum*) (Göttingen, 1927), pp. 253 ff. See also Geeraert Brandt, *History of the Reformation . . . in and about the Low Countries . . .* Translated from the Dutch (London, 1720–1723), Vol. II, pp. 21 f. The *Eirenicum* is discussed by F. W. Cuno in *Franciscus Junius der Altere* (Amsterdam, 1891), pp. 140–151. The *Eirenicum* well deserves translation and wide reading today.

10. James Nichols, *The Works of James Arminius translated from the Latin*, 3 vols. (London, 1825), Vol. I, pp. 371–476.

11. R. W. Lee, *Hugo Grotius*. British Academy annual lecture on a Master Mind (London, 1930), pp. 14–25.

12. David Masson, *Life of Milton*, 7 vols. (London, 1859–1894), Vol. II, p. 368; J. Minton Batten, *John Dury, Advocate of Christian Reunion*, pp. 46, 86.

13. Hugo Grotius, *Via ad pacem ecclesiasticam* (Amsterdam, 1642); *Votum pro pace ecclesiastica* (Amsterdam, 1642); Rouse and Neill, *op. cit.*, pp. 93–96; Fritz Blanke, "Hugo Grotius," in G. Gloede *et al.*, *Ökumenische Profile, Brückenbauer der einen Kirche* (Stuttgart, 1961), pp. 83–95.

14. P. Schaff, *Creeds of Christendom*, Vol. I, p. 515.

15. Under the title *Consilium de pace et concordia in ecclesia Dei colenda*, appended to his treatise *Praeneticus de theologia cryptica* (Bremen, 1615).

16. *Ibid.*, pp. 106–116. Ludwig Crocius is not to be confused with John

Crocius, 1590–1659, Marburg University scholar, who wrote *Pacis et concordiae evangelicorum sacra defensio* (Marburg, 1623).

17. The *De ecclesiarum separatarum unione et syncretismo* (Union and Syncretism of Separated Churches) is found at the close of Voetius' *Politicae ecclesiasticae,* being Part III, Book III, Tractatus iii of that work, published in Amsterdam, 1576. I have used a reproduction from the copy in the Richardson Library, Hartford Seminary, which was kindly provided by Professor F. L. Battles.

18. Timannus Gesselius, *Veritas pacifica* (Amsterdam, 1651). Gesselius was a Utrecht physician and the author of an ecclesiastical history written with irenical purpose (1659).

19. Cornelius Triglandius, *Idea sive imago principis Christiani ex Davidis psalmis centesimo prima expressa et adumbrata* (The Hague, 1666).

20. The quotation from Trigland is from Nesca A. Robb, *William of Orange: A Personal Portrait* (London: William Heinemann, Ltd., 1962), Vol. I, pp. 141 f.; see also pp. 143, 169, 298.

21. Ritschl, *op. cit.,* pp. 254 ff., supplies the German title and outlines the argument of the treatise.

22. Hans Leube, *Kalvinismus und Luthertum in Zeitalter der Orthodoxie* (Leipzig: Scholl, 1928), Vol. I, pp. 59 ff.

23. On Meiderlin, see Ritschl, *op. cit.,* pp. 445 ff.; Rouse and Neill, *op. cit.,* p. 67. Pareus had studied under Zacharius Ursinus and was himself a teacher of numerous advocates of unity. These included John Amos Comenius and John Forbes of Corse (to be discussed below), and the Polish Reformed pastor Bartholomew Bythner, author of the *Brotherly Exhortation* (1607) described by Martin Schmidt in Rouse and Neill, *op. cit.,* p. 96.

24. The distinction has, indeed, the sanction of Calvin. See, e.g., *Institutes* IV. i. 2.

25. John Henry Alting, *Exegesis logica et theologica Augustanae Confessionis.* Cf. Leube, *op. cit.,* Vol. I, pp. 42–47.

26. See Bard Thompson and others, *Essays on the Heidelberg Catechism,* pp. 27 ff.

27. I am indebted to Otto Ritschl, *op. cit.,* Vol. IV, pp. 445, 463, 468 ff., and to the *Allgemeine deutsche Biographie,* Vol. XXXVI, pp. 1595 f. Ritschl gives chief attention to the *Frank Inquiry,* i.e., *Ingenua in controversiis Evangelicorum inquisitio* (Frankfort-on-Oder, 1708). I have used the copy of the *Tractatus duo de unione evangelicorum ecclesiastica* (Leyden, 1711), in the Richardson Library of Hartford Seminary.

28. Rouse and Neill, *op. cit.,* pp. 116 f.; Ritschl, *op. cit.,* Vol. IV, pp. 469 f.

29. Jacobus Acontius, *Strategemata Satanae* (Basel, 1565). There were many editions and translations. Cf. Ritschl, *op. cit.,* Vol. IV, pp. 270–277.

30. Philip van Limborch, *Theologia Christiana ad praxin pietatis ac promotionem pacis christianae unice directa* (Amsterdam, 1686); English translation, *A Compleat System or Body of Divinity,* 2 vols. (London, 1713). The English edition contains the funeral oration by his colleague Jean Le Clerc (Clericus), who had previously written a memoir (*Eloge*) of John Locke, friend and correspondent of both Amsterdam scholars. For Limborch's argument against "hereticide," see especially Vol. II, Book VII, "On the

Church," Ch. 8. In Ch. 9 he discusses necessary and nonnecessary articles and asks for mutual toleration in the latter.

31. *A Compleat System,* II, 1017.

Chapter V
REFORMED UNITIVE ACTIVITY IN EASTERN EUROPE

1. Vasily O. Kluchevsky, *A History of Russia,* tr. by C. J. Hogarth, 5 vols. (Russell & Russell, Inc., 1960), pp. 100 f.

2. Nijenhuis, *Calvinus Oecumenicus,* pp. 22–35; Paul Fox, *The Reformation in Poland: Some Social and Economic Aspects* (Baltimore, 1924), pp. 33 ff.

3. Fox, *op. cit.,* pp. 34–83.

4. Calvinus Casninskio, 4 Calend. Jan. 1555 in *Calvini Opera omnia* XV, 902 f.

5. Cf. Fox, *op. cit.,* pp. 46, 49, 51.

6. The narrative letters of Utenhovius to Bullinger and Martyr, written from Wladislaw, Poland, June 23, 1557, are given in English in Hastings Robinson (ed.), *Original Letters relative to the English Reformation, 1537–1558* (Cambridge, 1847), Vol. II, pp. 596–604. Utenhovius had written to Calvin from Cracow on Feb. 19, à Lasco adding a hasty postscript: "Enemies and false brethren assail us, so that we have no repose." Calvin's extensive correspondence with persons in Poland is examined in some detail by Nijenhuis, *op. cit.,* pp. 10, 22–38, 74 ff., and elsewhere (see his index, "Polen"). In a single day, Dec. 29, 1555, Calvin sent off nine letters to that country. He was several times invited to Poland by the nobles, not by the king.

7. Fox, *op. cit.,* p. 54.

8. Jaroslav Pelikan, "The Consensus of Sendomierz," *Concordia Theological Monthly* (1947), 825–837; P. Schaff, *Creeds of Christendom,* Vol. I, p. 587.

9. P. Schaff, *op. cit.,* Vol. I, p. 588.

10. John T. McNeill, *The History and Character of Calvinism* (Oxford University Press, 1957), pp. 285 f.; Léonard, *op cit.,* Vol. I: *The Reformation,* ed. by H. H. Rowley, tr. by Joyce M. H. Reid (Thomas Nelson & Sons, 1966), pp. 288, 329.

11. P. Schaff, *Creeds of Christendom,* Vol. I, pp. 579 f.; William A. Curtis, *A History of Creeds and Confessions of Faith in Christendom and Beyond* (Edinburgh, 1911), p. 135. The Latin text is in H. A. Niemeyer, *Collectio confessionum in ecclesiis reformatis publicatarum,* pp. 819–851. See also the valuable article by F. Bednar, "The Ecumenical Idea in the Czech Reformation," *Ecumenical Review* VI (1954), 160–168, though the emphasis here is on Comenius.

12. Matthew Spinka, *John Amos Comenius, That Incomparable Moravian* (The University of Chicago Press, 1943), p. 16.

13. John Amos Comenius, *The Bequest of the Unity of Brethren,* tr. and ed. by Matthew Spinka (Chicago: National Union of Czechoslovak Protestants in America, 1940).

14. C. J. Wright, *A Religious Portrait of Comenius* (London, undated), p. 29. Comenius' *Via Lucis* was translated by E. T. Campagnac: *The Way of Light* (Liverpool: University Press of Liverpool, 1938).

15. See especially Ch. 18 in Matthew Spinka's translation from the Czech original, *John Amos Comenius, The Labyrinth of the World and the Paradise of the Heart* (Chicago: National Union of Czechoslovak Protestants in America, 1942).

16. John Amos Comenius, *De dissidentium in rebus fidei Christianorum reconciliatione hypomnemata.* See Spinka, *John Amos Comenius, That Incomparable Moravian,* pp. 100, 160.

17. Spinka, *Comenius,* pp. 145–149.

18. See the article "Jean Calvin, Théodore de Bèze, et leurs amis hongroises," by Charles d'Eszlary, *Bulletin de la Société d'histoire de Protestantisme français* CX (1964), 74–99.

19. Imre Revesz, *History of the Hungarian Reformed Church,* tr. George A. F. Knight (Washington, D. C., 1956), p. 16.

20. A brief informed treatment of the Hungarian Reformation is afforded in two articles by William Toth, "Highlights of the Hungarian Reformation," *Church History* IX (1940), 141–156, and "Trinitarianism and Antitrinitarianism in the Hungarian Reformation," *Church History* XIII (1944), 255–268. An unprinted master's thesis by Ronald Shipman Law, "The Development of the Reformed Church in Hungary During the Sixteenth Century" (Union Theological Seminary, 1948), offers much additional material. Law points out (pp. 58 f.) the early interest in missions on the part of the Hungarian churches. In 1664 Francis Picus was seeking to evangelize the Turks and preaching to many in Asia Minor and in Constantinople. I have also used various histories of Hungary. On leading personalities of the Hungarian Reformation, see also Mihaly Bucsay, *Geschichte des Protestantismus in Ungarn* (Stuttgart, 1959), pp. 26–33, 84–87.

21. George A. Hadjiantoniou, *Protestant Patriarch: The Life of Cyril Lucaris, 1572–1638* (John Knox Press, 1961). On the Confession, see pp. 94–109, and the translation, pp. 141–145.

Chapter VI
SCOTTISH AND ENGLISH ADVOCATES OF CHRISTIAN REUNION

1. For most biographical facts the reader may still safely follow J. Minton Batten's admirable monograph, *John Dury, Advocate of Christian Reunion* (The University of Chicago Press, 1944). Much additional detail can be found in Gunnar Westin, *Negotiations About Church Unity, 1628–1634* (Uppsala, 1932), and *John Durie in Sweden* (Uppsala, 1934), and in G. H. Turnbull, *Hartlib, Dury and Comenius* (Liverpool: University Press of Liverpool, 1947).

2. Batten, *op. cit.,* p. 19, quoting Dury's *Epistolary Discourse* (1644).

3. Batten, *op. cit.,* p. 20; Westin, *Negotiations,* pp. 208 f.

4. Batten, *op. cit.,* pp. 23 ff.; Westin, *Negotiations,* pp. 97 ff., 196 f.

5. Westin, *Negotiations,* pp. 108 f., 204–207; Batten, *op. cit.,* pp. 27–31, 56. For the Leipzig Colloquy, "*Colloquium Lipsiense,* 1631," in Niemeyer, *op. cit.,* pp. 653–668.

6. Above, p. 67. Cf. R. W. Lee, *Hugo Grotius* (London, 1930), p. 41, and for the preceding data, Westin, *Negotiations,* pp. 150–154, 216–241, 290–294; Batten, *op. cit.,* pp. 40–58.

7. It was at this time that Dury's marriage took place at The Hague. His wife was Dorothy Moore, a widow, whose aunt, Lady Ranelagh, kept high intellectual company in a circle that included John Milton and Robert Boyle, both of whom lent some support to Dury's efforts. Dury's only child, Dora Katherina, became the second wife of Henry Oldenburg, the celebrated Secretary of the Royal Society.

8. The Library of Union Seminary, New York, has a film copy of the Assembly minutes. See S. W. Carruthers, *The Everyday Work of the Westminster Assembly* (Philadelphia, 1943), pp. 4, 39, 187; Batten, *op. cit.*, pp. 96–110. Batten thinks Dury probably influential in the attention given to the Covenant Theology in the Westminster Standards. Batten notes also that Dury was censured by the Assembly for his part in the preface of the translation (1648) of Jacob Acontius' *Stratagems of Satan* (1565), a learned plea for religious toleration, which the Independent Thomas Goodwin had warmly approved. See above, Chapter IV, n. 29.

9. Gilbert Burnet, *History of My Own Time* (London, 1883), Vol. I, pp. 141 f.

10. Othon Cuvier, *Notice sur Paul Ferry, pasteur de l'église réformée de Metz* (Metz, 1870), pp. 13–19; Eugène Haag and Emile Haag, *La France protestante*, 6 vols. (Paris, 1877), Vol. III, pp. 511–519; Roger Mazauric, *Le Pasteur Paul Ferry* (Metz, 1964). Ferry presented a union proposal to the Synod of Loudun, 1659; it was warmly approved, but the text remained unpublished. Samuel Mours, *Le Protestantisme en France au XVIIᵉ siècle* (Paris, 1967), p. 40; Mazauric, *op. cit.*, pp. 92 f.

11. Westin, *Negotiations*, p. 221.

12. Batten, *op. cit.*, p. 74.

13. W. K. Jordan, *The Development of Religious Toleration in England* (Harvard University Press), Vol. III (1938), p. 321.

14. Jordan, *op. cit.*, pp. 316–327.

15. G. D. Henderson, *Religious Life in Seventeenth Century Scotland* (Cambridge, 1937), p. 47, quoting Patrick Forbes, *Defence of the Lawful Calling of the Ministers of Reformed Churches*, p. 5. See also Henderson, *The Burning Bush*, pp. 89–93.

16. John Forbes of Corse, *Irenicum amatoribus veritatis et pacis in Ecclesia Scoticana* (Edinburgh, 1629). Reprinted 1636, and revised from the author's notes, 1703.

17. J. B. S. Carwithen, *The History of the Church of England* (Oxford, 1849), Vol. II, p. 303.

18. William Orme, *Life and Times of Rev. Richard Baxter*, 2 vols. (Boston, 1821), Vol. II, pp. 187 f. Orme's biography is specially useful to us in Vol. II, pp. 54, 152–188. The treatises of Baxter here used are found in Vols. XIV–XVI of *The Practical Works of the Reverend Richard Baxter* [Including Orme's Life], 23 vols. (London, 1830). For Baxter's role in the general situation, see Rouse and Neill, *op. cit.*, Ch. 3, by Norman Sykes.

19. *Works of John Owen*, ed. by William Gould (Philadelphia, 1871), Vol. I, p. 492. The text of the Preface to the Savoy Declaration is given in P. Schaff, *Creeds of Christendom*, Vol. III, pp. 708–718.

20. United Church of Canada, *A Statement concerning Ordination to the*

Ministry (Toronto, 1926), p. 228. For evidence on English Congregational ecumenical interest, see also Norman Goodall, "Some Pathfinders in the Ecumenical Movement," *Transactions of the Congregational Historical Society* XX (1967), pp. 184–199.

21. Edward Calamy, *Memoirs of the Life of the Late Rev. John Howe* (London, 1724), p. 238. For what I have said here of Howe, the reader may profitably see also pp. 32, 47, 142 ff., 187 of Calamy.

22. A. H. Drysdale, *History of the Presbyterians in England* (London, 1889), p. 521.

Chapter VII
FRAGMENTATION AND REUNION OF THE CHURCH OF SCOTLAND

1. In this connection, see especially R. Stuart Louden, *The True Face of the Kirk* (Oxford University Press, 1963), Ch. 2.

2. One of the later and better accounts of the era of the tulchan bishops is found in William M. Campbell, *The Triumph of Presbyterianism* (Edinburgh: St. Andrew Press, 1958).

3. A reliable and sufficiently ample treatment of the sequence of events is furnished by John H. S. Burleigh, *A Church History of Scotland* (Oxford University Press, 1960), pp. 188–308. Lord Balfour of Burleigh's *Historical Account of the Rise and Development of Presbyterianism in Scotland* (Cambridge, 1911) treats the facts succinctly in Chs. 4 to 7. Robert Logan in *The United Free Church: An Historical Review . . . 1681–1906* (Edinburgh, 1906), Chs. 2 to 4, offers some details on the secessions. Indispensable for documents and other information on the Covenant is John C. Johnson, *Treasury of the Scottish Covenant* (Edinburgh, 1887). Consult also J. K. Hewison, *The Covenanters. A History of the Church in Scotland from the Reformation to the Revolution*, 2 vols. (Glasgow, 1908; 2d rev. ed., 1913); W. M. Hetherington, *History of the Church of Scotland . . . to 1843* (New York, 1870). On Thomas Gillespie, see the article "Thomas Gillespie" by Hugh Watt in *Records of the Scottish Church History Society* XV (1964), 89–101.

4. John Mackay, *The Church in the Highlands* (London, 1914), lecture vi, "The Awakening Church"; Alexander Haldane, *The Lives of Robert Haldane and James Alexander Haldane*, 2 vols. (London, 1852; 5th. ed., 1871).

5. Robert Buchanan, *The Ten Years' Conflict*, 2 vols. (Glasgow, 1849); A. Taylor Innes, *The Law of Creeds in Scotland* (Edinburgh and London, 1902). Innes gives essential portions of numerous documents, including the Claim of Right. Logan, *op. cit.*, Chs. 5 to 7, writes from a Free Church point of view a lively account of events leading to the Disruption; J. H. S. Burleigh, *op. cit.*, pp. 334–369, gives a judicial narrative.

6. Andrew J. Campbell, *Two Centuries of the Church of Scotland, 1707–1929* (Paisley, 1930), p. 90.

7. For some of the evidence, see J. A. Wallace (ed.), *Testimonies in Favor of the Free Church of Scotland* (Edinburgh, 1844). Typical is the language of John Lillie, American Dutch Reformed pastor of Scottish birth, "that fine, solemn, summer day, when Scotland's pious chivalry came forth, a spectacle to angels and men. . . . I have wept for joy, both as a Scotchman and as a

Christian." An emissary of the Kirk in Australia wrote: "It almost seems as if, whilst the Establishment is breaking down, the Church were rising up" (Wallace, *op. cit.*, pp. 77, 79).

8. Quoted by J. H. S. Burleigh, *op. cit.*, p. 362.

9. Logan, *op. cit.*, pp. 48–51; William Gregg, *History of the Presbyterian Church in the Dominion of Canada* (Toronto, 1885), pp. 132 ff.

10. Logan, *op. cit.*, pp. 79–84. Of the 49 ministers, 12 refused to take this course, two of whom changed their minds later. Eight of the others moved over to the Auld Licht Antiburghers.

11. William Hanna, *Memoir of the Life and Work of Thomas Chalmers* (New York, 1852), Vol. IV, pp. 243 f.

12. Logan, *op. cit.*, Ch. 9. Text in A. Taylor Innes, *op. cit.*, pp. 333–334.

13. Innes, *op. cit.*, pp. 244 ff.

14. Innes, *op. cit.*, pp. 334–337, gives these acts in parallel columns. In both churches these declaratory acts were adopted after celebrated heresy trials, and were designed to protect against further debilitating controversy. Protesting the 1892 act, a small group in the Highlands broke away from the Free Church to form the Free Presbyterian Church.

15. Innes, *op. cit.*, p. 316.

16. J. R. Fleming, *The Story of Church Union in Scotland: Its Origins and Progress, 1560–1929* (London, 1929), p. 44; Rolf Sjölinder, *Presbyterian Reunion in Scotland, 1907–1921* (Uppsala, 1962), pp. 318 f.

17. For an informing chapter on "Recovery in the Established Church," see J. H. S. Burleigh, *op. cit.*, pp. 370–393.

18. Lord Balfour of Burleigh, *op. cit.*, p. 158.

19. See below, Chapter XII.

20. Fleming, *op. cit.*, p. 53.

21. The Church of Scotland Act, 1921, with its appended Articles Declaratory, forms Appendix C to R. Stuart Louden's *The True Face of the Kirk* (cited above, note 1), pp. 104–109. Article V is here quoted.

22. For a somewhat ample account of the preceding events and of this meeting as seen by the biographer of "the chief architect of union," see Augustus Muir, *John White* (London: Hodder & Stoughton, Ltd., 1958), Chs. 7–15.

23. Louden, *op. cit.*, p. 109.

24. *Ecumenical Review* XXIV (1972), 364 f.: Report by Basil Gingell in *The Times*, October 6, 1972.

Chapter VIII
TRANSPLANTATION TO AMERICA AND CONSOLIDATION

1. Charles A. Briggs, *American Presbyterianism* (Charles Scribner's Sons, 1885), pp. 284–289; J. I. Good, "Early Attempted Union of Presbyterians with Dutch and German Reformed," *Journal of the Presbyterian Historical Society* III (1905), 122–137.

2. See especially Perry Miller, *Orthodoxy in Massachusetts, 1630–1650* (Peter Smith, 1965), and Edmund S. Morgan, *Visible Saints: The History of a Puritan Idea* (New York University Press, 1963).

3. C. C. Goen, *Revivalism and Separatism in New England, 1740–1800* (New Haven and London: Yale University Press, 1962), pp. 2 f.; and J. F. Maclear, " 'The True American Union' of Church and State," *Church History* XXVIII (1959), 41–62.

4. Goen, *op. cit.*

5. A. L. Cross, *The Anglican Episcopate and the American Colonies* (New York and London: Longmans, Green, and Co., 1902); C. Bridenbaugh, *Mitre and Sceptre* (Oxford University Press, 1962).

6. M. W. Armstrong, "The English Dissenting Deputies and the American Colonists," *Journal of Presbyterian History* XL (1962), 24–37, 75–91, 144–159.

7. Leonard J. Trinterud, *The Forming of an American Tradition* (The Westminster Press, 1949), pp. 255 f.

8. W. N. Jamison, *The United Presbyterian Story* (Pittsburgh: The Geneva Press, 1958), Ch. 3. Also W. Christy, "United Presbyterian Church and Church Union" (Ph.D. thesis, Pittsburgh, 1947).

9. R. H. Nichols and J. H. Nichols, *Presbyterianism in New York State* (The Westminster Press, 1963), Chs. 4 and 5.

10. C. B. Staiger, "Abolition and the Presbyterian Schism," *Mississippi Valley Historical Review,* Dec., 1949.

11. E. D. Morris, *A Book of Remembrance. The Presbyterian Church New School, 1837–1869* (Columbus, Ohio: Champlin Press, 1905); E. R. MacCormac, "The Development of Presbyterian Missionary Organizations, 1790–1870," *Journal of Presbyterian History* XLIII (1965), 149–173; E. R. Mac-Cormac, "An Ecumenical Failure: The Development of Congregational Missions . . . ," *Journal of Presbyterian History* XLIV (1966), 266–285, and XLV (1967), 8–26.

12. W. S. Jenkins, *Pro-Slavery Thought in the Old South* (University of North Carolina Press, 1935).

13. *Presbyterian Reunion: A Memorial Volume, 1837–1871* (New York: De Witt C. Lent and Co.; Chicago: Van Nortwick and Sparks, 1871).

14. Henry B. Smith, *Faith and Philosophy* (Scribner, Armstrong & Co., 1877), pp. 265–296.

15. H. Harmelink III, "The Ecumenical Relations of the Reformed Church in America," *Journal of Presbyterian History* XLV (1967), 71–94. See also D. H. Yoder, "Church Union Efforts of the Reformed Church in the United States to 1934" (Ph.D. thesis, University of Chicago, 1948).

16. A. E. Murray, *Presbyterians and the Negro: A History* (Philadelphia: Presbyterian Historical Society, 1966), p. 200. On the civil suits, see M. J. De Lozier, "A Presbyterian Property Dispute Before the Tennessee Supreme Court," *Journal of Presbyterian History* XLV (1967), 193–202.

17. E. T. Thompson, "Presbyterians North and South: Efforts Toward Reunion," *Journal of Presbyterian History* XLIII (1965), 1–15.

18. W. N. Jamison, *op. cit.,* Ch. 12.

19. S. B. Humphrey, "The Union of the Congregational and Christian Churches" (Ph.D. thesis, Yale, 1933).

20. W. E. MacNair, "Formation of the United Church of Christ" (Ph.D. thesis, University of Wisconsin, 1964), and A. B. Peabody, "Congregationalist Controversy Over Merger" (Ph.D. thesis, Syracuse University, 1964).

21. A. Peel and D. Horton, *International Congregationalism* (London: Independent Press, 1949).

Chapter IX
REFORMED-LUTHERAN RELATIONS:
UNION IN CONFESSING THE GOSPEL?

1. G. J. Planck, *Über die Trennung und Wiedervereinigung der getrennten christlichen Hauptparteien* (Tübingen: J. G. Cotta, 1803). F. S. G. Sack, *Über die Vereinigung der beiden protestantischen Kirchengemeinden in der preussischen Monarchie* (Berlin, 1812). F. Schleiermacher, *Zwei unvorgreiflichen Gutachten in Sachen des protestantischen Kirchenwesens* (Berlin, 1804).
2. D. H. Yoder, "Church Union Efforts of the Reformed Church in the United States to 1934."
3. C. E. Schneider, *The German Church on the American Frontier* (Eden Publishing House, 1939), p. 409.
4. Philip Schaff, *Principle of Protestantism* (Chambersburg, 1845).
5. A. J. Lewis, *Zinzendorf the Ecumenical Pioneer* (London: SCM Press, Ltd.; Philadelphia: The Westminster Press, 1962).
6. *Ekklesia,* Vol. V, *Die Kirchen der Teschechoslowakei* (Leipzig: Leopold Klotz Verlag, 1937). A. Molnar, "Zur Konfessionsunionistischen Tradition . . . ," in *Antwort; Karl Barth zum 70th Geburtstag* (Zollikon-Zurich: Evangelischer Verlag, 1956), pp. 647–660.
7. *Ecumenical Review,* 1961, pp. 501 ff.
8. *Lutheran World,* 1956, p. 385. This consensus, incidentally, drew an extended favorable analysis from Professor Torrance of the Church of Scotland, together with suggestions for further understandings. See *Lutheran World,* 1956, pp. 395 ff.
9. *Lutheran World,* 1960, pp. 57 f.
10. *Auf dem Weg,* ed. by M. Geiger, H. Ott, L. Vischer (Zurich: EVZ Verlag, 1967), pp. 93–109.
11. A. R. Wentz, *Basic History of Lutheranism in America,* rev. ed. (Fortress Press, 1964), pp. 234 f.
12. Paul C. Empie and James I. McCord (eds.) *Marburg Revisited: A Reexamination of Lutheran and Reformed Traditions* (Augsburg Publishing House, 1966).
13. *Ibid.,* Preface, pp. 191, 183.
14. *Reformed and Presbyterian World,* 1967, pp. 307–319.
15. *Auf dem Weg.*
16. *Reformed and Presbyterian World,* 1971, p. 216 .
17. *Reformed World,* June, 1972, pp. 70 f.

Chapter X
THE EVANGELICAL ALLIANCE:
THE ECUMENISM OF THE VOLUNTARY SOCIETIES

1. Lefferts Loetscher, *The Problem of Christian Unity in Early Nineteenth-Century America* (Fortress Press, 1969), pp. 7, 19. See also C. I. Foster,

An Errand of Mercy: The Evangelical United Front, 1790–1837 (University of North Carolina Press, 1960).

2. D. King, "Historical Sketch of the Evangelical Alliance," *General Conference, World Alliance* (London, 1851).

3. *Christian Observer*, Dec., 1845, pp. 728–761. See also E. R. Norman, *Anti-Catholicism in Victorian England* (Barnes & Noble, Inc., 1968), pp. 23 f.: "Those seeking an early false-start in ecumenicalism can find one here: serious attempts were made to turn the united Protestant opposition to Maynooth in 1845 into a sustained and permanent Evangelical organization."

4. R. Lovett, *History of the London Missionary Society, 1795–1895* (London: Henry Frowde, 1899), pp. 49 f.

5. Conder, in *Eclectic Review*, 1837, p. 181.

6. W. Canton, *History of the British and Foreign Bible Society* (London: John Murray, 1904), Vol. I, p. 12.

7. W. Jones, *Jubilee Memorial of the Religious Tract Society* (London: Religious Tract Society, 1850), pp. 74 ff.

8. *Christian Observer*, Dec., 1845, pp. 48 f.

9. Published in *The Christian Alliance. Addresses of Rev. L. Bacon and Rev. E. N. Kirk* (New York, 1845), pp. 38–46.

10. Cited by J. W. Massie, in *The Evangelical Alliance* (London: John Snow, 1847), pp. 309 f.

11. *Ibid.*, p. 294.

12. G. Monod, *Conférence de Chrétiens Evangéliques de Toute Nation à Paris 1855* (Paris, 1856), p. xi.

13. P. Schaff, *Creeds of Christendom*, Vol. III, p. 527.

14. Massie, *op. cit.*, p. 257.

15. King, *op. cit.*, p. 43.

16. Culling Eardley Smith, *Remonstrance . . . to the Christian Abolitionists*, p. 11.

17. Correspondence, Presbyterian Historical Society, Philadelphia, Sept. 2, 1851.

18. Philip Schaff, "The Evangelical Church Diet of Germany," *Mercersburg Review*, 1857, p. 1.

19. Philip Schaff, "The State Church System in Europe," *Mercersburg Review*, 1857, p. 154.

20. *Ibid.*, p. 161.

21. P. Schaff, "The Evangelical Church Diet of Germany," *Mercersburg Review*, 1857, p. 24.

22. Cited from *American Lutheran*, Feb. 21, 1884, in *Christian Observer*, April 3, 1884.

23. *Christian Observer*, Sept., 1884.

24. Philip Schaff, "Discord and Concord of Christendom," in *Christ and Christianity* (London: James Nisbet & Co., 1855), pp. 297, 301.

25. Philip Schaff, "Christianity in America," *Mercersburg Review*, Oct., 1857, p. 508.

26. David Schaff, *The Life of Philip Schaff* (Charles Scribner's Sons, 1897), pp. 351 f.

27. Philip Schaff, *Diary*, Oct. 11, 1873 (Library of Union Theological Seminary).

28. *New York Evangelist*, Nov., 1869.
29. Cf. Kalkar's observation in D. Schaff, *op. cit.*, p. 351.

Chapter XI

THE WORLD ALLIANCE OF REFORMED
AND PRESBYTERIAN CHURCHES

1. The official title was "The World Alliance of Reformed Churches Throughout the World Holding the Presbyterian System." The organization was frequently referred to also as "The World Reformed Alliance" or "The World Presbyterian Alliance." Since the merger of 1970, the title is "The World Alliance of Reformed Churches (Presbyterian and Congregational)."
2. D. Schaff, *op. cit.*, pp. 318 f.
3. Philip Schaff, in *New York Observer*, Jan. 17, 1877.
4. P. Schaff, in *Christ and Christianity*, p. 5.
5. Scrapbook (Union Theological Seminary Library).
6. Philip Schaff, in *Independent*, Oct. 28, 1875.
7. P. Schaff, in *Christ and Christianity*, pp. 153–183.
8. Philip Schaff, "The Renaissance and the Reformation," *Mercersburg Review*, 1891, pp. 464, 462, 461.
9. Philip Schaff, *History of the Apostolic Church* (1853), pp. 45 f.
10. Philip Schaff, "Other Heresy Trials and the Briggs Case," *Forum*, Jan., 1892, p. 625.
11. Charles Briggs, "Church and Creed," *Forum*, June, 1891, p. 378.
12. Philip Schaff, in Document XXXIII (New York: Evangelical Alliance Office, 1893).
13. Philip Schaff, "Christian Union," *New York Evangelist*, April 28, 1887.
14. *Alliance of the Reformed Churches . . . Twelfth General Council, Cardiff, 1925*, p. 137. For an expansion of the Barthian conception of a confession, see Ch. VII of *The Church's Confession Under Hitler*, by Arthur C. Cochrane (The Westminster Press, 1962).
15. *Proceedings of the Seventh General Council of the Alliance of Reformed Churches . . . Washington, D.C., 1899* (London: Office of the Alliance, 1899), App. 96.
16. *Proceedings: Ninth General Council . . . New York, 1909* (London: Office of the Alliance, 1909), App. 116.
17. *Report of Proceedings of the First General Presbyterian Council . . . Edinburgh, 1877* (Edinburgh: Thomas & Archibald Constable, 1877), p. 4.
18. *Report of Proceedings of the Second General Council of the Presbyterian Alliance . . . Philadelphia, 1880* (Philadelphia: Presbyterian Journal Company and J. C. McCurdy & Co., 1880), p. 603.
19. *Alliance of the Reformed Churches . . . Proceedings of the Fourth General Council, London, 1888* (London: Presbyterian Alliance Office, 1889), p. 386.
20. *Alliance of the Reformed Churches . . . Proceedings of the Third General Council, Belfast, 1884* (Belfast, Edinburgh, London, 1884), App. 21.
21. *Alliance of the Reformed Churches . . . London, 1888*, p. 194.
22. *Alliance of the Reformed Churches . . . Belfast, 1884*, App. 12.
23. *Alliance of the Reformed Churches . . . London, 1888*, App. 270.

24. *Ibid.*, p. 186.

25. *Ibid.*, App. 271.

26. M. G. Ellinwood, *Frank Field Ellinwood* (Fleming H. Revell Company, 1911), p. 214.

27. *Proceedings of the Sixth General Council . . . Glasgow, 1896* (London, New York, Chicago, 1896), p. 234.

28. *Alliance of the Reformed Churches . . . London, 1888*, App. 263.

29. *Executive Commission of the Alliance . . . Western (American) Section, Minutes, February, 1912*, pp. 12 f.

30. *Proceedings of the Tenth General Council . . . Aberdeen, 1913* (Edinburgh, 1913), App. 79.

31. *Proceedings . . . Washington, D.C., 1899*, App. 105.

32. *Executive Commission . . . Western Section, Minutes, October, 1905*, p. 4.

33. *Proceedings . . . Glasgow, 1896*, App. 116 ff.

34. *Proceedings . . . Washington D.C., 1899*, App. 101.

35. *Proceedings . . . Glasgow, 1896*, App. 125.

36. *Executive Commission . . . Western Section, Minutes, November, 1900*, p. 7.

37. *Minutes of the General Assembly of the Presbyterian Church, U.S.A.*, 1900, p. 96.

38. *Executive Commission . . . Western Section, Minutes, February, 1908*, p. 10.

39. *World Missionary Conference, 1910, Report of Commission VIII, Cooperation and the Promotion of Unity* (Edinburgh, London, New York, Chicago, Toronto, 1910), p. 88.

40. W. H. T. Gairdner, *Echoes from Edinburgh 1910* (New York, Chicago, Toronto, London, Edinburgh, n.d.), p. 65; cited by W. H. Hogg, *Ecumenical Foundations* (Harper & Brothers, 1952), p. 125.

Chapter XII
REUNION ON THE HISTORIC EPISCOPATE?

1. There was a significant Presbyterian opposition, but not primarily on predestination or synergism.

2. *Quarterly Register of the Alliance of Reformed Churches*, July, 1887, pp. 101 f.

3. *Report of the Committee on Church Unity*, 1890, pp. 17 f.

4. *Ibid.*, p. 10.

5. *Alliance of the Reformed Churches . . . Fourth General Council* (London: Presbyterian Alliance Office, 1889), p. 361.

6. *Report of the Committee on Church Unity*, 1890, pp. 12 f.

7. *Minutes, General Assembly*, 1887, p. 156.

8. *Correspondence Between the Committee on Church Unity of the General Assembly . . . and the Commission on Christian Unity of the General Convention* (Philadelphia, 1896), p. 34.

9. *Ibid.*, pp. 19 f.

10. For an application of the canon, see J. R. Nelson, "Pike, Hedley and Otwell," *The Christian Century*, March 9, 1960, pp. 279 f.

11. See B. G. M. Sundkler's reconstruction, *Church of South India: The Movement Towards Union, 1900–1947* (London: Lutterworth Press, 1954), pp. 62 ff.

12. J. J. Willis *et al., Towards a United Church, 1913–1947* (London: Edinburgh House Press, 1947), Part 1, "The Kikuyu Conference, 1913."

13. J. Scott Lidgett *et al., Towards Reunion* (London: Macmillan and Co., Ltd., 1919), and G. K. A. Bell (ed.), *Documents Bearing on the Problem of Christian Unity and Fellowship, 1916–1920* (London, 1920).

14. G. K. A. Bell (ed.), *Documents on Christian Unity, 1920–24* (London: Oxford University Press, 1924), pp. 1 ff.

15. Bell, *Documents, 1920–24*, pp. 120–141.

16. *Alliance of the Reformed Churches . . . Eleventh General Council . . .* (Edinburgh: Office of the Alliance, 1922), p. 193. Cf. pp. 87–97 and appendixes, 24–26 and 98–100.

17. Bell, *Documents, 1920–30*, pp. 213–222.

18. For a time it seemed that a limited achievement was promised in New Jersey, where some ten congregations of the Eastern classis of the Hungarian Reformed Church were to be given financial aid and episcopal oversight from the Episcopalians. Four Hungarian ministers were "ordained" again. But the laity rejected the arrangement in 1926. See A. Komjathy, "The Hungarian Reformed Church in America" (Th.D. thesis, Princeton Theological Seminary, 1962).

19. Sundkler, *op. cit.*, p. 166.

20. J. E. Lesslie Newbigin, *The Reunion of the Church: A Defence of the South India Scheme* (Harper & Brothers, 1948), pp. 15 f.

21. C. D. Kean, *The Road to Reunion* (The Seabury Press, Inc., 1958), p. 71. Cf. C. C. Richardson, *The Sacrament of Reunion* (New York and London: Charles Scribner's Sons, 1940).

22. Sundkler, *op. cit.*, p. 315.

23. *The Lambeth Conference 1958* (London: S.P.C.K.; Greenwich, Connecticut: The Seabury Press, Inc., 1958), 2.43 f. E. L. Mascall summarized the joint import of these two propositions as "Your Church is a true part of the One, Holy, Catholic and Apostolic Church, but the Eucharist ought not to be celebrated by its ministers." The word "true" in this context, he continued, must be compatible with "radically defective." *Lambeth 1958, and Christian Unity* (London: Faith Press, 1958), p. 16.

24. *Reformed and Presbyterian World* XXV (1959), 273.

25. R. M. Brown and D. H. Scott, *Challenge to Reunion* (New York, Toronto, London: McGraw-Hill Book Co., Inc., 1963), p. 271.

26. *Ibid.*, p. 14.

27. *Catholic Register*, Jan. 20, 1961.

28. *Nineteenth General Council of the Alliance of Reformed Churches, Frankfurt, 1964*, ed. by Marcel Pradervand (Geneva, 1964), pp. 235 f., 242 f.

Chapter XIII
PRESBYTERIANISM AND CHURCH UNION
IN CANADA, AUSTRALIA, AND NEW ZEALAND

1. Marc Lescarbot, *History of New France,* ed. and tr. by W. L. Grant, 3 vols. (Toronto, 1907–1914).

2. Charles W. Baird, *History of the Huguenot Emigration to America* (New York, 1885), Vol. I, pp. 21–147; William Gregg, *History of the Presbyterian Church in the Dominion of Canada,* pp. 27–35; John T. McNeill, *The Presbyterian Church in Canada 1875–1925,* pp. 1–5; Ian F. Mackinnon, *Settlements and Churches in Nova Scotia 1749–1776.* For the several histories, see John Bartlet Brebner, *New England's Outpost: Acadia Before the Conquest of Canada* (The Shoe String Press, Inc., 1965).

3. See above, p. 112.

4. See above, pp. 113 f.

5. Gregg, *op. cit.,* pp. 143–212, 589–595; McNeill, *The Presbyterian Church in Canada 1875–1925,* pp. 5–21.

6. The provinces added to the Dominion between 1867 and 1875 were Manitoba, British Columbia, and Prince Edward Island.

7. Among the most influential of these, in addition to Grant, who was to become Principal of Queen's University, Kingston, Ontario, may be mentioned: William Caven, Principal of Knox College, Toronto; John Cook, minister in Quebec City, and William Ormiston, minister in Hamilton, Ontario. For brief sketches of these and other leaders of the period, see McNeill, *The Presbyterian Church in Canada 1875–1925,* pp. 33–51.

8. For explicit data, see McNeill, *ibid.,* pp. 28–30.

9. McNeill, *ibid.,* pp. 16 ff., 245 f. Gregg, *op. cit.,* pp. 299 f., has the main articles of the Basis of Union.

10. On cooperation and the local unions, see S. D. Chown, *The Story of Church Union in Canada* (Toronto, 1930), pp. 50–60; C. E. Silcox, *Church Union in Canada* (New York, 1933), pp. 225–230.

11. Noted in McNeill, *The Presbyterian Church in Canada 1875–1925,* pp. 247 f.

12. William Moncrieff, "A History of the Presbyterian Church in Newfoundland, 1842–1966" (B.D. thesis, Montreal Presbyterian College, 1966), pp. 10 f., 55–58. I am indebted to E. Arthur Betts, Pine Hill Divinity Hall, Halifax, for verifax copies of appropriate pages of this thesis, and to Walter F. Butt of the Newfoundland Conference of the United Church of Canada for extracts from the session records of St. Andrew's Church, St. John's. J. R. Smallwood has edited *The Book of Newfoundland* with a section entitled "The Presbyterian Church in Newfoundland," by N. S. Fraser and Robert A. Templeton (St. John's, 1937).

13. The history of the formation of the United Church was treated as a chapter in the history of Presbyterianism by the present writer in *The Presbyterian Church in Canada* (Toronto, 1925). It has since been the subject of many books and articles. The book by S. D. Chown, cited above in note 10, gives the recollected and documented account of a prominent Methodist participant. The larger work by C. E. Silcox, also cited, attempts a complete

history. Tabulating the votes by congregations, Silcox reports the nonconcurrent Presbyterians as between 39 and 40 percent (pp. 275–282). John Webster Grant, in *A History of the Christian Church in Canada*, II (Toronto, 1972), p. 128, states that about two thirds of the Presbyterian membership entered the United Church "with a larger proportion of elders and an overwhelming majority of ministers." Canadian census records show that the growth of numbers adhering to the Presbyterian Church from 1931 to 1961 was slightly less than 2 percent, while in the same period the United Church made a gain of just over 80 percent. A succinct account of the making of the United Church is that by Kenneth M. Cousland, *A Brief History of the Church Union Movement in Canada*, which appeared as pp. 1–56 of *Our Common Faith*, by Thomas Buchanan Kilpatrick (Toronto, 1928). The first moderator of the General Council, George Campbell Pidgeon, made an indispensable addition to this literature in *The United Church of Canada* (Toronto, 1950). John Webster Grant, in *The Canadian Experience of Church Union* (Toronto and Richmond, Va., 1967), has thoughtfully analyzed the factors and motives involved and supplied some more recent data.

14. *General Assembly Minutes*, 1903, pp. 86, 150. The document was drawn up by the committee appointed by the Assembly in 1901 for the revision of the Confession. Credit for its authorship goes mainly to Henry van Dyke. It was not adopted as a substitute for the Westminster Confession, but diverges from it in laying emphasis on the divine love and the sufficiency of grace. See especially Lefferts A. Loetscher, *The Broadening Church: A Study of Theological Issues in the Presbyterian Church Since 1869* (University of Pennsylvania Press, 1954), pp. 83–89.

15. See Chown, *op. cit.*, pp. 61–79, and for the text pp. 139–156; Kilpatrick, *op. cit.*

16. Randolph Carleton Chalmers, *See the Christ Stand: A Study in Doctrine in the United Church of Canada* (Toronto, 1945), pp. 241–270.

17. Cousland indicates the fraternal relations established by the United Church of Canada with the worldwide Presbyterian, Methodist, and Congregationalist organizations, and with the several Presbyterian churches of Ireland and Scotland (*op. cit.*, pp. 50–56). For some later aspects of these relationships, see Grant, *op. cit.*, pp. 80–93.

18. Rouse and Neill (eds.) *A History of the Ecumenical Movement, 1517–1948*, p. 458.

19. I am indebted to Dr. Robert B. Craig, Executive Commissioner for the United Church of Canada in the General Commission on Church Union, for copies of the documents here referred to. For comments on Anglican and United Church relations and some suggestions for a future social emphasis in Canadian ecumenism, see George Johnston in Philip LeBlanc, O.P., and Arnold Edinborough (eds.), *One Church, Two Nations?* (Don Mills, Ontario, 1968), pp. 179–190.

20. Edward Jenks, *A History of the Australasian Colonies* (Cambridge, 1912), pp. 49 ff.; Marjorie Barnard, *A History of Australia* (Frederick A. Praeger, Inc., 1963), pp. 99–130.

21. *Dictionary of National Biography*, art. "Lang, John Dunmore, 1799–1878." Lang's numerous books include: *Religion and Education in America*

(1840); *Freedom and Independence for the Golden Lands of Australia,* a utopian scheme for a United States of Australia (1852), and *On Religious Establishments* (1856).

22. Above, pp. 113 f.

23. J. Gordon Balfour, *Presbyterianism in the Colonies* (Edinburgh, 1900), pp. 76–102, 157–162; John M. Ward, *Empire in the Antipodes* (London, 1966), pp. 87–96.

24. W. Scott McPheat, "History of Presbyterianism in Australia," in Clifford M. Drury (ed.), "Four Hundred Years of World Presbyterianism" (Typescript, San Francisco Theological Seminary, 1961), pp. 420–439.

25. The National Conference of Australian Churches held in Sydney in February, 1960, brought together 430 delegates from member churches of the Australian Council of Churches and proved gratifying to church unionists. For an extended report, see *We Were Brought Together: Report on the National Council of Australian Churches* (Sydney, 1960). A valuable exposition of the principles by which the conferees in the Australian unity movement have been guided is supplied by J. Davis McCaughey in his article "Church Union in Australia," *Ecumenical Review* XVII (1965), 38–53. See also Norman Young, "The Ministry of the Uniting Church of Australia," *Ecumenical Review* XVIII (1966), 321–330, and in this review "Ecumenical Chronicle" sections, XVI (1964), 423 f.; XVIII (1966), 323 f.; XXIV (1972), 361. Helpful also is J. F. Peter, *Church Union in Australia* (Melbourne, 1964). An informing letter was sent, on request, by Professor George Yule of Ormond College, Parksville, Victoria, January 1, 1968. Urgent inquiries recently made in order to bring up to date our information on the projected union of Australian churches have met with prompt response from Miss Barbara Griffis of Union Seminary Ecumenical Library, Dr. Paul L. Meacham of The Westminster Press, Mr. Cornish Rogers, News Editor of *The Christian Century,* and Rev. James Peter, of Artarmon, New South Wales. Items of news from Australian church periodicals have been enclosed with their answers. From these it becomes a safe forecast that final affirmative action by the ruling bodies of the three negotiating churches will be completed in the spring of 1974, and that the consummation of the union will take place in June, 1976. Some misunderstanding has attended the balloting in Presbyterian churches; as this has been cleared up it is expected that about a third of the Presbyterian congregations will not enter the Uniting Church. Congregational nonconcurring churches will be proportionately fewer.

26. Balfour, *op. cit.,* pp. 230–255; J. B. Condliffe and Willis T. G. Airey, *Short History of New Zealand,* 5th ed. (Aukland, 1935), pp. 90–105.

27. The positions of numerous critics of the plan are explained from a Roman Catholic point of view by John Pennington in "Crisis in New Zealand Church Union: A Catholic Appraisal," *Journal of Ecumenical Studies* IX (1972), 700–720.

28. R. M. O'Grady, *The Christian Century,* Oct. 25, 1972, p. 1076.

29. For stages in the New Zealand church union movement, see J. G. S. Dunn, "The Steps Already Taken," in Lloyd S. Geering, *Shall We Unite?* (Dunedin, undated), pp. 20–26; *Ecumenical Review* XVI (1964), 424 f.; XVIII (1966), 364 f.; XXII (1970), 264 ff.; XXIV (1972), 361 f.

Chapter XIV
CHURCH COUNCILS AND FEDERATIONS

1. J. A. Hutchison, *We Are Not Divided* (Round Table Press, Inc., 1941); Samuel M. Cavert, *The American Churches in the Ecumenical Movement: 1900–1968* (Association Press, 1968); Samuel M. Cavert, *Church Cooperation and Unity in America . . . 1900–1970* (Association Press, 1970).

2. See R. Pierce Beaver, *Ecumenical Beginnings in Protestant World Mission* (New York and Toronto: Thomas Nelson & Sons, 1962), p. 297.

3. *Reformed and Presbyterian World* (XII), 227, 536.

4. *Presbyterian World* (XXII), March, 1954, p. 203.

5. *Presbyterian Life,* April 1, 1970, p. 9.

6. *Reformed and Presbyterian World,* 1951, pp. 101 f.

7. *Ecumenical Review* XVI (1964), p. 554.

8. The text in *Ecumenical Review,* October, 1952, pp. 52–58, is somewhat condensed.

9. Katharine Hockin, *Servants of God in People's China* (Friendship Press, 1962), p. 122.

10. B. J. Marais, *Human Diversity and Christian Unity* (Grahamstown, 1957), p. 9.

11. *Mission in South Africa* (Geneva: World Council of Churches, 1961), p. 31.

12. Alan Paton, *Christian Unity—A South African View* (Grahamstown, 1951), p. 11.

13. Frank S. Loescher, *The Protestant Church and the Negro* (Association Press, 1948). See also A. E. Murray, *Presbyterians and the Negro—A History* (Presbyterian Historical Society, 1966).

INDEX

Abbot, Archbishop, 50, 67, 91
Aberdeen Doctors, 95, 101
Abolitionism, 142 f., 184 f.
Accommodation Plan (1808), 140, 148
Alliance, Pan-Presbyterian, 121. *See also* World Alliance of Reformed Churches
American Board of Commissioners for Foreign Missions (ABCFM), 177, 203, 211 f.
American Education Society (AES), 138–142
American Home Missionary Society (AHMS), 138–142
Amoy, Presbytery of, 204, 213
Amsterdam, Classis of, 128, 144; Evangelical Alliance at (1867), 189; World Council of Churches (1948), 272, 274
Amyraut, Moïse, 47–50, 68, 90
Anabaptists, 23, 63, 76
Andreae, Jacob, 29, 37
Andreae, John Valentine, 90, 94
Anglican Church of Canada, 248 f.
Anglicanism, 9, 15, 37, 40, 45, 49 f., 52, 55, 59, 63, 67 f., 73 f., 88, 91, 94–96, 105, 108, 125, 127, 130, 151, 156, 173–181, 194, 205, 215–234, 241–244, 254 f., 270 f., 274
Anglo-Catholicism, 209, 223, 226, 229
Antiburghers, 112, 116 f., 135 f. *See also* Associate Presbytery; Covenanters; Secession: First

Antichrist, 162, 197
Apostles' Creed, 13, 52, 56, 62, 103, 254
"Appeal to All Christian People" (1920), 224 f., 233
Arminians, 63, 66 ff., 74 f., 89, 133, 199, 216; semi-Arminianism, 197
Arminius, 66, 69, 74
Arnoldshain Theses (1957), 168
Associate Presbytery (1733), 110 f., 135. *See also* Covenanters; Secession: First
Associate Reformed Church, 136, 147
Associate Reformed Synod, 135 f.
Associate Synod, 136
Atkinson, Henry, 263 f.
Augsburg Confession, 9, 31, 47, 52, 58, 72 f., 74, 83, 87, 92, 149, 159, 161, 166, 217
Augusta, John, 78, 82
Australia, Presbyterian Church of (1901), 252
Australia, The Uniting Church of, 254
Austria, Evangelical Church in, 159
Awakening, Great (in American colonies), 131–133, 136; Second, 136 f.

Bad Schauenberg conferences, 171
Bangkok East Asia Conference of Churches (1964), 270
Baptism, 138, 162, 174, 197, 232; believers', 133

311